SunShines

The Astrology of Being Happy

Michael Lutin

A Fireside Book
Published by Simon & Schuster

New York   London   Toronto   Sydney

FIRESIDE
Rockefeller Center
1230 Avenue of the Americas
New York, NY 10020

For information regarding special discounts for bulk purchases,
please contact Simon & Schuster Special Sales at
1-800-456-6798 or business@simonandschuster.com.

Designed by Ruth Lee-Mui

Manufactured in the United States of America

1   3   5   7   9   10   8   6   4   2

Library of Congress Cataloging-in-Publication Data

ISBN-13: 978-0-7432-7726-6
ISBN-10:   0-7432-7726-0

CONTENTS

THIS BOOK HAS BEEN CHANNELED FROM GOD!

Life has a funny way of making you pay for everything it gives you. The good news is that it always rewards you for the things it takes away. This is a book about happiness, the thing everybody deserves, yearns for, and chases after, the thing you think everybody else gets. Of course, the trick is knowing what happiness is, mainly because what brings me joy might turn you off completely, and your bliss is probably something I don't give a damn about. So one of the things we shall do in this book is describe, astrologically, where your true happiness lies, what throws you off course, and what puts you back on the path.

I've been devoting my whole adult life to the study and practice of astrology, and have had the blessing and privilege of seeing people magically transformed right before my eyes. It doesn't happen all that often, but when it does, Technicolor appears where there was once black and white, humming birds start humming, and bumble bees buzz all over the place. Happiness comes when it dawns on you who you really are and what in the name of tarnation you are doing here on Earth. When we see the Sun and Moon rising and setting each day and observe the cycles repeated over and over with such stunningly accurate correspondence to our behavior, we feel connected to the Universe. And when we feel connected we assume there is meaning to the cycles and purpose to the situations, circumstances, and events we encounter throughout our life. Maybe, however, it could all be a giant coincidence.

Consider the noble kitchen cockroach. Turn the light off, and the roaches come out. Turn it on, and they scurry away. Turn it off, and they return. Back on and away they go. If you do it enough times with enough regularity, maybe they will think there's a higher purpose to all.

The fact is, though, that we are not roaches crawling over a melon. We don't merely respond mindlessly to stimuli. We have choices. Astrological cycles give us a chance to process information, record experiences and evaluate them, and creatively change our abilities to adapt and grow. Thanks to family, school, government, and religion, we often shun our raw emotions, never daring to acknowledge the volcanic forces that churn beneath the surface of our minds. In our efforts to be polite and social, we allow a crust of defense and propriety to form around our creative core. Astrology can help us break through to that core by putting us in touch with everything we know we could be but have been programmed to forget—our profound connection to our Sun Sign and all the forces that affect it.

In this book we are going to look at how our Sun Sign (and other major forces) can overcome almost anything if we are hip to all the forces operating from within and without. We'll see what residue from childhood drags us backward, throws us off course, and keeps us from realizing our potential, and we will look at the steps we need to take to get back on that path to fulfillment and stay on the road to happiness.

So just exactly where did I get my information for the material to be found on the following pages?

God told me, of course.

This book has been channeled straight from God. Actually, that statement is no more ridiculous than the claims of Moses and all the rest of the inspired prophets who "received" all the do's and don'ts found in the Bible, which, by the way, not too many people live by these days. And it's certainly no more absurd than the bazillion and one grandiose prophecies and visions touted by all the evangelists springing up everywhere, all with their version of heaven's latest press release. Astrologers believe that knowledge of how the planets and stars move around above our heads can help bring about great changes in human consciousness. Such transformations occur when we bring our behavior in line with our cosmic destiny and heal ourselves of false thinking. It's what Moses, Buddha, Jesus, Muhammad, and all the wise thinkers, prophets, and magicians throughout history have been after. It's all about the healing of the mind despite the pickle juice it's been steeping in since childhood. Yours. Mine. Everybody's.

As we move through the twenty-first century, no matter who we are or where we come from, everything that we ever thought was absolutely, immutably, 100 percent eternally true is going to be reexamined. Whether the Pope will don a flowered muumuu or be replaced by a college of women—only time will tell, but shocking and seemingly heretical and sacrilegious events will shatter forever our nice, safe, little beliefs about who made us and why we are here. Even atheists will not escape unscathed. Ironically enough, when they have their cozy little belief in Nothing all in place, BOOOM! they'll experience a miracle and have to deal with that. There will be more zealots and heretics walking the streets than Elvis impersonators.

Astrology must undergo the same transformation. If all belief systems have to go through the meat grinder, then we must add more dimensions to our study than simply finding astrological reasons for our behavior. We're going to have to take a journey deep into the basement of your mind to see why and how you got to where you are now.

But we won't leave you there. Astrology is an absolutely fantastic and useful tool that boggles the mind of anybody looking seriously into it. Taken to the level we shall achieve in the following pages, it will help you tap into that core of health, psychic energy, and creativity. We make no grandiose claims that reading this book will cure your lumbago or marry you off to a billionaire. I can promise, however, that by the time you get to the end of this book you will have practical techniques for developing, strengthening, and healing yourself. By the way, once you do that, any and all the miracles you might be waiting for are sure to follow, and a life of prosperity is guaranteed.

So it's not brain surgery. It won't hurt a bit, mainly because we'll be laughing at ourselves all the way through. There's work ahead, though. You're not just going to sit passively under the astrological hair dryer and come out with a gorgeous do. In fact, before you stick one pinky toe in the astrological ocean, I want you to look at the question below. Don't think about your answer. Just write down in the space provided the first three things thing that pop into your head:

What is happiness?

1. _____
_____
_____
_____
_____

2. _____
_____
_____
_____
_____

3. _____
_____
_____
_____
_____

INTRODUCTION

THE POWER OF THE SUN

Goals, Limitations, and Responsibilities

When people turn to astrology, they are usually at a spiritual crossroads and are searching for something. Is it possible they've stumbled on a path that leads toward greater fulfillment? Even if they cannot cope with the demands of everyday life, are reluctant to accept more traditional means of therapeutic help, or have difficulty adjusting to society or suffer from authority problems, astrology fills a void and answers questions other disciplines fail to answer. We could always ask if it is a mistake to look outside one's self for validation and guidance, but the truth is people do.

Enlightenment has so many paths, paths off paths, tributaries off tributaries, so many methods and approaches, all seeking to converge on the same point—the bright beam of truth that blazes from somewhere at the heart of the universe. Every approach to self-knowledge is an avenue leading to that same place. There are as many views on consciousness as there are people poking around at the heart of it. Astrology is no different, of course. That's both the beauty and the curse, of course, because astrologers everywhere are quibbling and squabbling over the meanings and definitions of planetary effects, not because general hypotheses cannot be made, but because the disagreements often stem from the prejudices of every astrological observer, which in turn emanate from his or her perceptions of life.

Whatever our approach to happiness, however, there is certainly one goal we all share as human beings plunked down here on Earth to scratch out our own shred of satisfaction:

We all want to feel good and get what we want.

Used appropriately, astrology can promise you that. The sheer truth of astrology is utterly awesome when you come upon it. Just to have your connection with the Universe confirmed is validating and inspiring. You're not crazy. All the conflicts, ambivalence, struggles, and opposing truths, the yin and yang of it all—it's all there. Astrology completely blows you away. The brain-crunching accuracy of it blasting through you has a healing effect in itself. Its brilliant light blinds you, fills you with its life-giving current. It raises you up, even when you're feeling weighed down by the apparent impossibility of getting your cheeks pinched raw by Great-Aunt Gertrude or having to sit through two separate Thanksgiving dinners on the same day because Dad won't sit down at the same table with Mom. There is astrology right there with its heartbreakingly simple explanations, its stark, implacable revelations of what, how, why, and of course the thing everybody wants to know—when.

But, alas! Eventually astrology loses its initial luster. After a while it seems not to work.

Doesn't work? Doesn't work? What blasphemy. Everything is always right there in the chart. Astrology *always* works.

Astrology is true, all right, but you still have to live your life. At first you think, "Thank God it's my Moon; I thought it was my mother!" Getting that first planetary high is fabulous. Eventually the crash comes, and when it does, it's as bad as the morning after a week of nothing but Coke and donuts. As any honest, seasoned, professional astrologer will tell you, that morning-after feeling always comes. It may be your Moon, but it *is* also your mother.

Of course you're dazzled in the beginning. Who wouldn't be? The astrologer tells you that in November, Saturn will be out of your fourth house and all your family issues will be solved. November comes and, voilà! right on the money—things clear up at home. One eensy little thing the astrologer has forgotten to tell you: Saturn is moving somewhere else. After a while you realize that astrology is doing no more than describing and predicting symptoms of deeper long-term questions and struggles. The problems persist, recur, even in exacerbated form.

Then you feel powerless. The depression and disillusionment that can follow that initial burst of insight evoke the powerlessness that many people experience in childhood. Astrology itself becomes another well-meaning but grandiose and controlling parent figure who foresees your future, knows what's best for you, can't bear your dependence, doesn't want to encounter any resistance from you, and—most destructive of all—refuses to be present for your pain. To rely solely on astrological definitions of human events often leaves us feeling empty and alone, even more separated from wholeness than when we started out. Just because we can see it in a horoscope is not enough. After a while you don't really care that Mars is doing this or that or Venus is in your whatever house. If you don't feel healed, you don't feel healed.

Religious or philosophical beliefs aside, if true healing is possible, then what's the dish? What does all that mean in real-life terms? Healing involves the gaining of confidence. It's about waking up to your creative potential and fulfilling yourself. You can't do that unless you possess the confidence that you're a whole person capable of making decisions based on real insights and healthy instincts.

We may think we spend our lives struggling over issues of love, money, or health, but we are really always fighting for our autonomy. We don't want to be categorized, boxed up, and sent down the conveyor belt with the rest of the cream pies in the factory. We are always seeking to validate our own feelings, establish our competence, confirm our sanity, and liberate enough creative energy to feel good and get what we want.

A true and permanent healing of this kind cannot come through a flat interpretation of the horoscope. And that's all a horoscope is. A flat circle on a flat piece of paper. Certainly knowing you're connected to the Universe is one step, but to go the distance, to have this awakening in its totality, there are other steps you have to take. You have to see how childhood has molded you, and you also have to open up to the possibility that the life you are leading is but one small leg of a greater journey leading you to a greater destination, a cosmic destiny that has spiritual, even divine connections and significance.

True confidence is achieved when you have been freed from notions of what you should be, what you'd like people to think you are, or what you're afraid you might become. Real confidence expands your sense of personal power and trust and eventually leads you toward greater sharing and intimacy. True confidence is that thing inside that tells you you're all right, you're cool, you can cope, and—contrary to what some members of your family might think—you can even thrive. Strength and confidence come only when we can break through the crust of defense and false thinking and liberate the core of energy and health we all have burning inside. To achieve a true healing in ourselves we have to have a fearless desire to go into our own hearts and face some dark truths about our wishes and instincts, no matter how terrifying some of them may be. If we keep our eyes on the goal we eventually rise back up again into the light of triumph.

The Power of the Sun

If you've ever stepped onto a plane during a fierce winter storm and then stepped off a few hours later into a sunny paradise, or if you've ever simply awakened in the morning with golden light streaming across your bed, you don't have to go to college to know and believe, first hand, in the power of the Sun. Its healing and restorative qualities on body and mind are known by all. Yeah, sure there's a downside to everything, like when you fall asleep on the beach and then for days afterward if someone so much as breathes on your blistered shoulders you see stars. And yes, we know . . . sun block 39 or else.

The Sun gives another kind of healing light, too: astrological light. Astrologers aren't sure to this day if it's actually a stream of energy passing from Sun to Earth that influences our lives, or if it's just some fabulous coincidence of clocks clicking simultaneously everywhere in this tick-tocking universe. Astrological light is both real and symbolic, physical and spiritual. We observe characteristics shared by people born, say, during the month the Sun appears in Leo or Sagittarius, but we still don't understand *why* they share these traits.

Astronomically, of course, the Sun is the center of our system. It is connected to our heartbeats (scientific investigation has demonstrated a relationship between sunspot activity and heart rhythm). We are wedded to that Sun. It's great to think that Captain James T. Kirk and the rest of the crew of the Enterprise could go gallivanting off to other star systems, but until some currently unthinkable advances are made in the biosciences, for now we Earthlings are bound to our center, the Sun. It's what stabilizes us, feeds us, makes all growth possible, creates and maintains an environment favorable for life (in spite of great odds, from some efforts of some major corporations). The Sun is our fire, our fuel, the one constant source of natural light and warmth in an otherwise dark world.

One can see why it forms the core of astrological thinking, and why, even if you accept only the beauty of the metaphor, its position at the time of your birth—your Birth Sign—could possibly symbolize your core, your source of constancy, creativity, and warmth.

The Sun is everything you want to be. It's your center of power, the potential you have for health and wealth, and it's your birthright to pursue your own little bluebird of happiness. It is everything you could become, thanks to the union of your father's seed and your mother's egg plus your own will to grow and change. It is the center of your being around which everything in your life will always revolve. In astrology the Sun is said to represent personal warmth, and if you but step out of your house after a horrible thunderstorm or feel a gentle solar kiss on your cheek as you doze in a garden, you can easily make the metaphoric jump and understand why. To astrologers the Sun means creativity, brilliance, and stability. Each Zodiac Sign is centered and kept on the right path by the Sun. We all exhibit magnetism and genius because of the Sun in our horoscope. The Sun symbolizes your flawless potential, your fertility and potency—and above all it is the metaphor for the Life Force itself. Of all the planets, asteroids, and stars that fill the sky, the ever-changing sequences of events that toss and turn you through life, the people who come in and go out of your life, the Sun is your source of energy and describes the fulfillment of the promise of constancy. In astrology the Sun is said to rule the heart.

Astrological symbolism is rich with magic and meaning. A skilled astrologer knows the proper time and place to evoke it. This symbolism goes back thousands of years and is based on both empirical observation and gifted insight. We use the motions of the planets, positions of the Signs of the Zodiac, and astrological houses to interpret behavior and predict events. The Scorpion, the Twins, the Bull, all have their special magical meanings that correspond—even just in a symbolic or metaphorical way—to human personality. Looking at each Sign is our first step toward realizing all the potential contained within the heart of the Sun. So that is the point from which we are going to start, mainly because the Sun in your horoscope represents your ability to function in fire and in flood, for richer or poorer, in sickness and in health, and it is therefore always the starting point on your road to happiness and prosperity. It is even said to rule over the heart.

But wait. How is it possible that everybody born during a given month could be destined to have the same fate?

The answer is, it isn't possible at all. Lots of other factors come into play in determining your destiny. It depends on the year you were born, time of day, place on Earth, and all that jazz. Whether you are a family-type person, a whiz at business, or a restless raconteur depends on a lot of other celestial influences. Those factors determine the planetary forces that bring people and situations into your life to support or thwart your great plans. Later in the book we'll deal with the most profound of those forces—the path of the Moon across the Zodiac.

We're going to put it all together for you. We are going to examine not only the Sun's position in your horoscope, but especially how the path of the Moon across the Zodiac can explain why some Aries are tough and dominant and others are soft and submissive, why some Capricorns are career oriented and others are happier loafing about.

This book will instruct you in techniques to tap into that core of health, psychic energy, and creativity. You will use your Sun Sign as well as the Moon's path—another equally powerful tool—to explore other, deeper levels of your path and personality in an effort to solve problems and resolve issues in an adult way. For example, let's say you're a Leo. That's the sign of the Lion, with all the mythology and connotations implied by that noble wild animal. What could have happened in your childhood, though, that encouraged or harmed your development as a Leo? Whether you're brave and noble, bossy and obnoxious, generous, dangerous or cowardly—what happened in childhood? Also, how do your economic background, and ethnic and religious teachings influence how you view yourself as a Leo today? Is a white Jewish male Leo different from an African American female Leo? How does a Leo woman born in the United States differ from one born in Iran? How did your parent's marriage affect your sense of autonomy and gender role as a Leo? How best can you exploit strengths gleaned from childhood or rise above problems caused back then? What path must you take to become the best Leo you can be?

That's the sort of thing we'll begin tackling. After we look at the psychological effects of the childhood, we'll go a step further. We'll explore the most important conflicts you experience and use them as springboards toward understanding more cosmic dimensions of being. We always need to look at astrology as a perfect blueprint of what you could become—no matter what your mother said to your father, what he did to her, or any other of the countless conflicts our origins inevitably produce in us as adults. Viewed from a spiritual as well as practical point of view, we can chart the path you are destined to take.

Consider Libras. Libras are very often secretly angry. They're angry because in their childhood (because of what went on in the home) they became confused between confrontation and hatred, anger and rejection, so they tend to get mad at all the wrong people, fearing true communication with those closest to them. In a metaphysical sense, what's the best healing path for that anger? What are the healthiest outlets for aggression? What cosmic reason could there be for you to have been born having to worry all the time about what other people are going to think, say, or do? In higher terms, what purpose do you have on Earth as a Libra? Without this vital spiritual dimension of interpretation added to the astrology, astrology alone has little lasting or useful meaning.

But we must go still further. Few of us have the luxury of sitting up on the mountain top and contemplating the clouds. We have kids to raise, spouses to relate to, and bills to pay. If astrology doesn't help you in those areas, forget it, what the hell good is it? In order to complete a transformational healing, we need to delve into your Sun Sign to explore how you relate to other people. How do these three other factors—your astrology Sign, your childhood, and your spiritual path—impact the way you deal with and have relationships with the people in your life? This particular area of study will help you deal better with yourself and other people. It will provide insight into your own habitual patterns in relating as well as giving you a unique perspective on why your loved ones, bosses, and children do the ridiculous things they do. This will help Virgos stop blaming other people, give Capricorns a way to trust, maybe even help Tauruses with that appetite problem. The examination of your Sun Sign in the light of how you connect (or don't) with the outer world is probably the most important level of all on which to use astrology. Astrology can help make relationships better.

No one can deny the profound research that has been done in the area of human behavior. The lasting effects our childhoods have upon our lives underlie everything we accomplish or fail to accomplish in our adult lives. Your parents and their marriage, as well as your racial, religious, ethnic, or socioeconomic heritage will mark you deeply and forever. Your attitudes to relationships, family, or sexuality are direct results of your early conditioning—especially the first five years of your life. How do these factors affect your Zodiac Sign and vice versa? Are there any astrological signs that are typically "Christian" or "Muslim" or "Jewish"? If you are a German born in Berlin in 1945, which affects your life more: that fact or the fact that you might be a Capricorn? And how can such a powerful influence be seen in the horoscope itself? By finding connections between your astrology chart and your early life, astrology gains new relevance. You have more options. You can see what happened and why. You can do something about it.

Astrologers, philosophers, and students of metaphysics have been asking the same questions for millennia: Have we lived before and experienced incarnations in distant times, faraway lands, even in another gender? Did we choose to be born? If so, to what end? If not, why have we been thrust here amid the noise, violence, and temptation? Who dunnit? And why? Is there anything we can do about it? Human beings cannot survive without meaning. Each one of us yearns for a connection with the great, dark, and yawning Universe. We have to find a reason for enduring. We need something of the nature of light to strive for, so we can feel—true or not—that we have come here to help turn the Great

Wheel of Life. Unless you gain a sense of awe, wonder, and respect for our own presence on Earth, the horoscope is a dead circle. Perhaps we did live another life in another time. In the following pages, we will take a fanciful tour into such a possibility to help define the strengths and weaknesses you have brought into this life with you. The spiritual, mystical view of the Zodiac opens the mind to new possibilities and burns away conflict, prejudice, and early negative conditioning; opens our eyes to a greater purpose; and liberates us from limited thinking and the strict view that all our problems come from childhood. When we envision our lives from such a greater perspective, we see how perfect the path is. We see more clearly where we have come from and where we are going. Seeing the perfection that is already there gives us new vitality, provides us with something to work toward, wakes us up to spiritual morning.

No matter how astrological, analytical, or spiritual we want to get, nothing can make you feel good or help you get what you want if you can't relate to other human beings, Oh, it's a definite prank they played on us, all right, but one we all have to live with: You can't consider you've lived on this planet until you've connected with another being and tasted love. That's for damned sure. But—and here's the kick in the head—the last thing you do before departing from this place is experience the reality of separation when you leave it all behind. The punchline of the great joke has something to do with attachment and separation and how we handle both.

Nonetheless, everything you come from and are striving to do and be will have no meaning or purpose unless it defines how you look at other people, use or abuse them, and ultimately connect, communicate with, and show your love for them. How your astrological makeup affects your interaction with other people is probably the most vital level of exploration of all. By raising the level of expression of your Sun Sign, based on some of the other factors that influence it, you draw other people to you. When you are manifesting to the highest possible degree that you were put here to do, no one can resist you. When you connect and communicate with other people, you are joined once again with the Universe.

(P.S. Secret message to astrologers: This *is* the Node book, based on the Solar Chart.)

How to Read This Book

The author would prefer that you start on page one and read straight through to the end, but nobody ever does that. We know you're not going to want to wade through all the introductory material—although if you do, you'll get a heck of a lot more out of the book. Some of it is hysterically funny, and some of it is really dark. There's a purpose to it all, however, and that purpose is to bring you to a greater ability to fulfill your destiny and be happy at last.

But we know you're probably going to turn immediately to your sign and the signs of all the people you would like to control. When you do, here's how to get the most out of this book:

1. Read your sign in the first part of the book.
2. At the end of the opening section, look through the charts until you find the year during which you were born. Beside it is a number. Read the section corresponding to that number.
3. When you've read that section, note the key words assigned to you. They describe two of your biggest issues. Turn to the part called Going Deeper, and read the chapter corresponding to those key words. Since all people work out their issues and act out their obsessions in different ways, once you read about those key words, maybe you should sit quietly for a minute or two and think about exactly how it all applies to you. Don't worry—it will.
4. Repeat this method for all the people you're dying to know about.
5. Optional: Then eat an entire chocolate cake. You'll probably need one.

PART ONE

Your SunShines

ARIES

March 20–April 19
Dates vary from year to year—consult your local astrologer

Aries is the yellow crocus that pops up through the snow, premature maybe, but there to remind Ole Man Winter to get the hell out of here because spring can't wait a second longer. Aries is hydrogen, not only because it's the first element on the periodic chart, but because Aries rules the most primitive force of life. It is the quickening in any being that sets it on fire to live, not just to live or survive, but to triumph over life.

Aries is there when antlers are sprouting and the males begin eyeing each other in discomfort and pawing the ground. It's the first light of dawn in the Big City. You can see morning pushing through its pink streak visible behind the buildings to the east. A cab driver zooms by sipping his coffee, beating the light. He's the first one up on his shift. He's an Aries.

Maybe the first man alive was Adam. Maybe it was Homo erectus or *Australopithecus,* because Aries rules over the first anything that is alive, is ignited.

Try to imagine the mad, insane, fabulous rush the astronauts must have when they hear it's a go, and the rocket engines beneath them roar into magnificent flames, and they think, "Son of a bitch. It's really happening. We're going to the stars." It's the thrill of the new that is Aries.

Forget the head-banging, cajoling, convincing, hondling, and fooling around any early explorer had to do before he got the damned ships and actually set sail on an unchartered ocean; that's Aries at work. When there's a one-day half-price sale on expensive food processors and the store opens at nine, who's at the head of the line at 7 AM? Aries. Of course.

Whatever the mechanism is that differentiates an ant from an elephant on the DNA chain is ruled by Aries, because Aries rules the uniqueness of identity. It's what made you irreplaceably, irresistibly you, me me, and Brando Brando. It is the face you never forget, the name the mere mention of which evokes a thousand associations like Joan Crawford or Reese Witherspoon.

Aries is the force within you that liberates you from the tyranny of guilt and regret and kicks you into positive action. It is believed by some researchers that a baby chooses its own time of birth. The fetus produces from its pituitary gland a substance that eventually leads to the contraction of the mother's uterus and the expulsion of the baby-to-be in to the world. It's called the "I'm-outta-here" hormone, and it's definitely Aries. The moment when day becomes longer than night in the northern hemisphere is called the first point of Aries. It begins the cycle of life over again. It is the light. The Sun god Ra and the triumph over fear, darkness, imprisonment, and even death is Aries. It is the exaltation of the Sun with its life-giving and healing power, ceaselessly generating warmth and life-giving properties to all living beings. It is the woman who forgot she had cancer twenty years ago. The guy who was told five years ago he had one month to live, but last night he went out to dinner with friends and had three vodka martinis.

Aries is the fearlessness and courage that sent firemen bounding up to the eightieth floor of the World Trade Center, with no thought of anything but saving people and the belief that nothing could ever happen to them. If you're Aries, your goal is heroism, foolhardy or not.

One has to wonder, then, why so many members of your noble sign are just plain pushy and obnoxious or the opposite—totally yellow-bellied chickens?

One has to realize that Arians come in all shapes and sizes. There are more aggressive types, milquetoast types, spiritual types, blue-collar types, and other assorted characters, each with a unique way of expressing their divine identity. Then, too, were you the first born? If so, did siblings follow? The way your parents dealt with the fact that the Sun no longer rose and set around your little heinie affects the way you relate to other people. If you were the first born, naturally you're going to have a great sense of responsibility, and you're bound to be a bit bossy. And if you were not the first born, that in itself can create a somewhat bizarre contradiction, since in your mind you are the first, the only, the one and only. So you see that it is quite difficult to gather together all the possibilities and put together one simple picture of an Aries without turning your sign into a Frankenstein thingie. We can however isolate the major fundamental themes and issues and let you take it from there, mainly because you can't stand anybody telling you anything anyway and you can listen for only two seconds without your mind wandering back to the only subject of any interest: you.

Open wide, here comes the big medicine: male dominance.

Man or woman, whoever and wherever you are, Iranian fundamentalist or hip-hopper from the East Bronx, who's on top is your key issue—is, was, and always will be. Now, if you're a woman under a black burka reading this by flashlight, better not let the imam catch you. It's blasphemy. Or if you're a Catholic woman and wondering why the hell members of your sex aren't being ordained yet, quickly think something else. Those thoughts are impure. And conversely, if you're an Aries man who prefers sewing to snowboarding, better be careful. Aries is all about the issue of what it means to be the man in charge, even if you're a woman, a straight woman or a lesbian, doesn't matter. The story is the same. All members of all signs get a little defensive when it comes to gender identity, and the louder, more boisterous, and aggressively some display their pride over it, the more defensive they probably are underneath.

The western countries are lightening up on the subject, so it's not so important any more for a woman to wear a lot of pearls and pretend her husband is right when she knows he's talking through his butt. She doesn't even have to get married to prove she's normal. And an Aries man can cry when Melanie dies at the end of *Gone with the Wind* and not be labeled a sissy. Well, that's not always true, because some people are still stereotyping and probably always will.

If you're an Aries, you must prove your dominance and it doesn't have to be by hitting somebody over the head with a club or a fourteen-inch penis, either.

Just by being born an Aries you're lucky. You're a powerful person, period. The life force within you beats with unceasing certainty. I am here, I am here, I am here, I am here goddamit, I'm here, I'm here, your heart seems to be saying. You will not be ignored. You cannot be ignored. Your energy streams from you in an unending flow of invisible particles that radiate outward in all directions. And that's why you have to take hold of yourself. Otherwise you're all over the place.

You're obnoxious—screaming, impatient, bossing everybody around constantly, furious at people because they can't read your mind and grant your wishes before you even say them. You're enraged at the latest outrage of someone who failed to spread their cloak across the puddle so you could pass. Everyone annoys you because they're all moving in slow motion, as if they're in another dimension made of honey and glue. You certainly can't hold a job indefinitely because all bosses are morons, and you know way more than they do—than everybody—so you have to fake your résumé as you get older so you don't look like a bipolar maniac.

Relationships? Come on. When you're not in control of yourself and all that energy, how can you expect to carry on a normal sane relationship? Everybody bores you. Nobody can keep up with you. You're like a cat that yearns to be picked up but then jumps off a lap and runs away. On a date the person sitting across the table from you will be bombarded by your latest, nonfascinating tale of your most recent travels over molehills you've made into mountains until that person has to excuse himself or herself to go to the john either to throw up or call their roommate and beg them to ring the cell phone in five minutes to say their mother died so they can grab a taxi and go home—alone. When you are *not* the master of your energy, you can be like a suicide bomber who's just swallowed a bottle of Dexedrine, screaming, "Lemme at 'em! Lemme at 'em!" without even knowing who the enemies are or stopping to think what they may have done to deserve your blind, atavistic wrath.

Don't forget you're an animal, and a primitive one at that. Wearing shoes and eating with silverware is a chore in itself, and because you've had to fend for yourself since God knows when, it's not easy for you to be kind and sweet and patient if people don't just get up and tip their hat after you run them over. You're more into wielding your power than using it. You can be like the guy with the electric drill that's been souped up to such a degree that he's not handling it, it's handling him.

Where this kind of rage and self-absorption comes from is hard to say. It could stem from either too much early repression or too little discipline. If somebody beat the hell out of you from the time you can remember, you were destined to be one pissed camper when you got out on your own. And a beating doesn't have to be physical. A systematic destruction of your identity and confidence could create later outbursts of anger and violence. It's a vicious cycle. Men strike their wives. Women strike their little boys who grow up to strike their wives who continue to strike their sons. Your rage could also come from the fact that you were not given good guidelines when you needed them. So you are an animal let loose on the streets, and you have no idea that there's anybody else in the world except you—much less a society populated with individuals whose needs and wishes you have to bother with addressing.

On the contrary, when you don't understand your powerful energy and it frightens you, you may go the other route and be the turned-inside-out Aries: the tip-toeing little timid person always afraid to make a noise, take up space, speak your mind, exercise your will, even insist on a restaurant. This is the passive-aggressive sort of Aries who needs lots and lots of hard-core therapy—even more than the loud-mouthed, pushy, know-it-all bores. If you're one of these, male or female, you've been castrated, and you've got to grow back your organ of open self-assertion. Granted, people are rarely just one kind of Aries or another. In some instances you can be confident and self asserting—say in business—and then when you get home at night you're running back and forth to get your sweetie coffee, then milk, then sugar, then, oh sorry, sugar substitute. Moderation of course is the secret to all success, but in your case, it's vital. So many Aries are terrified of living without the daily fix of caffeine and/or nicotine. They get their courage from coffee, and they are so terrified of losing their edge they don't dare allow themselves all the joys of intimacy and sharing that go with living in a happy family setting. So they're constantly seeking a new high, a new thrill, always upsetting the status quo just because for them the status quo means death. Same in business. If the challenge isn't impossible, quit and go elsewhere. Comfort and safety become anathema to the Aries spirit of adventure and thirst for newness.

Nonsense: Your power comes from how you direct your energy. You are in complete control of it when you decide to be. When there is someone to be defended, a cause to be fought for, wrongs to be righted, you can be as focused and able to cope with a hundred impossible tasks at once as a certified public accountant at 11:30 PM on April fourteenth, and fortified with the determination and accuracy of a missile on its way to a target. You may bitch and moan as you whack your machete through jungle after jungle, but when the challenge is there all your fears vanish along with your self-absorption. This is the moment your dominance surfaces. Hand you a job other people wouldn't dare touch and you laugh. For you the driving force is the competition. Isn't it funny? As selfish as some people think you are, you are able to do for them what you can't seem to do for yourself. You'll support them, push them forward, speak for them when they're too shy, anything that involves being brave for those who cannot help themselves. In your own life you may still have problems speaking up for yourself or avoiding intimidation by partners or other people to whom you have yielded dominance.

Never ever forget how lucky you are to have been born an Aries. Of course, nobody could ever appreciate your wonderfulness enough, nor could you ever in one lifetime realize all the potential you've got stored up in one little pinky. Gathering those forces and directing them—that is where you can take no advice, have no help, get no guidance. That ability is something that is in you: a potential, an innate divine talent. When you are inspired, you catch fire. What inspires you to channel that energy is totally, completely, eternally, and forever an individual choice. We all hit the speed bumps fate has placed in the road, but you and only you can make certain decisions about how you want to react, which roads to travel and which to reject. The choices you make have to be yours, as well as the responsibility for making them. Your horoscope may suck and your childhood may have been a nightmare, but individual morality comes from the strength you find within yourself to alter the course of your own destiny. This is what "male" dominance is all about, not pushing a fat kid in glasses down in the schoolyard or screaming at coworkers or family members. Nor is it about going belly-up because somebody's bigger or pushier than you. True dominance is about looking for and finding courage within yourself. You don't have to run into a phone booth and come out in a blue suit and a red cape. Courage Aries-style comes any time justice needs someone to step forward and fight for it.

So how do you focus your power to achieve your goal of heroism? What are the forces that drag you backward and keep you from reaching the highest manifestation of your Sun? What are the energies that can support you, guide you, enhance your positive qualities, and make your Sun shine bright? The fact is you're not just an Aries. There is another energy operating, one that either cuts across your efforts and undermines them, or spirits you to heights of joy and fulfillment. That energy depends not on the month you were born, but the year. Later on in this book the technical aspects will be explained more fully. We'll examine how you waste time chasing your own tail, why you do it, and how to pull yourself out of self-destructive obsessions and put yourself back on the road to success. But for now, check out the following table. Find your birth year and note the number beside it. Then read the section corresponding to that number.

Year–No.	Year–No.	Year–No.	Year–No.	Year–No.
1901–2	1915–5	1930–8	1945–10	1959–1
1902–2	1916–5	1931–7	1946–9	1960–12
1903–1	1917–4	1932–6	1947–9	1961–12
1904–12	1918–3	1933–6	1948–8	1962–11
1905–12	1919–3	1934–5	1949–7	1963–10
1906–11	1920–2	1935–4	1950–7	1964–10
1907–10	1921–1	1936–4	1951–6	1965–9
1908–10	1922–1	1937–3	1952–5	1966–8
1909–9	1923–12	1938–2	1953–5	1967–8
1910–9 until	1924–12	1939–2	1954–4	1968–7
4/20, then 8	1925–11	1940–1	1955–4 until	1969–7
1911–8	1926–10	1941–1	4/14, then 3	1970–6
1912–7	1927–10	1942–12	1956–3	1971–5
1913–7	1928–9	1943–11	1957–2	1972–5
1914–6	1929–8	1944–11	1958–2	1973–4

Year–No.	Year–No.	Year–No.	Year–No.	Year–No.
1974–3	1986–8 until	1997–12	2009–5	2020–10
1975–3	4/7, then 7	1998–12	2010–4	2021–9
1976–2	1987–7	1999–11	2011–3	2022–8
1977–1	1988–6	2000–11	2012–3	2023–8
1978–1	1989–6	2001–10	2013–2	2024–7
1979–12	1990–5	2002–9	2014–2 until	2025–6
1980–11	1991–4	2003–9	3/22, then 1	2026–6
1981–11	1992–4	2004–8	2015–1	2027–5
1982–10	1993–3	2005–7	2016–12	2028–4
1983–9	1994–2	2006–7	2017–12	2029–4
1984–9	1995–2	2007–6	2018–11	2030–3
1985–8	1996–1	2008–5	2019–10	

Aries 1

If you hear that you don't have the greatest reputation in the world for being sweet, wonderful, and kind, that will hurt and surprise you. You do try so hard to be nice to people and bend over backwards to please them. Trouble is, you do so but then at a certain point you snap. And when you get angry, pal, do you get angry! You can't stand all that smiley baloney that people throw at you when you know they want to kick your butt. So you're not really all that great at long, boring meetings with Japanese businessmen. As sweet and charming and romantic as you can be, you can sound like a bullhorn when you're pissed, loud enough to send a flock of birds flying from a branch five miles away. As thoughtful as you try to be, it's easy for you to snap back into a very selfish mode. You do make lots of efforts to listen to the needs of other people, but your knee-jerk reaction is to grab back control to regain dominance. In an undeveloped state, you think about yourself first and can hardly carry on a real two-way conversation without bringing the subject back to you, where you're at, what happened to you, and other insignificant details about you you you.

This is actually very possibly a gender issue, one in which your masculine side—macho, if you will—is overdeveloped, no matter if you are male or female. The animal part of your Aries nature still thinks it's okay to pee with the door open—if you even bother to not go on the carpet. That's a bit of extreme hyperbole, but the fact is you're great at playing a wild, uncontrollable, free-spirit hothead. It's natural for you. It's not the path to lasting happiness in relationships, however, unless you believe in wife-beating or husband-bashing and that will only land you in the clink. Besides, once you've dominated somebody you only end up feeling bad and guilty anyway and then have to spend double the amount of energy making it up to them. So it would be worth the effort to get on the more balanced path of caring about your effect on other people and not doing such a hit-and-run job on them. You're a lot less concerned about the feelings of other people when you're young and full of defensive anger. By the time you are old enough to have had plenty of run-ins with authority figures, you become interested enough in what other people think about you to be able to take the message to heart in the loving way it is intended and not just throw this book down, screaming "This guy's a moron!"

So it doesn't mean you're a little wimp just because you're mature enough to think before you speak or ask for advice before you make moves and decisions out of reactionary anger. You don't lose your autonomy or independence when you can hook up with people. You can gain your civilized self and connect with society in a way more fulfilling manner.

At this point you need to probe a little deeper into your obsession with being on your own. In the next part, Going Deeper, reading the chapter called "Independence" will help you pass through the illusion of being controlled by others and on to a higher expression of your Aries nature that will help you express your needs more fully, develop and maintain healthier relationships, and make your Sun shine bright.

> *Celebrities Who Share Your Issues*
> *James Caan, Pete Rose, Ryan O'Neal, Anita Bryant,*
> *David Hyde Pierce*

Aries 2

Although you may think all your energy has to be put into making money, that is not true. Sometimes your best creative work will be done for love and not money—probably most if not all, in fact. Such a statement stirs all sorts of feelings within you. Number one: You know that is correct. Number two: It scares the hell out of you. You feel that, in some ways, you've gotten screwed financially (probably have); that somebody has made big money and profited from your efforts, creativity, and genius; that you should have been better at business and not just given in. But how rich do you have to get before you won't think that somebody is richer? Somebody is always going to be richer than you, and it is *not* about the money.

No matter how much you make, if you feel poor, you're never going to enjoy a moment of peace or prosperity. And it's odd, too, because when it comes to your art or work or some project or cause you are deeply involved in, you don't care what anything costs. But then you'll turn around and you'll take a bus or skimp on food because the price of pickles went up. You may never really know how much you're worth, literally or figuratively, mainly because sometimes you see yourself as the world's gift to genius, and at other moments, you're some immigrant kid stealing apples off a cart. The secret to success lies in not looking back at the way things were when you felt like a slave.

You get so angry when you start thinking about having been taken advantage of because you were a young stupid dreamer. You are always in a struggle between your higher self—a proud healer and creator of great integrity—and the lower self that has trouble resisting sticking your hand in the cookie jar once in a while. In a world that measures you by your bank account, it's really tough to stay above cheap commercialism and still turn out top quality work. That, however, is the big challenge. To get all your needs met without being compulsive, greedy, or dishonest is the task at hand. To remain true to yourself and your cause, you cannot hide your desires or suppress them. You have to assuage your earthly appetites without being engulfed by them. None of this celibacy routine for you, enforced or otherwise. Truth comes out anyway, eventually, so there's little sense in thinking you can hide your desires in a box on the top shelf of the closet.

Part of your growth will be to accept sharing financial control, even if it bugs you to be hooked into people who, once they fund you, think they have a say in what you do and how you do it. Writers and their publishers, artists and their dealers, directors and their producers—whoever has control of the money is not to be ignored, looked down upon, or hated.

Gratitude and economic savvy have somehow to be united so you can get your stipend, allowance, advance—whatever you want to call it—and not think it's a paltry handout, doled out to a beggar.

At this point you have to go on a journey through the illusion of money. In order to be proud of yourself, you have to find a way to be connected to other human beings. In the next part, Going Deeper, read the chapter called "Money" to find your secret word or phrase that will help you make your Sun shine bright.

Celebrities Who Share Your Issues
Francis Ford Coppola, Howard Cosell, Jack Webb,
Elizabeth Clare Prophet, Jennifer Capriati

Aries 3

Energy is one thing, frenetic running around is quite another. You'll live in a lot of places, sometimes all at once. You're here, you're there, you're everywhere. Actually most of the time you're not exactly here and you're not exactly there. You're someplace between here and there, and to look at your current place of residence it would be hard to tell if you are moving in or moving out, if you've just arrived or you're in the process of throwing a few things in a bag before a trip. It's a wonder you ever got out of high school. Actually it wouldn't be surprising if you didn't. So many members of your sign go so far in life with an interrupted education.

It's not the attention deficit thing everybody seems to suffer from these days. You are on the run most of the time, and that's not a criticism. You cover a lot of territory in a short period of time, and one has to wonder exactly what fuels your restless resistance to settling down. Maybe it's just that you've got a bigger bag of wild oats to sow than other people and therefore want to stay young longer in true Peter Pan style.

You have to develop confidence in your own brain power, which you lacked in youth. Not the intelligence—the confidence. And you'll have to work hard to overcome social, ethnic, or racial prejudices that make you feel stupid or inferior. Great moments of suffering come when you are not listened to or when you know you have solid wisdom to impart that is ignored and your advice goes unheeded. That is one cross you have to bear: You know more than you can say, and are therefore not taken seriously at crucial moments when it is vital to be heard and understood.

Sometimes it's a lot easier to give up, play in your own sandbox, and let everybody laugh and think you're just another face with nothing upstairs. But you do have strong ideas and convictions. You do have rather high moral standards—even religious convictions in some cases—even if your behavior and actions make some people think you're one of those in-name-only Catholics, very devout but not monogamous, or a not-so-observant Jew who adores BLTs. There's bound to be a gap between what's in your head and what comes out of your mouth.

Communication is easy, too easy sometimes, if you're talking fast and selling a used car or trying to seduce someone, but it's very difficult when the subject is more complex or deep. There is, however, a whole other side. The fast-talking wiseguy is just a defense for fear that the profound philosopher in you will be ridiculed, laughed at, or ignored. The religious issue persists and eventually needs to be addressed.

At this point in order to make the best use of your energy you have to pass through the illusion of communication to tap into your real gifts as an Aries. In the next part, Going Deeper, read the chapter called "Communication" to find the word or phrase you need to develop your talents and make your Sun shine bright.

Aries 4

Who would ever guess in a million years the big, strong, I-don't-need-anybody-I-can-do-it-myself Aries you are is also a weeping, lost little puppy all alone and abandoned by its mommy. So naturally family is going to be the gigantic tail that wags your dog. It will be very important to you to disguise this lost-little-puppy-dog aspect of your personality, mainly because it is *so* un-Aries. You're supposed to be brave and self-reliant, unmoved by petty emotions, and certainly not fixated on the past. Your sign is supposed to live only for right now—this minute, a self-created future built solely on your immediate actions. It's not typically Arian at all to dwell upon the past and search for lost roots, or to operate in response to what happened long ago, with your behavior fueled by reactions to what your parents did to you or didn't do for you. So maybe that's why you get nuts on the subject of having a home and creating a family, and why you get so inextricably wound up with and tied into your parents. Extreme case: You freeze at the thought of walking out the door and leaving the house.

One thing you cannot escape: being known by the public in your area. You don't have to be world famous, but life, fate, or whatever you want to call it will not permit you to rot away in your little nest of coziness or self-pity. You have a job to do in this world. You must put yourself in your high-functioning mode (with or without the aid of substances). You have the potential to become a total dynamo/CEO/leader/boss/governor/entertainer/fireman/mom and dad combined. There's always a pull between the dependable competent professional and the weak or dependant child. Even if you elected to vedge out and stay in bed for the next twenty years, you'd have to give interviews to the press from your darkened room.

Nobody can say for sure where this conflict comes from. It either propels you forward and upward in business—mainly because you are scared of ending up like your parents—or it compels you to spend too much time (way too much time) puttering around the yard or the kitchen as a way to avoid the drain and drudgery of office politics— unless you're a chef or a landscaper/developer, in which case you've got the best of both worlds. No matter how hard you try, though, you're unlikely to recreate the illusion of the 1950s: Wife kisses hubby good- bye, hubby goes off to work, wife puts on her apron and bakes cookies while singing until it's time to throw the roast in and kiss hubby hello. Uh-uh. Oh, you'll try. A balance between home and work is certainly the answer.

At this point you need to probe a little deeper into why you are not the to- tally typical, free-wheeling Aries. In the next part, Going Deeper, reading the chapter called "Security" will give you a chance to pass through the il- lusion of abandonment and into a higher expression of your Aries nature to ensure your success in the world and make your Sun shine bright.

> ★ *Celebrities Who Share Your Issues*
> *Dennis Quaid, Dudley Moore, Henry James*

Aries 5

Some people will certainly call you narcissistic. They'll say you have to bring everything back to yourself, that you have to be the center of atten- tion every minute, that you're always on, that you're obsessed with your image, and that you've got the personality of the stereotypical Holly- wood actor. How cruel. Don't they know how hard it is for you to sit there with your hands folded in your lap when all your natural instincts are telling you to get up and show them all how it's done? They just think "obnoxious, self-absorbed Aries." People would be totally blown away if they knew how shy you really are. Not shy, exactly, but how difficult it has been for you to learn how to relate socially. And yes, you're a born performer. There's nothing wrong with that. It's a great thing. It's a gift to be able to perform or get up in front of people and speak. If some people think you hog the stage and that you get hammy now and then, that's their prerogative. You just want to be loved. That's normal, isn't it? Sure, but you and love, that's another story. Who in this world could ever give you all the love you need? One person? Ten? A million? You have a bit of a hole in your heart that is tough to fill, and your quest for validation could become your raison d'etre: self-assertion, being known and accepted for who you are, dammit!—and if people don't like it, tough!

You are not just an egomaniac, mad at the world and trying to control everything and everybody. That's bull. You have a real desire to help other people. Nothing turns you on like being the watchdog for the underdog and the champion for those who can't champion themselves. And maybe that's why people think you're so brave and strong and able and capable. Because even though you do seize the floor whenever there's an opportunity, it's not just because you want the spotlight. In fact, you do want to make a generous contribution and you do want to be remembered not just for your looks but for what you did for other people. Sure, that's ironic. You do have an inordinate need to be loved and your personal life has been a rose garden comprised mostly of thorns. You're not about to advertise your heartaches and moan and whine and sob, because that's not your way. But you certainly must advocate for people's rights to express themselves freely, even if in your own childhood, children and young people were beaten down and discouraged from showing who they really were. So naturally you're still mad about that, and you can either beat down and discourage young people or stand up for them and be a shining example of how people can overcome shame and rejection and social embarrassment and become powerful members of society.

Although it takes guts to rise above self-loathing or embarrassment for how you look or how you feel, the rejected lover is a role you've played more than once, and the fact that you are always asked to love on a higher plane and be a friend is the way to happiness.

At this point you need to probe more deeply the issues in your personal life that have interfered with the contributions you want to make. In the next part, Going Deeper, reading the chapter called "Love" will give you a chance to pass through the illusion of love and move to the higher vibration of your Aries nature to make your Sun shine bright.

Celebrities Who Share Your Issues
Richard Chamberlain, Gloria Steinem, Shirley Jones, Orrin Hatch,
Rick Moranis, Billie Holiday, Barry Sonnenfeld, Ewan McGregor

Aries 6

Heigh-ho, heigh-ho. It's off to work you go, heigh-ho, heigh-ho! No question that you are a worker bee, a soldier with blue-collar blood coursing through your veins—nothing fancy or grandiose about you. Fussy? Yipes! Some say you're a perfectionist; others claim you're just a royal pain. You know how to work late into the night until you're bone tired, and although you bitch from dawn to dusk, you still carry on even though your feet are sore or your back is aching or you're coughing and feverish. You can still show up as faithfully as the U.S. mail. In fact, the sicker or more exhausted you are, the bigger the challenge. The bigger the challenge, the more you can prove you can do it. You've had to take some crappy jobs in your time, but then work is work, and it does make you feel better, sick or well, to be able to make yourself useful and be independent. God knows, no angels are going to fly out of the clouds with a cup of tea and a butter biscuit holding a pair of furry slippers. Or are they? You've had a few scary bouts with trust in your day, but you ended up guess where?—*working again.*

Maybe you're not an easy person to bring tea, biscuits, and slippers to. The tea is cold, the biscuits too sweet, the slippers too hot for your feet. Or something. There is always some sand in your bathing suit: It's a scary prospect for you to *not* work, to be somewhat dependent. And the funny thing is, you love doing things for other people, even if your motive is to maintain control. Your kindness and generosity are great assets, even if it is very hard for you to be on the receiving end. Sooner or later, however, you can't be afraid to believe there's a plan in the

Universe, a force, a current that moves everyone including you, even when you're outside the boat pulling everyone else in it, by a rope through the swampy reeds.

You're part of a vast rhythm of the Universe that does not hinge on whether you get up at six and do your stretches or not. Intimacy is not just a dangerous seduction designed to lure you into a dulled, dazed, chaotic state that impedes your functioning; it's actually the antidote to your obsessive fear of becoming obsolete and to the ferocious urge to remain young, unspoiled, untouched, uncorrupted, in control, and unattached.

It's utterly impossible to live in this world and avoid the cooties of existence; contamination is unavoidable, emotionally as well as figuratively. Will intimacy cause chaos and interfere with your work if you allow yourself to be tempted to lose an innocence you're clinging to in desperate fear of being unable to cope and survive? Probably, but it will also enrich your life.

At this point you need to probe your obsession with work a little deeper. In the next part, Going Deeper, you will get a chance to examine this need to be useful and practical and pierce the illusion of work by reading the chapter called "Control." It will help to soften your hold on what you consider reality, and help you make your sun shine brightest.

> *Celebrities Who Share Your Issues*
> *Mariah Carey, Christopher Walken, Debbie Reynolds,*
> *Jayne Mansfield, Vince Vaughn, Haley Joel Osment*

Aries 7

Apart from the fact that you're the one who has to do everything and you rarely if ever get properly thanked or taken care of . . . you're a lucky person. You are lucky to be gifted with a life force that flows within you and gives you the strength to support as many people as you do, especially those helpless, even inferior beings who haven't been endowed with the powers you have. That could sound like a gigantic rationalization when you think about all you've done for people and how damned little you've gotten back. The truth is simple. Some people, like yourself, grew up early, took responsibility early—not because they were thrilled to give up their childhood long before they should, but because when there's nobody who's going to do it for you, you have to do it for yourself.

What happens all too often, unfortunately, is that you get very unbalanced and unrealistic about all relationships, business and personal. You don't really trust or believe anybody is going to be there for you the way you are for them, so you wait for the moment of disappointment or abandonment, knowing it's going to come sooner or later. Or you go the opposite route and imbue the other person with magical powers they don't have in the hopes that maybe this time, somebody will care for you as much as you care for them.

So why do you always—or almost always (maybe a bit less than you used to)—gravitate to needy, dependent, hopeless or helpless cases? It's a habit, getting hooked and thinking you have to save people then resenting them for it—a habit mighty hard to break. You get sucked in, lose yourself, then have to break away because you're pissed off that you got put right back into the hero/savior role, which—pardon the frankness— you've allowed to happen too often. You have to be brave and free yourself from guilt. You need to be liberated from your grandiose sense of your own importance. You have to be able to help when you can but also to allow people to live with their pain and their issues without thinking it's your fault or your job to fix them. You have to develop the strength to be alone and not think you're bad or wicked or a total loser if you choose to stay on your own path and not collapse into somebody's arms and be engulfed in their problems.

The role of true leader is what you, as an Aries, must assume. Setting an example for others, less gifted and mature, to follow. The healthy spirit that you have been given has to help you develop not only your compassion but your self-reliance.

At this point you need to probe a little deeper this issue of being alone. In the next part, Going Deeper, you will get a chance to read the chapter

"Marriage" and gain greater balance between your wish to be connected to another person and the strength you find in your independence to make your Sun shine bright.

Celebrities Who Share Your Issues
Leonard Nimoy, Sir Alec Guinness, Ram Dass, Booker T. Washington,
Paloma Picasso, Clarence Darrow, Ron Perlman, Christine Lahti,
Patricia Arquette

Aries 8

Aries stands for the fight for truth and justice. That's a given. You're usually a bright spot in any darkness, because you can't stand for things to be covered up or swept under the rug. You'll go down into the valley of the lepers with coffee and danish, especially if you have to break down a fence to get there. Sometimes the urge to surpass those boundaries and thumb your nose at taboos can get you into a heap of trouble. Such acting out is usually associated with the wild folly of youth, and the older you get, the slightly tamer you become. Your horror of being a petty bourgeois, however, can fuel your penchant for misbehaving, and it will take enormous restraint for you not to sneak in a few secret snorts of pleasure now and then. Sex is a problem only when you're overattached to either your desirability as a sexual object or the gender role you are required to play in society. You've got a serious sexual issue that goes way back.

Periodically it comes back again like an old army wound. Arians work this out in different ways. Some are on sexual watch and continually act naughty until they are caught in a motel at the edge of town. Others reform and repent and lead monogamous, stainproof lives that make up in loyalty what they lack in passion. Then you've got the Arian watchdogs, who go peeking around corners to make sure nobody's "doing it" or that everybody is doing it when, where, and how they're supposed to. It's a really tough obsession to unhook from, whether you practice promiscuity or abstinence, when you don't have a sound sex education from the start. Aries overcomes everything, however. Your will can always end up at least as strong as—if not stronger than—your obsessions, so whatever fears you have of inferiority usually get well compensated for. When you turn your attention away from the dark side, prosperity and recognition flow toward you. It's like an artist who finally capitulates and understands that in this society, business is part of everyday life. It is not easy for you to acknowledge that your path is part mission, part passion, but also very largely part business and politics. It's business that will help (force) you to take your mind off the dark side, gain wealth, and when you come down to it—live a better and probably longer life.

At this point you need to probe yourself a little deeper. In the next part, Going Deeper, when you read the chapter called "Sex" you will get a chance to see how best to manifest all your creative talents and bring greater prosperity into your life, and make your Sun shine bright.

> ### Celebrities Who Share Your Issues
> Pat Robertson, Sandra Day O'Connor, Harry Houdini,
> Mary Pickford, Thomas Jefferson, Keira Knightley, Robin Wright Penn

Aries 9

What are you looking for? What do you think you are going to find over the next hill or the next or the next? Your Aries mind is thirsty for experience and knowledge, but it gets a bit much when you can't ever be satisfied where you are. You're like the tourist who arrives in London and after two hours starts reading the Paris guide book. Your life could become a whole if-this-is-Tuesday-we-must-be-in-Venice kind of trip. It's not that you don't enjoy yourself. You always enjoy yourself. You're curious about absolutely everything and you don't want to *not* know anything. You probably have some kind of weird phobia about being thought of as ignorant or stupid. It's not so weird when one thinks of the role that education, or lack of it, played in your childhood. You can't stand pedantic, know-it-all teachers who actually get off on messing with their students' heads and making them feel dumb, but you can also get a kick out of games of one-upmanship, proving your moral or intellectual superiority by speaking above the heads of your peers so only a select few get the joke. There's actually a lot of defensiveness in your behavior sometimes. Class, racial, religious, or social differences that make you feel inferior can prompt you to overcompensate in outrageous ways. Not all your Arian brothers and sisters act this way, of course. Being successful doesn't mean you have to be accepted and loved by everyone, of course. You have your own standards of morality and behavior that many of the hypocrites around will judge in their own way. But to be successful in love, to be really fulfilled, you have to overcome your fear of being laughed at for your ideas. You need to develop your own mode of communication and even a whole new language. There is a hearing-impaired woman who, in her parents' effort to protect her from hurt, was never told she was hearing impaired until she got to kindergarten. Until that time she thought everyone was like her. How her family managed to keep it from her during the first five years of her life is a mystery. In any case, Aries that she was, she decided at five that communication was not going to hold her back. She now holds two PhD degrees from two of the highest-rated Ivy League colleges in the United States. The two degrees are actually less of an achievement than her ability to communicate with many individuals on many levels in the hearing world.

Obstacles, although they annoy you no end, are your fuel. If there's one thing you have to do on this planet, you must find a link between what goes on in the head and what comes out of the mouth.

At this point you need to probe more deeply the illusion of education and its impact on your life. In the next part, Going Deeper, you will learn in the chapter called "Religion" how to articulate more readily your gifts to the world, and make your Aries Sun shine bright.

> *Celebrities Who Share Your Issues*
> Tim Dalton, James Lovell, Elton John, Maya Angelou,
> Ethel Kennedy, David Letterman, Sarah Jessica Parker,
> Kareem Abdul-Jabbar, Tom Clancy

Aries 10

Fighting a corrupt system can be the noblest of missions. Righting the wrongs of wicked politicians could become the path you were born to take, no matter how unpopular your views or philosophy. You could go against the whole tide of society in your battle for what you think is right. The thing is, you could get on a crazy high horse and become totally misguided, totally off the mark, totally power-crazed yourself in your efforts to unseat the power-crazed. It's a tricky business, because when you get your back up, God help those you consider to be unjustly in positions of power. You could hate 'em all, just because they are in positions to make the laws you find untenable. You're discontented with society as it stands, and you want to change it? Fine, just try not to lump all people into one category and judge them too harshly, even if you have been victimized by The System. Well, you'll probably be branded as an upstart or troublemaker in any case. You have to know, though, that the whole problem with authority goes a lot deeper than you might think. Therapy would help, except the minute the shrink disappoints you in any way, he or she is history. You'd bolt and overthrow the process. Of course, the answer to your crusade against unjust laws and lawmakers is not, as you might think, to get rid of them all. Quite the contrary. Invite them all into your house for drinks and dinner. Setting up a home for people to come to and feel safe and secure in: That's the real accomplishment. Give people a shelter from the political storm they live in. Have a family—the thing you think is going to impede your progress is the very thing that will be your progress.

Every life is filled with irony, and that's yours. Turning away from a society you believe to be corrupt, and creating a haven of refuge from it, may not unhook you from your angry war against what you perceive to be intolerable injustice. It will, however, provide you with the base from which to operate. The more fanatically you fight society, the further underground you will be driven. You may never join them, but inviting the enemy to dinner will turn out to be your greatest secret weapon, and you won't have to slip anything weird into the drinks, either. It's the old honey-or-vinegar trick, and all you have to do is learn the recipe.

• • •

At this point you need to probe your issues with authority figures a little deeper. In the next part, Going Deeper, when you read the chapter called "Recognition" you will see best how to move your ship through political waters without losing Arian integrity and come out into the wide ocean of possibility, and make your Sun shine bright.

Celebrities Who Share Your Issues
Julian Lennon, Hugh Hefner, Gus Grissom, Charlie Chaplin,
Elle McPherson, Conan O'Brien

Aries 11

Some people are just not the groupie type. It's the old saying about not wanting to join any group that elects you to be part of it. And that's funny, too, because you will probably be a powerful advocate for freedom First Amendment rights, legalization of drugs, or the protection of disenfranchised peoples of the world, AIDS victims, or any other group suffering discrimination or mistreatment. If you get hooked on a cause, you know congress will have to pay attention to it. When you get angry over a bully beating up someone, you're going to wake up a lot people about it at 6 AM, and dammit! laws are going to change. No greater champion could anyone find for gay activists or stray kittens. Of course, as usual one of the dogs you give shelter to will bite you. When the group you're fighting for disavows you, once again you'll wonder why the hell you are bothering to get your fur in a flurry for a bunch of ungrateful people who didn't really give a hoot about you.

Yet here you go, still doing it, still caring, still making the effort. Of course, some would say if you stayed home and took care of your kids once in a while instead of running around picketing and marching and getting people to sign petitions, you'd be a lot better off.

You know you should stay home more, but it's stressful for you. Personal life is not easy. It's very hard to be in an enclosed space, and it takes too much time away from what you think is your real life. That's the joke. Where is your real life? Does it involve the battle for human rights? Or does it really and truly lie in your acceptance of your role as mom or dad, and in the ability to be in a loving situation with one other person, not thousands of downtrodden strangers. It's a lot easier for you to embrace the concept of an entire race of people than to hug and hold or be hugged and held by one single, solitary individual who needs you without getting itchy, nervous, and restless and thinking you've got to go. Developing your ability to be present on a personal as well as impersonal basis will give you depth and empathy and an understanding of intimate relationships you simply cannot get by loving people anonymously from afar. You've got to leave the group and shine on your own.

At this point you need to probe your obsession with your own independence a little deeper. In the next part, Going Deeper, read the chapter called "Freedom" to pass through the illusion of freedom to go on to bring out the warmth and love your Aries nature is capable of, and to make your Sun shine bright.

Celebrities Who Share Your Issues
Doris Day, Eric Idle, Diana Ross, Matthew Broderick,
Marlon Brando, MC Hammer

Aries 12

Maybe only a few people will ever know the depths to which you've sunk and how you've had to pull yourself out of quicksand just as you were about to disappear and get swallowed up. Loved ones, therapists, and employees will certainly know and hopefully not publish a tell-all book about you, because the less that gets around about your periodic descents into the cellar of darkness, the better. Unless you're a writer of horror or other spooky or tear-jerking fiction. Of course, as an Aries you can't resist those dangerous forays into nowhere. In some cases it's downright bipolar. In others, it's just the Arian need to plunge periodically into oblivion just to be able to rise again like a phoenix out of your own self-destructive ashes.

So there will definitely be more comebacks than Frank Sinatra had. There are damned good reasons why you have to escape now and then to nurse an old wound and indulge in some bad behavior. It gets serious if you keep upping the ante, escalating the danger, and spending more energy on the downslide. Then you run the risk of going that one step over the edge and not being able to pull yourself back.

Sobriety and hard work are the paths away from self-indulgence. Both, however, are colossally boring to an individual who refuses to grow up and be more grounded. Granted, you can't remain too long at sewing or whittling little figurines without going out for a few drops of escape. The trick to decent living and long life is not simply to swear off your naughtiness. You probably never will. It's just that nobody can live a fulfilling, productive life with such intense highs and lows. After a while it takes its toll on your health, and if you don't curb your appetite for pleasure you start having that ravaged look way too early for your age.

The sorrows you secretly bear for a past that has many ironic, tragic twists are many, and the only thing that's really going to pull you out of deep water is the life preserver of simple, practical, down-to-earth, regular old work and normal nonmagical health remedies like vegetables and fruit juice.

At this point you need to probe a little deeper into why you can't take being around people all that much. In the next part, Going Deeper, when you read the chapter called "Escape" you will get a chance to pass through the illusion of seeking refuge from a boring world. It will help you to channel your energy and make your Aries Sun shine bright.

> *Celebrities Who Share Your Issues*
> *Aretha Franklin, Michael York, Erica Jong, Marshia Mason,*
> *Wayne Newton, Norah Jones, Christopher Meloni*

TAURUS

April 20–May 20

Dates vary from year to year—consult your local astrologer

Taurus is the grassy meadow in full springtime. Daisies and daffodils are in full bloom. All of life is cherry pink and apple blossom white. Trees are exploding with green. If there is a goddess of fertility, she's pregnant again. This is the moment of glory of life on Earth; Nature is giving up its bounty. Indoors it's just as lush, luxurious, and natural as it is in the meadow outside. In the house rich Oriental rugs cover the sturdy wooden floors. There are couches you could sink into forever, watching TV and eating about a thousand pounds of Ben & Jerry's Giant Chocolate Chunk. A maid is ringing a dinner bell, and in the dining room duck à l'orange is being served on beautiful china on a long shining mahogany table. Seated at the table are a pair of elegant people. They may be rough and crude in some ways, but even if they are covered in tattoos with pierced body parts (some Tauruses just have to prove they're rebellious), they still exude breeding. On their backs they sport Ralph Lauren or some other designer whose fashions will go out of style somewhere in the year 3059. There is a forever quality to the whole scene. The happy couple will be married until death do them part, but if they're Tauruses, probably a lot longer than that. In fact, forever is written all over the place.

So many Tauruses have so many problems either amassing such a fortunate life or keeping it. Do you have any idea how lucky you are to be a Taurus living right now in the world? Even at this time, with the whole planet spinning out of control, you should kiss the floor your couch is nailed to and be thrilled you are here. Just imagine yourself in Stalinist Russia in the 1950s, when you couldn't even own one lousy cow, much less a condo in the Caribbean. Here in capitalism country the New York Stock Exchange is also a Taurus, so you're in pretty snazzy company. Whatever it goes through, you go through, whether you're heavily invested in the market or not. In fact, the changes that you go through will be reflected in the activity of the NYSE as well. Change: not your favorite thing.

And to think of the un-Taurus state of the world, golly! Some morons today run around wearing their underwear outside their clothes and call it fashion. Only a nut wouldn't think that was nuts, because it *is* nuts. It's a complete offense to normal sensibilities, and that's what Taurus is, normal sensibilities. You're something anyone can count on all the time, a volume of Shakespeare you pick up twenty-five years later and it's exactly the same, only better. Like the redwood forest, the trees get wider, the roots get deeper, not only over the years, but over the centuries.

You've heard the song, "the Rockies may crumble, Gibraltar may tumble, they're only made of clay." But Taurus is here to stay. One mind-set. All the way. Mellowing like good wine. No hiccups. No surprises. No deviations. No divine deus ex anythings. Always and forever. You might even say is was and shall be. World without end. Just take a walk down to Wall Street some time and look at the edifice that houses the NYSE. It's not prefab. One look and it tells you, "Come back in the year 3000 and I'll be here, looking just as I do now." Let's hope so.

Just good ole Mac over at the gas station, been there since long before the interstate went in, and he'll be over there, pumpin' gas, we reckon, 'til the corn grows sideways. If you're a Taurus, you can definitely identify. You're as reliable as the old cars the Chrysler Corporation used to put out in the fifties, and you can withstand ups and downs even better than Detroit. You're as clear as an Ella tune which, even when it was Memorex, was still very much alive. Taurus is the great pre-Castro Havana cigar, TV before the Elvis went on Ed Sullivan and ruined everything, the clip-clop of horses in town before there were cars, and things were right and servants lived downstairs. In short, Taurus is the gritty determination of the bull as well as the bulldog Michael Moore, although with a definite swing to the right. It's not only the sign of the bull. It's the sign of the bull market.

It's not that you're snobby or anything, although you have to admit that your ears do perk up a little and your eyes sort of sparkle like a kid at Christmas when you hear somebody mention Beverly Hills, Shaker Heights, Westchester, or Sixteenth Arrondissement. That's why you are torn between voting for protection of the environment (you love nature) and voting for whatever will raise the value of your 5000 shares of Boeing. Hell, why not live well while you're here? You're only here once, and as long as you are here you want to fulfill every last one of your appetites. Taurus is the sign of appetite, usually without an off button, and that's why as they get older the waistlines of some Tauruses are equal to their age.

As far as roughing it goes, you'll go to the Moon when you don't have to go coach and they've got nice fluffy towels up there. Not that you're ever turned on by phonies who speak French in French restaurants when they're sitting right there in Dallas, Texas. And even if maybe you did the whole cruise thing in an upper cabin and saw the Aegean and Montego Bay, by golly, there's nothing like that restaurant down the block, "your" restaurant, the one that's been serving you your pot roast since—it's gotta be going on twenty years now, two years before Sally the waitress went and got herself pregnant (and she had your regular order down pat, too, dammit). And dadgonnit! That's the way you like pot roast, well-done, and a waitress who knows your name.

It must be said here that you are certainly not a boring old party pooper, just because you like things the way you like them. Tauruses have been known to party on into the wee hours until they've snorted everyone else under the table. Fact is, though, there's a set of beliefs you have about the way things are supposed to be. And what's a right way for folks to live, and that's that. Some Tauruses—not you of course, but some Tauruses—would be a lot happier today if all that ruckus back in the sixties had never happened.

But it did. And that was just the beginning. Now, it's almost hard to find a spot that doesn't make you uncomfortable any more.

Up until now you've been able to figure out a way to understand and even rationalize your position in this insane world full of caprice and whimsy and nonsense, even if it seems stubborn and old-fashioned to some. Maybe you are swimming against the current direction society is going, which is actually to hell in a handbasket as far as you are concerned. What's happened to service?

What's happened to politeness or tradition or morality? All of society, in fact, is currently in the process of, in plain English, falling apart. Nobody believes in anything any more. Social mores are for the birds, and proper ways of behaving have been thrown slap into the garbage can. In fact, there's nothing left to guide us through the darkest night, except, God help us, rap music. Up until now you have believed that the human condition could improve (you're not a cynic, after all), could improve dramatically, in fact, if only the people of the world would open their eyes and see the light. If only they thought the way you did.

Well, wind my watch and call me Dizzy, because no matter how you resist the mad fads of the fickle mob, you and every other Taurus will eventually undergo a shift of perspective and achieve a greater understanding of how and why the world changes the way it does. In fact, you eventually experience an enlightenment and change of consciousness the likes of which haven't been seen since the Buddha himself sat his butt down under a tree and figured out the Secret of Life. But you don't have to go sit under a tree minding your own business to find yourself suddenly thinking, "Eureka! That's it! I've got to leave my job and family and start a psychotherapy practice that could turn into a religion!" That's Enlightenment for you. One day you're living a life you think is just peachy perfect (aside from a few major life crises and minor irritations you're willing to overlook because you'd rather suffer than change), and the next thing you know you can't tolerate one more minute of it. Then it's just as if everything in your Kodachrome life seems more like an old black and white photograph from someone else's album. More likely, however, the process of Enlightenment takes place over a much longer period of time. Many Tauruses have to go through major therapy just to change their brand of toothpaste.

Every Taurus is at a different stage of mental and intellectual evolution. No matter where you are on the ladder, spiritually or intellectually, something quite miraculous is going to happen inside your brain. So don't pay attention to the critics who think you are dull and slow-witted. It just takes a little longer sometimes for Tauruses to get a joke. Your particular form of Enlightenment brings a broadening of mind, and while it often begins with nothing more than a trip or a simple exotic vacation, it sets off a chain reaction of ideas that eventually transform your entire view of life. Whatever the experience may be, it begins with some objective experience that connects with something being born within you.

You take one look at the NASA pictures of Mars or Saturn or an outer galaxy, and something stirs in you. This has nothing to do with your kids or your relationships or your business or any other of the daily joys and miseries we who are chained to the flesh are doomed to experience. Maybe you climb the Pyramids, or view starving children in Africa on TV, or make a pilgrimage to the Holy Sepulchre, or do something that is outside your normal routine, even if it is a routine you've loved and clung to all your life. At first it's just an image on your digital camera— something to tell the folks at home about. Not long after, Enlightenment hits you, and at that point it is no longer enough to be alive and prosperous. You want to know *why* you are alive, and whether it's financially practical or not, whether your search is considered heretical or not, you are on your path. Thus begins your real education, an explosion of thought that will obliterate every belief you have ever had concerning what your true reality is all about. This philosophical transformation raises questions of faith and dogma that will change all your ideas about why you have been put on the Earth and where you are going. The expansion of consciousness on this sort of scale overturns your entire belief system and liberates your true intelligence, no matter how long it takes. Don't get nervous, though. You won't have to throw out your good dishes.

It is scary when your whole paradigm shifts. At first you freak out, of course, get totally defensive, and retreat to your old way of thinking, clinging a hundred times more ferociously to everything you have been taught to believe. You could even become more conservative and orthodox in your approach. Some Tauruses will become rabid fundamentalists during this period, and that is the big joke. Whether you turn into a foaming-at-the-mouth conservative or something else, the people around you will think you've gone nuts. They will want to hustle you in for a CAT scan or rush to put you on some "stabilizing" medication, so you can come back to your senses and be normal again. Most likely they'll be wasting their time. An awakening of awareness of this magnitude cannot be suppressed or denied forever.

While it is true that you could do the Buddha-bop-on-the-head/ Eureka thing, it is more likely that this profound and permanent transformation takes place slowly. When it happens, you may think at first that your whole view of life and lifestyle have been put in jeopardy, but in the end you see that you've taken the only path to growth and freedom there is for you. It is a voyage you take voluntarily, inspired by your own natural curiosity, by a discontentment you already feel, and by your need to rediscover meaning and purpose.

Your most challenging task will be to confront your own prejudices and even hypocrisy—a belief and moral system and rules for behavior you accepted but have not followed as religiously as you have pretended to follow or wanted to follow, just because they have not been convenient or conducive to the way you've chosen to live. So it's when you're out there, on the thinnest limb of the spiritual tree, that something magical happens. A light bulb goes on. You think, "Hey! Wow! I never saw it like that before. Why didn't I discover this before?" The spark of Enlightenment ignites your whole soul, illuminates your path as if for the first time. It is there and then that you come to see exactly what you have to do to become a spiritually whole human being. Then will come the split with the party line. You will disavow some form of accepted belief or orthodoxy and espouse an entirely fresh, new philosophy, based on your own beliefs. It's enough to turn a dyed-in-the-wool Republican into a Democrat, and even stranger, the other way around. Oh, it's scary, all right. It's Martians attacking your lawn party. It can be terrifying when you first catch a glimpse of what's happening, what's out there, what's *really* out there.

You come to see that what encompassed a worldview you considered to be universal and sophisticated was at best parochial and at worst paranoid and xenophobic. You will be exposed to your own prejudices and challenged to challenge them. Once you have seen what you consider to be the light, there is no going back. Eventually courage overtakes anxiety and conviction replaces guilt. Once you've crossed the threshold of new awareness, there is no longer any fear of ridicule or reprisal. In its place is perfect clarity in your understanding of how men and women should live, free from mental or moral restriction. Conscience is at last liberated from conditioning and suppressive dogma.

Can you, a Taurus, think truly independently of the issues and ideas planted in your head by family, church, state, and your own perceptions of your own experiences? If you believe in the evolution of human thought, creative freedom, and the ability of an individual to step away from automatic, unconscious knee-jerk behavior, then the answer is yes. To do that you need to go in deep and restructure your inner personality. This is possible. Somewhere, somehow, you are going to turn over a rock, stumble on a clue, get the prize in a box of Cracker Jack. Something will let you know you're on the right track and there is life beyond your annoying brother-in-law, beyond the rings of Saturn, and beyond what they have pounded into your head as true.

Since you're a Taurus, God only knows what it will take to put this new head on your shoulders. It will happen, though. Count on it. There is something out there, something shining, thrilling, and blissful. It's as vast as an ocean and as bright as the sparkle of the Sun on the water. It is called Higher Law, a law we all answer to. You've always been interested in the laws that govern human behavior and morality. Now you need to discover how to feel compassion toward the baboon sitting across from you at the board meeting or the dinner table. How can you experience this broadening of perspective and still keep your values and sense of morality and codes of behavior? If you are living in a world you consider low-minded and crass, how can you integrate your ideas of material wealth and prosperity into a world you see as too vulgar and too concerned with money and wealth? There has to be a way for you to be able to enjoy the world with all its rich gifts and still not be dragged into the selfish and greedy hell you see going on around you.

So how you do you retain your sanity in a crazy world and gain greater stability and prosperity and achieve your goals? What are the forces that drag you backward and keep you from reaching the highest manifestation of your Sun? And what are the energies that can support you, guide you, enhance your positive qualities, and make your Sun shine bright? The fact is you're not just a Taurus. There is another energy operating, one that either cuts across your efforts and undermines them, or spirits you to heights of joy and fulfillment. That energy depends not on the month you were born, but the year as well. Later on in this book the technical aspects will be explained more fully. We'll examine how you waste time chasing your own tail, why you do it, and how to pull yourself out of self-destructive obsessions and put yourself back on the road to success. But for now, check out the following table. Find your birth year and note the number beside it. Then read the section corresponding to the number.

Year–No.	Year–No.	Year–No.	Year–No.	Year–No.
1901–1	1924–10	1947–8	1970–5	1991–3
1902–1	1925–10	1948–7	1971–4	1992–3
1903–12	1926–9	1949–6	1972–4 until	1993–2
1904–11	1927–8	1950–6	5/6, then 3	1994–1
1905–11	1928–8	1951–5	1973–3	1995–1
1906–10	1929–7	1952–4	1974–2	1996–12
1907–9	1930–6	1953–4	1975–2	1997–11
1908–9	1931–6	1954–3	1976–1	1998–11
1909–8	1932–5	1955–2	1977–12	1999–10
1910–7	1933–5	1956–2	1978–12	2000–9
1911–7	1934–4	1957–1	1979–11	2001–9
1912–6	1935–3	1958–1	1980–10	2002–8
1913–6	1936–3	1959–12	1981–10	2003–8 until
1914–5	1937–2	1960–11	1982–9	5/14, then 7
1915–4	1938–1	1961–11	1983–8	2004–7
1916–4	1939–1	1962–10	1984–8	2005–6
1917–3	1940–12	1963–9	1985–7	2006–6
1918–2	1941–12	1964–9	1986–7 until	2007–5
1919–2	1942–11	1965–8	4/22, then 6	2008–4
1920–1	1943–10	1966–7	1987–6	2009–4
1921–12	1944–10	1967–7	1988–5	2010–3
1922–12	1945–9	1968–6	1989–5	2011–2
1923–11	1946–8	1969–5	1990–4	2012–2

Year–No.	Year–No.	Year–No.	Year–No.	Year–No.
2013–1	2017–11	2021–8	2025–5	2029–3
2014–12	2018–10	2022–7	2026–5	2030–2
2015–12	2019–9	2023–7	2027–4	
2016–11	2020–9	2024–6	2028–3	

Taurus 1

It's really hard sometimes to respond to the passionate, well-intended sexual advances of partners if you feel angry, empty, or even dead inside. You do pull away, though. Plenty of times. And not because you don't love someone or they don't turn you on or you don't love to make love. Even though you love somebody and want to unite with them, you can be such a royal pain in the ass. There are moments when, gobble gobble, you're snorting somebody in as if they were a line of coke. It's not for a lack of appetite, God knows. When you want, you want; and as the song goes: the shark, dear, has such teeth, babe, and it shows them pearly white. When you're in that mood, you can be the most loving and passionate partner alive. Then, too, when you start to feel controlled or dominated, or a demand is made upon you that you can't or won't meet, the animal in you stops. That's when the ox in you refuses to budge. It's no go. No show. Turn on the lights. The star is late. So no matter how many adoring fans are out there who would love just one hour with you in the sack, when you need to regain control you will not move your butt for any amount of love or money.

This is not just about sex and personal relationships; it's about business as well. You're not easy to negotiate with. Sometimes you're a fanatic about the money and whether you're getting your fair share or getting screwed and what they are getting out of it and who has the longer end of the stick. But mostly, it's not really the money or position you give a damn about. You really shouldn't anyway, because not many people have the good fortune to be as sought-after, admired, desired, and wanted, or offered as many deals as you are. But when you get in that strange, absent, I'm-not-really-here mood, it's understandable how you could actually send in your clone to pick up the check or accept the Academy

Award for you, because to you at that moment it would mean nothing and couldn't fill the emptiness you feel inside.

So the goal is to be more present, cooperative, and appreciative of all your opportunities despite these periodic feelings of malcontent or the inexplicable despondency that cannot be traced to anything in your current life.

Man, what an appetite. That is one throat you've got there. Sword swallowers, eat your hearts out. You have such a drive to earn money that you could make, lose, and make back fortunes during your lifetime (depending on how self-destructiveness balances with a healthy belief that you deserve to be prosperous and happy). As always, you have to wonder how much of what we accomplish (or undo) is really all a matter of choice, and whether we come into this life with baggage we have to get rid of. And of course, blood too plays its own role in shaping the strange attitude you have toward money. How you seek to be not anything like your parent of the same sex when it comes to financial dependence reveals oodles about how you see yourself and in what role, male or female.

It's not only the money you want. It is also important for you to be perceived as a person of means. In fact, you can get dangerously over-attached to your social identity. You're like the hidalgo, an archetypal character in Spanish novels. Although he was an impoverished nobleman, he never appeared in public without a gold toothpick between his teeth, whether or not he had eaten.

You have to wonder what makes a person so obsessed with an image of wealth and prosperity. Such a preoccupation could actually be totally fine, because if you want something to be true about yourself, you certainly have to project it, even if it is only half true. You could go along that way, provided you've got the goods to back up the image. Okay, so part of it is hype, but if you follow through and deliver, everybody is a winner.

It's only those closest to you who know how hard you can be to live with—the moods, the bossiness, the ego, your impossible ego. You can be like a diva who screams at her agent then blames the agent when she has a sore throat and can't go on. It's odd, too, because deep down you yearn for a close, loving bond that can take away all the pain of the past.

Somebody has to be tough as nails to handle you—the tougher the better. You don't need necessarily to be smacked around, but from time to time you can certainly benefit from an occasional kick in the butt (metaphorically speaking, of course). You need someone you can't completely read, someone who keeps a few secrets from you. You'd be surprised how that can help you behave. In fact, despite your ferocious need to control the world around you, what you really need is a partner who holds you responsible for all your actions and whose actions are always a little beyond your control.

At this point you need to probe a little deeper your obsession with your own issues about control in a relationship. In the next part, Going Deeper, read the chapters called "Independence" and "Money" to pass through the illusion of fear of losing yourself to someone else, and on to a higher expression of your Taurus nature that will help you enjoy the prosperity of relationships more and make your Sun shine bright.

Celebrities Who Share Your Issues
Emperor Hirohito, David O. Selznick, Annette Bening, Gary Cooper, Sid Vicious

Taurus 2

It's unusual for a Taurus to not be into money, although you scream about it constantly. You may tell yourself it's all about money and keep your secret stash either in the fridge or in Switzerland. In the end, though, you could live in a hole in the ground and be happy if people would just let you be. Your fortunes will probably rise and fall periodically, partly because you're not all that smart about money or consistent, and partly because the Universe is trying to teach you how to accept from others as well as control them. Of course, you think you're smart, because you know how to move money around, write post-dated checks, and even sell pirated videos. You're basically an honest Taurus, but sometimes could have trouble resisting the temptation to receive a TV that fell off a truck or a fur coat offered to you by an old lady in an alleyway. When you're in your very cheap mood you could buy chicken necks on sale and try to pass them off as a rare delicacy, but then you could turn around and squander away an entire fortune in a big basket of forbidden fruit or some other crap you don't need.

Even when you have a gold-trimmed toilet, you could suddenly get the old starving artist–hungry pig feeling, and then you can forget that you are supposed to learn how to accept the generosity of other people, not take from them what they have just because you want it. Choose the right road and you can become a prolific artist or a dedicated, successful professional, especially in any field where communication is demanded. Because it was difficult for you to make yourself heard and understood as a child, language is a huge issue in your life. It is maybe for that reason that it's so important for you to be able to speak and master any language, whether it is foreign to you or not.

Sex must be part of your education in this lifetime, and it's a big part. You'll have to deal with more offers and propositions in one month than escort services have during the entire time they're in business. Not that you will, should, or can take advantage of them all, but it will be hard to pass up a few of the hotter ones. In this area you are both very Taurus and very un-Taurus: Taurus in the sense that if the danish pastry is on the plate in front of you, you're probably going to at least nibble if not gobble up the whole thing, and un-Taurus in the sense that sleeping with only one person your whole life just doesn't seem natural to someone with an appetite like yours. You'll buy things for everyone else and not yourself, then eat off everybody's plate.

At this point you need to probe a little deeper your obsession with poverty, real or imagined. In the next part, Going Deeper, read the chapters called "Money" and "Communication" to find the words you need to remember to gain greater stability and to help you move closer to your goals of prosperity, and make your Sun shine bright.

Celebrities Who Share Your Issues
Jack Nicholson, Chow Yun-Fat, Shakespeare, Duke Wallace, Saddam Hussein, Penelope Cruz

Taurus 3

Talk about your mother much? Now there's a subject with no end. Your shrink could buy Versailles on what you'd end up paying to get to the bottom of that dry well. Everybody's got one of course—a mother, not a shrink—and everybody's got a story they could tell about how she was and wasn't there at the same time, how there was and is absolutely no real communication but a nagging ongoing longing to make that mental/emotional connection with her. In an effort to disguise that sense of longing and deprivation, you could project your feelings onto other people or issues and not even realize you are doing it.

Ever find yourself screaming at some innocent person just because they didn't call when they said they would? In astrology it is said that Taurus is female and silent, but if anybody has ever incurred your wrath they have heard you roar like the bull you are. How silly to say you're still mad at your parents after all these years, but anger can create a more fierce attachment than love, especially if a person feels they were left to fend for themselves and not properly looked after.

That, of course, is the great irony of your life. Left to look after yourself, you eventually learn to use the power of your own wits and intelligence. That's when you really take off. When you stop hanging around the neighborhood street corner and actually venture into the world of adults, your education begins in earnest—not to mention your happiness. Even if it's hard for you to express, at least verbally, what is going on inside your mighty brain, it's the intelligence you once thought you lacked that will bring you the most success. But you'll probably never totally get off the abandonment thing. Somebody or other will have always stopped talking to you or you to them.

It's amazing to see how far you can go when you put your mind to it, but then a button is pushed and you're acting like an angry five-year-old. There's a huge gap between your potential and your ability to manifest it. The sculptor and painter are at first paralyzed, the writer and actor struck dumb until he or she figures out a way to move what is in the head out into the world. Greatness is in you. You definitely can't be lazy, though, or think there's a shortcut to wisdom. Patience of mind doesn't come easy or early for someone with as much going on in their head as you have. Putting the mind in order means eliminating the chaos of misunderstanding and poor communication. It means finding new significance in and respect for a morality or religious training that at first seems to have no meaning other than to control your thoughts and actions.

At this point you need to probe a little deeper into your obsession with being abandoned and your problems expressing feelings appropriately. In the next part, Going Deeper, read the chapters called "Security" and "Communication" to pass through the illusions that hold you back from prosperous self-expression, and to help you find the words that will make your Taurus Sun shine bright.

> *Celebrities Who Share Your Issues*
> *Michael Moore, Albert Finney, Glenda Jackson, Leonardo da Vinci*

Taurus 4

Losing too early the warmth and safety that parents can provide leaves its mark on you. It can either completely stunt your growth and leave you cowering in insecurity the moment you have to be alone for five minutes, or it can propel you to heights of achievement, success, and popularity. Usually, however, it is likely to be a little of both. You could be up there performing before a crowd of 100,000 people with complete confidence and ease, provided you could bring yourself to walk out the door and leave that thumb-sucking, yowling infant at home. No, not your kid. You. The terrified, agoraphobic, narcissistic, attention-grabbing, almost autistic child who was so ignored and deprived in the distant past still hasn't developed any other emotion but hunger. That kid is always there and it's always screaming for its mommy or daddy. One can't tell which, because your parent's gender roles could have gotten switched, as they well may be in your own life. You're determind to have a home and family, even though life insists on taking you far away from the home and family you'd like to create. If you were to build your whole identity solely around your image as a warm and loving head of household, you could eventually be exposed as a fraud. You belong more to the world than you do to the family, even though you can't wait to get home and take your shoes off.

You have a gift that needs to be developed and a talent for edifying, entertaining, or inspiring people that has been given to you for a reason. The people out there may not give a hoot whether or not you're getting enough lovin' on a hot night in August, but your job doesn't depend on that.

It can really be crippling, though, when that old feeling comes over you. No matter how confident and competent you are—and you could be a great leader—something happens and you buckle. No Taurus likes to show that, so you have to make every effort to put on a big smile, step onto the balcony, and wave to the crowd. Not only to keep up their faith in you, but to remind yourself this is where you should be and the career path is the right path and leading a professional life is what you should be doing. In a public setting nobody has to know what's going on inside. Is it hypocritical of you to stand for the Age of Aquarius let's-all-love-one-another when deep down you don't even feel loved yourself half the time? Some might say yes, indeed, your public persona is the real you, at least while you are out there in front of people. You do believe in tolerance and mutual respect and cooperation. It's when you forget that and start getting too clingy and needy and way too personal for your own good that the situation can get mighty messy.

Reconciling your professional self with your personal need—it's quite a task.

At this point you need to probe a little deeper your obsession with feeling unloved and uncared for. In the next part, Going Deeper, read the chapters called "Love" and "Security" to pass through the illusion of being abandoned and to help you carve the secure place in the world you deserve to have, and to make your Sun shine bright.

★ *Celebrities Who Share Your Issues*
Shirley MacLaine, Tony Blair, Frank Capra, Machiavelli,
Moshe Dayan, Pierce Brosnan, Sofia Coppola

Taurus 5

Love is supposed to warm you up, raise your fever, and boil your bananas, not leave you feeling cold and empty and unsatisfied. True enough, it takes a lot to satisfy a Taurus. You need a lottalotta lovin' and frankly it doesn't look as if one little person is going to be able to give you all you need. This doesn't mean you lack a deep sense of loyalty or commitment, because dammit! you can be loyal and committed. It's just that you've got this notion about an absolutely pure, unspoiled, spotless love thing, so you would probably be better off to wait a while to choose your ultimate lover. That, however, could take forever, considering how critical you can be when the glow wears off. When they start producing androids to customized specifications, then you can put in your order and your particular desires, needs, and fetishes can be much more easily satisfied. You can be picky and critical, especially when the shine rubs off and you see that once again you have projected onto your current love object a set of blueprints from which it is virtually impossible to construct a real relationship.

No matter how many times you've been hurt or disappointed, you don't stay in your bitter and cynical "never again" phase, though. You always go back for more, because you are fundamentally a deeply loving person and terminally romantic. You just have to avoid the notion that you are either a sick child or a nurse, put here on Earth to nurse sick "child" after sick "child." You are a highly evolved being, however, when you open up to all people without being attached too deeply to any. It's when you get hooked on the inappropriate or unattainable love objects that you need to step back and look at your own history in personal social situations. Some people are capable of enormous waves of unconditional love. They can pour it out and receive it, as long as there is distance between them (meaning you) and all the rest of the people in the world.

It's possible that your destiny involves more than a hot love affair, making it in the shower while music plays on the stereo.

Maybe your love has to include all the beings of this world and all other worlds. What if you haven't been put here to fit into the little normal life out in NoTown, Ohio, but to do something for the world at large you haven't been able to do for yourself? Wouldn't it be a kick it if all the love affairs you think you missed back in high school, all the adoration and attention you've thought you wanted, didn't really make you feel all that much better in the end, because there was something unreal and selfish about your fantasies? What if it were to turn out that the secret to being truly fulfilled and happy was not to be found in how many valentines you got, but how deeply you were able to love people? Maybe that's why you used to dump on people who did love you and always chose someone you couldn't have. That's a great realization to wake up to.

At this point you need to probe a little deeper into your issues about being loved in a healthier way. In the next part, Going Deeper, read the chapters called "Control" and "Love" to pass through the illusion of fear of not being able to have a fulfilling personal life, and to move on to a higher expression of emotion, find the words to give you a greater sense of your talents, and make your Taurus Sun shine bright.

> ★ *Celebrities Who Share Your Issues*
> *Renée Zellweger, Louis Farrakhan, Rudolph Valentino,*
> *Peter Ilyich Tchaikovsky, Javier Bardem, Kim Fields,*
> *Cate Blanchett, Robert Zemeckis*

Taurus 6

Wouldn't it be fantastic to have a full-time maid named Monique, a butler named Jeeves, and a pool boy named Renaldo, just like in the movies? They could stay with you your whole life through, run around after you, pick up your socks, bring you the mail with your coffee, remind you about your four o'clock rendezvous, pay all your bills, lay out your dinner attire, and meet all your other needs as well? Well—that's just what it would be: fantastic because you're not one of those Tauruses who has that kind of life. Well, of course you could keep the same one or two employees, if you could put up with incompetence and deal with the fact that just when you need them, they're not there. Actually that is one of the big problems: getting too involved with the blue-collar types and becoming so enmeshed in their problems and dependent on them that you end up serving them. Servitude and relationships—a very tricky mixture. Messing around with the babysitter or the gardener is the stuff TV movies are made of, and good tabloid reading, but what will it do for your life in the long run?

Such behavior crosses a line many people consider a big no-no. For you, though, it's sometimes (often) a temptation you seem to have a lot of trouble resisting. You've got a few hereditary relationship issues to contend with, and a whole thing about the dominant master and the submissive servant that merits at least a couple of solid years in therapy. Of course, even in therapy, you'd have to be vigilant to see how subtly the boundary erosion takes place, because when there's money changing hands and one person is working for another, there is danger.

Your jobs don't always pan out the way they promise to, either. When the great résumé meets the perfect position, step back, take a deep breath, think of the times you've fallen into the same trap, and give yourself time to think deeply before you move ahead. Be aware also, that you could want to stay in a job that's all wrong for you, just because you don't want to admit, God forbid, you've made a mistake.

And what about your health? You need the same ability to gain perspective there as well. You could read something accidentally in the newspaper or on the Internet about a certain topic—say, kidney function or lower back pain—and suddenly you have a ferocious commitment to pursue every possible cause and remedy for renal failure or osteoporosis, because the fear of loss of control over your body overtakes you. You just seem to have a hypersensitivity to your body that sometimes borders on hysterical hypochondria.

So what is the link between fear of loss of control over your body and desperately clinging to a lousy job or incompetent employee? It is your lack of belief in your ability to survive on your own. There's a powerful spiritual force of courage and initiative buried deep within you, sometimes clouded by a terror of change and a dread of being alone to fend for yourself. You must get beyond the clouds and tap that source of strength.

At this point you need to probe a little deeper into your issues about not wanting to work at all, and needing to be needed and staying too long in relationships. In the next part, Going Deeper, read the chapters called "Marriage" and "Control" to pass through the illusion of fear of being fired, let go, or abandoned, or even worse of being sick and alone, and on to a higher expression of your Taurus nature that will help you work more efficiently, conduct your affairs with more joy, and make your Sun shine bright.

> *Celebrities Who Share Your Issues*
> *Stevie Wonder, Sigmund Freud, Willie Mays, John Muir,*
> *Jay Leno, Tim Russert, Billy Joel, Tony Hawk*

Taurus 7

You're either the noblest, most generous creature ever born or quite the sucker. And at times you know you have been taken for quite a ride by people you trusted. Some would say that should teach you a lesson about accepting rides from strangers. Imagine! Some other people dare to say you're stubborn or inflexible. They should only know how many times you've taken a sip of wine from a cup you thought might have been tampered with but drank anyway just to prove your loyalty.

One thing let's hope you've learned: Sometimes it's better to be alone than to be dragged through the sewer by the Phantom of the Opera. On the other hand, you don't have to join a religious order and renounce your earthly desires. That might certainly be a more appealing notion than playing the fool for every flashing-eyed stranger who whistles at your wiggle. Besides, it's doubtful you'd remain chaste forever. You would never stop wiggling, even after you were ordained, and you know you could never resist turning around if you heard a whistle.

You just have to learn that a promise is not always a deal. People may not mean to deceive or disappoint you, but you can be damn well sure they'll use every bit of whatever they've got when they want to sell you their soap. So you've got to get more savvy as you get older and learn how to resist sales pitches and advances, because they come from the same source: somebody who wants what you've got. Very flattering indeed. But they've got to hold up their end of the deal. And you, a trusting soul, aren't about to start following somebody around to see what they're up to when they're not with you.

When you find yourself doing that, STOP, you're on your way down a one-way rat hole. You've lost your sense of pride and your confidence in yourself. When you become more involved in a partner's clandestine activities than you are in your own fantasies of what you yourself are capable of, you won't be satisfied until the private detective brings you hurtful pictures shot in a seedy motel at the edge of town. Then all your suspicions can be confirmed, and you'll be faced with the hairy decision of whether to put up with deception or get out and start looking for a new mate or business partner.

Of course it's an issue of trust. And why not? Look at what people have done to you, how they have mismanaged your affairs, squandered your resources, abused their power. It's positively untenable, but you can't live in a bubble, afraid you're going to be robbed, violated, and poisoned just because you make a deep connection with somebody. Of course not. You are a connecter and you need people. You just have to be a little more resistant to the come-on. Stay in your own place at least half the time. Don't be in such a hurry to compromise. Don't project your own fantasies about what you would do if you weren't so loyal onto what you think the other person is doing.

At this point you need to probe a little deeper into your obsession with being seduced and led astray. In the next part, Going Deeper, read the chapters called "Marriage" and "Sex" to pass through the illusions about the kinds of people you are attracted to, and relationships in general and their outcome, and on to a higher expression of your Taurus nature that will help you have relationships without being devoured by them, and make your Sun shine bright.

Taurus 8

Sex, money, and religion: What a combo. If you had been born in the year 900 it would be one thing. But being a modern person in a modern world is hard for you. A kiss on the hand may be quite continental, but if you will remember, Lorelei Lee knew the score in *Gentlemen Prefer Blondes.*

Of course, today the show would be blasted for its politically incorrect lines (sexual and probably racial), but oh, what a message there is in that show for you. You probably didn't figure it out back in high school, but merely hooking someone for the sake of hooking them is not the same as having a loyal, fulfilling relationship. You were too worried about being desirable, or rather *not* being desirable. As a result of poor sexual education back then you were either the type who had no idea what the sex organs of adult members of the opposite sex looked like until you were embarrassingly too old to admit it, or you were into oral sex the day after you hit puberty. Sex was always an issue, and probably still is.

Both kinds of Taurians exist, and neither should be ashamed of their history. Neither had the benefit of wonderful sex education, so it's no big whoop to find out you've had to learn a lot the hard way. In either case, at the age of nineteen you had a very rude awakening with regard to the importance of sex education and its impact on your ability to relate to others in an adult way. Whether this experience resulted in glut or ignorance, it certainly involved a lot of unfulfilled fantasies, repression, and rejection, and a huge desire to be desirable and popular. There is often an upside to unfulfilled fantasies. They can lead you to channel your imagination in a thousand creative directions, despite the fact that you tend to waste much time chasing the Big O. Some Tauruses just throw away money and other resources in the search for a pleasure that ultimately eludes them. They reject more practical material values as superficial, and thus fail to create the flow of economic prosperity of which they are enormously capable.

Eventually you have to try to reduce your belief that somebody is coming along to sock it to you as it has never been socked to you before. You have to get over the notion that the doorbell will ring some morning and there will be the FedEx person, delivering the package you've been waiting for, your ticket to Paradise. Uh-uh. Your real fulfillment will come from good, honest, simple communication and a sincere appreciation and awareness that every relationship has a business component to it. Commerce and money need not destroy love. They could, of course, but that's the trick.

At this point you need to probe a little deeper into your obsession with being a desirable sex object, or guilt over the same issue, as well as an obsession with hanging onto your image as an artist who rebels against commercialism, even to your own detriment. In the next part, Going Deeper, read the chapters called "Religion" and "Sex" to pass through the illusion of sexual or financial fears, and on to a higher expression of your Taurus nature that will help you enjoy relationships more and make your Sun shine bright.

> *Celebrities Who Share Your Issues*
> *Cher, Shirley Temple, Catherine de Medici, Sergei Prokofiev,*
> *Charlotte Brontë, Candace Bergen*

Taurus 9

A famous writer who happens to be a lapsed Catholic and a Taurus recently published a scathing denunciation of the abuses of power perpetrated by the Catholic Church. He wrote the entire book in India where he was studying Eastern philosophy and practice under the strict discipline of his new spiritual mentor. He never saw the irony in it. It's not easy for any of us to see our own issues, but this Taurus absolutely denied there was any humor or irony in the fact that he had denounced one rigid system for another. Sometimes Tauruses do take a bit longer to get jokes and figure out puzzles. In your case it's a subject you should look at more deeply. You should be able to relate to this story, since you too have gotten angry because you've been misled by the inflexible laws, rules, rites, and regulations of one patriarchal system or another and rejected it, only to find yourself attracted to another.

Laws and judicial and educational institutions have an odd, magnetic pull that draws you ever closer to them, and no matter how many times you expose their flaws and fight against the corrupt politics that pass for legal and moral practices, you can't quite pull yourself away. You still believe your teacher is out there, someone who can give you the direction and structure you don't believe you can live without. Funny—you're so enamored with the rituals that have in some ways provided you with necessary structures, but at the same time they have hampered your ability to think independently and develop confidence in your own intelligence.

It's pretty much a father thing, or rather an absent-father thing. You can certainly remember a time when certain rules were laid down that you were required to follow blindly and absolutely (with no reasons or explanations given) or risk the fear of reprisal for disobedience. It could be years before you dare to question the laws, and once you do, you pull the curtain back and expose the Wizard of Oz. He's not some thunderous image of an awesome specter clouded in green smoke at all. He's just a guy, a guy who made up the rules and figured out a glitzy way to get you to follow them. Still, that sort of imposing, all-knowing figure has power over you in one form or another, even in a mate. The trick is to be able if not to reject those omniscient figures totally, then at least to discuss things with them, test ideas, challenge laws and philosophical/psychological approaches you think are outdated and with which you—horror of horrors—dare to disagree, without becoming more dangerously closed-minded than the system you question.

At this point you need to probe more deeply into your issues about being intelligent and being recognized for it. In the next part, Going Deeper, read the chapters called "Recognition" and "Religion" to pass through the illusion of fear of losing yourself to someone else and on to a higher expression of your Taurus nature that will help communicate better on an intimate level, form more lasting and deeper connections, and make your Sun shine bright.

Celebrities Who Share Your Issues
Queen Elizabeth II, Vladimir Lenin, Coretta Scott King,
James Stewart, Lucrezia Borgia, Kirsten Dunst,
Edward R. Murrow, Johannes Brahms, Kelly Clarkson

Taurus 10

If you can't go along with the program, you can't complain too loudly when you are publicly criticized for your actions. They say there's no such thing as bad publicity, as long as your name is mentioned.

Gotta wonder, though, if some people will do anything to avoid their greatest horror: being an anonymous member of society, stuck in the suburbs raising a family. What is really amazing is that some Tauruses who avoid it for years usually end up with a family they didn't even want, or at least one they spend half their life running away from. For you the career area has always been and will always probably be one hell of a hair-raising amusement park ride. *Amusement* is not the right word, because it sometimes leads you right into haunted house—a house haunted by your eternal struggle for validation. And it's a funny thing about recognition. Once you have it, it usually comes at a very high price, and sometimes even scandalous accusations. Even though you are a Taurus, there's part of you that actually loves a good scandal. You'd better love it, because you can't maintain total privacy and still carry on the dangerous games you play in politics without being photographed with jam on your face, your hand in the cookie jar, or the authorities hauling you in on charges of some sort of fraud or misbehavior. And you can't have it both ways. Nobody can. If you're irresistibly and constantly drawn into impossibly unpredictable political situations, you know there are bound to be factors you didn't consider, so you'll always be risking being caught in an avalanche when you can't resist climbing that icy political mountain.

Since you were raised under a completely unconventional (read chaotic) regime, it's no surprise you can spot insanity in every authority figure you run into. You have to realize, however, that even if you can quickly spot fraud and corruption, your idealism and sense of justice can sometimes prevent you from seeing that you can be as implacable, rigid, unyielding, and inconsistent as the people you're overthrowing. Yes, yes, it's your mission in life to help all those who cannot help themselves, all those who have been trapped and fooled and downtrodden because of the misuses of power by the rich and powerful.

What is also true, though, is that you don't want to be just a mom or a dad. You see your role as more important, more global, grander than picking up the kids at school or painting the shutters. That kind of normalcy makes you shudder. Love itself, the one ingredient that will give your life real meaning, threatens you because it will force you into an intimate setting where you will have to admit the need for comfort, support, and emotional security. The trick is in balancing your outer and inner lives.

At this point you need to probe more deeply into your obsession with avoiding love and intimacy because you think it will trap you and keep you from a more independent life in the world where you can be recognized for your achievements. In the next part, Going Deeper, read the chapters called "Freedom" and "Recognition" to pass through the illusion of being too dependent on the family, and on to a higher expression of your Taurus nature that will help you enjoy your private life without having to totally give up your career, and make your Taurus Sun shine bright.

Celebrities Who Share Your Issues
Bing Crosby, Bob Woodward, Irving Berlin, Malcolm X, Yogi Berra

Taurus 11

Maybe you don't have as many friends as some other people—real friends, that is, not just a ragtag collection of people you have nothing in common with. It's not for lack of trying. You've sacrificed so much personal happiness and really dedicated yourself, very unselfishly some- times, and do people appreciate it? Oh, yes, thank you for saving human- ity, now, bye! It's got to make you wonder why you still feel the urge to prove what a wonderful and evolved human being you are to a world full of people who don't give a damn, a world which, according to this morning's news, seems still to be headed straight down the tubes. Some- times no goal seems worthwhile, and everything you ever dreamed of doing seems like a big fat waste of time. No wonder so many Tauruses start indulging themselves in sugar, starches, and substances that provide delicious escapes but are ultimately lethally destructive.

If you didn't have to get up and take care of the kids or get out on the stage and work, you could just wallow in your disappointment over all your broken dreams. Fortunately, no matter how absolutely satisfying self-indulgence may be, you have services to perform for the people who you think, in your downbeat moments, don't give a good goddamn about you. And performance is a service. It's work. It takes work for you to take a shower, put yourself together, and go to the party or stand before that canvas or do anything that demands a high level of functioning, focus, and discipline. You need the sense of mission and purpose, ridicu- lous as it seems to you half the time, to inspire your creative genius and motivate you enough and get your juices flowing. So whether or not the "mission" turns out to be one big laugh doesn't matter. However, you tend to get too far out in the galaxy, way farther than any respectable Taurus should go—and that is dangerous. You need to be sober when you perform, even if sobriety is a strain. It is that sense of responsibility that allows you to practice your craft, hone your skills, and become a perfect artisan in your chosen metier, so that you can produce with utter unique- ness. Since you are so hooked on being the odd duck in the pond (as out of it as that made you feel in high school), you might as well put your de- sire to be different to work for you. It could get you in the hall of fame, or your picture on the post office wall.

• • •

At this point you need to probe more deeply into your issues about being unappreciated by the people you're making sacrifices for, and about how often you have couched love in the guise of friendship because love scared you. In the next part, Going Deeper, read the chapters called "Escape" and "Freedom" to pass through the illusion of disillusionment with everybody and everything, and on to a higher expression of your Taurus nature that will help you accept the personal happiness you are destined to have, and make your Sun shine bright.

> *Celebrities Who Share Your Issues*
> *J. Robert Oppenheimer, Barbra Streisand, Salvador Dalí,*
> *George Lopez, Dennis Rodman, Bono*

Taurus 12

On the surface you're cool. Tauruses are cool. They don't seem to get ruffled. Secretly, however, it's a different story. You're often terribly unsure of yourself, horribly self-critical, and at times you've been known to fly into self-destructive rages (only to feel guilty afterward and make amends), especially when you're young. The self-hating thing could come from some physical or genetic attribute that makes you privately embarrassed about who and what you are, or it could come from some way you were put down as a kid. As a Taurus you would probably keep that totally under lock and key somewhere, buried 300 feet below the bank vault. You do not like to show weakness or self-doubt. Any self-loathing you harbor secretly for yourself, which must be overcome as you grow into maturity and gain confidence, could come also from a deep-seated and deeply buried fear of not being masculine enough, no matter if you are a man or a woman. Your fulfillment comes when you learn the difference between healthy self-assertion and the violent outbreaks that could harm relationships, lose you good jobs, or even get you locked up.

So you can see how protecting your sanity after having it shaken in childhood can bring you to a life devoted to hiding who you are. Sometimes it's about shame, and the reasons could most definitely be linked to shame about the family or your parent of the same sex. The internal strife roils and boils incessantly within you, and it is usually the worst when you're alone. But because you find working with and talking with people a strain, sometimes the release you need is just to run away and hide for a while, only to find that the more alone you get, the worse you feel.

So of course work is the answer. Looking forward to retirement may be a big fantasy—it could be the carrot held out in front of a very exhausted donkey, but pal, you'd better always keep busy, or hope you'll just slump over someday on the job. You need to work with people, learning to cooperate and share and trust, trust, trust—oh, definitely. Learning how to depend on help and advice (control freak that you can be, you ultimately have to be in charge and be the one who makes the big decisions) is the big lesson for you. Of course you fear the dependence. Even if you're lost in the desert, asking for directions will make you nervous until you realize none of us can get there completely on our own. So you don't have to start imagining yourself as an invalid who can't get to the john without a health care worker's arm to hold you up. It's the spirit of interdependence that will wake you up and keep you functioning at a high level.

At this point you need to probe more deeply into your issues about being weak or needy. In the next part, Going Deeper, read the chapters called "Escape" and "Independence" to pass through the illusion that needing people is a sign of weakness or that a life of good old-fashioned work is something to be avoided, and on to a higher expression of your Taurus nature that will help you be more in the world and make your Sun shine bright.

> *Celebrities Who Share Your Issues*
> Dr. Benjamin Spock, Sugar Ray Leonard, Al Pacino,
> Harry S. Truman, Samuel F. B. Morse

GEMINI

May 21–June 20
Dates vary from year to year—consult your local astrologer

Gemini is the spark of consciousness. It is the magical process by which perception takes place. It is your keen awareness of the outside world and your ability to discern in a dispassionate manner the difference between objects. It is your urge to join and connect with other human beings. Gemini, therefore, is everything that joins human minds from the first grunt of *Australopithecus* to broadband. It is the smoke signal at the top of a distant mountain. It's every town crier from ancient Rome to nineteenth-century London. Gemini is the intelligence of the Egyptian scribe, and what kept Gutenberg up nights until he figured out what he was supposed to be doing. It is the morning paper and the evening news. Gemini is the process of perception, thought, and voice all perfectly integrated in a ceaseless searching for new information, as watchful as a sleepless eagle that circles the prairie.

Let's be real. Gemini can be so skitzed out it's not funny. Of course, it all depends how you look at it. With Gemini the right hand very often doesn't know or doesn't care what the left hand is doing. It's hard to describe Gemini without using the word schizo, although that term is so often wrongly used in connection with your great sign. It's just too darned difficult to figure out whether you are a multifaceted genius with varied interests and an array of unusual talents, or someone so filled with nervousness and anxiety that you get impatient waiting for a microwave to boil water. You do require lots of mental stimulation from a wide number of sources to satisfy your thirsty, active mind. Your fascination with people compels you to seek out conversations with individuals from all walks of life and areas of culture. Some people, however, still claim that Geminis suffer from a mild form of ambulatory multipersonality disorder, which allows you to get away with an entire life of double-dealing and two-faced deception.

Being a Gemini is a blessing and curse. The sign of the Twins, that's you. And in astrology, Gemini is one of the only human signs. It is your powerful mind that separates you from the lower animal kingdom. Granted, you have your moments of feeling like a total vegetable, but despite a spooky detachment you can call up at any time, you are most human. Gemini is human in the sense that it is the sign of the sentient being with the ability to respond to other sentient beings in their own language. Because of the eight hundred and forty-two thousand gazillion thoughts that run through your head in any given period of two minutes, Gemini represents instantaneous change, unexpected turns in behavioral weather, just as capricious as the clouds that scud across the sky, turning a sunny day into a driving rainstorm and vice versa.

You know that you are not always in control of your moods. Sometimes you're bright and chatty, smiling and gabbing intimately with the teller at the bank as if you've known her all her life, making her feel that you really know and care about her, but also distracting her just enough so she will cash your check whether you've got enough money in your account or not. And then a flash across the brain occurs and you can mouth off and chew the poor woman out, so it takes her a week to recover from the tongue-lashing. Oh, you're not like that? That's just the stereotype of the split-off Gemini? Think back a few days. You haven't been screaming at your kids and then turning all honey and sweet on the phone to someone else—or the reverse? You're changeable and restless and that's the truth.

Back in the 1970s when people wanted to calm their minds, they had themselves lowered into tanks filled with water. Then the tanks were shut and the people could just float in the dark for hours in utter silence, cut off from the world, senses shut down. Outside stimuli all but utterly extinguished. You can be sure not too many of those people were Geminis, because if there is one sure way to turn you into a screaming maniac, it is to cut you off from contact with the outside world for any extended period of time. Rather than calm your mind, such a practice would depress you. Separated from people and with no one to talk to, you would slump down in a corner like a widowed penguin on a block of ice in Antarctica. You're not the loner type. Far from it.

In fact, if a friend needs, say, a plumber quickly, they should call you immediately. You either have the phone number and email of the best plumber in town right there in your cell phone, or you live around the corner from him, or he's someone you are currently sleeping with. Or coincidentally, last night you just happened to be watching the Home Channel and you learned just enough plumbing from the show to be able to solve your friend's problem. That's how your life works. That's how your mind works.

You're a human coaxial cable, a conduit between people, a link between two individuals who five minutes ago didn't know each other but now are glued together for one reason or another, thanks to you.

Remember in *2001: A Space Odyssey*, when one of the apes suddenly had a thought that it could string together with another thought? Right there one could see the spark of intelligence being born, illuminating a brain that would forever in function differently. That ape *had* to be a Gemini. Unfortunately many members of your sign haven't progressed a whole lot further than the ability to string together two disjointed, unrelated thoughts. If you are a highly evolved Gemini you have become the master of discourse, not lies or gossip, and you have learned how to speak, not with a forked tongue, but in many tongues. You have become the epitome of Aristotelian discourse, the center of information on an endless number of subjects in whatever sphere of interest has captured your vivid and thirsty mind at the moment.

Some people think you've evolved all right, but from a race of fast-talking alien chameleons who came to Earth to sell used cars to old ladies. Few people understand the way that brain of yours operates. They think you just plain operate, work a room, say anything anybody wants to hear. You are different and that's all there is to it, alien or not. While most people's brains are located entirely inside their heads, yours has thousands of invisible antennae that extend outward on all sides from your head in all directions. These wires are all invisible to the naked eye, of course, and they are all simultaneously seeking connections. Although your eyes, ears, and other sensory organs look like normal human organs, they are not. You can be looking deep into your lover's eyes and at the same time wink at the bartender. You can be listening intently to Debussy, Guns N' Roses, and CNN and actually be able to repeat the news (condensed of course) to the person you are on the phone with at the same moment. For you the greatest miracle of modern life isn't the Salk polio vaccine. It is call-waiting on cell phones.

It's not that you are terminally superficial or disloyal. These days they're calling it ADD, but back in the old days it was known as just plain old Gemini. You're in motion from day one, doing a perpetual Yosemite Sam, dancing around to avoid the bullets blazing all around you. You like it that way. You need it. You crave it.

Without the noise and the confusion and the four hundred messages and errands that are scrawled across your chaotic date book, you are a lost soul, at loose ends, washed up, depressed, with nothing to do. So, when that yearned-for moment of repose finally does come, one wonders if you can actually sit for two whole hours or minutes and watch a movie without fidgeting or going to the john five times, or making phone calls even before the commercials go on. If you say you have seen *Gone with the Wind*, certainly it is not because you sat and watched it for four hours. You probably pieced it together after watching it twenty-four times on TV for ten minutes at a time. This is not necessarily a sign of a brain disorder, but you certainly have to figure out what causes the boredom and the restlessness. Is it anxiety or just a thirsty mind? Are you an objective reporter? Or are you just cold enough to watch an autopsy while eating a tuna sandwich and listening to your iPod?

You are brilliant. There's no denying that. You can think of the fastest way to communicate with other beings. No saddling up and riding three hours to the next farm for the doctor for you. Speed and restlessness permeate the Gemini personality. Your span of attention is getting shorter and shorter, and your thirst for novelty is always battling your hunger for permanence. In some all too very real ways you are a skitzed-out speed freak with an incurable streak of Tourette's Syndrome.

You are not the type to be tucked in beddy by 8:30 PM. The influence of Gemini can make you a Dunkin' Donuts insomniac tuned into all-night talk radio and flipping the channels on TV looking for an information fix. You may preach love, but you can get carried away to such an extent that you bolt the door against the expected break-in, emotionally speaking. You're as warlike as you are peace-loving and you can turn on a dime. Bomb somebody's ass one day, send flowers the next. And unfortunately, vice versa. Is that Gemini or what?

Just think of the vast amounts of time, money, and effort that have gone into Geminis' ability to save time so they can run around town: ice box, fridge, Crock-Pot, Hamburger Helper, microwave cookies— everything imaginable so you can prepare food, eat it, and get out of the house as fast as humanly possible. This isn't crazy? You work like a dog to own a house, so you can wolf down a meal and scram. This is exactly the conflict that lies embedded in the Gemini consciousness. The dichotomy between permanence and transience is what brought the first settlers to the Western Hemisphere, and then had them packing their dishes and setting off in a covered wagon.

This is why some people insist you're wacko: your obsession with the new, the latest, most superficial snippet of life in the now. It's totally what Gemini is about. Where to go, how to dress, the new and improved all-purpose cleaner that will make every household job a breeze, every spot in your sink or underpants fade and disappear in the blink of an eye. Telephones and gadgets that speed your life along? Gemini.

What happens to that slowpoke, ambling-in-slippers attitude of "don't bother me I'm having a beer in my hammock" when the other side of your Gemini kicks in? You become agitated. If you're in one place too long, you get itchy. You're antsy when you're idle. The Gemini effect has you ceaselessly dreaming up new ways to do everything faster. Be sure of one thing. When scientists start beam-me-up-Scottying, Geminis will be the first to start flinging their atoms all over the place. The Gemini mind wishes for peace, yet it is the fear that its security will be disturbed that brings on war. What does Gemini do to your information abilities? It over loads them and skews them, one day one way, the next day another.

Do you "cause" the war? The Gemini Sun shows that your dark side is perfectly capable of sneaking in through the back door and setting fire to the whole joint. You know you have done it. Personally. Professionally. Emotionally. You can point to events in your past and say, "Was that paranoia? Was that my imagination?" Some would say that all Geminis have a streak of paranoia, and that's what makes them stay on the run. But you are not looking over your shoulder all the time. Sometimes you're casual, breezy, and full of trust. It's when the other thing kicks in that there's no talking to you. If brothers, sisters, associates, lovers, mates, or neighbors are seen as a potential threat, they eventually become one.

You have an underlying awareness of potential danger that makes you ready for flight at any time. Whether it's a San Francisco earthquake, a Kansas twister, or a Florida Category Five hurricane, the potential for some disastrous event for which you must always be ready keeps your life in a state of temporary suspension. It keeps you on yellow alert. It always has. It distracts you from your search for tranquility and keeps you alive, alert, ready to move in a moment, and definitely always awake. You keep one eye open for the way out, the open door, the open window. Although you'd much prefer to split and change your phone number than fight, if need be you keep your rifle cocked. No matter what happens, you have an amazing ability to forget almost instantly whom you have shot.

Beyond it all, there will always be your marvelous Gemini ingenuity—the products, performances, and services for which the world always ends up owing a Gemini a debt of gratitude. Maybe in the great scheme of things a George Foreman Grill that will cook burgers fast without grease isn't what we all need to get into heaven. The Gemini mind, however, even hopped up on caffeine and tobacco, will continue its marathon race against nature. In fact it's just that amphetamine fuel that juices up Gemini Wall Street brokers and gooses scientists, engineers, and architects on to bigger and kookier discoveries and inventions. It's Gemini that created Detroit, or rather, the Detroit that *was,* in its heyday. Gemini was Ma Bell and Gemini is Silicon Valley. It's the baldface ballsy habit of saying one thing and doing another. It is the antithesis of family values, not because it abhors tradition, but because it doesn't have a lot of time for such things. Gemini represents a collective boredom that covers up a profoundly anxious dread behind a confident, warm-hearted exterior. Putting your thoughts together in a meaningful way, channeling the enormous mental energy that surges through you at every instant of the day and night—that's the goal. To remain active and mobile, but focused and productive—that's the trick.

So how do you create a life for yourself that gives you the freedom to move around and explore, but keeps you grounded enough to carry on coherent relationships and stick with ideas long enough to see them come into fruition? What are the forces that drag you backward and keep you from reaching the highest manifestation of your Sun? And what are the energies that can support you, guide you, enhance your positive qualities, and make your Sun shine bright? The fact is you're not just a Gemini. There is another energy operating, one that either cuts across your efforts and undermines them, or spirits you to heights of joy and fulfillment. That energy depends not only on the month you were born, but the year as well. Later in this book the technical aspects will be explained more fully. We'll examine how you waste time chasing your own tail, why you do it, and how to pull yourself out of self-destructive obsessions and put yourself back on the road to success. But for now, check out the following table. Find your birth year and note the number beside it. Then read the section corresponding to the number.

Year–No.	Year–No.	Year–No.	Year–No.	Year–No.
1901–12	1911–6	1920–12	1930–6	1940–11
1902–12	1912–5	1921–11	1931–5	1941–10
1903–11	1913–5 until	1922–11	1932–4	1942–10
1904–10	5/27, then 4	1923–10	1933–4	1943–9
1905–10	1914–4	1924–9	1934–3	1944–9 until
1906–9	1915–3	1925–9	1935–2	6/4, then 8
1907–8	1916–3	1926–8	1936–2	1945–8
1908–8	1917–2	1927–7	1937–1	1946–7
1909–7	1918–1	1928–7	1938–12	1947–7
1910–6	1919–1	1929–6	1939–12	1948–6

Year–No.	Year–No.	Year–No.	Year–No.	Year–No.
1949–5	1967–6	1983–7	2000–8	2016–10
1950–5	1968–5	1984–7	2001–8	2017–9
1951–4	1969–4	1985–6	2002–7	2018–9
1952–3	1970–4	1986–5	2003–6	2019–8
1953–3	1971–3	1987–5	2004–6	2020–8 until
1954–2	1972–2	1988–4	2005–5	6/4, then 7
1955–1	1973–2	1989–4 until	2006–5 until	2021–7
1956–1	1974–1	5/29, then 3	June 20, then	2022–6
1957–12	1975–until	1990–3	4	2023–6
1958–11	6/13, then	1991–2	2007–4	2024–5
1959–11	12	1992–2	2008–3	2025–4
1960–10	1976–12	1993–1	2009–3	2026–4
1961–10	1977–11	1994–12	2010–2	2027–3
1962–9	1978–11	1995–11	2011–1	2028–2
1963–8	1979–10	1996–11	2012–12	2029–2
1964–8	1980–9	1997–10	2013–12	2030–1
1965–7	1981–9	1998–10	2014–11	
1966–6	1982–8	1999–9	2015–11	

Gemini 1

Can you believe that many people think that sometimes you're really hard to talk to? And you're a very engaging person, too. People like you. They admire you. You bring out the best in them. Half the time, however, you are only half there. And since there are always two of you present at one time, that means you are only there one quarter of the time. It's impossible to tell exactly when you are going to be there and when the "Out to Lunch" sign is going to be up. Your eyes glaze over while someone is trying to have a normal conversation with you, and you get a blank expression on your face. It's as if somebody has pulled the plug out of your brain. Or maybe some radio receiver inside your head has been switched on and now instead of listening to the conversation going on in front of you, you are receiving messages and instructions from the beings in the mother ship above your head.

Your mind does wander. Definitely. And goes to places the person you're staring at would be stunned, shocked, or horrified to know about. But there's a big difference between you and crazy people. A moment or two later, as if on a delayed satellite radar, you come back and miraculously respond correctly and appropriately to what the person was saying just as if you had actually been listening, though the whole time you were thinking one of your weird thoughts or just deciding what to order from the Chinese restaurant and thinking about the next person you had to call. Really crazy people actually think they are listening to messages and instructions from the mother ship. But of course you don't, do you?

For some reason you're very into your own head and it's really a stretch for you to keep your attention on anyone else for very long. It's the sporadic absences that mess up relationships and can keep you from being connected to the rest of the world, mainly because the key to happy and fulfilling relationships is the ability to listen fully and totally and not tune out. It's the secret to doing well in school (which you may have to return to when you're more mature and less resistant to what teachers have to say). You need to engage with people a little smarter than you, who can see through your games and who know how to snap you back to attention. Why would marriage to someone from a different culture or religion keep you interested longer and help you be more focused and present? Nobody knows but in the case of many Geminis, some sort of mixed marriage often seems to work best.

At this point you need to probe more deeply into your obsession with your own thoughts and ideas. In the next part, Going Deeper, read the chapters called "Independence" and "Communication," which will help you pass through the illusion of losing yourself to someone else, and on to a higher expression of your Gemini nature, help you enjoy relationships more, and make your Sun shine bright.

Celebrities Who Share Your Issues
Lauryn Hill, Kenny G, Joe Montana, Alanis Morissette, Jewel

Gemini 2

Starvation fantasies may actually compel you on to make a nice pile of money, but they might not help you keep it. They could even create a kind of eating disorder in some folks who binge on everything then deny themselves everything. Whether you come from more money than you could ever earn or not, the family and finances will forever be linked in your head.

Oddly, the hole in your pocket and the growl in your stomach, if you ever were poor, remain to this day, so it's not that you're greedy and you want money for it's own sake. To you, a fat bank account is akin to a full tummy and a warm bed. Maybe it's completely ridiculous to fear being poor and homeless, because you'll always have a cushion, inherited or otherwise. But you definitely equate money with security, and it can become a pathology. You could be a total pack rat, saving everything, being cheap at the stupidest times, and God forbid anybody moves your stuff. Half the time you don't know where anything is, but if anything is missing, you sense it, feel it, perceive the absence. Oddly there is a connection between your wealth and security obsession and your over-controlling but punitive or absent mother, and maybe that's why you translate money into a reward for good behavior. And even if you know the old adage "Do what you love and the money will follow," it doesn't always ring true when you see how some people manipulate the feelings of others and play power games and trade favors and throw their weight around just because they're the ones with the money, and therefore they're the ones who make the big decisions for you. Often it's the family money that tries to direct your life—and often it succeeds.

So in your attempt to bypass the sharing of control it's very tempting (irresistible, in fact) to take jobs or accept offers and opportunities that will give you security on your own, apart from the income from people or other sources. It's rarely enough, though, to satisfy the hunger that gnaws at the pit of your stomach when you start feeling poor. Sharing financial control and sharing resources can remove that empty feeling and bring you a passion and intimacy you never thought possible.

• • •

At this point you need to probe more deeply into your obsession with the lack of resources and the fear of being financially or sexually engulfed by another person. In the next part, Going Deeper, reading the chapters called "Security" and "Money" will give you a chance to pass through the illusion of poverty, and on to a higher expression of your Gemini that will help you enjoy intimacy more and make your Sun shine bright.

> ### Celebrities Who Share Your Issues
> Dean Martin, Norman Vincent Peale, Nicole Kidman, Gena Rowlands, Heidi Klum

Gemini 3

Phone out. Disconnected. Not speaking to anybody. It's awful to be cut off from people you've loved. An incomplete conversation or premature interruption ends up making you feel angry or bitter or even more attached than you'd feel if all the parties involved had a chance to iron out their differences and have their points of view heard, especially when dealing with siblings, relatives, or neighbors. You've certainly been on the outs with people in your day. We all have. But with you there's a pattern of getting close quickly—the whole thing heats up fast and then goes cold just as quickly. Not to say that you are superficial or capricious. You can be pretty deep when you want to be. It just doesn't last that long.

The whole not talking thing is funny, too, because being listened to and taken seriously is your life's ambition. It's so painful when you're about to make a long story short, and you see the person you're trying to communicate with stifle a big, fat yawn. Even then you've been known to press on, more determined than ever to finish your story, which is usually about your latest heartbreak, until you realize people have stopped listening and several members of the audience, if not coughing, have already gotten up to go to the bathroom. That's because if you always bring the subject back to yourself, people will turn off. You'll get all the attention you crave when you turn your attention outward, away from your soap opera, toward the betterment of all sentient beings. There may always be a huge gap between what you practice and what you preach, because as lofty and noble as your desires to help model a better humanity are, part of you is still a needy, narcissistic child doing anything for love and attention.

It's hard to shift your attention off yourself, especially if no matter how hard you try to let people see your good, noble, brilliant, humanitarian self, you still can't stop your ego from peeking out from behind the curtain and mooning the audience. And yet you have such highly noble goals. You really do. It hurts you that some people see you as a souped-up caricature of a typical Hollywood actor. At least in your own town. The farther away you go from your birth place, the better it gets. Is that running away? If there's one thing you have to do, it's to be understood, to make yourself understood—in any language.

At this point you need to probe more deeply into your own issues about taking things so personally and being hurt to the point that you stop speaking to somebody. In the next part, Going Deeper, reading the chapters called "Love" and "Communication" will give you a chance to pass through the illusion of not being heard or understood, and on to a higher expression of your Gemini nature that will help you enjoy being connected to people (definitely your thing), and make your Sun shine bright.

Celebrities Who Share Your Issues
Joan Collins, Isabella Rossellini, Sir Arthur Conan Doyle,
Ralph Waldo Emerson, Noah Wyle, Mark Wahlberg

Gemini 4

Although it may take you years to see how or why, the best thing that could have happened to you is somehow, at the age of three, to have gotten separated from your parents and started making it on your own. Traumatic, yes, but in the long run, a blessing. Whether you ran away or not, the family pursues you, hangs on, and haunts you. Maybe that's a bit harsh, because in most cases parents don't really set out to embarrass you, constantly cut you down, criticize you, and make you feel that you can't do anything right, if not abandon you completely. They probably don't intentionally make you think you're sick or weak and that you have to drive yourself and keep everything in your life pristine and pure because if you let down your guard for one moment you're going to be swept away in the tide.

Whatever their intention, you end up trying to please people you totally can't stand. All your life. Until that great post-therapy day when you realize you have to walk out that door and go find your fortune and cast your fate to the winds. If the son of an orthodox rabbi has one dream and that's to be in show business, then that's what eventually has to happen. The idealistic dreamer who believes in everything will always rebel against the blue-collar family belief in the struggling underclass, clinging together in ethnic desperation. "Papa, this is America. I can be anything I want to be." "Big shot," cries Papa, "but don't come crying to me when. . . ."

And at the end of the movie, after you've pulled away from the tyranny and become famous, you rush to the hospital to care for the parent who never held you and never let you go, while in the theater the audience is in hysterical tears.

It goes something like that, with all the million Gemini variations. You run away. You come back. You run away. You come back. You're terrified of having the bottom drop out of your life, but you're actually relieved if it ever does happen. You're always half expecting it, and as painful a feeling as it is to be left, it does liberate you to pursue your own life— provided you don't rush right out and tie yourself down again to a sick "parent" you have to take care of. You've got a few really intense food fetishes that can become obessive (and in some people's eyes, completely nuts), and probably have something to do with not being properly fed emotionally at a time when you really needed it. But all that is such a total waste of time and energy in the end, because no matter what your feelings are toward the dysfunctional family that poses for holiday photos as if everybody were normal, your greatest achievements will be in moving away even on a part-time basis from an exaggerated sense of responsibility to a family heritage and set of traditions that don't work for you.

You have a destiny out in the world that may require you to give up your fantasy about what healthy family life is. There's a path you have to walk on, it's a career path, but in a way you don't even choose it. It chooses you. It's one thing you have no control over. It's one thing you cannot explain or approach rationally. You just have to allow yourself to be guided, elated, excited, disappointed, buoyed up, and let down a million times. In short, your career is your foray into naive idealism with all the perks and consequences that go along with it.

At this point you need to probe more deeply into your obsession with sick family relationships and the toll they have taken on you. In the next part, Going Deeper, reading the chapters called "Control" and "Security" will give you a chance to pass through the illusion of the fear of abandonment, and on to a higher expression of your nature that will help you enjoy your professional successes and make your Sun shine bright.

> ✦ *Celebrities Who Share Your Issues*
> *Isadora Duncan, Joan Rivers, Richard Thomas, Steffi Graf,*
> *Mario Cuomo, Sally Ride* ✦

Gemini 5

The perfect love object exists in your own mind only. Do you think it's someone who serves all your needs, clips your toenails, and goes along with everything you say, think, or do? Wrong. That person may be a great friend and lifelong pal, but he or she is not your passionate love object. You need a challenge. In fact you have such an enormous need to be romantic that it's doubtful one person could satisfy it. Besides, you're the kind who can get whacked when you do fall in love.

You totally lose your sense of yourself and you become powerless. Of course that's okay when you're in ninth grade, but you can't carry on like that when you're forty without looking like a jerk. On the other hand, who cares? Being a jerk is no sin when you are as romantic as you are. Come to think of it, though, you've got to learn to draw the line between romanticism and masochism, since you are happiest when you're miserably smitten by somebody you can't have. At least you were that way in junior high school. Let's hope that these days you're more able to handle relationships that are a little more appropriate—although you probably still can't resist that wonderful feeling of being blown away by somebody who rips your heart right out. It's not that you love to be dominated and a little mistreated, rejected, or walked out on. Who could ever want that? It's just that until you realize that you are a lovable human being, can accept a real person with all their flaws, and don't feel you have to either be a love slave or have one, you'll always be looking for the perfect love object, which in an unevolved state is one who will hurt you.

The answer lies, of course, somewhere between being so afraid of giving your heart to anyone that you totally shut down, and on the other hand becoming the toy of anyone who's savvy enough to know how to play you like a harp.

As a friend you are impeccable, confident, loyal, fun, and full of energy to inspire and encourage others. Friends will always rally around you when you need them, because you are there for them as well. You're always strong and courageous when people need help, as full of altruistic zeal as a firefighter on a mission to save a family or get a kitten out of a tree. So why can't you have that same confidence in personal and intimate situations that you have with friends? All you would have to do is find some healthy middle ground between being masterfully detached and objective and being obsessed with whether you are being loved the way you want to be loved.

At this point you need to probe more deeply into your obsession with proving your worthiness to be loved or your need to fall in love with all the wrong people. In the next part, Going Deeper, reading the chapters called "Marriage" and "Love" will give you a chance to pass through the illusion of idealizing someone or being horribly disappointed in them, and on to a higher expression of your Gemini nature that will help you enjoy being both in a relationship and on your own, and make your Sun shine bright.

Gemini 6

You know when you should turn the TV off? During the evening news when you hear them say "And now a word from our medical expert." Turn off the TV and run. If you don't, you'll be sure to catch every disease they mention. Your immune system isn't necessarily compromised, but you are too attuned to the possible calamities, contagion, contamination, and general cootie transfer that take place when you step out of your bubble and interact with this grimy world.

In this day and age, with AIDS and other STDs so rampant, and strains of bacteria appearing that are resistant to antibiotic treatment, one can't be too careful, especially if you've already succumbed and caught something from getting too close.

Here's the funny part. Your fear has really absolutely nothing to do with health. It is all about your fierce need to be in control. If you're afraid of what happens to people when they let go of control, you will have trouble interacting freely and fully. You could even find yourself getting hung up sexually as well. Often this enormous fund of controlling energy is sublimated or displaced onto work, so that you have a perfect excuse to avoid the danger of intimacy by being spotlessly dedicated to your work, which can send you deep into the dark. As a researcher or a performer you're known as an annoying perfectionist. It scares you to let nature take its course until you come to respect nature and allow it to guide your life, a life which has its own peculiar destiny, much of which will demand privacy, intimacy, and seclusion.

Money is an issue you'd rather not touch, but as you grow older you realize that you can't work for peanuts just so you'll be kept around and can continue to be useful. Such naivete is laudable, but it won't pay your rent or health insurance. So what a strange combo you somehow have to figure out: faith in the plan that the Universe has for you and smart business savvy. How are you supposed to relax and be carried by the current of the Great Ocean and wait for miracles to occur, if you're destined to smarten up and not be such an innocent dope when it comes to business? It should be easy for a Gemini to compartmentalize and divide your head so you can be both cosmic and rich. Gemini should be readily able to work hard and play. But for some reason you have to get older to know exactly how to relax, how to allow prosperity in your life, and how not to think that your life is one long struggle.

At this point you need to probe more deeply into your obsession with your health or working hard because you don't dare get really close to people. In the next part, Going Deeper, reading the chapters called "Sex" and "Control" will give you a chance to pass through the illusion of contamination, and on to a higher expression of your Gemini nature that will help you enjoy not only working but intimate relaxation as well, not to mention gaining greater prosperity, and make your Sun shine bright.

> ✱ *Celebrities Who Share Your Issues*
> *Rosemary Clooney, Vincent Price, Jacques Yves Cousteau, Anne Frank*

Gemini 7

There are so many possibilities for relationships. What a pity you simply don't have time to take advantage of them all. And what a Gemini you are. Talk about a love in each port. A wildly romantic untameable soul. Behave? Oh, you can promise. But the French are so sublime. And the Scandinavians are like strawberry sundaes. And African Americans are so cool. And who can forget hot-blooded Latins? And Italians, ciao, baby! And what a joy, Eskimo kisses are on a snowy night up there beyond the Arctic Circle. And you're not a faithless, heartless wretch at all. You're actually a kind, loving, and happy soul who adores the idea of being married. In the case of many Geminis, they love to get married, not be married. They can't resist the exotic. Once they have it, though, they find that after a while, there's nothing to talk about. And for a Gemini to lose a mental connection is death on wheels to a relationship. You love to explore people, not necessarily move in with them and be stuck with them for the rest of your life. Does that make you an irresponsible rat or a Jezebel heartbreaker? Some would say yes.

It's not just your "Gemini-ness" that makes you a fickle seductive rejecter. You've been walked out on plenty of times, so, yes, you're wary. Yes, you're particular. Yes, you often try to control a relationship, even if your history reveals how hard it is to change people's minds. And that is usually the deal breaker—your lack of tolerance and understanding. Not only does communication break down at that point, but the irreconcilable differences between you could start a war. At best communication can be a fruitful, healthy exchange between the student who asks the questions and the teacher who is challenged to answer—an ongoing dialogue between individuals from different backgrounds, lifestyles, and philosophies. At worst it's a tower of Babel situation in which, try though they might, the parties involved are speaking two different languages with two different alphabets and two different approaches to life that can never meet. You have to find a way to bridge the gap between minds, to be able to enter a new relationship with wide-eyed hope and optimism and not have it plummet into a disappointment so you feel alone again. The soul mate you long for, the perfect business connection you seek—they have to exist somewhere in this galaxy, because God knows, you're really not a loner.

At this point you need to probe more deeply into your own issues about getting too involved too quickly, or dumping someone who bores you. In the next part, Going Deeper, reading the chapters called "Marriage" and "Religion" will give you a chance to pass through the illusion of first idealizing someone then being crushed when they turn out to be someone whose whole world you cannot enter or understand, and on to a higher expression of your nature that will help you enjoy relationships without giving yourself up totally to them, and make your Sun shine bright.

Gemini 8

You have to wonder why some people get themselves deep in debt, when if they could just curb their spending binges, that's right, binges, they could easily amass fortunes and never have to worry about money again.

Many do have sensible values, of course. They grow up early and learn to accept a life of wealth and economic security. No matter where you fit in along the prosperity–panic continuum, it is worth it to understand the roots of your need to be financially supported. These roots lie in early near-death experiences, situations, circumstances, or events that exposed you to danger. It's usually not some dim nonmemory you can't pin down. It's a set of memories that define your life. They often involve not only money or early confrontations with mortality, but also sexuality issues, more specifically conduct and behavior that is considered proper, correct, moral, and in line with the laws and social practices of the day. That's why one has to wonder how much choice we actually have in these things.

Seriously, when it comes to being sexually "liberated," do we actually get to choose whether we swing one way or the other way, or in the case of some people, no way? Or are we herded into behavior by our wish to be obedient to parents, church, and school—and do those various orthodoxies determine our preferences and practices? Is it in our DNA? Or is it all a matter of getting control of our desires? Maybe we make a decision, consciously and deliberately, to forego certain pleasures and indulgences in favor of more practical, traditional forms of security. Or, as some Geminis end up doing, maybe we just let the edgy obsessions take over and let the bad publicity and gossip and politically suicidal antics do what they will as long as we get our rocks off one way or another. And you can be sure there will be sexual gossip, even jokes in bad taste, about your proclivities and carryings on. The more you are in control of your urges, the less bad press you'll get and the more money you'll have in the bank. Your sex life may be lousy at times, but in the end what will save your life is your life savings. And you will have to learn exactly why it's called "life savings": your desire for financial security has to end up being as strong as if not stronger than your desire to throw it all away out of anger and frustration. In youth the money doesn't matter. You fight the bourgeois strings attached to it. As you get older, however—and even Geminis do—you come to appreciate the value of economic security.

At this point you need to probe more deeply into your obsession with being financially supported and/or sexually desirable in socially acceptable terms. In the next part, Going Deeper, reading the chapters called "Recognition" and "Sex" will give you a chance to pass through the illusion of not being wanted and on to a higher expression of your Gemini nature that will help you enjoy a more prosperous, fulfilling life, both financially and sexually, and make your Sun shine bright.

Celebrities Who Share Your Issues
Miles Davis, Sir Laurence Olivier, Johnny Depp,
Paula Abdul, Prince William, Barbara Bush,
Priscilla Presley, Mike Meyers, Marilyn Monroe

Gemini 9

You're supposed to be an observer of humanity. You're not supposed to get crazy because the Catholic Church is rife with scandal and hypocrisy or because discrimination against African Americans and Jews is still going on in this country today or because the Arab terrorists caused 9/11 or for any of the other nine million reasons you have to be outraged about the human injustice that supposedly fine, upstanding citizens perpetrate against each other. You do, though. In fact you are way too prejudiced against prejudiced people. Your powers of objectivity are lost when you start chasing truth down the rabbit hole.

You're here to observe people with a dispassionate eye, not spy on them in the hopes of exposing their altruistic motives as mean-spirited evil wishes to control people's minds.

Something that happened to you early in life left you scarred and hurting with regard to religious groups, college fraternities and sororities, or any exclusive club that judges people and accepts or rejects them on the basis of what you consider to be nincompoop ideas. You're here to report human behavior, not judge it. You're actually a fortunate person who can discover the path you're destined to follow. You're a journalist, a scribe, a photographer, whose function it is to observe and document the absurd antics of human beings you will never completely understand but whose language you must master, mainly because your goal here is not just to gather information but to disseminate it in any form or medium you choose.

Your feelings of anger or inferiority or rejection do not matter, or rather should not matter. It's your creative perception that not only counts, but will get you a lot further than anything else in life. Standing up in front of a board of college examiners for your oral exam is probably the most horrific image you could imagine. You might freeze, and at that moment you could begin to see more about the examiners—what they're wearing, how they sound, who they look like. It would be more about the experience of being there than parroting back a bunch of bull you read in a book.

For this reason you are an army brat, a gypsy, a peripatetic poet, an expatriate, a heretic, a person who is not of any group except maybe by adoption, or for the time being. There's a fascination with every group you don't belong to, and while that will definitely cause you to beat yourself up for not being what you aren't and will never be, you eventually see that you're a lucky son of a gun to be born with the faculties of perception you've got. You've got what it takes to see in a nanosecond a situation in its total essence, and while you may not be the valedictorian of your class, the important thing is the heart you bring to all your communications.

The fact that you are a Gemini, the sign of the Twins, means you may try to run away from your other self, just to prove you have a different separate identity from family and siblings. Eventually you come back to reality: You are half of your other half.

• • •

At this point you need to probe more deeply into your obsession with intellectualizing everything and your difficulties realizing the true gifts of communication that store all your potential. In the next part, Going Deeper, reading the chapters called "Freedom" and "Religion" will give you a chance to pass through the illusion of fearing you are stupid or crazy, and on to a higher expression of your Gemini nature that will help you articulate and communicate on the highest levels, using your own ideas, not somebody else's, and make your Sun shine bright.

> ⋆ *Celebrities Who Share Your Issues*
> *Joe Namath, Patti LaBelle, Josephine Baker, Tony Curtis,*
> *Boz Scaggs, George H.W. Bush, Margaret Bourke-White*

Gemini 10

Il prezzo di fama means the price of fame. What a vain and illusive pursuit. Not so if you take a stage name so you can enjoy celebrity and anonymity at the same time. You wouldn't like that, though. It's one thing to fantasize about being pursued down the street by screaming fans, but when you can't even walk into a drugstore to buy toilet paper without reading about it in the paper the next day, then you feel more like Frankenstein's monster being chased into the woods by torch-bearing villagers. Fame is actually awful in some ways—the cheapening humiliation and stinking corruption you have to endure, the slobbering drunken sycophants who try to proposition you and get you to compromise your ideals, and the countless demeaning tricks you have to pull to get your name on the bill, when most of the time they'll end up spelling it wrong. And yet, it's like crack. You get one snort and you're hooked. As tiresome as it gets when people nose into your most private business, you go out of your mind if you think you're being ignored, passed over, or forgotten.

There's such total madness in the pursuit of glamour. Madness in the pain of being invisible. Madness in the illusion that you could ever be made truly happy by pursuing something that isn't even really there.

Even if you do get it, some sort of disillusion or even scandal will eventually follow, because no matter how straight you try to be, you can't be a member of a society you don't want to belong to. It's enough to drive you to drink, which you could easily fall into if you didn't have an anchor at home, some sobering influence waiting for you with a vegetarian dish to yang you back to reality after you've nearly yinned yourself to death on your latest ego binge. It's a vital balance to achieve, between being drenched and intoxicated by the search for recognition (a thirst that's as hard to quench as an alcoholic's for booze) and the need to grow up and stop running away from home.

The family thing can be so stifling and boring, not to mention the fact that small-minded, hard-working relations are forever putting down the dreams of artists and idealistic altruists who have a burning need to do something meaningful in life and not just mow the lawn or prepare food. Odd, though, how as you progress through life, those petty jobs and menial tasks you fled from turn out to be refreshing antidotes to a public life which, while deeply gratifying, is always fleeting and, without constant vigilance on your part, can turn out to be just plain toxic.

At this point you need to probe more deeply into your issues about what success is and what you have to give up to get it. In the next part, Going Deeper, reading the chapters called "Recognition" and "Escape" will give you a chance to pass through the illusion of anger for not being seen for who you really are, or being manipulated and pushed around by mindless people, and on to a higher expression of your Gemini nature that will help you enjoy both worldly success while cultivating simpler and purer relationships with your family, and make your Sun shine bright.

Celebrities Who Share Your Issues
Bob Dylan, Paul McCartney, Prince Rainier of Monaco,
Henry Kissinger, Boy George, Paul Gauguin, Melissa Etheridge

Gemini 11

Nobody's going to tell you what to do, dammit. You are one free bird who is never going to get locked in a cage like some poor, miserable little parakeet with clipped wings. Yes, you're an oddball and no, you don't always feel like you fit in, but by golly, you are going to make your oddballness pay off. You've always felt weird. Actually, that's not true. In your own head you have always felt normal. You only feel weird when you are compared with everyone else in your high school class. Or your family. And you've adapted to that ugly duckling feeling darned well. In fact, it's become your badge of courage, your stamp, your trademark.

As time goes on you value your freedom more and more. You can develop an aversion to normalcy and a fear that being in a deep relationship will take control away from you and impede your freedom.

You could start confusing your freedom with dominance and love with submission. Think about that for a minute. You'd even be running away from having children until they stopped needing you. It's a lucky and highly evolved Gemini who can do the single, solo, humanitarian bit and have a rich and highly fulfilling personal life. That usually doesn't happen when you're young. Even if you do hook up with someone, fall in love, take a lover, get married, and have a kid early, you have a huge amount of resistance making and keeping a commitment. And it's not like you have one consistent burning goal or mission you have to fulfill that keeps you unattached. You always love to do things for people, but you have trouble giving over control long enough to receive love from those who need you, at least when you're young and busy with your wild oats. If you are ever going to be able to settle down and become a good lover, mate, or parent, you will need maturity, and you will have to get whacked but good by love when you are ready to accept it. It's easier to keep the whole relationship open, see each other once in a while, have random encounters. It fits your personality so much better not to make vows and long-term commitments, as much as you'd like vows and commitments from others. Keep it loose, that's your motto, even though uncertainty about the future bugs you. When friends diss or dump you, it hurts or cuts you deeply, and yet you have been known to latch onto people and then when it's over, dump them on the side of the road and keep driving without looking back. Developing love relationships and dealing with children won't come easy or early, but it will be your reward for good behavior.

At this point you need to probe more deeply into your obsession with making sure you never get snagged, to the point that you actually pass up golden opportunities to be happy. In the next part, Going Deeper, reading the chapters called "Independence" and "Freedom" will give you a chance to pass through the illusion of how love and marriage affect your right to be your own person, and on to a higher expression of your Gemini nature that will help you accept love, and make your Sun shine bright.

> ★ *Celebrities Who Share Your Issues*
> *Rennie Davis, Christopher Lee, Bob Hope, Prince, Judy Garland,*
> *Jane Russell, William Butler Yeats, Drew Carey, Betty Shabazz*

Gemini 12

Everybody's a little bit crazy on the subject of money. Your case is especially tricky, however. Money is your bête noire. Financial stability (or instability) pursues you like a specter. You run away from money but are irresistibly drawn to all the things it can bring—mainly the freedom and mobility. Ironically, though, when you become obsessed with acquiring enough money to give you the freedom, your freedom of mobility is hampered. What a conundrum! And what a ball of wax that can turn into. You already know how many times the issue has turned you inside out and brought you to the edge of your own private apocalypse. Wealth or poverty, it doesn't matter. If you're poor and have nothing, you're free in a way, but not mobile. You're out of touch. No car. No cell phone. You're cut off and stranded and grounded, a situation that is not healthy for a Gemini. Then, too, when you're rich you've got the car, the cell phone, the house, the mortgage, bills, furniture, electronic equipment, jewelry, and eleven thousand other items that hang off you and keep you chained and weighted down like the chains on Marley's ghost. And it's not easy to get you to stop thinking and worrying because you feel as if you are being followed around by a live piggy bank that oinks every fifteen seconds to remind you to fill it up.

How do you get your mind off the pig without slaughtering it and choking on the bacon?

Nobody in this world has the powers of sharp concentration, determination, and diligence you have when you put your mind to it. No one else could be a total sugar and white flour addict the way you can be and then decide, screw it! and never touch the stuff again. When you turn your mind to a task, one that is both creative and serves others as well, you're off and running. The trick, of course, is to be able to work steadily at that creative service task without yielding to tempting distractions. Work has to be creative, deep, somewhat edgy, not totally commercial (that will make you nervous), a bit on the esoteric side, but ultimately practical. It's just as difficult to apply all your discipline and perseverance to a diet and not get distracted by chocolate. Sexual hygiene may make you seem cold and clinical in certain situations, but you of all people have to know how to curb your appetites on all levels. Developing honest sexual behavior is a task of yours, although you're likely to be more clinical than spontaneous and liberated. So if you have to shower before and after, that's just you.

At this point you need to probe more deeply into your obsession with being cheated, to the point that you are freaking out over every transaction, professional or personal. In the next part, Going Deeper, reading the chapters called "Money" and "Escape" will give you a chance to pass through the illusion of being constantly taken advantage of, and on to a higher expression of your Gemini nature that will help you work more creatively and productively, and make your Sun shine bright.

Celebrities Who Share Your Issues
Igor Stravinsky, Richard Benjamin, Tommy Chong,
Peter Yarrow, Susan Strasberg, Joyce Carol Oates

CANCER

June 21–July 22
Dates vary from year to year—consult your local astrologer

If you want to know what Cancer is, just think of the most peaceful, remote spot existing in nature and you've got it. It has to be someplace at least out of the flight path of jet planes. Water is nearby, birds are tweeting and chirping hello to each other everywhere. Roots go deep, nourished by rain, and bees are deep in flowers. Green is everywhere, because it's summer. Cancer is the sign of summer in full. It represents life in its grandest, fullest experience. In case you never met one, Cancers are kind, gentle, God-fearing folk who always cook up an extra pan of lasagna or matzo ball soup for an ailing neighbor or unexpected cousin from Florida. They often live at the end of a tree-lined driveway (sometimes you don't even know a house is there), and from the windows of the gabled second floor appear cute little smiling faces, and hands excitedly waving, "Welcome home, Papa!" At mealtime mounds of mashed potatoes and other yummy starches are generously passed from plate to plate. All things considered, the family has a certain *The-Waltons*-R-Us quality to them you just can't beat.

Now let's be real. What are you so afraid of? The answer: everything. You're not necessarily so crazy that you think prowlers are crouching in the bushes under your window, but you certainly do your share of worrying about the inevitable onslaught of an army of unwelcome in-laws marching toward you with hunger in their eyes. That's a big one for Cancers. It's not that you are selfish or cheap (the latter is a debatable point if you've ever taken a good look at yourself while shopping and comparing prices). It's not that you don't want to be generous or lavish. You'd love to be. Aren't Cancers supposed to be the nurturers of the world? You're supposed to feed the hungry. That's your karma. But God help anyone who dares to remind you of your nurturing responsibilities when you're not in the mood, especially if they want to keep all ten fingers. You do love to nurture and feed people, but that's only one day a month. Maybe two. The rest of the time you're growling and grinding your teeth and resenting humanity's heartless and endless drain on your dwindling resources. But . . . on those two days a month, everybody better be ready for some major carbs. During that short period you will let go of all the resentment you've been storing up the rest of the month. And woe to any poor soul who happens to be lactose intolerant, because at Cancer happy hour loved ones will be offered more dairy products than have been produced by the state of Wisconsin in the last 150 years.

Just take one look at that stash of comfort foods and then try to say you don't hear Rosemary Clooney singing "Come-On-A-My-House." And what about the old movie, *I Remember Mama*? No matter how divisive she was, the old girl abhorred separation and would not tolerate any disunity she herself did not create. One family, indivisible by God, and by God you get here for Thanksgiving or she'll break your goddamned neck.

Male or female, when it comes to those you have come to consider family, you are the ferocious protective mother who, unlike a female hamster, may not go so far as to eat her children, but pal, those kids are tethered with a steel leash around their neck, and Heaven help the one who dares to try to break away. Individuation? Don't even think about it.

Cancer is the sign of the mother, so this is not a personal attack on mothers. We're looking at what it means for you to have been born under the sign of the Mother. The Mother gives birth to but never completely separates from her children. Because the kids are of her flesh, she and they are one and don't you forget it! What you carry forward from that sort of bond is that on some level you see yourself as the world's mother, as loyal as a penguin. Because you have such a sense of attachment and responsibility, naturally you love and hate all the people you are attached to.

No matter what, however, you must have an extra supply of meat, pies, rhubarb, corn, and Cornish game hens stocked in the freezer, just in case.

In case of what?

Gotta remember that the Mother always protects her children from everyone and everything but herself. The sign of Cancer rules over the unconscious, and the honest, sincere conscious wish of every Cancer, as it is of most mothers, is to make sure that all under her wing remain safe. Don't touch a hair on a head of anyone she holds dear, or God love ya, you can expect a visit from the Marines, or Uncle Vito, or both. The funny thing is, you will protect people as long as they continue the illusion that they are the weak, helpless little children who need protection. You feel threatened when loved ones are all grown up and want to get married or set out upon a life path which, horror of horrors, doesn't include you. That's when there's trouble in River City. You will do everything to prepare your little charges for life in the world, but you know best that they are never quite ready to go off on their own. Not quite yet. That is the fatal flaw of Cancers: the clinging and the clutching, the fainting spells and heart attack scares, the sub rosa manipulation, and if all else fails—war.

There's a definite positive side to this automatic, unconscious wish to hang on. Cancers abhor open confrontation. Usually. You are fundamentally a seeker of peace. No matter what sort of unspoken and indirect passive-aggressive hostility exists between you and the rest of the world, there is still usually a sincere love of unity and connection that sets you apart from all other signs. So no matter how much you scratch and claw, you'll bring your mate child boss lover perceived oppressor hot chocolate afterward. You will put yourself in harm's way to stand between evil doers and those you love, whether those you love want it or not. You will make willing sacrifices in times of crisis—most of which you create—and for all your million anxieties about starvation, you will dig into your wallet or make a stack of pancakes when someone is in dire straits.

Fundamentally, whether you've got kids or not, you are fertile. All you have to do is buy one lousy tomato plant at Home Depot, and before you know it you're producing Mama Gianelli's Homemade Marinara Sauce, authentically churned out in Mama's own factory right there in good old New Jersey, mostly composed of $C_6H_{12}O_6$—sugar, of course, the thing that all Cancers coat their rage with.

It is also helpful to bear in mind that by this point you have probably been driven emotionally indoors by the driving rainstorm you consider life in the world. This is true for all Cancers, whether you run a big company or not.

Even when you accept the First Lady role, à la Nancy Reagan, and put yourself in charge of huge operations, in the end you are still an introvert. The origins of this tendency to curl up in a fetal ball and escape from life's coldness lie shrouded somewhere in the past when you were first ejected from amniotic fluid and never really got over being born. Of course it goes back to the way in which you were separated from your mother, and that's probably the whole story right there in a nutshell, one that explains this obsession with finding security.

Security, then, is one of the primal drives of all Cancers. Always has been. Back in caveman times the first person to be called a caveman was probably a Cancer, because he was the first person to have sense enough to go indoors to escape bad weather and wild animals. Many Cancers shrink in horror from the idea of a permanent home. Every two years they move, often further and further away from their birthplace, probably because they dread the thought of ending up like their mothers, which they risk doing anyway sooner or later. Even they, however, always set up some version of home, even in a trailer park or residence hotel, and all you have to do is look around you right now. It's amazing. You're in a place for two weeks and anybody would swear you'd been nesting since the Ice Age. Even if it's sparse and unfurnished and seems more like a murderer's hideout than a home, it always looks as if it's home, because home is where you have to be, even if it means living out of a rolling suitcase.

You're really all about real estate, period. Whether you own or rent, you are territorial to the nth degree, no matter how trashy and transient some Cancers try to be. You sincerely believe your home should be free of all pests, from cockroaches to nosy in-laws. Territory, for Cancers, is everything. What do you think is your real spiritual mantra? "There's no place like home"? Wrong. "Blood is thicker than water"? Uh-uh. It's "Location, location, location," because the essence of the Cancer dream may involve intimacy and tenderness, but at the end of the day, it's all about a low mortgage rates.

"Own your own home!" People tell you. Then you'll be happy.

What a fabulous come-on, dreamed up by the bankers, of course. It's brilliant. You buy land, which you can sell later and buy more at a bigger mortgage, or you can leave it to your kids to fight over. And because you're fundamentally an honest and moral person, you don't like to think that you are buying land from somebody who bought it from somebody who inherited it from somebody who bought it from somebody who stole it from the Indians. You'll pretend that didn't happen, because as a Cancer you are great at pretending things didn't happen, then remembering them better than they were, especially childhood, most of which you've totally blocked out. Let's just say that Cancers need a home and will do just about anything to get one, most of the time from honest, hard work. There are a few ruthless members of your sign who, when greed and insecurity take over, are not above giving smallpox to anybody who lives where you see value in the property and natural resources therein. Well, you wouldn't go quite that far, but it wouldn't be wise for anybody to try to kick you out of any square footage you're squatting in, unless they don't mind spending a fortune on lawyers.

You sincerely welcome people with open arms, but you've been known to treat them afterward as if they were Ralph Kramden's mother-in-law or a locust, until they "prove" themselves, which means God-only-knows what rites of passage and loyalty they have to pass through before they are considered family. At that point they are free to go to the fridge and help themselves. Essentially, Cancers are by nature a more live-and-let-live bunch than the aggressive marauders linked to other signs of the Zodiac. But you can certainly be piggy about your resources. You can be as dangerous as a Doberman that hasn't eaten since last Tuesday when your resources appear to be dwindling. Yours is a very conservative point of view, sometimes to the point of actual xenophobia.

Unfortunately, not all Cancers are spiritually liberated, a fact that causes a disparity between philosophy and practice among the members of your sign. Some Cancers are overwhelmingly obsessed with their personal comfort, which erodes their sense of practicality. In some ways you can be like a flea on a sheep dog. Once you burrow in, forget it. Even bug spray won't work. You just won't leave. You can reject, manipulate, and turn someone inside out, but if you think a person wants to get rid of you, you come back like malaria. And it's not malice or pure masochism that guns your motor although, if truth be told, along your DNA chain there is a gene for a naughty little girl who got spanked too often, and liked it.

It's just that when you get comfy, when you've established yourself in a spot, when your fanny has worn a perfect cranny in the couch, there's just no moving you. As peaceful as you are, when your personal comfort is jeopardized in any way, watch out. While the pursuit of a better and easier life is certainly one goal everyone deserves to have, it's also the reason so many Cancers are fat. Personal comfort, when emphasized above purpose and diligence, leads to sloth and laziness. Eventually your brain shrinks. Your limbs disappear, and you're a blob of enjoyment rising as you sleep, like a ball of yeasty dough in the oven. This is the clear and present danger when you're not vigilant and alert.

Some unevolved Cancers have a dread of appearing dependent, so no matter how desperately they need what others have, they will manipulate the situation to make it appear as if they haven't a care in the world. You are caring and loving and sincerely unselfish when it comes to comforting and protecting those you love, but when someone attempts to squeeze you in any way and exercise power over you or let you know that you are not in control, they'd better prepare for armed conflict.

One of the most magnificent qualities of the Cancerian is the sense of abundance and prosperity that evolved Cancers have. Evolved Cancers are free of the fear of the future. They don't think they're going to starve to death out in the cold. They don't fear that foreigners are going to take their jobs or snatch the potatoes off their plates. They welcome them. They have utter faith in their own ingenuity and ability to work hard and be productive, mainly because they know that industry results in reward. Evolved Cancers also know that they can always afford to be generous and share what they have, mainly because they belong to a bountiful Universe whose function it is to provide amply for its inhabitants.

Herein lies the first secret to changing your fate. How do you develop your faith in everyone and vanquish the fear of invasion? What drives you toward fear and insecurity and how can you get back on the right path of your destiny? Those are a couple of the big questions, ones you need to explore deeply on your way to happiness and fulfillment.

So how can you put all the swirling emotions together in one integrated whole? What are the forces that drag you backward and keep you from reaching the highest manifestation of your Sun? And what are the energies that can support you, guide you, enhance your positive qualities, and make your Sun shine bright? The fact is you're not just a Cancer. There is another energy operating, one that either cuts across your efforts and undermines them, or spirits you to heights of joy and fulfillment. That energy depends not on the month you were born, but the year as well. Later on in this book the technical aspects will be explained more fully. We'll examine how you waste time chasing your own tail, why you do it, and how to pull yourself out of self-destructive obsessions and put yourself back on the road to success. But for now, check out the following table. Find your birth year and note the number beside it. Then read the section corresponding to the number.

Year–No.	Year–No.	Year–No.	Year–No.	Year–No.
1901–11	1915–2	1930–4	1946–6	1961–9 until
1902–11	1916–2 until	1931–4	1947–6 until	6/27, then 8
until 7/19,	7/4, then 1	1932–3	7/12, then 5	1962–8
then 10	1917–1	1933–3	1948–5	1963–7
1903–10	1918–12	1934–2	1949–4	1964–7
1904–9	1919–12	1935–1	1950–4	1965–6
1905–9	1920–11	1936–1	1951–3	1966–5
1906–8	1921–10	1937–12	1952–2	1967–5
1907–7	1922–10	1938–11	1953–2	1968–4
1908–7	1923–9	1939–11	1954–1	1969–3
1909–6	1924–8	1940–10	1955–12	1970–3
1910–5	1925–8	1941–9	1956–12	1971–2
1911–5	1926–7	1942–9	1957–11	1972–1
1912–4	1927–6	1943–8	1958–10	1973–1
1913–3	1928–6	1944–7	1959–10	1974–12
1914–3	1929–5	1945–7	1960–9	1975–11

Year–No.	Year–No.	Year–No.	Year–No.	Year–No.
1976–11	1987–4	1998–9	2010–1	2022–5
1977–10	1988–3	1999–8	2011–12	2023–5 until
1978–10 until	1989–2	2000–7	2012–12	7/12, then 4
7/20, then 9	1990–2	2001–7	2013–11	2024–4
1979–9	1991–1	2002–6	2014–10	2025–3
1980–8	1992–1 until	2003–5	2015–10	2026–3
1981–8	7/5, then 12	2004–5	2016–9	2027–2
1982–7	1993–12	2005–4	2017–8	2028–1
1983–6	1994–11	2006–3	2018–8	2029–1
1984–6	1995–11	2007–3	2019–7	2030–12
1985–5	1996–10	2008–2	2020–6	
1986–4	1997–9	2009–2	2021–6	

Cancer 1

This is a tough world and if you want to survive in it, you have to protect yourself. It's ironic, because just as easily you can get stuck in your role as caretaker and then resent it like mad. You might find it hard to juggle your need to avoid messy dependencies with your need to be present to wipe everybody's nose, when it's actually your own fear of being walked out on that drives you, by golly, to be their mommy whether they are six or sixty. Some might say you keep people in line by keeping them dependent on you, which might seem crazy since you're the one who is actually trying to get away. Your "come to Momma, honey" thing provides a source of refuge, not only for the clinically depressed, but also for anyone who is trying to find a replacement for the parent they never had. That's a colossal bit of irony when you think about it, since you probably identify too closely with your mother, an issue that, when left unresolved, renders it hard for you to accept a mature role of parent yourself.

When you resent your role, you display an angry form of nurturing: "Here! Eat this, dammit. I cooked it especially for you!" It reveals both your desire to care for someone else and your resentment of the responsibility inherent in having a relationship. Despite all your attempts to worm your way into someone's life and erode the boundaries between you, you'll actually thrive best when up against someone who has the will to resist you. You need someone who draws you out—out of yourself and especially out of the house. Someone who helps you, and sometimes even forces you to respect healthy distances and live up to your word. You are searching for a father and yet you resist the traditional male attitudes. You love to engage in and play a very traditional "Mrs. & Mr." game (regardless of gender or sexual orientation), but in reality you have enormous struggles accepting the mommy role you so desperately love to play. Of course, if you could just stay home and cook and do the laundry and let your significant other go out and kill the lions, that wouldn't make you happy either, mainly because you know you weren't put here on Earth to be Mrs. Mary Smith of Duluth or Frau Kleinschmidt from Salzburg.

Somehow, some way you need to find a healthy way to care for people without invading their lives. You have to participate in politics and career even though you don't enjoy leaving the house for more than two hours. If you don't become the president, then you should probably marry the president so you could spoon feed him or her your ideas and get to rule the world without ever leaving the house. How can you be caring and avoid enmeshment?

At this point you need to probe more deeply into your obsession with your own issues about being so self-protective that you fight people off, turn on your answering machine, and prefer to be (miserable) alone rather than in the company of others because they demand too much of you. In the next part, Going Deeper, reading the chapters called "Independence" and "Security" will give you a chance to pass through the illusion of fear of being controlled by another person who is not sensitive to your needs, and on to a higher expression of your Cancer nature that will help you come out of your shell long enough to fulfill yourself in business or personal relationships, and make your Sun shine bright.

Celebrities Who Share Your Issues
The Dali Lama, Carson Daly, Athena Starwoman,
Donald Sutherland, Jack Kemp, Billy Norwich

Cancer 2

How could money be linked to a feeling of being loved? It's easy if you were unloved or mistreated as a kid. Then financial security becomes everything. Even if some people say it's better to be loved for your money than not to be loved at all, can that be true? You've got to wonder what propels some guys and gals to spend precious days out at the track praying for the ponies to deliver them from financial worries. When you come to think of it, though, any mad speculation, from investment in a Broadway play to pork belly futures can become an insane obsession, especially if you think that it's going to save you from your fear of fiscal ruin. You win some and you lose some and as long as you have the spirit of the game, it's okay to spend a weekend in Vegas. It's not easy for anybody, especially a Cancer, to have to depend on other people's money for subsistence, so you are always thinking of ways to pull away from such a dependency and have resources of your own. If you could find some magical commodity that would never depreciate in value, you could then be totally, eternally economically secure. Gold, for instance. Gold is precious. Maybe it goes up or down a little depending on the dollar and the euro and the yen and the ruble, but gold is always gold. If you get fixated on money and hang your whole portfolio or future on one dream, you can be sure all your fears of starving and ending up homeless could come true. What you consider to be your talent for generating income is your gold mine, metaphorically speaking, but when your ego becomes too attached to your image, you become overidentified with yourself as appearing richer than you are.

At that point you could start acting like the French nobility before 1789. This is a false identity, and you're going to have a heck of a time adjusting when you realize that the pursuit of wealth is all a vain illusion. You need to trust people more and allow your funds to be managed by people who know more than you do and have objectivity—which you don't have.

Equating money with love is a danger to us all. If you're feeling guilty about being too financially secure, humanitarian efforts will help to satisfy your need to throw away all your money and be poor. They call it tithing, and it has nothing to do with wealth. Being sensitive to the needs of humanity can help you gain perspective and achieve objectivity, and reduce ego identification with your financial status in the world, so you're less likely to make an ostentatious and defensive show of fiscal power, which only winds you up behind the eight ball. In fact, and here's the whole secret: Your true prosperity will come as you develop a healthy and open attitude to, of all things, your own sexuality.

At this point you need to probe more deeply into your obsession with being identified with your net worth, to the point that you forget you are an organic being with lusty emotional desires that also need to be fulfilled. In the next part, Going Deeper, reading the chapters called "Love" and "Money" will give you a chance to pass through the illusion of fear of losing your shirt in the game, and on to a higher expression of your Cancer nature that will help you be more balanced and confident as a person who deserves to be loved and desired in your own right, for richer or for poorer, come out of your shell long enough to fulfill yourself in business or personal relationships, and make your Sun shine bright.

> *Celebrities Who Share Your Issues*
> *Jamie Farr, Alan Born, John Quincy Adams, John Bradshaw, Sydney Pollack, Kristy Yamaguchi*

Cancer 3

Recently there was a piece in the newspaper about a set of twins, conjoined at the head, who were successfully separated. It turned out they were Cancers. The metaphor is perfect, mainly because when siblings are separated for one reason or another, sometimes their attachment becomes inexplicably deeper and more powerful than it would have been if they had remained together, especially if one thrives and the other one doesn't. Then the healthier, more successful one has to deal with the guilt of being healthier and more successful! Alienation from siblings, relatives, or neighbors can affect mental and physical health positively or negatively, depending upon your consciousness and your ability to accept your destiny. It can also send you into years of therapy in an effort to free yourself from thinking you have to be everybody's big sister or brother, although frankly, you'll probably never be able to shake that obsession entirely. Even if you lose contact with a sibling you will probably keep the connection on a spiritual level.

While these talents lead you to unmatchable expertise as a researcher into nutrition, a scientist glued to a microscope, a telephone repairperson, an auto mechanic, a critic, or a mathematician, all these roles could mask a deeper need for an emotional and spiritual connection with the life you're afraid to pursue for fear you'll be thought of as a fool. In the attempt to avoid the chaos of emotionalism you could easily be cheating yourself out of rich experiences that have nothing to do with a rational approach to life or science. There usually comes a striking epiphany when you realize that you need to develop a whole other side of your life, explore other dimensions. You eventually need to step out of the little world you have created for yourself in an effort to avoid operating on blind faith and having to forgive the people closest to you who deceive or desert you. It's the sort of thing physicists go through when they have gone so deep into studying quarks that the only thing left to do is take up the guitar.

You get very caught up in the minutiae of the day and totally lose perspective. You have to be forced to take off your shoes and walk along a beach, just to allow your mind to wander into the vast sea of possibility, which is the mental refreshment you desperately need. It's much easier to make observations and dwell on infirmities, real or imagined, but actually your answers lie outside the mundane, physical world. The trick, of course, is to remain deeply rooted in reality and communicate with people, but not fear that your beliefs will be ridiculed, laughed at, or totally ignored. There will be moments, however, when silence will be a wiser choice.

Some perceptions have no rational explanations, and for a rational person like yourself, fulfillment will require a leap of faith in your own mind, your own intelligence, and your ability to step away from what people usually call common sense.

At this point you need to probe more deeply into your obsession with being rational to the point that you don't trust your own mind. In the next part, Going Deeper, reading the chapters called "Communication" and "Control" will give you a chance to pass through the illusion of fear of being thought of as crazy because you don't think like other people, and on to a higher expression of your Cancer nature that will help you have more faith, and make your Sun shine bright.

> *Celebrities Who Share Your Issues*
> *Cheryl Ladd, Jesse Ventura, Pat Morita, Della Reese, Gerald Ford,*
> *Geoffrey Rush, Julia Duffy, Chris O'Donnell, Angelica Huston*

Cancer 4

You are a Cancer to the nth degree. The nth to the nth degree, in fact. If it's possible to be too much of what you should be, you are it in spades. At least that's the risk you run when you try too hard to create a perfect family scene out of Norman Rockwell, *The Waltons*, and every sitcom ever broadcast during the 1950s. Not that it's a bad thing to want a decent home and a happy marriage. That's a totally normal desire. The problem arises when you invest so much energy into family and marriage that you turn away from your professional responsibilities and opportunities and then begin resenting mate or kids—especially when they grow up or leave you and there you are with a plate full of baked potatoes and nobody to eat them. Because of the marriage your parents had, which nowadays would be called dysfunctional, you're determined (read obsessed) to create a better life for your own kids. The irony is that you can't control what goes on in a household. In fact, chaos is inevitable. One-parent families are common today and not the stigma they once were. Divorce and widowhood used to be thought of as devastating events that scarred children forever. Nowadays it is often thought that kids are better in a happy home, even if it's not a traditional Mom-and-Pop thing.

The guilt factor is still pretty huge, however, and when you try too hard to compensate for domestic problems, you find it hard to be both nurturer and disciplinarian. One thing is sure: You have to try to have a life outside the house, whether the house falls apart without you or not.

As selfish as it will appear, you have to fight the urge to be swallowed up in the abyss of family and marriage. While it's normal for most people to tend to their families, you've got to be careful you don't live for or through yours, because you have such an issue with abandonment and guilt when a marriage fails or ends. Your lifeline is your career. Even though you'll be irritated to have to tear yourself away from the house, or you'll get annoyed when torn between family needs and professional responsibilities (which you will be all the time) when you do drag yourself across that threshold, you cease either feeding or being an insecure and needy little infant and become the leader you are destined to be. Nobody ever knows what goes on behind closed doors in people's homes. And since you can be such a powerful person in the marketplace, one would never guess how desperately you can hang on to a scene at home that may not be emotionally fulfilling, but satisfies a need you have for a place to run to, a base of operations, a showplace to prove to the world that you're not just some dried up career freak and that you are just as able to have a fulfilling personal life as you are to run a company. The trick is to prove the opposite as well. When one receives a Christmas card from a Cancer CEO, picturing the happy little family by a fireside, one is never aware that behind the photo a soap opera saga is going on. So how to be the successful businessperson and not reveal your deep insecurities about being abandoned?

At this point you need to probe more deeply into your own issues about setting family boundaries, as well as your leadership capabilities. In the next part, Going Deeper, reading the chapters called "Marriage" and "Security" will give you a chance to pass through the illusion of fear of abandonment and on to a higher expression of your Cancer nature that will help you step away from home, fulfill yourself in business, and make your Sun shine bright.

> ★ *Celebrities Who Share Your Issues*
> *Lindsay Wagner, Jimmy Walker, Leslie Caron,*
> *George Steinbrenner, Tab Hunter, Vera Wang*

Cancer 5

Your story doesn't necessarily have to be as dark a tale as *Rosemary's Baby,* but the longer you live you come to understand that no matter what you do in this life, one thing is always certain: Children are a blessing and a curse. If you don't have them, you wish you did. When you have them, half the time you're madly in love with them and the other half of the time you could put a contract out on them. That may be a bit harsh, because maybe you don't even want kids or aren't destined to have any. Not all Cancers have kids. Some are happier being Aunt Jodi or Uncle Matthew. It's not that you shouldn't have children. It's just that some Cancers choose not to. They prefer to channel their protective instincts—maternal if you will—into what they perceive to be more creative endeavors. One thing is sure, though: Whether it's flesh and blood or works of art on canvas, you'll approach your creations with a ferocious attachment some people will consider unhealthy and even unnatural. Even if you have normal, wonderful kids, you've got to be careful not to project all your negative fears and dark fantasies onto them. You may still find it hard not to identify with or feel responsible for their behavior, no matter how outrageous. It's one thing when people tell you to let go. It's easy to say that each person has his or her own path (or karma) that has nothing to do with the parents. It's quite another thing when you see the horns and the tail sprouting from your own kid. Your attachment is deep—too deep maybe.

It's the same with people you fall in love with. You don't love lightly—and that is an understatement. Maybe that's the issue. Maybe your needs are so complex, so intense, so rife with melodramatic fantasies that border on Greek tragedy, that the only way to overcome this sort of possession is to walk away from it completely. That's way easier said than done in your case, mainly because that's what it can become: a sexual possession—an emotional, almost incestuous, lust that can never be satisfied. It's what makes artists the obsessive creatures they are, but it doesn't do a damned thing to calm down their personal lives. As you get older, of course, you do calm down and you recognize the value of a loyal friendship over a taboo love affair. What you give up in intensity you gain in support and longevity. Watching one of your affairs unfold, you can see how ancient people could believe in demonic possession.

Your salvation lies in finding a group of people who can ground you, bring you back to reality, remind you of the business of living. You need to be in the company of earthy, practical, prosperous individuals who can lift you out of the emotional swamps you could easily end up splashing around in. Your particular form of genius/madness/ecstasy/grief is your own snake pit, of course, but as you develop your talents for the benefit (and profit) of a common good, your life becomes fuller, richer, more connected to the world.

At this point you need to probe more deeply into your obsession with being sexy and lovable, to the point that you forget you have to conduct business and have relationships based on loyalty, not passion. In the next part, Going Deeper, reading the chapters called "Sex" and "Love" will give you a chance to pass through the illusion of fear of being undesirable or unloved by a child or another adult, and on to a higher expression of your Cancer nature that will help you remain creative and passionate while being able to step away from your own needs long enough to make friends with the world, and make your Sun shine bright.

Celebrities Who Share Your Issues
Kathy Bates

Cancer 6

Finding a job in health care—mental or physical—is one sure way to discover the link between psychic and somatic well being. Whether illness is caused by the cooties you find on any doorknob or by genetically traceable immune strengths or weakness, or simply by the mind will remain for researchers to determine over the next several centuries. Even then it is doubtful they will every completely agree. You do need to take care of people, as much as it bugs you. And you are interested in health—or, as you probably look at it most of the time, mental illness.

How about teaching kids with learning disabilities? You certainly must know a lot about that.

Why focus on work? Aren't you supposed to be home whipping up a batch of brownies from scratch? Not you. You're a working mom or dad and part of you always remains at least partially single, in service, like the lamplighters of old times who went around each night lighting street lamps, or the town criers' "Nine o'clock and all is well. Ten o'clock and all is well." You definitely have to work.

Odd, too, that no matter how empty or meaningless a job is, you can too easily get glued to it. You find your security there, like a diligent priest who never misses mass or confession but stopped believing long ago. The job becomes rote. You stop thinking. You do it all by the book. You love the ritual. You love the routine. You love the regularity. Round and round you go—like running a kiddie carousel. There's a hypnotic magic within the monotony that gives you an odd sort of comfort. It helps reduce the feeling of not being needed.

Obviously the psychological and spiritual health thing is no joke, and sooner or later you have to realize that the body is animated by some form of intelligence that medical science is now only beginning to understand. Awareness of what makes the body work is certainly a big part of your day (and night, when you're not freaking out over some weird malady you just saw on the National Geographic Channel).

There is another aspect to your life, of course, other than bandaging boo-boos. It could be called a coffee break, because you can't stay away from work more than 20 minutes without getting nervous. Little breaks. That's all you need. That's all you'll allow yourself. You have to have them, though. Otherwise you're as stale as last week's corn bread. Sure you're likely to be a tad hypocritical, because when you do have your few moments away, what you do will be quite contrary to what you preach during working hours.

So much of your day is devoted to proving you're sane and sober that your moments of escape are likely to be breaches of etiquette and deviations from doctrine. Paradoxically, your sanity depends on your being a little crazy from time to time. Your sense of humanity and your ability to empathize depend on your deviation from critical, analytical intellectualizing and mentalizing in favor of feeling with your soul's eyes. Like Luke Skywalker who had to learn to use his feelings to see and to communicate, you need to develop new methods of perception.

• • •

At this point you need to probe more deeply into your obsession with staying healthy and proving your intelligence and sanity, to the point that you become a slave instead of serving gladly. In the next part, Going Deeper, reading the chapters called "Religion" and "Control" will give you a chance to pass through the illusion of being indispensable as well as your fear of communicating, and on to a higher expression of your Cancer nature that will help you develop your powerful mental gifts, enjoy life more, and make your Sun shine bright.

Celebrities Who Share Your Issues
Bob Fosse, Sylvester Stallone, George W. Bush,
Gilda Radner, Neil Simon, Fantasia Barrino

Cancer 7

Remember the little old lady who lived in a shoe and had so many children she didn't know what to do? Where the hell was her husband or her boyfriend? Can you relate to that tale? You do, you know. You are obviously a very wonderful and sweet person, a spiritually developed, matured-way-too-early individual who is happy when other people are happy and sad when they are sad. Of course, there are always cynics who will start screaming, "codependent enabler!" And certainly it cannot be denied that you have been known to breast-feed an awful lot of people in your day. For some reason you look for the depressed, I'm-such-a-loser-nobody-sees-how-great-I-am type of lost soul, and immediately you start lactating. Yet you loathe the role. What's a Cancer to do?

You've always been the nurturing type and the grown up. Had to be from day one. Maybe that's part of the problem. You have been so conditioned to offer comfort to the control freaks who act like lost little lambs but end up running your whole damned life that you have to shoo them off like flies. Then, dammit! you're alone again. Whether you've ever been in a long-term relationship or not, you have to empathize with those perfect hairdo housewives back in the 1950s who got married out of high school, stayed married, had Tupperware parties, and made cupcakes for the school bake sale and roast beef for her hubby's boss, and yet, was alone her entire life without one single person ever really knowing her. Why? Because she put everyone else's needs before her own. That cannot—must not—happen to you.

Unless, of course, you want to be the reincarnation of Eleanor Roosevelt, which might not be so bad as long as you fix your teeth. You could become the strength behind the power and be recognized some day, *finally*, although probably not by the people you want to be recognized by or in the way you want to be recognized.

Who? How? You want that *one certain person* to honor you and acknowledge you and thank you and give you the credit you deserve for being supportive, especially during the times when *you* needed support and didn't get it. Until somebody invents a time machine that may not be possible.

You can't really go back in time to those moments of yesteryear when you had to be the parent although you were supposed to be the child. Just can't do it. Be grateful, however, that you are healthy, wise, mature, able to handle any situation, willing to help those in need, able to open your door and give shelter and allow the cold and hungry to sit by your fire. Your task is to be able to do so without becoming robotically controlled by someone who knows how to take advantage of your dread of being alone.

At this point you need to probe more deeply into your issues about being so responsible that you stay in a bad relationship too long or leave one prematurely before you can be abandoned. In the next part, Going Deeper, reading the chapters called "Marriage" and "Recognition" will give you a chance to pass through the illusion of fear of either being alone or controlled by another person's problems, and on to a higher expression of your Cancer nature that will help you keep a piece of your own life but still be able to relate to people on a healthy level, and make your Sun shine bright.

Celebrities Who Share Your Issues
Courtney Love, George Michael, Carly Simon, Deborah Harry

Cancer 8

It's great to be desired by everyone on the planet—no agenda, no deep, dark emotional attachments to impede your needs for gratification. The longer you're alive, however, the more you will know that you cannot escape from developing your talents in business and putting a lid on some of your libidinous desires. Such repression may make you angry, mainly because of the early events and circumstances that messed up your head sexually and ultimately inhibited your need for a fulfilling love relationship that includes healthy sexual expression. You know you can push that little button when you want to. You're not really cut out to star in one of those naughty movies involving a scantily dressed French maid and a Latin pool boy, but you're not exactly home-sweet-home the way Grandma defined it, either. You can't help it, though. Your kind of mothering is the kind soldiers need the night before they go into battle. As a man, it's Valentino all the way. Not!

Not that you act on it all the time. You don't get the chance as much as maybe you'd like. You are not a nice-nice little Cancer. You are deeply and religiously rebellious, especially when it comes to issues of sex and sexuality. Some call it deviant behavior. According to standard and practice, you are way over at the far end of the bell curve. You may not like to admit it, but the element of sex is present all the time. Whether you are hailed as a kooky eccentric cross between Betty Crocker and Marilyn Chambers (male or female) all depends on the society and time you live in.

Fortunately your acts of rebellion can be a great asset to you, providing a necessary valve to let off steam from a very responsible and (what most people would consider) a very normal life, which will usually end up being centered around business and finance. Issues of money and personal relationships with children, mates, or lovers may sometimes seem like a drag that pull you back to reality when you get tempted to go off on one of your humanity-saving missions or sexual financial binges. The fact is that once you face your urges for intimacy and aren't afraid of them, you are grown up and you can knead your obsessions into shape, throw them into the oven, and have them come out as a golden brown product that normal people can swallow and digest.

That's a gift. Even though you consider commercialism repulsive and crappy, you are always torn between developing your creative gifts for their own sake and being too concerned with what material rewards they will bring you. You don't respect the empty values of commercial society. You've got to bake from scratch and hope for the success produced by mass-market, prepackaged donuts. Your capacity to produce quality and still retain your uniqueness, and your stubborn refusal to knuckle under and sell out—these are qualities you can take to the bank. Keeping your integrity while remaining practical is your path to prosperity. Growing up means dealing with the financial world without being totally corrupted or driven mad by it. A little monogamy wouldn't hurt, either.

At this point you need to probe more deeply into your obsession with being creative and sexually desirable to the point that you hinder prosperity. In the next part, Going Deeper, reading the chapters called "Freedom" and "Sex" will give you a chance to pass through the illusion of fear of being trapped by your own needs for love and sex, controlled by society's values, and on to a higher expression of your Cancer nature that will help you fulfill yourself on an artistic and personal basis, and make your Sun shine bright.

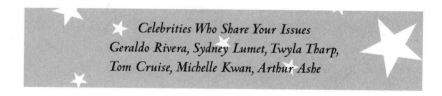

Celebrities Who Share Your Issues
Geraldo Rivera, Sydney Lumet, Twyla Tharp,
Tom Cruise, Michelle Kwan, Arthur Ashe

Cancer 9

Cancers are often thought to be a bunch of overly emotional hysterics, swimming madly around like fish in a barrel. You're reputed to have no real analytical, thinking brain. It's all supposed to be on gut. You, however, are not like that. You do have a brain. In fact, you are thinking all the time.

Many of your thoughts involve either escaping from work or trying to run away from some drudgery-laden routine that doesn't allow you five minutes rest. The fact is, you can be a deep thinker and an unusually analytic person, plagued with many doubts about things you've been taught as a child—half of which you're afraid to look at or challenge until you get fed up enough. Is it crazy to believe in anything at all? You read the Bible, the Koran, Eastern texts, the Torah, and the rest of the good words wise men have passed down through the ages (and it was *men* of course), and then what? While in reality it was probably the women who had the insights and connections to spiritual wisdom, it was the men who were in charge of publishing and promulgating ideas and beliefs, so you can just imagine what the New Testament would have been like if the Virgin Mary had written it. It would have probably been titled, *Dammit! I told Him He should have been a doctor!*

If we seek comfort in religion, why is it always about misery and sacrifice and being a good sport when perfectly good people are forever getting screwed and buried under a ton of crapola? So many people are suckers for it, even though they don't really believe it is wonderful to suffer. They keep going back for more. They keep on searching. We all keep on searching.

Sometimes, the bigger the deal some clerics make out of their piety, the more empty you know they must feel inside. They don't really find true comfort spouting chapter and verse. They're probably just rationalizing a frustration they don't dare express until they finally explode and become total atheists.

That's rarely the end of the story, however. So desperate are they to find order in the chaos, and discover meaning in a Universe that has turned out to be a collection of impersonal, random events, that they keep on searching, pretending to feel what they are supposed to feel. The betrayals are devastating, and it causes great pain and consternation to articulate what they have discovered to be true, especially when they know that their point of view could be looked upon as cold and jaundiced and bitter and cynical. Truth, like beauty, is in the eye of the beholder and not everything can be defined in black and white.

You must be able to relate to all this. How this plays out in your life comes down to the religion into which you were born. Whether you would rather be boiled in vegetable shortening than eat a slice of bacon or take a bite of a Big Mac, eating habits of different ethnic or racial groups will be your fascination, at least until you have had your fill of rites and rituals. You are a philosopher, and no matter how much it pains you to defrock the priests and teachers of beliefs that have disappointed you, you must not completely lose your objectivity or be drowned in false thinking and gullibility.

At this point you need to probe more deeply into your own issues about being trapped and lied to, to the point that you don't trust your own brain. In the next part, Going Deeper, reading the chapters called "Escape" and "Religion" will give you a chance to pass through the illusion of the dread of consistency and the rigors of education, and on to a higher expression of your Cancer nature that will help you develop your learning abilities and find fulfilling work, and make your Sun shine bright.

Celebrities Who Share Your Issues
Mick Fleetwood, Michelle Lee, Vicente Fox, John Elway, Harrison Ford

Cancer 10

You may strive to be the biggest honcho the company ever produced, just so you won't end up walking around in sandals followed by a brood of little Cancerlings as mindlessly clueless as a gaggle of geese waddling along on a country road. You've got big issues concerning the old, a-woman's-place-is-in-the-home thing, and because of your conflicts over being "just a parent" you will probably be bouncing back and forth between career and family your whole life. The male dominance factor is the big fat tail that wags your dog. It's not even funny.

And you are not likely to laugh it off without a whole lot of life experience to teach you that you are both attracted to and repelled by it. Of course being a big shot is a false identity, but one you cannot seem to shed. As private a person as you are, you cannot bear to be thought of as someone who can't make it in a career and has to "settle," move back to your hometown, marry your high school sweetheart, and work in Dad's pharmacy. You've got plans, hopes, and dreams—the stuff Hollywood movies were made of: small town yokel comes to the Big City and makes it big. Of course, what do you encounter the minute you try to make your starry-eyed visions real? Male domination in politics, dirty games, and plenty of personal humiliation that hurts your dignity.

Some Cancers even avoid marriage and family like the plague, because they think that having a personal life is a compromise for success. Ironically, when you do trudge home at the end of a long day of being maligned or ignored, it can be wonderful to have a gentle velvet glove touch your cheek.

Your life may always be a contest between you and a corrupt world. No matter how frustrating it is, you may keep knocking your head up against the same wall, beating out the competition, struggling to rise above a mediocre crowd, being the big shot by day, the housewife or dad at night. You will probably find yourself being two parents in one, always fighting a role you consider too passive or too "female."

Ultimately you do come to appreciate the support of family. You eventually realize that a relationship is not the seductive devil, keeping you from achieving your life's ambition. Quite the opposite, in fact. It is the foundation without which you can build nothing in this world. An intimate relationship is not the booby prize for failure. It is the gift the Universe is giving you for being a loving person. You are one of the fortunate Cancers in the world, able to realize your potential as a public leader—but only if you are attentive to your own personal needs for emotional security.

It's a known fact that married people tend to succeed more readily. A happy home life affords you a stability that gives you the drive, courage, and confidence to do battle in this rotten world. Will it demand your time, attention, caring, and love, and not permit you to waste all your time chasing after the recognition you didn't get from one of your parents? Yes. Will your life be better for it? Absolutely.

At this point, you need to probe more deeply into your obsession with being somebody on your own, apart from the family. In the next part, Going Deeper, reading the chapters called "Independence" and "Recognition" will help you balance your need for a public identity with the need to build successful, intimate relationships, and make your Sun shine bright.

Cancer 11

What are you trying to be, the Statue of Liberty? What's with the give-me-your-tired-you-poor-your-huddled-masses-yearning-to-be-free jive? Admit it. You like to be associated with the rich. Well, not really. In fact, part of you loathes them with their fancy, exclusive, restrictive country clubs and goofy golf outfits and charity balls. Loathe isn't exactly the right word, either. You disapprove of their sloth and greed and shallow values, but God forbid they turn up their snooty noses at you or dare to exclude you from activities and discussions you don't even value at all, and you're absolutely furious. Exclusion from any association because of money is enough to turn the golden retriever you try to be into a snarling Doberman. You aspire to a level of financial success you don't even respect, especially because the sacrifices of personal integrity demanded to be a "money person" are far beneath you. You always seem to be struggling between your wish to be among the Fortune 500—or at least among the fiscally fortunate—and your intention to prove that's not who you are at all.

You can be so absolutely phobic about getting hooked emotionally that you may even deny sexual attractions, putting yourself instead into the role of loyal friend. "It's not romantic," you'll hear yourself saying. "It's not about sex." Not that you are not romantic or sexual. You are, and those vibes are always operating. It's a lot easier, however, to keep things open, not go the traditional route and get railroaded into a situation you are not ready for. Although, jeez, isn't that just what happens? The so-called, unwanted pregnancy. Accidents do happen, of course, but there are people who don't believe that. They say that there are no accidents. They claim that all too often the unconscious takes over your life, knocks the conscious mind over the head, slips it a mickey, and makes you go against everything you think you are trying to do, guiding you, forcing you toward everything you think you are trying to avoid. You find your-self saddled with kids you don't know how to deal with, all because of a moment when you allowed yourself to be touched by a romantic tune, night blooming jasmine or some other madness that has you forced you to kiss bye-bye to all the freedom you see other lucky people able to take advantage of, just because they weren't stupid like you.

Or you could react in the completely opposite way. You could try to be one of those people who never let down their guard. You could never permit love to blind you to the fact that you must remain free and open to relationships with no commitments at all. Even if you do avoid inti-macy for a long time, though, a moment will come—and you may be turning gray when it happens—when you see that the Beatles were right. Love is all there is. The pursuit of eternal freedom can be a juvenile Peter Pan behavior that gets old and loses its lustrous appeal. Overcoming your fear that sex will trap you is your destiny. It's your path to fulfillment. It is not freedom or money that must drive you to produce. It has to be the urge to express yourself creatively, liberated from the need for reward or the fear of social ostracism for revealing who you really are.

At this point you need to probe more deeply into your obsession with fi-nancial independence, to the point that you impede your own creativity and avoid your needs for love and intimacy. In the next part, Going Deeper, reading the chapters called "Freedom" and "Money" will give you a chance to pass through the fear of being trapped by your own need for love, and on to a higher expression of your Cancer nature that will help you fulfill yourself on an artistic and personal basis, and make your Sun shine bright.

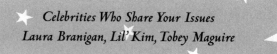

Celebrities Who Share Your Issues
Laura Branigan, Lil' Kim, Tobey Maguire

Cancer 12

You are an atypical Cancer. Cancer in the usual sense, anyway. Some would swear you've got a screw loose, which can be either your charming eccentricity or a freaky streak of behavior that could get you on the evening news. People will have to accept this if they are going to get involved with you. It could be just a minor case of *lifus interruptus,* and it's not really all your doing. It is true that you cannot sit still. It is true that you have been known to jump from one thing to another. It is not something you do on purpose. It just happens. Life seems to be a series of unavoidable disconnects—the way your cell phone blinks out in the middle of an important conversation. No matter how hard you try to create permanent bonds or put down permanent roots, you have an inexorable need or compulsion or unconscious wish to run that makes your existence episodic, picaresque, and downright disjointed. As much as you want and need steadiness and consistency, routines are periodically broken. There is even a wandering gypsy, nomadic, and even "carny" twist to the way you lead your life.

The antidote takes will and effort. As hypocritical or insincere as it may appear to others, you can teach other people to be more consistent healthwise than you are able to be yourself. It bugs you so much when people stand you up or change the rules without giving you notice. This comes from many disruptions over which you had no control in childhood. Your salvation lies in setting a better example for others than was set for you.

The helping professions in health care, education, and psychology are perfect avenues for such a transformation. You don't have to have a big, fancy position. Somehow the dissemination of information is your outlet. You could be a cheap gossip, a court reporter, or a lunch lady serving soup in your kid's school cafeteria. You need some task that demands you show up rain or shine to serve and to educate.

At this point you need to probe a little deeper into your need to cut corners, take shortcuts, and avoid what you consider to be the boring road to healthy habits. In the next part, Going Deeper, reading the chapters called "Escape" and "Communication" will give you a chance to pass through the illusion of the dread of consistency and the rigors of education, and or to a higher expression of your Cancer nature that will help you develop your learning abilities and find fulfilling work, and make your Sun shine bright.

Celebrities Who Share Your Issues
Tom Stoppard, Montel Williams, Derek Jeter, Chris Isaac, Tom Hanks

LEO

July 23–August 22
Dates vary from year to year—consult local astrologer

Leo is the wonderful miracle and potential of a chick when it pecks its way out of an egg. Sometimes, if Fate wills it, the chick turns out to be a western omelet, which is just a chick in a different form. Leo represents the potential of becoming anything at all. It's a baby's first cry, the song of the infant whales in the wild, in fact any and every birth. It's not only birth, but the awareness of being born. Awareness of Self is the key to Leo. Leo is not blind, unconscious existence. It is a deliberate presentation of Self: self-awareness, conscious of its effect. Leo is a tiger perfectly poised on a branch in Africa or on a stage in Vegas. It surveys the people in the audience and can feel the admiration, awe, and fear emanating from them. It knows its power to devour or entertain. It makes its choice each day, each night, at the start of each performance. Leo is also the pedigree dog that wins best in show at the Westminster Kennel Club Dog Show at Madison Square Garden. It knows it's the best and it loves the truth of it. Don't ever make the mistake of thinking Leo is tame or domesticated. It's not. It is pure animal, but an animal in full control of its motions and actions, as lithe as an Olympic swimmer. Leo is an odd blend of the studied and mannered with the primitive and carefree.

When anything chooses to be born, there is risk, and Leo is always in a game of chance. Leo must always gather its forces and use them, not dissipate them in useless displays of power. It provides warmth, light, and direction, much like a lighthouse in the midst of a stormy sea. In fact, it is the whole light and power system of a large city. Leo tests itself against the impossible, ever proving its supremacy and excellence. It is noble blood no matter what station it finds itself in during its lifetime. Utterly aware of its greatness and potential, its comportment is stately, elegant, and with unmatchable grandeur. It is the essence of what is produced by an artist. Leo rules every painting, sculpture, ceramic vase, architectural wonder, Pulitzer Prize–winning book, or anything else that has issued from the mind of a creative individual. It is summer at its max. Green everywhere, flowers in full bloom, beachgoers and campers in gear, a time when nature is high on itself. It's Romeo waxing poetic over Juliet and the ecstatic night they spend together. It's every young person who ever fell in love because of a love song. It's the model on the cover of *Vogue*. It's mascara. This season's color.

It's Jagger, Marilyn (she was Leo Rising), every icon people have drooled over since the first crooner ever crooned a tune. It's Vegas, even the crappy, vulgar side. It's the roll of dice, the feathers of showgirls. It's the thunderous roar of the crowd, and the hoofbeats at the Preakness. It's Arnold's muscles—anything and everything that lets the world know "Here I am, everybody, yes this is me, this is my work. I'm responsible for it. I'm proud to present myself because I've produced something for you to applaud. I know you love me, so come on, admit it." Leo is the pride of having produced beauty and greatness. More often than not, however . . .

Why do so many Leos have such problems with ego? Either you're hiding behind a faceless gray mask or flashing more gold than could ever have been found in Saddam Hussein's bathroom. Of course, a lot depends on where you come into the family, and when—first born, middle, or only child or baby. Were you treated like the Second Coming or did you have to do your own laundry from the time you were seven? Whether you are a privileged Windsor or shabby product of the Dickensian household will have a lot to do with how you present yourself, or don't, to the world. If you were encouraged to follow your own path, have faith in your own instincts, and believe in yourself, it will be so natural and normal for you to step out on the stage of life and expect to be rewarded. It's a bigger battle, however, when you have to invent yourself, create an identity, and follow in nobody's footsteps but your own.

We have to examine your father's role in the family, mainly because it is one you wish either to follow or forget. In astrology Leo is often thought of as the sign that rules the father. It's the captain of the vessel, so you have to think about who your father is or was in relation to you, of course, but also to your mother and to the rest of the family. That is going to provide you with the image you have of men, leadership, the power to project one's self onto the world, and the ability to move about with confidence and self-assurance. Gender is a big factor here, of course. It's a lot better for women Leos today than in olden times, and that includes a good chunk of the twentieth century. Back then a Leo woman had to content herself with letting her husband think he was the head of the household while she ran the entire operation. She had to smile and wear a lot of perfume and earrings and stand at the front door waving hello and good-bye and be content to run the bridge club. If her male side began to peek out of her hoop skirt, she had to move to Paris to smoke cigars. Men didn't have it easy, either. They could come home at night and announce to the family, "We're moving to St. Louis," and have everybody say, "Yes, Papa," whether they wanted to jump him and wring his neck or not. He had to appear as if he did not feel the crushing burden of pretending to be sure of every decision he was making, without showing a scintilla of doubt. Otherwise, uh-oh. Was that a pinky raised on the teacup? Not masculine.

Thank God people can be bit more real now. A bossy Leo woman can at last have an office with a corner window and a man can wear a pink tie. Now, too, there are all kinds of ways to be creative that don't carry the stigma of being bohemian (another Leo idiosyncrasy). You want to be thought of as creative, but you're still nailed to normal. Maybe that's why you're so attracted to the weirdest, out-of-step duck in the whole duck parade. You linger there, impaled on the fence between outrageous on-stage behavior and off-stage regular life. Or in the case of most Leos, the opposite. You act totally normal at work during the day, but at night, pull down the shades.

There are, of course, very twisted egos among your sign mates. They're the Mussolinis of your crowd. They have no sense of their nobility, no awareness of their true greatness, and absolutely no regard for their effect on other people other than the fear and obedience they wish to instill. Who can say why some Leos have such a brilliant sense of love and loyalty, and are able to blend kindness and strength, warmth and leadership, while others constantly threaten to kick your ass if you don't do exactly as they say? They act like the Terminator before he turned good. In the case of the Terminator (the sequel), it was an updated chip that told him to kill only the bad guys, and never bring harm to those close to him.

In the case of humans it's not a chip. It's a choice. If as a kid you were treated like a little prince or princess, you're naturally going to have a sense of noblesse oblige. It's breeding, and you'll know instinctively not only which one is the salad fork but how to treat people with deference and respect. But if you were told every other day you were stupid or ugly, your rage will simmer, because inside you know it's not true but as a kid you were not in a position to protest.

Then you have to exercise the Leo God-given gift: will, for good or evil. No sign of the Zodiac has the strength of will that you have. You can heal people or scald them to death. There's lower will and higher will. You've got the Leo woman who treats you to a video presentation of her round-the-world trip: "This is me in Rome. Here I am crossing the Rubicon. And don't I look cute in that yellow thing against the Great Wall of China?" etc. until you wish you had brought along a cyanide tablet. Or there's the guy who drives by your house every day and beeps the horn on his unpaid-for Porsche, then goes home to experience his version of Tantric sexual union: masturbation in front of a mirror. The most narcissistic and tiresome Leos are actually very insecure. They have to boast and show off, get fake boobs, take steroids and penis enlargers, spend their earnings on facelifts and fancy rugs. Not that image is not important—it is for everyone. But Leos especially.

You know only too well that when you look good, more doors are open to you, so it's worth it to primp a little and spruce yourself up before a meeting, a date, or even before you get in bed with your long-term other. It's when you have nothing but the outer image that you get pompous, grandiose, and downright silly. You're not exercising your higher will at that point. You are living through your own effect on people. Inside, you don't exist at all. You are only an image reflected back to yourself from the eyes of other people. You can't possibly be creative at this point, because all your efforts must be directed toward how you are perceived. In that case it's an understatement to say you are mannered. You are downright ludicrous as long as you are centered on your external appearance. You become so sensitive to criticism at that point that you can tolerate no input or feedback from anyone other than worship and blind obedience. If one imperfection is picked up and mentioned, then your whole sense of self falls apart and the person who saw it must be squashed like a bug. This is Leo narcissistic autocracy at its worst. And if that's the case, behind the Armani get-up, Bruno Magli shoes, and Oakley sunglasses, there just ain't nobody home.

Living through your higher will is another situation altogether, and it doesn't really depend completely on your upbringing. Higher will is your ability to create and nurture a strong inner identity that radiates outwardly. That is pure confidence gleaned from your own abilities to love, relate warmly, guide, and help others to shape their lives and their creations. That is beauty as only Leo can project it. When you overcome whatever forces seek to repress or cloud your light, you become who you are supposed to become. The light at the end of everyone's tunnel.

Leo is the sign of the heart. You have to be the center and the source, the pump that distributes the life-giving juice to those around you. That's not just ego. That's your destiny. How you ascend to that position is up to you and that will of yours. Usurped power can never last; earned respect can never be taken away. There is no one more ardent and romantic than Leo. You can be a plain Jane who doesn't wear lipstick or a bald-headed guy with a bit of a paunch, but that won't stop the valentine heart from going all out and making a big fuss over your sweetheart's birthday, or celebrating his new job.

Confidence comes not from the obsession with making yourself loved, but from the joy of loving. This is how Leos put themselves on the line emotionally or professionally. You have to be able to step over yourself and totally adore your life, your work, and the people around you, and not be overly attached to what comes back. This is the essence of Leo business acumen, artistic potential, and romantic success. When you love what you do you can sell anything, as long as you believe in the product.

You're a hard but just negotiator, always wanting to win—but not by cheating. There are the traveling salesmen and frauds among you, foolishly thinking they need smoke and mirrors and sleight of hand to win the deal. It's all to no avail, because the inner conscience of those people will eventually lead them to do themselves in. Artistically, you identify with everything you produce, so you have to love everything you produce, and it better not be secondhand, leftover, rehashed crap. It's got to be original and totally, undeniably, uncopyably you.

You can see what a strain this could put on you eventually. Kids who God forbid are not what you dreamed they'd be. Fortunately, Leos don't usually have lots of children anyway. So the test is usually limited to one or two, three at the most, if any at all.

And what a test for you when it comes to loving. Ah, love. Hey, you're just a kid yourself. You've got a teen romance thing in you that needs always to be satisfied one way or another. Of course, if it gets to a point where you've got more hair dye and Botox coming through your body than red blood cells, then you're definitely not exercising your higher will. And if you want to scare yourself silly into remembering your beauty is inside as well as outside, just go find a picture of Mae West at the end and place it on your mirror.

Real Leo love is that couple celebrating their fiftieth holding hands, still in love—and only their kids know what holy hell they went through to make it that far. If you can do one thing as a Leo, it's hang in there. But more than that, you are constant. As constant and forever and humorous as any of the *I Love Lucy* episodes, which are still running, still hysterically funny, full of affection and warmth and without the prurient sick jokes that pass for comedy today.

Leo is a flower opening when you see it through stop-motion photography. It can be, when the higher will is employed, a long-lasting moment like the one in the musical *Little Shop of Horrors,* when Seymour and Audrey, two goofy individuals, suddenly discover the beauty in each other. You'd better perform or produce. Integrity breeds authenticity—that's your goal.

So how do you move more with right action as a way to achieve your goal of heroism? What are the forces that drag you backward and keep you from reaching the highest manifestation of your Sun? And what are the energies that can support you, guide you, enhance your positive qualities, and make your Sun shine bright? The fact is you're not just a Leo. There is another energy operating, one that either cuts across your efforts and undermines them or spirits you to heights of joy and fulfillment. That energy depends not on the month you were born, but the year as well. Later on in this book the technical aspects will be explained more fully. We'll examine how you waste time chasing your own tail, why you do it, and how to pull yourself out of self-destructive obsessions and put yourself back on the road to success. But for now, check out the following table. Find your birth year and note the number beside it. Then read the section corresponding to the number.

Year–No.	Year–No.	Year–No.	Year–No.	Year–No.
1901–10	1920–10	1941–8	1962–7	1983–5
1902–9	1921–9	1942–8	1963–6	1984–5
1903–9	1922–9	1943–7	1964–6 until	1985–4
1904–8	1923–8	1944–6	8/3, then 5	1986–3
1905–8	1924–7	1945–6	1965–5	1987–3
1906–7	1925–7	1946–5	1966–4	1988–2
1907–6	1926–6	1947–4	1967–4	1989–1
1908–6	1927–5	1948–4	1968–3	1990–1
1909–5	1928–5	1949–3	1969–2	1991–12
1910–4	1929–4	1950–3 until	1970–2	1992–11
1911–4	1930–3	8/18, then 2	1971–1	1993–11
1912–3	1931–3	1951–2	1972–12	1994–10
1913–2	1932–2	1952–1	1973–12	1995–10 until
1914–2	1933–2 until	1953–1	1974–11	8/11, then 9
1915–1	7/27, then 1	1954–12	1975–10	1996–9
1916–12	1934–1	1955–11	1976–10	1997–8
1917–12	1935–12	1956–11	1977–9	1998–8
1917–12	1936–12	1957–10	1978–8	1999–7
1918–11	1937–11	1958–9	1979–8	2000–7
1919–11 until	1938–10	1959–9	1980–7	2001–6
8/11, then	1939–10	1960–8	1981–7	2002–5
10	1940–9	1961–7	1982–6	2003–4

Year–No.	Year–No.	Year–No.	Year–No.	Year–No.
2004–4	*7/28, then*	*2014–9*	*2020–5*	*2026–2 until*
2005–3	*12*	*2015–9*	*2021–5*	*8/18, then 1*
2006–2	*2010–12*	*2016–8*	*2022–4*	*2027–1*
2007–2	*2011–11*	*2017–7*	*2023–3*	*2028–12*
2008–1	*2012–11*	*2018–7*	*2024–3*	*2029–12*
2009–1 until	*2013–10*	*2019–6*	*2025–2*	*2030–11*

Leo 1

When you're getting the love and attention you crave, you're okay. As loving and generous as you try to be, you've got ego problems, up the wazoo. In the best of all possible worlds, you will outgrow them, or at least find somebody who can put up with your attention-getting antics. The need for attention is the least of it, though. The worst-case scenario is irrational acting out. There's a spot on you that you can't rub off, a scar made long ago, some act or even genetic marker that has had a serious effect upon your personal pride, ability to relate to people, and give and receive love. People see much more in you than you see in yourself. That is the irony, of course, because you can be brash, blustery, self-aggrandizing, and narcissistic, even if it is just a flimsy cover-up for how crappy you really feel about yourself.

You are really good at driving people away with your spooky antics, which can be ferociously controlling. There may not even be a word to describe it adequately, except maybe totalitarian. Or always focusing on the negative, such as "who hates me now" or "who is ignoring me today" -type things. You are battling a childhood memory you spend much of your life hiding, compensating for, or taking out on everybody else.

A shadow follows you, one that makes you feel unworthy. Something that impels you to prove yourself, pulls you from crime to sainthood, from chronic misbehaving to reforming. You like to show everyone that you can be a rat to be turned out of the house and then you have to show you are truly a hero who is just a kid at heart who needs an awful lot of reinforcement. You can be so affectionate, loving, ardent, romantic, and impossible to resist. When you are in your "I know I'm a great person" mode, you have an irresistible pout that says "All I need is a good person to love me." Who can pass that up? Especially when you are singing the hymn, "I've repented."

It is probably the love me–hate me syndrome that messes you and everyone else up the most, not to mention how it plays with other people's heads. How can you appear to be a person of such sterling integrity and then turn around and reveal what a childish, petulant, scoundrel you can be. And emotionally manipulative!

You know how to play people like xylophones, and if you think you are losing control, you'll do it. You've got the charisma of a sexy Hollywood villain whose dastardly deeds the audience gasps at in revulsion and horror but blurts a teary "Awww!" in unison at when the villain is brought down by the cops at the end of the flick. You truly can be lovable because you are lovable at heart, even though you can look into the camera at the end of the film and cry, "I was framed!" and make everybody in the audience believe it.

Why would you desperately try to make yourself look good no matter what? You are loaded with talent. You're creative. You're gifted. It's just that as soon as people start to believe in your abilities, you reveal some dark truth that makes them either shrink away and make them think you're a monster. Why don't you feel authentic?

At this point you need to probe more deeply into your obsession with your own pain, to the point that you push away people who want to love you. In the next part, Going Deeper, reading the chapters called "Independence" and "Love" will give you a chance to pass through the illusion of fear of being held too closely even though you need it, and on to a higher expression of your Leo nature that will help you develop your enormous talents and form healthier relationships where you grant as much freedom as you need for yourself, and make your Sun shine bright.

★ *Celebrities Who Share Your Issues*
Judith Regan, Pete Sampras, Robin Quivers, Tom Green, Jeff Gordon

Leo 2

Whether you were born in a shack at the edge of Coaltown, USA, or your first bite of solid food came from a sterling-silver spoon, you've been made aware of the difference that exists between royalty and commoners. So much so, in fact, that half the time you don't know whether you should be wearing a jeweled crown or a miner's cap with a light on it. It might be a bit of hyperbole to say it has created a split in your identity, but part of you believes you are a wealthy celebrity while the other side of you is a lowly worker whose only goal is to keep your head above water and make ends meet. You could really keep yourself in that state of poverty by either making sure you stay deeply in debt from a lifestyle that stays ahead of your income, or simply comparing yourself with everybody who makes more money than you do and thus feeling inferior, unappreciated, and drained of energy and resources.

On the positive side, you're a tireless worker, perfectionist, and very disciplined when you're honing your craft and perfecting your metier. Because you tend to be competitive and have to be the best, nobody can touch you when you're busy or at the top of your game. You think it's the money that drives you, intent to rise above your humble origins, or come down from your royal perch to prove to the common man or woman that you're just like them. Not afraid to get your hands dirty. So it's always back and forth between a privileged life and the sad sack, dreary existence of the downtrodden worker who never gets ahead of the damned game. No time for fun. Too tired (or scared of disease) for romping in the hay.

Being terrified or resentful of having your sense of financial security tampered with or compromised by having to depend on someone else for your bread or benefits is the source of all the problems, financial or emotional. Being able to let yourself go seems like a simple enough remedy for all your uptight ills. Sexually this is a tall order for you, and you have good reasons for keeping a tight lid on your libidinous desires.

Health, however, demands interaction on a deep level, even if it takes the occasional glass of wine to loosen you up. Losing control terrifies you, but it's the path to fulfillment. You have to accept mystery, passion, and especially the sharing of resources with others and, to some extent, financial dependence on others. This requires loosening the hold you have on your whole life and trusting in the generosity of others and the integrity of your own powerful creative imagination.

At this point you need to probe more deeply into your obsession with resisting outside control, to the point that you become tyrannical and hurt the ones who love you most, rather than be too close to anybody. In the next part, Going Deeper, reading the chapters called "Control" and "Money" will give you a chance to pass through the illusion of fear of being dominated by another person, and on to a higher expression of your Leo nature that will help you be a creator, performer, or leader, connect in a deep relationship, and make your Sun shine bright.

Celebrities Who Share Your Issues
Carroll O'Connor, Magic Johnson, Christian Slater,
Menachem Begin, Mata Hari, Edward Norton

Leo 3

Ever wonder why some people can't stand to be alone? They pick up the phone and call somebody and say absolutely nothing but call anyway. Since it's your task to expand your mind and see the world alone or not, you can't be afraid to be on your own. And it's really a shame to sacrifice life's adventure just because you have got to stay glued to someone you really have nothing to say to. People do it all the time, though. You can easily get yourself tied to people you can't be honest with, because the pleasantries make it more of a détente than a relationship. If it's a brother-sister thing you've got going here and you're hooked on it, move on. There's something both seductive and abhorrent about all relationships. They often have a totally hollow ring to them. They can be devoid of joy, drained of any realism or passion, and the only thing that can honestly be said of them is that they are comfortable and safe. Comfortable and safe? How can anything be comfortable and safe when nothing of any profundity dares pass anyone's lips? This is the change you have to make, whether the people you wish to communicate with you have the capacity to hear and understand you or not.

Have you got any siblings? Or are you the only child? This is the issue to consider here, mainly because it is the link to other human beings on a mental level that either joins or alienates you from the species. Sometimes it's a neighbor, or a cousin, or some daily associate you get attached to. Some person all of a sudden becomes your shadow, alter-ego, advisor, or at least someone you have to check in with every single day to gab and gossip with. It's probably just anxiety, too. Of course, that whole problem stems from a childhood in which you weren't listened to, your views were silenced or ignored, and nobody even had the slightest inkling of what was really going on in your head.

Forget test scores. Teachers freaked you out and demanded more of you than you ever dreamed you had. As an adult you have to come more and more into your own brain power and rely on raw intelligence. But it's a groundbreaking thing you have to do. Your path to freedom demands you go on a quest in search of yourself. You can't do that if your shadow is tailing your butt every second. The search for an individual entity demands that you find out for yourself, by yourself, who the hell you are. That's it. You have to take yourself by the hand, take yourself to school, discover your talents, discipline yourself, reveal what unique talents you display, and develop them on your own by yourself with no guidance, advice, or support. Your confidence in your intelligence has been shaken and seriously undermined, intentionally or not. You must strike out on your own, even if it means challenging the religious doctrines and political dogmas that do not define your personal need to develop yourself as you see fit, and to find out for yourself what you believe God to be. Get out and travel. Do something you've never done before. Go someplace you've never been where you don't know the language, the customs, the geography, the culture, the terrain, the weather. Challenge yourself in subjects you think are beyond you. Study something nobody, including yourself, thinks you can master. Stop talking and start doing. Quit obsessing over the people in your life, relatives especially whom you can't or won't talk to, and move into higher consciousness state. Break all rules. Make discoveries.

Challenge clerks and teachers. Do not go along with the program. You can't anyway. Be the first to break new ground against all odds, against all advice.

At this point you need to probe more deeply into your obsession with having someone to talk to. In the next part, Going Deeper, reading the chapters called "Marriage" and "Communication" will give you a chance to pass through the illusion of fear of being alone, and on to a higher expression of your Leo nature that will help you develop yourself intellectually and psychologically, open you up to new experiences, and make your Sun shine bright.

> ★ *Celebrities Who Share Your Issues*
> *Karl Jung, Aldous Huxley, George Bernard Shaw,*
> *Herbert Hoover, Willie Shoemaker, Neil Armstrong*

Leo 4

Leos are supposed to be beings of light. They're supposed to be the steady torchbearers, stalwart and ever positive. How can that be true when you know you've experienced a kind of darkness deep in your soul that bats wouldn't live in? The murky swamp into which you were born may well be the bayous of Louisiana, but more likely it's metaphorical. It's a story in which, unlike many members of your sign, you were exposed very early to elements of survival on the most primitive of levels. Deserted and abandoned, or in even a more atavistic sense struggling to breathe and live in a world that was alien and uncompromising to your sensitive soul.

You learned quickly, however, where to find food, how to not get killed, and it may have hardened you emotionally. Deep down maybe you don't trust people to take proper care of you without abusing their position or pulling the rug out from under you just when you're beginning to trust or rely on them. And excuse you if anybody tries to tell you your emotional cynicism is unfounded. You have a damned good reason to believe your "protector" is liable to mess with you, walk out or even die on you. It has happened! Of course, it can become an addictive expectation, so if a loved one gets a little cold, right away you're calling the coroner. And the slightest deviation could spark a major war, mainly because deep down you could create a whole calamity in your head, long before it happens. In a way you cannot ever relax totally in the most intimate situation, because you're afraid of what will happen if you do.

Some people would read you then as unresponsive, controlling, emotionally manipulative, and even sexually deviant or repressed. Those closest to you may be let in on some of the family secrets that led you to this place, but quite ironically, in your public life nobody would ever guess in a million years what goes on in the basement of that mind of yours. How could they? When you turn toward the light, you are the consummate professional. Wealthy, prosperous, rich with good, wholesome values, and reaping enormous rewards for a talent and expertise nobody in their right minds would ever try to top or even match. You could become a lasting icon in your field, a personification of loyalty and dignity and majesty that really wins you back your title as a true Leo. To do it you have to tear yourself away from the darkness.

At this point you need to probe more deeply into your obsession with being abandoned or emotionally abused, to the point that you could become desperate to create a normal family. In the next part, Going Deeper, reading the chapters called "Sex" and "Security" will give you a chance to pass through the illusion of fear of being left all alone in the dark, and on to a higher expression of your Leo nature that will help you have the family you want, and still always remember that you have a career of success and prosperity out there waiting for you to make your Sun shine bright.

Celebrities Who Share Your Issues
Jacqueline Kennedy Onassis, Lucille Ball, Tipper Gore,
Vin Diesel, Danielle Steel, Arnold Schwarzenegger

Leo 5

You have to learn to talk to people, not just perform for them like a seal with a beach ball, even if that means making a fool of yourself in public a million times. People will laugh and make jokes and think you're an awful comedian, or worse—an egotistical self-promoting hypocrite. That's always what happens when you do try something out of the ordinary, and you're definitely an out-of-the-box, off-the-top Leo. No doubt about that. Your performance is the kind of iconoclasty people love to mock when they're really in awe of your moxie. The prejudice you have to face when you get in front of people could intimidate most normal people. But Leo can never be intimidated by fear of prejudice of any kind. Language barriers, ethnic, social, and racial boundaries are actually the challenges which, instead of spooking you into silence, actually turn you on. And even if your critics think you're a clown who forgot his makeup, your stigma must become your badge of honor and the mark of your courage and talent.

It can, however, be an emperor-with-no-clothes ego trip, where you become a caricature of yourself and do the outrageous buffoon thing merely for the effect and because the audience expects it. It's all defensive, of course. You haven't exactly had the advantages of social interaction that some people have, so if you exploit the talents you are born with, who's to criticize? Your intelligence and sincerity will most likely be impugned because your artistry will be hard to separate from your desire to prove your uniqueness and brilliance. If only you could get over this adolescent muscle-flexing "Look at me, look at me, look at me, love me, love me, love me" thing. There is a way. Your goal to communicate with people on a global level is sincere. Your search for a common language sets you apart from and above your fellow human beings in the search for understanding, brotherhood, and sisterhood for all. For all your antics that seem bestial to a lot of folks, you're definitely a human being with an honest goal to unite people, raise their consciousness, and open their eyes and ears to new approaches to life. All you have to do is get off the "look at me" trip.

At this point you need to probe more deeply into your obsession with being on stage, to the point that your self-involvement and desperate need to be loved interfere with the job you have to do in this world. In the next part, Going Deeper, reading the chapters called "Love" and "Religion" will give you a chance to pass through the illusion of fear of being thought of as inferior, uneducated, or unsophisticated, and on to a higher expression of your Leo nature that will help you develop your public skills, improve communication, get your head together about being a lovable human being, and make your Sun shine bright.

Celebrities Who Share Your Issues
Wesley Snipes, Bill Clinton, Connie Chung,
Fidel Castro, Andy Warhol, Peter Jennings

Leo 6

Leos are supposed to have this fabulous personal life, full of romance and golden glitter floating down over their lives. They're supposed to be marvelous, amorous mates and brilliant role models as parents, with a home life the Waltons would have killed for. So how to explain the fact that you work like a damned dog, are rarely around for mealtime, and take a rest only when you're rushed to the hospital? Work could be no more than a desperate attempt to escape what you perceive to be the mediocrity and claustrophobic morbidity of bourgeois, stifling family life. Irony, irony, irony: the personal interaction, the soothing of the brow, the plate of your favorite dessert—those are the things that actually save you from the constant slave-driving and the impossible political machinations you have to cope with just to stay on top of a completely unjust system that rarely gives you the credit you deserve for all the effort you put into everything. Irony again: You work like a damned dog in a system you despise to support a lifestyle you rarely get to enjoy. You need the respite from the fray, but vacations make you nervous unless they're working vacations. That means being on the beach but feverishly meeting yet another deadline or defeating yet another would-be assassin. The ferocious attempt to maintain control over all systems extends to your own body as well. Granted, if you don't stay awake and frosty, you're likely to get mauled or run over in this life. Diligence is not the same as obsessive, self-indulgence and fear of contamination.

The trick for you is to learn to float on the river. Get in an inner tube and let the current take you while you close your eyes and bask in the sunshine—without digging your nails into the tube and screaming. Face-lifts and all medical procedures aside, your heroic image depends not on how you look but how you serve your fellow beings.

Learning to trust Mother Nature is hard for a person who sees life as an obstacle course. Only when you develop the cosmic mind you've been blessed with do you come to see beyond the trees. Not only the whole forest, but the village, the town, the country, the world, and the great plan that put you in the family you need to come to respect and appreciate.

At this point you need to probe more deeply into your obsession with being important, to the point that you turn your back on much needed intimacy. In the next part, Going Deeper, reading the chapters called "Recognition" and "Control" will give you a chance to pass through the illusion of fear of being passed over, ignored, not needed, or forgotten, and on to a higher expression of your Leo nature that will help you be rewarded for your serious efforts, be able to rest when you need it, have a family, and make your Sun shine bright.

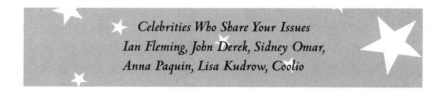

Celebrities Who Share Your Issues
Ian Fleming, John Derek, Sidney Omar,
Anna Paquin, Lisa Kudrow, Coolio

Leo 7

Know this: People are completely unpredictable. At least the ones you choose. Not you, of course. You can hang in there until the last sunset. And probably have, sometimes, when you should have cut rate and run. But talk about the center of life, stability, and loyalty. Of course, some people think you seduce them, draw them in, and then clamp down in maniacal control and attempt to repress or stamp out the very same idiosyncrasies you found fascinating in the first place. And you do seek the wild child, the anomaly, the person least likely you'd ever be wish to be with, because they are not polished, or are ill-mannered, or somehow the product of a mold that was broken or banned by law once they were born. And then you think you can get them to spit-shine their shoes and salute to the "general" when you walk in.

Or the opposite. You give yourself over to the newest, most recent crush, then reject him or her for not being what you "really" need in another person. Oh it's a wild ride, your venture into relationships. And you are a definite marrier. It's just very hard to commit yourself totally when a) you expect the person to drop out at any time or b) you're already deeply committed—to yourself. That's hard. That's really hard, because while the idea of being the center around which the whole world revolves is attractive, it's not pleasant to see yourself as Mr. Lucky Old Sun, all by your great and shining lonesome, surrounded by people you can never ever really get close to because of their motives, instability, and unpredictability, or some terminal lack of trust from which you suffer because of the screwed up relationship your parents had.

So it doesn't have to be one extreme or the other. You don't have to keep such a tight rein on someone for fear they will run away with the cart and leave you flailing and out of control. On the other hand, you can't just let people run your life into the ground because you don't want to appear controlling, either. If you refuse to have grown-up relationships because you fear losing your own youthful edge, your partners keep getting younger and younger until you get yourself arrested. Success comes in allowing people their eccentricities, without permitting those eccentricities to disrupt your life entirely. More to the point, however, is your need to control not others but yourself—and most important of all is to understand and accept the qualities in others you find irresistible over and over, but eventually push you to the edge.

At this point you need to probe more deeply into your obsession with being with someone, to the point that you give yourself up and forget that you too have a life of your own. In the next part, Going Deeper, reading the chapters called "Marriage" and "Freedom" will give you a chance to pass through the illusion of fear of being walked out on unexpectedly, and on to a higher expression of your Leo nature that will help you have your relationships, always keeping in mind that you can't cure other people's hang-ups if you don't keep a piece of your own life for yourself, and make your Sun shine bright.

Celebrities Who Share Your Issues
Mick Jagger, Robert DeNiro, John Huston, Arlene Dahl,
Mme. Blavatsky, Count Basie, Laurence Fishburne

Leo 8

How you manifest your oddball vibrations in a lower or higher way takes will and stamina. You have to come to terms with how out of control you can get after one half a beer, not to mention the stimulants you could get into if you let yourself. Let's just say that by nature you are a most passionate person of many desires. Diverse desires. Some might even call their overwhelming desires. For a creative artist, this is music to your ears.

As a Leo you are supposed to have one persona, one strong identity for all the world. In your case, so not true. You have a thousand roles you play, struggling to maintain the dominant image you project (man or woman), while being able to find release and gratification in a game of mouse-submissive-to-cat.

This sexual identity is secret, submissive, masochistic at times, and may stem from early experiences that twisted your view of what normal healthy emotional expression was all about. As a result you could go from intoxicated self-destructive bouts of emotional frenzy, begging to be allowed to prove you are desirable, to a sober renunciation of all acts considered deviant in favor of staid and long-lasting monogamy. The former when you're younger, the latter when you see just how far you'll go to when you are feeling rejected.

Artist, businessperson, or politician, you eventually have to sober up and go to work, mainly because working and supporting yourself and your family turn out to be the only way back from escapist binges and forays into mind-altering experiences of any kind. Your intensity could flip people out, so anybody coming close should be told you're no lightweight. When you go all the way with something—sex, work, alcohol—they're going to have to join you, because they are sure as hell not going to beat you.

Thank God for maturity, however, provided it comes before you burn out completely. With maturity comes the ability to enjoy yourself and to remember it the next morning. Maturity brings the capacity to work and enjoy prosperity without being either greedy or throwing away valuable resources in self-indulgent fantasies or questionable financial practices. It means having good business sense and prudent economic practices without fearing you'll be just another middle class clone. It means turning away from unbridled desires in favor of a productive prosperous life.

At this point you need to probe more deeply into your obsession with sex, to the point that you could mess up your head as well as your financial security. In the next part, Going Deeper, reading the chapters called "Escape" and "Sex" will give you a chance to pass through the illusion of not being desirable, as well as the wish to be financially taken care of and on to a higher expression of your Leo nature that will help you find a fulfilling resolution to your passionate but poorly disciplined nature, gain material wealth, and make your Sun shine bright.

> *Celebrities Who Share Your Issues*
> *Jerry Garcia, Myrna Loy, Clara Bow, Percy Bysshe Shelley,*
> *Dag Hammarskjöld, Deng Xiaoping, Sean Penn*

Leo 9

If you think you're far removed from some of the pressing philosophical issues of the day, think again. And again and again. Consciously or otherwise you are steeped in the traditions that have set in motion male-female patterns of behavior in relationships for hundreds if not thousands of years. The roles have made it difficult for passive Leo men and assertive Leo women to be real and still proud of themselves. So many times you have had to cover up how you really thought because of how you thought people would take it. There is still so much stilted, twisted thinking in society today, especially on the subject of what it means to be a man or woman. And it's not really so much a statement of one's sexual preference, although that issue seems always to be raging in religious and political circles. That totally burns you, because liars and bullshitters make your blood boil, the way they either swagger and throw their weight around or pretend to be nice and sweet when you know they're really out to manipulate and control you any way they can.

As much as you loathe both the bullying swaggerers and the shuffling, hat-in-hand pussyfoot-arounders, you have to look at yourself to see what sorts of prejudice or self-hating mind-sets could have conceivably created in you—the very sort of premixed, snap judgment, narrow-minded thinking you yourself have had to overcome in order to have better relations, even with the people whose minds you are trying to open up and whose consciousness you care to raise. It's the paradox of paradoxes. You can't hate people who hate or you are just like them.

Your integrity is at stake. Everything you say you are has to be what you really are. You can't believe one way and speak with forked tongue and not expect somebody to expose you. Your interest in equality can't be just hype. Your desire to see people treated equally has to extend to your own personal life. Racial, religious, or cultural differences will always be an attraction and a stumbling block to overcome if you are to achieve a deep mental connection and honest truthful communication. So how to be real and kind is the trick.

At this point you need to probe more deeply into your obsession with being intelligent, well-educated, and well-traveled, but still unable to communicate on a simple level. In the next part, Going Deeper, reading the chapters called "Independence" and "Religion" will give you a chance to pass through the illusion of fear of the loss of your autonomy, and on to a higher expression of your Leo nature that will help you remain a free agent while developing your skills at communication and being in relationships, and make your Sun shine bright.

Leo 10

You are such a proud human being, and so intent on presenting an honest, credible image of yourself, that you loathe those phonies who flash their wads of hundred-dollar bills around and act like divas when they're just regular people like the rest of us. You have been dazzled, however, by big money and fancy lifestyles, as much as you can't stand their fraudulence. You like to be thought of as prosperous and successful. Who doesn't? But your great paradox is being angry with the fraudulence of fancy cigars and stretch limos and all the other perks and frills the big stars and CEOs get, but you've also gotten hooked on wanting to be identified with big leaguers. The identification with money and success is your bête noire, mainly because you know how ridiculous it is to measure a person's soul value in terms of net worth. You're not completely free of the notion, however, that recognition and financial compensation are inextricably linked, and that a project is successful only if it makes money for the greedy overlords whose ability to see quality and beauty cannot get past the dollar sign. You loathe being tied to them and their piggy values, but their corrupt system still has a spell over you that you can't totally break. Sometimes you're fine with it, until there's a clash of values. Then you growl under your breath and vow you're going to run away to the heart of the Amazon where you can play your guitar naked if you want to and never have to answer to a system that is organized around money instead of the beauty of human passion. You can be as cheap as they are, too, especially when that old fear comes over you—a memory of poverty or joblessness that was instilled into you from you-probably-can't-even-remember when.

It is the paradox between financial stability and recognition and the yearning for intimacy and emotional security that fuels both your need for family life and the driving need to escape it periodically to be part of the money-making work force. You couldn't ever be enough of an icon of recognition and worship as a Leo, unless they deified you in your life-time. And at the end of the day it's sex, love, and art that hold your soul, not money at all. So you have to find a way to achieve an intimate family connection without fearing the dependencies those traditional roles can engender, have your hand in the world of art and magic, and still render unto that damned Caesar what is his.

At this point you need to probe more deeply into your obsession with being included in a system the values you don't really respect. In the next part, Going Deeper, reading the chapters called "Recognition" and "Money" will give you a chance to pass through the illusion of fear of being broke and a nobody, or stuck in some conventional family role, and on to a higher expression of your Leo nature that will help you take your place in the world without losing the need for personal intimacy and art that make you feel whole, and make your Sun shine bright.

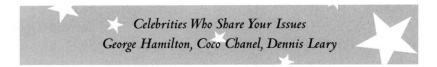

Celebrities Who Share Your Issues
George Hamilton, Coco Chanel, Dennis Leary

Leo 11

If scattered goals and 800,000 interruptions have marked your history, be of good cheer. Your real story is not about how many flat tires you've had or how often you've run out of gas, but how wholeheartedly you have been able to throw yourself into your creations without running away from your commitment to them. God knows there are enough sand-filled socks waiting around every corner. It's a wacky life, all right. So many unforeseen twists of fate to impede your course, and the worst thing you can get hooked on is those interruptions. If you think something is going to come along and mess up your plans, hopes, dreams, or wishes to produce something meaningful for the world, you'll never be able to commit yourself to completing anything. Commitments of any kind—love, art, children—may fill you with dread, because they will demand that you give completely over to them. In your younger days, that was a threat to your sense of freedom and curiosity.

Frivolous, capricious, scatterbrained, and irresponsible people infuriate you. People who speak without thinking hurt others, and you hate that. You've certainly seen enough of them come and go in your life. Here's a question you can ask yourself someday: Why do you draw yourself to friends who desert you? One reason: Your own reluctance to be responsible to your own commitments, in your desire to stay free and unattached, draws you to the same type of person.

When you grow up, those kinds of enfants terribles and eternal children hold no further magic for you. You gain better friends, have more permanent, longer-lasting love relationships, and healthier relationships with your children, and are far more able to be better educated and deal with creativity.

Part of you always remains childlike and likes to appear unattached and available, as false or unrealistic as that is. But it's the unexpected turns, never-expected-in-a-million-years plot twists, and jerky starts and stops that have to become your trademark, and eventually put you back on track. You shouldn't care about belonging to the club. You're supposed to mind your own business and find the courage to express yourself creatively.

At this point you need to probe more deeply into your obsession with being liberated from the conventional roles people are always trying to assign to you, to the point that you could run away from your own love life because it scares you to be too close to people. In the next part, Going Deeper, reading the chapters called "Communication" and "Freedom" will give you a chance to pass through the illusion of fear of being pigeonholed, and on to a higher expression of your Leo nature that will help you explore all the possibilities that lie before you, while also gaining the maturity to accept the perks of love and children when they come your way, develop your creativity on a deeper level, and make your Sun shine bright.

Leo 12

No wonder you have to run away and go into hiding. This world would be happy to turn us into tireless clones who could work sixteen-hour days, seven days a week, and eat by a tube while we were working. So for you it's a matter of survival to put on the answering machine and pretend to not be there. It's not laziness or an unwillingness to be of service. You want to do your bit, and you're thrilled that you are given as many opportunities as you are given, and well-received and rewarded for the hard work you put into being as good at what you do. But . . . you're not a machine somebody can just stick coins or a few bills in and out comes the Coke. Yes, thank God, you can be honored and recognized but a) you can't spit out performance after performance with no breaks and b) you cannot work and live among them, them being the people who make it possible for you to do your thing. The danger is a serious form of anti-social behavior that could in extreme cases be considered paranoid. The world is a dangerous place. There are poisonous snakes not only among the rocks of the desert, but right there in office buildings. The former spit venom, the latter threaten you with canceling your contract. The world is a dangerous place all right, and no amount of insulation can prevent invasion. Your need for privacy and intimacy is also an escape from the pressures of business and grown-up responsibility (which you find burdensome and exhausting), so it's easier for you to take your marbles and go home than it is to stick around and negotiate. Until you get the joke, that is. Then you can become a skilled negotiator as well as an ardent worker. The services you perform are unmatchably masterful, and you don't have to run away like a child.

Good business practices demand your full presence, just as good physical health demands the regimen of regularity, consistency, good diet, and sobriety. Granola floating in a bowl of vodka or God-knows-what-else is not what we mean by a balanced diet.

The reason you have to work as much as you do is so you don't end up a crazy old recluse living in the woods. And if you weren't commanded by your doctor to lay off the hard stuff and go natural, heaven knows where your antics and pain and fear of abandonment could lead. The balance is the desirable alternative.

At this point you need to probe more deeply into your obsession with the need to get away from it all, to the point that you could shirk the success the world is offering to you. In the next part, Going Deeper, reading the chapters called "Security" and "Escape" will give you a chance to pass through the illusion of fear of being drained and overworked by the system, and on to a higher expression of your Leo nature that will help you find the peace, tranquility, and intimacy you desire while enjoying the rewards of fulfilling work, and make your Sun shine bright.

Celebrities Who Share Your Issues
Robert Redford, Wilt Chamberlain, Davy Crocket, Isabel Sanford

VIRGO

August 23–September 22
Dates vary from year to year, consult your local astrologer

Virgo is the harvest. What poets haven't said, painters have painted. Grapes are purple in their time. Vegetables are green when they're supposed to be. Everything that has been seeded, planted, watered, and protected from prowling predators is now in its proudest moment of bloom. It's the kind of harvest the Bible predicts for God-fearing, hard-working people. Whatever is considered the best made car on the road today came from some Virgo craftsperson who supervised the whole operation from the first pencil sketch to the first sale on the market. It's the detail in the Pietà, the tiny cross-hatching in a little wooden box you buy on the Ponte Vecchio in Florence. It's the Oriental rug you have to pay an arm and a leg for because somebody, somewhere, took two years to weave it. Virgo is whatever comes out of talent, channeled into discipline, and tempered with patience, all underlayed by pure and totally focused dedication to the execution of the task.

Virgo rules fishermen and weavers, butlers and housekeepers, farmers and milkmaids, wheelwrights and blacksmiths, seamstresses and tailors, leather tanners and shoemakers, masons and bricklayers—craftspeople who put their hearts, souls, and minds into what they do. Of course, that was before the days of throwaway everything. Today Virgo still rules the steady hand of the chemist who, drop by drop into the beaker, helps to create medicine. It's not the price of a Rolex that makes it valuable, but the effort that goes into producing one.

If you've ever grown your own tomatoes and fed them as if they were your own little babies, you have to have some shred of Virgo in you. None of this "I'm-too-tired-I'll-water-them-tomorrow" baloney. But then, if you've ever plucked one off the vine when it's just turned the deep blush of red and taken a bite, now that is a real Virgo reward. Virgo is the FedEx guy who rings your bell with a package during the century's worst blizzard, the Red Cross worker risking typhoid and parasites galore to help with the latest African catastrophe.

Virgo rules smoothness of operation on the highest level of functioning. It is the reason airplanes really are safe, and why we don't get poisoned from eating a can of sardines. It's the lemniscate design that some brainy Virgo architect adapted so that it now serves as the entrance to I-59, part of a perfectly choreographed plan for the flow of all traffic. Virgo is responsible for the magical way the human body operates, from digesting a taco to expulsion of a baby-to-be. It's what prompts scientists to want to go poking into the heart of the atom to discover the smallest particle in the universe. It's the spirit that moves Mr. Gardner to ring Mrs. Rocchio's doorbell when the pollen count is high because he knows about her asthma. It's Sarah the tutor who has actually created quite a little reader out of Shawn after everybody else had given up long ago.

It's the feeling you get when you wake up early, sober and refreshed after a good night's sleep, shower, and hit the deck before rush hour. It's the fun of the first apple bobbing contest, and apple pie, and even the apple on the tree in the Garden of Eden. Virgo is the innocence of anything that's unspoiled. It is the lotus in bloom. Maturity.

More often than not, though . . .

So many Virgos are hysterical, phobic slobs. It probably has something to do with being ruled by Mercury, which makes all Virgos somewhat touchy and nervous. And then there's toilet training: big issue for Virgos. So much about Virgos depends on what book your mother read and her own toilet training, and whether she thought doo-doo was a no-no or natural process of life. That's probably why when the slightest thing goes wrong you nearly crap in your pants. To err is human. Admitting it is almost impossible for Virgos. Your perfectionism probably goes all the way back to diaper days and whether you were made to feel like the worst little baby in the world if you did it in your pants. But we can't blame everything on your mother, although Virgos do tend to have that *"J'accuse!"* look in their eye every five minutes. It could take years of blaming and rejecting people and thousands of dollars in therapy before you realize that, horror of horrors, you're a flawed, hung-up human being yourself, who clings to an innocence you lost long ago and seeks to place the responsibility for your failures on the deception, trickery, and deceit played up on you by others.

Many members of your sign are sweet, well-balanced, and they can laugh at themselves, and not just list the shortcomings of all the people who limp into St. Virgo's hospital for "treatment." Other Virgos are cold and untouchable. They look upon others as weak, wounded animals without a lick of common sense.

When you come to see that you're just as screwed up as the hordes of people you dispense advice to, the field is leveled and it's much easier for you to form and maintain long-term, successful relationships. Until then, however, you could be Nurse Ratched in your own version of *Cuckoo's Nest:* tired, frustrated, repressed, and horny, but on duty, channeling the exhaustion, horniness, and frustration into anger toward those who look to you for comfort—and love.

On another note of health, there are as many types of Virgos on that issue as there are germs on the doorknob of a public john. You've got those Virgos who use every sterilizing agent but radiation on their kitchen sink because some poor fool came for lunch and God forbid put a fork in there without first passing it under scalding water. And since AIDS, forget it. They have a home testing kit that's used every morning even though they sleep alone, because in 1982 somebody told them you can get it from masturbating.

This is where you absolutely have to get hold of yourself and gain a wholesome equilibrium, because some Virgos are such disgusting slobs— privately, of course. To the world they are pristine and immaculate, but in the privacy of their own personal hygiene, the only word is *Calcutta.* You're either living in a plastic bubble or courting leprosy, and that can't really be very conducive to happy relationships.

As far as your body is concerned, Virgo rules digestion and the intestinal processes that lead to elimination, so we're back to the toilet training issue again. In general, if you eat normally, have grains and fruits and vegetables, and avoid raw eggs, steak tartare, and monkey brains, you should be okay. Obsessively worrying about mad cow disease because one case of it was discovered in Ghana last week only increases your fear of poison and contamination from outside sources, which is also how you view any trouble you have in relationships—as contamination. You're always one to blurt out "I was doing fine until you came along," when troubles arise. Or, "How could you treat me this way? After all I've done for you!" You have a lesson to learn: You make choices and they are your choices alone. Nobody forces you to eat the things you put into your mouth, so whatever happens after you eat the whole jar of hot pickles, you really have to take responsibility for. Crazy fad diets or obsessive behavior based on research you read on the Internet or on the information you get inside a fortune cookie end up making you fear life itself. There is contamination everywhere. Bacteria have a right to live, too.

On the other hand, things go wrong. They just do. The best made machines need repair, maintenance, and overhaul once in a while. You're lucky because you have a body that retains its vitality, skin that keeps its elasticity, and most of your working parts are well made. They have to be to withstand the abuse that so many Virgos put their bodies through—and not just with drugs and alcohol either. What some members of your sign will do and call it working out to stay healthy would be cause for a lawsuit and criminal prosecution if you did it to someone else. The jogging twenty miles a day, the overuse of colonics, and the horrible tasting green goo you'll drink—all for what? You don't think your body can heal itself?

Granted if you get a major illness, you should try all remedies, and you'll have to purify your diet and change your behavior accordingly. But under normal circumstances Virgos are like everybody else. Sometimes you can imagine you've got the flesh-eating disease when all you've got is a mosquito bite. Conversely—and this is more serious—you can deny something bigger because the prospect of dealing with major illness can be more than you can cope with. Rule number one: You have to believe in the healing power of your body. It's not a crappy, knock-off watch that will tick for an hour after you buy it on the street, then blow. It's a mystical machine powered by the human will to live, and by other forces we know nothing about.

You're also lucky to look as young as you do, provided you don't fill yourself up with too many stimulants and too much garbage. Until you're thirty it will probably annoy you that you get carded whenever you order a drink, but you'll love 'em for it every year thereafter. Looking young also can make you look innocent, and in the case of thousands of Virgos, that is a laugh and a half. A Virgo can give a lover that "Be gentle, it's my first time," look, and then think privately, "Well, today anyway." That's the thing you have to watch out for: pretending to be innocently swept off your feet and then blaming someone for sucking you in. Don't ever make the mistake of thinking that Virgo has anything to do with the modern term "virgin," which refers to anyone, male or female, who hasn't had sex. Virgo refers to a goddess, actually quite fertile and prolific, responsible for the harvest. Virgos *are* passionate and sexy, although usually not spontaneous, so the conditions have to meet their particular idiosyncratic standards. Virgo is a female sign, so all Virgos are female. It has nothing whatever to do with your sexual preference. It's the way you orient yourself toward life and relationships, accepting opportunities rather than chasing after them. Virgos can play the aggressive cop to the alienated outlaw, but it's still a feminine, almost scoldingly and motherly way of relating to people. You share certain characteristics of this motherly attitude with all Virgos, male or female.

Because you've been blessed with a major brain, people are going to look to you for guidance. You can't stand people around you all the time, but you need them to make you feel needed. That can be dangerous indeed, because you can trap them into feeling small, or wrong, or weak, or crippled, so that they keep coming to you for inspiration and healing. That is called codependance and is one of the big pitfalls anybody getting hooked up with you has to look out for. Because you are so clearly logical, and because you have an uncanny ability to get to the heart of any issue and reduce the most complex stories down to their simplest, comprehensible levels, people think you know everything and that you are always right. You often do nothing to disabuse them of that notion. You are often disingenuous and manipulative, although you'd rather be burned at the stake than admit it.

But aren't you always right? Didn't you say Nick and Rachel would break up when they were going hot and heavy? Didn't you warn Ahmed to get his papers in order before he got his taxi license? You are so right so much of the time, it's easy to think you can never miss. Of course, none of those people you wag your naughty-naughty finger at have any idea how many times you've gone and landed yourself in sticky business, all by your own impeccable guidance.

There's a cynical side of you that runs around like a nun at a Catholic school dance holding a twelve-inch ruler between the dancers to make sure they leave room for the Holy Ghost. You have a gift for troubleshooting—which you have to remember is to be reserved for use only when people ask for it! To resist giving unbidden advice is one of the most difficult tasks for any Virgo. If they didn't ask for your opinion, shut the hell up until they do. How much would you appreciate it if every time you sat down to a big bowl of Häagen Dazs, the doorbell rang and there was somebody in a uniform standing there shouting, "Remember cholesterol!" Or you're on a first date and as you gaze adoringly into the eyes of the angel across the table, a waiter shows up not to ask you if you're ready to order, but just to say, "Another relationship? Don't blow this one like you did the last two."

You're gifted with practical wisdom and profound insight, but you have to hold your tongue until your counsel is sought. Liberating others from the bondage of ignorance and their own unconscious behavior can be your greatest contribution to their lives. Holding them prisoner by making them feel stupid, ashamed, or like incompetent nincompoops is an abuse of your power, and serves only to keep yourself indispensable, needed, and important.

This goes for your mate and kids, too, and this is why so many people in relationships with Virgos end up on medication, prescribed and otherwise. In the light of your apparent saneness and practicality, it's easy for other people to feel as if they are staggering through a fog and you are their only beacon. As a result they may want to act out and break away from what they perceive as iron-fisted control, or else they can start doubting their ability to function effectively without your input. "But I was only trying to help," is the harumph Virgos often utter when their efforts are unappreciated, their advice not followed, and their warnings not heeded. You tend to take other people's wish to make their own mistakes as a personal rejection. You have to remember that you are there to provide recovery from the storm, not a way to avoid getting wet.

You're the one who has to find the balance between an existence of icy, bitter alienation and one of blind, total immersion in self-destructive relationships that leave you lost in a sea way over your head with no way back to land. The purity and ordered simplicity of the life you lead always needs to be blended with the entropy brought to you by other people. It's hard to live with dirty socks on the bedroom floor, if they are somebody else's.

You have been put on this Earth to work, so roll up your sleeves, wear something you can wash out and wear again tomorrow, and if you think the world owes you a living, get help. Whether you were put here by Fate or you came here of your own free will, your life this time around is not just about cruising the Greek islands. It doesn't have to be a fancy or glamorous job. You may be here to run a household and hold a family together, so don't think work is always about career or money. In fact, in a Virgo's case it rarely is. You are here to find work that will bring you contentment and prosperity. Many Virgos have jobs dealing with money. (When you play Monopoly with a Virgo, he or she will have to be the banker to be sure it's all kosher when you mortgage your property.) The job doesn't matter as long as it's work you are doing from your heart. It's not a good sign if a Virgo hates his or her job. You are your work, so you have to pick something to which you are suited and which you love to do with all you heart. The train conductor who loves the railroad is happier than the waitress who is really an actress. We all have to do things we're not mad about. Earning a living in the modern world is never a picnic—unless of course you love to provide picnics for picnickers. You have talents and brains, and your intellectual prowess and general street smarts can be directed in a thousand ways. The trick is to place yourself in a situation where your talents are best used and to put your finger on the pulse of need. You'll never be content just as an esoteric artist sweating in a loft, creating some brilliant and dazzling but incomprehensible piece of art. You need to have a function, a utilitarian objective, to operate most effectively.

When you have found your true calling, whether it's to be a CEO or a mom at home, it's not work. You don't bitch and moan and complain about how tired you are or how nobody helps you. It's your life, so you don't need those lousy two-week vacations American companies give you because, rather than being drained by your work, you are energized by it. So if you're currently in a stinko job you may not be able to quit right away, you'd better start thinking about it, no matter how old you are. A Virgo without fulfilling work has no life.

What is fulfilling work? Imagine an old man holding up a lantern leading someone through a dark cave. Or a woman sponging the forehead of her feverish child. You are here to provide light and comfort. Maybe you are a minister, or maybe you work for the electric company. Maybe you're a nurse or you work for the ad agency that handles the latest miracle pain reliever. You can't take all this too literally and suddenly set up a comfort station at the edge of the next natural disaster. We all have families, maybe elderly parents to look after, mortgages, car payments, and responsibilities that don't always permit us to indulge in our nobler fantasies. But if you want to be a totally self-realized Virgo, you have to choose a life that serves others and eases their burdens. Even if you are right about everything and the rest of us have to lie in the beds we made for ourselves, you'll be the one to bring us cool water, some insight, and best of all a bitingly funny chiding for the predicament we have landed in. Your goal is right livelihood.

So how you develop more of your right livelihood, or find it if you don't yet have it? How do you have a personal life as well? What are the forces that drag you backward and keep you from reaching the highest manifestation of your Sun? And what are the energies that can support you, guide you, enhance your positive qualities, and make your Sun shine bright? The fact is you're not just a Virgo. There is another energy operating, one that either cuts across your efforts and undermines them or spirits you to heights of joy and fulfillment. That energy depends not on the month you were born, but the year as well. Later on in this book the technical aspects will be explained more fully. We'll examine how you waste time chasing your own tail, why you do it, and how to pull yourself out of self-destructive obsessions and put yourself back on the road to success. But for now, check out the following table. Find your birth year and note the number beside it. Then read the section corresponding to the number.

Year–No.	Year–No.	Year–No.	Year–No.	Year–No.
1901–9	1928–4	1955–10	8/26, then 5	2008–12
1902–8	1929–3	1956–10	1982–5	2009–11
1903–8	1930–2	1957–9	1983–4	2010–11
1904–7	1931–2	1958–8	1984–4	2011–10
1905–7 until	1932–1	1959–8	1985–3	2012–10 until
8/25, then 6	1933–12	1960–7	1986–2	9/2, then 9
1906–6	1934–12	1961–6	1987–2	2013–9
1907–5	1935–11	1962–6	1988–1	2014–8
1908–5	1936–11 until	1963–5	1989–12	2015–8
1909–4	9/1, then 10	1964–4	1990-12	2016–7
1910–3	1937–10	1965–4	1991–11	2017–6
1911–3	1938–9	1966–3	1992–10	2018–6
1912–2	1939–9	1967–3 until	1993–10	2019–5
1913–1	1940–8	9/10, then 2	1994–9	2020–4
1914–1	1941–7	1968–2	1995–8	2021–4
1915–12	1942–7	1969–1	1996–8	2022–3
1916–11	1943–6	1970–1	1997–7	2023–2
1917–11	1944–5	1971–12	1998–7 until	2024–2
1918–10	1945–5	1972–11	9/18, then 6	2025–1
1919–9	1946–4	1973–11	1999–6	2026–12
1920–9	1947–3	1974–10	2000–5	2027–12
1921–8	1948–3	1975–9	2001–5	2028–11
1922–8	1949–2	1976–9	2002–4	2029–11
1923–7	1950–1	1977–8	2003–3	2030–10
1924–6	1951–1	1978–7	2004–3	
1925–6	1952–12	1979–7	2005–2	
1926–5	1953–12	1980–6	2006–1	
1927–4	1954–11	1981–6 until	2007–1	

Virgo 1

You probably see yourself as just a regular person trying to do your job and do it well and help people out when you can. Some individuals, however, might interpret your zeal as controlling, interfering, and obsessive. In fact, they would say you can be a real pill. That is so sad. And totally unfair as far as you're concerned. You have a gift for seeing into a situation and instinctively knowing what's up with people, what's wrong with them, and how to fix it. The problem is you sometimes don't know when to offer your help and when to keep your mouth shut. Your need to be helpful and needed is seen as maiden-aunt-picky meddling. The problem lies, of course, in your own insecurity about being wanted. You have to admit you're hard to please and not really a very happy-go-lucky person. In fact, you have moments that border on hysteria. You can be a total work or health nut. And not without good reason. You've got a lot on your plate and are always nervous when you're not working. That's why you're good at what you do. It also makes you impossible to satisfy and, at times, to work with. You are most annoying when nobody can help, comfort, or come near you, no matter how desperately you need closeness and comfort.

On the subject of health you can really be over the top: terrified of being seduced, shrinking from contact, but at the same time needy. It's so hard for you to relinquish the ferocious hold you have on yourself (and everybody else). It's not just a question of being a perfectionist or health conscious. Your fear of being led astray can easily turn into a Chicken-Little-sky-is-falling nervousness that makes mountains out of molehills and has everyone scurrying for shelter when you show up.

How unjust. All you want to do is stay healthy and do your work. The fact is, your real path is not just about work at all. You real path involves shutting down, at least once in a while, that beehive mind of yours that is always humming and buzzing. You need to surrender and allow yourself to be enfolded by an embrace that by the sheer force of emotion overwhelms you, blocks your sense of reason, numbs your critical ability, and lifts you out of yourself. You can't reach such a state of ecstasy or enlightenment if you are hanging on to work, practicality, or any other rational faculty. But that means you would have to go against everything you think keeps you sane. It's crazy. It's emotion. It means encountering someone you can't analyze, control, or even reason with. It means allowing yourself to be taken by the current, cared for. That means faith is your ironic twist: To achieve happiness you have to allow your normally sharp mind to be clouded. You have to conduct a relationship not with your eyes wide open, as you try to do, but with your eyes half closed. That's tough since you're always trying to splash yourself with cold water and come back to your senses. You're a whole person only when you lose your common sense, suspend the rational, allow someone to flood your life.

Oh, you'll fight it like mad. You'll be terrified of surrendering, but surrender you must. You cannot hang on to an innocence that no longer serves you. Allow yourself to be seduced? Hoodwinked? Fooled? Proceed on faith and suspend the cynicism? Go with the heart and not the head?

At this point you need to probe more deeply into your own issues about the fear of getting sick, letting yourself go, and making a mistake. In the next part, Going Deeper, reading the chapters called "Independence" and "Control" will give you a chance to pass through the illusion of thinking you're falling apart, or it's a sin to be taken care of, and on to a higher expression of your Virgo nature to have greater faith in others and in life, and make your Sun shine bright.

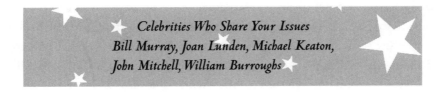

Celebrities Who Share Your Issues
Bill Murray, Joan Lunden, Michael Keaton,
John Mitchell, William Burroughs

Virgo 2

If business deals that were sure bets fall through, don't panic. Certainly any collapsed agreement that disturbs the economic equilibrium is upsetting. You do, however, tend to think it's the end of the world. No matter how many times it may happen, you've got to get back out there and keep making connections that could potentially bring in increased revenue. And when you're on the brink of a big one and suddenly, for some reason, the whole enchilada goes kaput you've just got to understand that there must be a cosmic reason for it. What else can you do beside tell yourself that you're a loser? That the Universe has a better plan waiting for you. But it's not just the crumbling of a money deal that gives you an aching back. It's the fact that people have led you on, made you think something was in the bag, and conveniently forgot to tell you that there was a great big hole at the bottom of the bag. It's the drop-off-the-face-of-the-Earth people who drive you more cuckoo than the loss of the deal itself. On top of that, it would be hard, even humiliating, for you to have to turn to people for advice, help, or a loan to tide you over. You do that. So you are forced to wheel and deal your butt off just to remain financially independent. And get this: It's your fantasy to hit it so big so you never have to worry about money again.

It's way too complicated in your case. You want the support, need the support, eventually have to go to somebody for support, but in the end you don't have confidence enough to let somebody handle your financial affairs without sticking your hands in the machinery.

On quite another note, your sex life could be very exciting, if you let it happen. Sex is an area where, if you're honest enough, you can achieve unparalleled mastery. A Virgo and sex? That's not an oxymoron. Virgos can be very passionate and sexy, as long as it doesn't take too long. Nobody should make the mistake of thinking, that just because you are a Virgo, you sit alone under a weeping willow tree doing math problems with never an impure thought crossing your spotless mind. You're not only easily turned on, but once you are, male or female, gorillas run for shelter! You need novelty, challenge, and in the game of sexual dominance and submission, nobody should think you are not vying for the top, in-control position. Because you are, if you let yourself be honest about what your needs are—which, sooner or later, will come out anyway. Your liberated sexuality will be the source of your big time success, and not necessarily in porn. Allowing your passion to be unleashed will open the door to the creativity you know lies dormant within you.

It requires complete courage, faith in your powers to conceive of and produce innovative material, and the ability to be a sexy figure and still retain that simple aw-shucks identity that invites people in without threatening them.

• • •

At this point you need to probe more deeply into your obsession with your high hopes in relationships of all kinds, which only mask your fear of being unable to sustain them. In the next part, Going Deeper, reading the chapters called "Marriage" and "Money" will give you a chance to pass through the illusion of unrealistic expectations, positive and negative, and on to a higher expression of your Virgo nature that will help you grow creatively and emotionally, make you more prosperous in business or personal relationships, and make your Sun shine bright.

> **Celebrities Who Share Your Issues**
> Sean Connery, Richard Gere, Twiggy,
> Anne Bancroft, John Cage, Gustav Holst

Virgo 3

Aren't Virgos supposed to spend all their time in silent meditation, thinking up good works they can perform for the poor, the downtrodden, the unfortunate, and the needy? Members of your sign are not really supposed to be taking little side trips to hell, which you certainly do—or at least you do in your more fragmented moments, hell being defined as the place you run to in order to satisfy habits that can eventually come to own you. You're not just the humble and sweet "Will-that-be-all-mum?" servant type people expect Virgos to be. You've got a fascinating, creative, but spookily dark side to your brain and a very weird twist of mind. And when somebody ticks you off, disappoints, or deceives you, and the situation warrants it, you've got a sailor's vocabulary that even parrots wouldn't repeat.

Those side trips to Darkville, the place wild dogs wouldn't even go, can get really scary, but you seem to be rather comfortable there. You are even on a first-name basis with people down on levels Hieronymus Bosch never imagined. You have lived out the Cain and Abel story at least a dozen times, and you have had pretty creepy—if not downright unprintable—interactions with neighbors and siblings along the strange albeit exciting road you have traveled this far. If you're helping your fellow men and women, there might be some moral justification for hanging out in the gutter. But if you're just looking for some cheap high and your forays into the back alley of consciousness don't have some higher purpose, you could turn out to have just another addiction, rationalized as only a Virgo could: an addiction to the seamy side of life as an escape from prosperity, security, and a lifestyle that follows traditional moral values.

Frankly, you'll never be able to stay totally on that straight and narrow, but as long as you don't preach fidelity and practice promiscuity, they won't be able to fault you, or arrest you. Even if your behavior is seedy now and then, in thought if not necessarily in deed, you have a gifted intelligence and a noble aspiration to raise the level of consciousness of others and, hopefully, yourself.

You need to go to places you haven't seen and step out of the habitual local hangouts that provide only empty conversation and cheap contact. In fact, not only will that clean up your head and give you a more fertile perspective on life, it will turn your attention to making money and being heard by people who really appreciate your brain and either don't know or care about your less hygienic habits. It's easy for someone to tell you to stop thinking one way and start thinking another. Even if you're going to put your brain ten or twenty times through a Maytag cycle, you've still got to figure out how to unify a higher and lower mind.

At this point you need to probe more deeply into your own issues about being sexy as well as smart. In the next part, Going Deeper, reading the chapters called "Sex" and "Communication" will give you a chance to pass through the illusion of being a person of high morals with naughty thoughts, and on to a higher expression of your Virgo nature that will help you deal more successfully with money, develop your business abilities, come to terms with your desires, and make your Sun shine bright.

> *Celebrities Who Share Your Issues*
> *Mother Teresa, Arnold Palmer, Jeremy Irons,*
> *Stephen King, Terry Bradshaw, John Ritter*

Virgo 4

Unless they saw you in your off moments, it would be hard for any casual observer to imagine that such an accomplished public speaker, an expert in your field whom people listen to and respect for your ability to communicate, could have so many deeply rooted insecurities and such shame, embarrassment, or anger whenever the subject of your family comes up. At the same moment you're up there on the stage talking, being the great communicator, part of you is still thinking about that little boy crouched under the eaves in an attic, alone and terrified by the sound of marching soldiers. That's how disparate the two sides of your mind are. On the one hand you're totally on top of your game, cheerful, humorous, likeable, and masterful. Then buried deep inside you there is an insecure little immigrant who thinks she's stupid, was told she must hide and not speak out, and even now fears ridicule or even worse if she just opens her mouth. That's the part of you that must not be allowed to take hold and drag you back.

Attachment to family members whose values and beliefs you're ashamed of can sabotage all your efforts to overcome the very prejudices and mental constructs that have come down from generation to generation and kept people in ghettoes. Strict religious or educational upbringing usually makes people rebel angrily against ethnic or social origins they feel has stunted their intellectual or moral growth. They throw off restrictions and resent parents who either mislead them or allowed their thinking to become skewed and distorted. Such resentments rarely free you from the grip of the past. On the contrary, they tie you to it. There are always likely to be loose ends, mysteries, hurts, and unfinished business that drag you back in longing or anger to times in your life you can't get away from. Even if you were not left to fend for yourself and survive on your own, if you are obsessed with either glomming onto or escaping a family, you do yourself a tremendous injustice. And you've already seen enough injustice to last you another lifetime.

Besides, it's not your true path. You have to separate yourself from yearning for the parent you wish you had and carve your own way, develop yourself professionally, and make your own mark upon the world through communication. Formally educated or GED-certified, you have to speak out fearlessly and unabashedly, and be able to overcome that crying child who seeks to distract you and hold onto you every time you attempt to leave the house.

Of course, you'll be torn between your responsibilities to a nagging but unsupportive family and the responsibilities to a demanding career. You're a Virgo and although you need your personal life, your fulfillment comes through the work you do, what you have to say to the world, and how you manage to juggle your public life (which can be enormously successful and simple if you give time to it), and a private life that is rarely simple. The trick is to avoid becoming enmeshed in ideological disputes with the family, whether their views embarrass you or not—which they will. To be loyal and still speak your own views is the path to freedom.

At this point you need to probe more deeply into your obsession with being taken care of, to the point that it hurts your career. In the next part, Going Deeper, reading the chapters called "Religion" and "Security" will give you a chance to pass through the illusion of thinking you're not smart enough to move ahead with or without family support, and on to a higher expression of your Virgo nature that will help you come out of your shell, become the communicator you are destined to be, and make your Sun shine bright.

Celebrities Who Share Your Issues
Charlize Theron, Mary Shelley, Joyce Brothers, Paul Volcker

Virgo 5

If parents put too much energy into controlling and directing the course of their children's lives, they're bound to end up disappointed or heartbroken. Virgos are not known for having a whole passel of kids, but if you have any, then you know exactly what it means to need distance and detachment. You've wondered if you could or should have children in the first place. You can be way too serious and heavy. Even though you are eager to do the best job you can raising them, you can be the type of Virgo who gets neurotic about something dire happening to your kids, and you're almost relieved when your fears come true. You have a tough time letting them have their own lives, so naturally, like all kids, they turn around and accuse you of destroying them, no matter what you do. In many cases you're a wonderful aunt or uncle or godparent—the best, in fact, because you're not nearly as maniacal in your desire to direct their destiny. Sure, Virgos are diligent, but when you don't dare have a life outside, you're setting yourself up for major heartache.

In love? Same deal. It takes years before you believe any person you love isn't going to fly away or drop dead. You can have such a notion about being jinxed that you lack any sense of fun, fair play, or good sportsmanship. You're a wonderful friend, the best, but since you equate love with control, the minute it gets personal, handcuffs get slapped, all the insecurity kicks in, and before you know it, you squeeze the juice right out of the orange. Get hung up on the taste of forbidden fruit, and the depth and loyalty you seek eludes you. Everything is personal. Suddenly everything is about you. You have to be the center of attention. The star. The patriarch. The diva. These are bad trips for Virgos to go on, because when you forget your humility, your goose is cooked. In romantic love you could lose your ability to trust, along with the clarity and objectivity you're famous for. Somehow you have to step back and restore yourself to yourself. And you can't do that by fear or threats or intimidation or control.

You're the best, most nurturing friend anyone can have. Because you are there for others, you will always have people to comfort you in your moments of crisis. You will always have people you can turn to when your personal life threatens to interfere with your real happiness. You're a born performer and creator, even if you don't feel you're adequately recognized or honored for your creative efforts. Your exploits and "romantic" antics are a way to avoid more traditional responsibilities to the family you create to make yourself feel more secure. So you constantly run from it toward affairs that give you a rush and make you feel temporarily loved, but not fulfilled in the end.

If you can learn how to be as nurturing, understanding, and loving toward one human being in a personal, romantic situation as you are toward all the people in Tibet, you'll be on top of the world. Your needs are not conventional. Your path is to entertain and improve society. Along the way if you have a thousand dalliances to fulfill your need to be validated and loved, in the end it's friendship, not romance, that will make you feel whole.

At this point you need to probe more deeply into your obsession with being adored, to the point that you scare people and opportunities away because they don't satisfy you. In the next part, Going Deeper, reading the chapters called "Recognition" and "Love" will give you a chance to pass through the illusion of fear of being ignored, and on to a higher expression of your Virgo nature that will help you display your talents, develop your ability to love without fear, and make your Sun shine bright.

Celebrities Who Share Your Issues
Lyndon Johnson, Warren Burger, Joseph Kennedy, Sr.,
Jose Feliciano, LeAnn Rimes

Virgo 6

You call it being busy and productive. Some people would call it plain, old overcompensation. You find your freedom in dedication, which some people perceive as a fanatical slavishness to work. For you, though, it's a perfect fit. You have a desire to serve mankind and a wish to remain free and unattached enough to do so. As a result the body of work you produce could be priceless as well as voluminous. It permits you to have an icy, detached affect that is as alluring as it is off-putting. It's a dream job—no matter how draining, exacting, demanding, repetitive, or even boring. You find safety and solace there. Work keeps you sober and clean. It prohibits too much nightlife where you could get into trouble. Perfect. You can't even involve yourself too deeply or too long in a romantic scene. You need your rest to restore your health, get your energy, and be able to work. Perfect. A Virgo's dream.

Except it's not perfect at all. If you work work work to that extent, you'll dry up like dust and blow away. Your diligence and chastity become emblems of repression, sooner or later the statue of the goddess crashes down, and people find out that the image you've tried so hard to develop and create is fake. What a surprise to find out that underneath it all you're quite a hot little cookie, and far from being your undoing, falling deeply in love could be your saving grace. Undoing, yes, in the sense that falling in love and having kids and/or secret affairs does blow the picture of Rabbi Jeff of Hollywood or Our Lady of St. Louis, but it refreshes your soul, opens your heart, and enters you as a member of the human race, not as the cool detached observer image you've created. As a fallen angel, a participant with just as much emotion, vulnerability, and foolishness as the rest of us. Oh, you'll fight it all right. After an episode of ecstasy, you'll find a million perfect reasons to jump out of bed and rush back to work—not so much because you're required to punch in on time, but because you are compelled to show that you're not a lazy, self-indulgent, damned fool whose heart rules your head, but a busy, committed, indispensable cog in the great machine of society. Your humility may be sincere, because you are honestly trying to serve people selflessly and be a friend to all. Your irrepressible ego cannot be hidden forever, however. You're the scientist who sings in the shower, the coquette who pretends to be uninterested and plays hard to get, but in the bedroom, watch out!

Why you hang on so ferociously to a self-image of purity that is empty and ultimately not fulfilling is a sad mystery, mainly because it keeps you from the love you are destined to express when you finally fall from grace. And you will. It's the secret affair that makes your work have meaning.

At this point you need to probe more deeply into your own issues about being unwilling or unable to give yourself emotionally. In the next part, Going Deeper, reading the chapters called "Freedom" and "Control" will give you a chance to pass through the illusion of fear of letting go and letting the Universe take care of you with its plan, and on to a higher expression of your Virgo nature that will help you continue your work, stay healthy, still have a private intimate life, and make your Sun shine bright.

Virgo 7

Everything would be fine if you were a registered nurse or a prison guard. But if you're a regular person who wants to have a happy, prosperous relationship, you've got to be able to allow people their self-destructive addictions without becoming addicted to their addictions. Become addicted and you can kiss your own life goodbye. Not that you'd necessarily become a druggie or boozehound yourself, but you'd become addicted to their addiction in the sense that it would be your sworn self-imposed duty to cure it. You'd become the personification of the cold shower and black coffee. You could identify too strongly with keeping someone from going over the wall and out of your life (or out the window to the pavement below). And not without reason. You have a history of such things. It angers you, and has since childhood, that some person could use another as a crutch, dominate them through fear of abandonment, and could, through outlandish, outrageous, and childish acts of self-destructiveness, steal someone's life away. Oh, does that ever make you mad. And yet, how many damned times have you taken the bait and been manipulated by someone just like that?

It's natural for a Virgo to want to provide a voice of clarity and be the note of sanity in the life of another person. It's generosity, not grandiosity, that has put you in the position of trying to save the ignorant, slothful, blind, or ungrateful. When it does become your cause célèbre and raison d'être, and you're not getting paid for it, an alarm bell should sound. But how can you achieve an appropriate boundary when it's not a clinical or professional situation? If it's your nature to "help" how can you turn it off when relationships are personal? Can you just stand by and let a person flail around like a drowning swimmer and not intervene? Is it wrong to remain silent when you see so clearly how to fix a situation, or rather help fix a situation, or rather help a person help himself or herself? The answer is simple to define, hard as hell to follow:

1) Never offer help or advice until it is asked for.
2) Keep yourself clean and sober and set the example.
3) Remain focused on yourself, especially when you start to feel plagued with guilt that you're not doing enough or when you're afraid you'll be ditched and dumped if you don't do your job better.

A personal relationship should not become yet another moonlight job you take on and live in fear you're going to be fired from if you rest for a moment. You've got to be aware that when you're insecure, you make the other person feel weak and sick and unable to function without you—a sure way to begin the end of any relationship.

It is not always clear who is the masochist and who is actually controlling the relationship through unspoken and often unconscious messages. Success comes when you can feel love and compassion without losing yourself in the process. Abandoning yourself to prove selfless love is folly. Keeping your head is the trick.

At this point you need to probe more deeply into your obsession with being responsible for everyone, to the point that all relationships become a burden. In the next part, Going Deeper, reading the chapters called "Marriage" and "Escape" will give you a chance to pass through the illusion of fear of being alone, and on to a higher expression of your Virgo nature that will help you stay on your course, conduct your relationships with more balance, and make your Sun shine bright.

Celebrities Who Share Your Issues
Otis Redding, Lyndon LaRouche Pink, Hugh Grant,
Branford Marsalis, Damon Wayans

Virgo 8

People worry about such nonsense, like penis or breast size. Are those things the real measures of a person's desirability? People love you best because they know they can count on you. That may be hard for you to accept when you're younger and concerned with whether or not you're sexy. You're the most loyal and gently supportive, enduring partner anyone could want. Sexually, however, you don't believe you can hold people, and it's usually a disaster the minute you get undressed and into bed with somebody. The event itself is not a disaster. Far from it. Your whole being goes into making it a smashing success, whether you're acting or not. Some Virgos have the capacity to have intimate relationships in a normal, nonhysterical way. You, however, have to make a conquest, and in the process pretend to lose your virginity every single time. You are always seeking to create or recreate the first moment, the first kiss, the first oral, the first penetration.

Besides being inordinately insecure about your body, you may lack confidence in your ability to sustain an ongoing sexual relationship combined with deep companionship. There's shame involved, shame that goes deep, along with the fear of what will happen if you become sexually submissive. In fact that's root of much of the problem—heterosexually or otherwise. Who can say if religious training, the fear of castration, and penis envy are actual factors in your sexual behavior? You do have some deeply-rooted phobias, fetishes, and fantasies that impede your ability to sustain ongoing sexual relations. An exercise in companionship and monogamy would be stressful, but it would help you gain confidence in your own desirability and trust others enough to reveal your actual passivity.

Your reluctance to reveal yourself can keep you in a masturbatory state, and not only sexually. The inability to share yourself keeps you locked up creatively as well. That's fine if you want to be a consumptive poet who keeps stale bread and cheese on your window sill. Giving up the self-absorbed life brings financial prosperity as well as the companionship you cannot prosper without. It demands a maturity in your attitudes toward business and money that jeopardizes the safety you have found in isolation. It requires renouncing your addiction to the fantasy sex life of a prostitute or hustler for an existence more grounded in honest sharing. Your passions have to be honored, because complete abstinence is definitely not good for your health. Going way over the line with abusive self-indulgence, on the other hand, will shorten your life. Unless you have already transcended this plane of carnal desires, being a Virgo doesn't mean being repressed. It means enjoying the fruits of this Earth, the grapes, the harvest, the wine, but learning what moderation is.

At this point you need to probe more deeply into your own issues about being in control and being desirable, to the point that your obsessions hinder your ability to allow you to be deeply known. In the next part, Going Deeper, reading the chapters called "Independence" and "Sex" will give you a chance to pass through the illusion of fear of losing yourself to another and of sharing your gifts, personally or artistically, and on to a higher expression of your Virgo nature that will help you develop bonds of loyalty, generate more money and prosperity, and make your Sun shine bright.

> *Celebrities Who Share Your Issues*
> *Pee-Wee Herman, Michael Jackson, Brian DePalma, Lily Tomlin,*
> *Darryl F. Zanuck, Ivan the Terrible, Tim Burton*

Virgo 9

Ethics and money—there's always an issue. No matter how Scout's-honor honest you try to be, it seems you can never escape that blot on your school record, the indelible mark that is behind all your defensive behavior about honesty, integrity, and intelligence, especially when it comes to the IRS. Thinking that anything you say could be held against you—which it well might be—you could get hung up in the legal/philosophical mumbo jumbo that screws up people's lives the minute they get involved with money. Virgos are not supposed to worry about financial remuneration? You're just supposed to live your life pro bono? Volunteer? Be a public defender or feed the hungry and homeless out of your own pocket? You're supposed to go barefoot to preach the good word? Forget it. As they used to say (before everything got so politically correct and oversensitive), no tickee no shirtee. Money may not be your path but it sure is a perk when choosing a profession. Why be a ditch digger for minimum wage when you can go to law school and charge five hundred dollars per hour, or business school, yes business school, so you can figure out what to invest in and how to run companies. Yes, that's the secret.

Except how is it that some jerks who didn't get past ninth grade own buildings and cars and fly to Transylvania first class if they want to? Financial success can't be just a function of education. Some people have luck. Other people may not have all the benefits of family and education but they do possess a certain kind of street smarts. They know how to get apples off carts and not call it stealing. Some guys have an ethical philosophy they stick to right through the entire trial, believing that there's no gaping hole in their logic and that they were really always on the up and up. And yet they know. They know about the padded deductions and unclaimed cash and everything else they wouldn't want dragged in as evidence of their hypocrisy.

Besides, in your case, the money isn't even the real issue. You can use it as a monumental distraction—Look over here! Look over here!—when your real hang-ups lie elsewhere. Gender and sexual preference play a much more significant role in your psyche than anyone but the most astute observer would ever suspect. The money is the red herring. While the big red herring is being waved in everybody's face, you have ethnic, racial, and sexual issues that need to be addressed and resolved. As a profoundly rational and intelligent Virgo, you have to understand the insanity that surrounded money in your family, and how hard you have to work to shed all the notions and prejudices that have been handed down to you. It takes tremendous effort to not be taken in by wrong thinking, but to draw your own conclusions, make your own observations, and come to the conclusion that creativity and your power of communication are stronger than any false thinking you once accepted without question. Observe and then communicate the truth as you see it.

At this point you need to probe more deeply into your obsession with the philosophy of prosperity and chasing financial rainbows, to the point that you become reluctant to be creative, productive, and prolific, with or without money. In the next part, Going Deeper, reading the chapters called "Money" and "Religion" will give you a chance to pass through the illusion of what it means to be rich enough to travel first class, and on to a higher expression of your Virgo nature that will help you develop a healthy faith in your own mind, develop your creative communicative abilities, understand your sexuality, and make your Sun shine bright.

> ★ *Celebrities Who Share Your Issues*
> *Alan Dershowitz, Craig Claiborne*

Virgo 10

As you grow and mature in this life you are bound to gain appreciation for the deep wisdom gathered from generations of matriarchs and patriarchs who have sat on porches with shotguns, waiting for invading bears and interlopers who dared to threaten their brood. Getting stuck taking care of that homestead has often made you embarrassed to be just a mom or just a dad, so you've probably made desperate flights into career and actually been successful at it. You're embarrassed that you have not always been amply rewarded or sufficiently recognized. It's not that you lack drive or motivation to achieve status, position, fame, or notoriety out in the world. Far from it. It's just the course you chose to follow isn't always hailed as wonderful by the masses. Besides the fact that you absolutely loathe, detest, and despise any authority figure mindlessly blaring incoherent and inconsistent orders at you (wonder why?), you also have a feverishly busy and curious brain that doesn't really stay on one thing for long. So your mind skips along like the bouncing ball on the lyrics of an old tune, and you're not willing or able to stick with one job, one company, and certainly not one boss until Medicare kicks in.

Your greatest achievements may not even bear your real name, although their impact could stick in people's heads for eternity. Funny, after all your attempts at public validation, it's the message that remains, not the messenger. And the message is that all the family values, rules, and regulations you thought were meaningless actually have greater significance in your fulfillment and success than you would have ever dreamed when you were younger and attempting to reject them. These once-annoying beliefs and practices grow on you once you stop wasting time running away from them and trying to get the world to listen to you. When you are coming from a loving place of deep wisdom and wishing to unite people of different backgrounds, all doors open. When, however, you run away from home, cut yourself off from family, culture, and tradition, you're running nowhere, getting nowhere. If you're out there spewing anger, you're going to have a lot of deaf ears (not) listening to you.

Either way you're not going to please everybody, and you know it damned well. Sibling rivalries, gang feuds, and communication breaches of all kinds will interfere with all the love and unity you are preaching. The monster you are trying to beat could be called political schizophrenia. It's the constant switching loyalties and the impossibly inconsistent changing of jobs under a chaotic and irrational regime. Scream all you want to, but in your golden sunset years you'll find it comforting to retreat from the exhausting attempt to be understood by people who do not now, never did, and probably never will speak your language. Deeply rooted beliefs in family values can either unify or separate people, depending on how open or closed their minds are, especially when it comes to bossy, irrational parents, two-faced professionals, and all politicians.

At this point you need to probe more deeply into your obsession with speaking out and being recognized, to the point that you run from the very people who will support you, just because they are family. In the next part, Going Deeper, reading the chapters called "Communication" and "Recognition" will give you a chance to pass through the illusion of losing confidence in your intelligence because you're at odds with society, and on to a higher expression of your Virgo nature that will help you come to terms with your need to balance professional responsibilities and your need for deep, intimate bonds, and make your Sun shine bright.

Celebrities Who Share Your Issues
Leonard Bernstein, George Wallace, Margaret Sanger

Virgo 11

A group of friends, closer than family could ever be, gather round a long table in a noisy restaurant and lift their glasses in a cheerful toast to their long-lasting bonds and a future nobody can predict. That's a photo op, and when you look at the yellowing snapshot, you have to wonder what ever happened to so-and-so. You heard such-and-such died last year. And who's-it's is now a big shot in Washington, but of course you never hear a word from her. You have a sense of being abandoned by people you adopted as family. It's happened to you more than once. You've got a thing about looking for a "family," family in quotes because, as a group, these people are tight but not linked by blood or DNA. They can be adopted kids, stepchildren, other people's families, and every other possible combination of motley crews. It's aliens from the planet Zorcan who treat you like family (not your real kin). Your attachments can be immediate and possessive. But you do have a deep need to belong, be connected, to nurture and be nurtured. But you also can't stand to be pushed, crowded, or helped too long, because as much as you want to be connected, you also want to be completely free. Your friendships are real while they last and you have certainly replaced one mother-child relationship with another. All that is easy for you. Too easy. What's hard is taking care of your own personal life, which often needs attention. Understatement.

Growing up means not being afraid to express yourself. You're spooked at the thought of getting trapped or being pigeonholed. Your career probably will involve creativity and/or kids. There is no escape from either. If you avoid your emotional life when you're younger because it threatens your liberty, you'll eventually have to reconcile the conflict between your freewheeling emotional life and your conservative need to be a more acceptable member of a society. You're trying to be a conventional icon and a rebel at the same time. You're not an all-for-one-one-for-all democratic musketeer. You may hide in the group and find safety in numbers, but eventually you will have to reveal your need to be the star. It's not easy for Virgos to assume the royal purple robe and live the life of a successful diva. You have to work at that. You have to work also at accepting your need for love so you don't keep running away from it.

Being a lead performer and playing the romantic lead in your life will mean you have to stand up, take the credit and the hits, and actually allow yourself to be deeply and permanently committed, as well as hurt.

At this point you need to probe more deeply into your obsession with being mothered from a distance, to the point that it could hinder your ability to commit yourself deeply personally or professionally. In the next part, Going Deeper, reading the chapters called "Security" and "Freedom" will give you a chance to pass through the illusion of what family is all about, and on to a higher expression of your Virgo nature that will help you develop your talents fully, be able to accept commitments deep enough to fulfill yourself in career and love, and make your Sun shine bright.

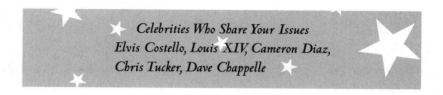

Celebrities Who Share Your Issues
Elvis Costello, Louis XIV, Cameron Diaz,
Chris Tucker, Dave Chappelle

Virgo 12

Once you put your mind to it and get off one binge or another, the body of work you could produce is enormous, and that is the point, isn't it? Isn't a Virgo destined to perform a unique and lasting service? It's not about glitter and glamour. It's about working for a living. You're not royalty—you don't even like all that phony, kiss-ass nonsense. You're simple person with simple needs and simpler tastes. You could even be a vegetarian. But how in the name of heaven and hell do you get so mislead and so far off track? It's probably just the folly of youth, because in your youth you could be bedazzled by the shine of what looks like gold, but pal, when it turns out not to be gold does that ever turn your finger green. You will have to be lead way astray by seductive forces about 200 million times before you cool off, sober up, and get back on the road of hard effort, good health, and a love of the work you do. You're a silly romantic fool of course, quite un-Virgo-like with a deep streak of romanticism that makes you so vulnerable to distraction, seduction, and fantasy. Dreams of being loved and adored are your undoing, but they have also saved you from totally slavish, dried-out work and a dead, boring existence. You need to establish some sort of healthy equilibrium between the two needs.

Trouble really comes, though, when you are seduced by any and every sweet-talking salesman or pretty girl with long eyelashes who promises you eternal adoration. These people can undo you totally, mess you up emotionally, and imprison you in a relationship of nonlove—which is based on the belief that the five minutes of pats on the head you get will make up for months of being mistreated and ignored. It's not true, and that's an easy lesson for you to learn. You think if you resist the temptation, refuse to give in to the distraction, you'll pass up a chance for the great love you are looking for. And then you could end up being some dried-up, bitter old fool who shakes a cautionary finger at any and all young and idealistic love.

Not so. Healthy detachment will not only make you productive and help you fulfill your destiny as a Virgo, but it will make room for love on a higher plane that is free from dangerous escapist dependencies. Even if you have to walk away from your visions of love and reject traditional parent-child roles, your life comes more sharply into focus when you make manifest your contribution to humanity and meet your destiny. It's about real love.

At this point you need to probe more deeply into your obsession with chasing gratification and personal validation in all the wrong places, to the point that it damages your health, distorts your mind, and keeps you from being productive and successful. In the next part, Going Deeper, reading the chapters called "Love" and "Escape" will give you a chance to pass through the illusion of thinking that fiction is a place you run away to in order to escape work, and on to a higher expression of your Virgo nature that will help you enjoy your secret moments but still gain enough distance and sobriety to be productive, and make your Sun shine bright.

Celebrities Who Share Your Issues
Regis Philbin, Sophia Loren, Ingrid Bergman

LIBRA

September 23–October 22
Dates vary from year to year—consult your local astrologer

Libra is the beveled edge on Steuben glass. It's the embroidered rose on an elegant pillow on an elegant sofa in an elegant room in an elegant house. It's the diamond, once it has been perfectly cut and polished and placed in the perfect setting. In short, it is impeccable taste in fashion, furnishings, decor, clothing, accessories, and human relationships. Libra is the dispassionate judge who metes out a form of higher justice worthy of the ancient Greeks. It is the wisdom of the Supreme Court and the grace of Gwyneth Paltrow. Libras seem to have instinctive gyroscopes inside them that help them steady the ride and avoid capsizing, no matter what drunken fool stands up and starts rocking the boat.

Libra is the garter flying toward the group of tipsy young bachelors and the bouquet caught by some lucky bridesmaid. It's the first dance at the wedding, when all envious eyes are turned toward the happy couple swaying in the middle of the dance floor. Libra is their complete unawareness of the crowd of family and friends as they gaze into each other's eyes and see only happiness in the future. Libra is that picture-snapping moment when a momentous contract is signed and everybody involved is beaming as they shake hands. It's a happy meeting they know will make somebody else's life easier. Libra is waiting for the signal, a violin bow poised in expectation of the stroke of a conductor's arm and the beginning of heavenly music.

If you're a Libra you have an uncanny ability to understand the plights of both the Arabs and the Jews, the Democrats and the Republicans, your mother and your father, with compassion for their insoluble predicaments. You are not above the law. You are the law, in the sense that you have a love of and an abiding belief in the existence of true justice.

What some people may perceive as an inability to take a stand, is just your way of viewing both sides of every case without prejudice, and you are not satisfied until all sides of an argument are completely explored. Libras are called in to tame a wild animal, show a dog where it needs to make doo-doo, teach a single guy how to chew with his mouth closed. You're the level-headed answer to a question, and your grandest wish is to be on the arm of someone who needs your input, trusts your advice, and considers your opinion. You embody romance in the sense that, for you, joy is found in transcendental union. Your own personal needs and wishes can be joyfully sublimated in favor of another's. Your function is to restore calm, stand before violence and diffuse it, and submerge ego drives, petty angers, and resentments, to demonstrate how intelligence can overcome primitive instincts. Surrender is your most sublime emotion. More often than not, however . . .

You're in a lifetime battle for dominance. How you enter that battle depends largely on the extent somebody (a parent?) tried to beat you down, beat you up, put you down, destroy your confidence, and in general obliterate your natural drive to exercise your will.

They didn't? You grew up in a home where peace, joy, and love radiated throughout the household? Yeah. Sure. Right. If you think that, your shrink can put a down payment on a new summer home. Now, it must be said that some Libra children *do* learn how to shut up, shut down, yield to anyone's dominance, never say boo or "Goddammit! I don't want Chinese food!" They learn how to be charming and pleasant and completely unauthentic. They are so accustomed to be moved around like pawns on a chess board, that they just give up and pretend to be content every time their desires are crushed by somebody else who was more aggressive. So they resort to guerilla tactics: denying their rage, seeming to agree to anyone's demands, but undermining those demands in any and every sneaky, aggravating way possible, which only serves to incite their more hostile counterparts and cause even more strife.

If only they could come out with what's really ailing them, spit it out, scream, kick, bite, scratch. Oh, they scream, kick, bite, and scratch all right, but always to the lady at the phone company or the mailman, to all the wrong people, the people who don't have emotional control over them. When it comes to the people they are most deeply connected to, the ones they most urgently need to communicate with, they've learned to displace all their anger, because any outward sign of hostility will be met with even more dangerous retaliation, putting their very life in peril. So they go through life smiling a smile that could cause diabetes in anyone daring to gaze upon it. Is that you?

If you are, you're no fluffy little teddy bear. You're a snarling, toothy animal that snaps at everybody—not just the mailman. You're always mad, but you never reveal your displeasure toward the true object of your anger. You kick everybody else's ass, still cowering in the shadow of someone you're either trying to please or trying to protect. So the little poodle morphs into a Doberman and vice versa. Do you always have to live in such a violent extreme? Certainly not every Libra in the world is an unstable borderline case. But until you learn the difference between a healthy expression of anger and an atavistic murderous hatred, you're going to be scared of your more aggressive side, either in the form of a person you're always hiding from, or the animal in your own nature. And that's why you can't always decide whether you want to serve your loved ones breakfast in bed or just go ahead and kill them while they sleep.

If you've been raised in a home of poodles and Dobermans, you're going to see relationships as a strain, and you would rather sit home alone with a bowl of chips and a good movie than have to deal with another person who drains you. If your home was full of smiling Connecticut WASPs who never argued, never fought, and lived their life politely dabbing their mouths after nibbling cucumber sandwiches on white bread, you're not going to know how to fight. If, on the other hand, you were born into a den of rutting wildebeasts, then you're still avoiding honest confrontation during which differences can be ironed out, disappointment discussed, and problems resolved to everyone's satisfaction.

That's the rub. You probably experienced both extremes. Picture a mouse scurrying around the edge of a boiling volcano (i.e., your parents). Somebody was always appeasing somebody else, trying to avert a major conflagration. You could have been raised in a scene of divided loyalties where you had to diffuse bitterness, resentment, and aggression while expressing your own feelings was considered acting out and inappropriate.

So you learned to live a nonexistence, permitting violation of boundary after violation of boundary. You say this is a much too extreme of a description of your childhood? Perhaps you've blotted out much of it, reassembled cuss words into niceties, and covered your memories with a wash of thin white paint. There has to be some reason you are always angry.

Oh, you're not? Wow, your brain cells must have been more reassembled than originally thought. You're here on Earth to integrate traditional male aggression and female acquiescence, and it doesn't have anything to do with what lies beneath your pubic hair. Your challenge is to deal with brute force—other people's and your own. Success in relationships (which, let's face it, is what you are here to accomplish) depends upon your ability to unravel the mystery of dominance and submission. You are seeking a perfect blend of self-assertion and surrender, a dynamic balance between the Viking's crude desire to take what he wants, and the refined Lady Plushbottom taking a genteel tiny little bite into her crumpet and apologizing for the noise she makes sipping her tea. You are looking for someone who can help you resolve your own conflict between wanting to be the Big Kahuna, Number One, the Boss, "the Man," and wanting to be seized, taken, carried off on the horse of an outlaw, and ravished in the hayloft of an abandoned barn.

To put it bluntly: Can you decide whether you want to be a top or a bottom? Do you want to "do it" to somebody else or do you prefer to "have it done" to you? This does not have much to do with sexual preferences as one might first think. Submissive men are not necessarily stereotypical gay interior decorators, nor are dominating women growling militant lesbians on Harleys. Millions of heterosexual Libras are dealing with this issue at this very moment. Success in relationships depends almost wholly on whether you can accept the kinds of people you are attracted to, and can handle them. If you like wild animals, go to school and become a veterinarian and move to the jungles of Africa. It's as simple as that. You're attracted either to very aggressive people who know how to kick your ass when you need it, or to sweet little cookies you can put in the blender and use as pie crust. It's not, however, a case of "Why can't I ever like the ones who are nice?" You need the challenge of someone bossier than you to create the balance. You often prefer the other person to be the aggressor, even if you'll go to all sorts of lengths to undo their aggression. If somebody is too sweet or too kind you become the wild-haired bitch-bastard of the Universe.

Your happiness depends on your ability to come to terms with any problems you have in creating and keeping boundaries, and to accept the kinds of individuals you are most drawn to. Strong, self-directed, self-made people do not have to be crude abusers. An individual who carves his or her own way through life need not be a selfish rat. Self-motivated innovators need not be alienated loners, who can't be let loose on other human beings because they will either maul them to death or strangle them with their need. A strong sense of self doesn't have to be raging narcissism. Direction and guidance doesn't have to descend to a level of cruel tyranny and violent control.

The goal is equality, mutual respect, cooperation, and sharing without one person being crippled by the other. A relationship is not the crushing of one gladiator by another, or the squashing of a flea under the heavy foot of a thundering giant. The goal is union, and there's no reason that your life in a relationship need stray too far from the vision in the gaze of that bride and groom on the dance floor, provided you understand and accept the true meanings of the words top and bottom.

Can't people be flexible—dominant sometimes, submissive at others? Can't you be dominant in some areas and submissive in others, while your partner complements you by being strong where you are weak and weak when you are strong? Can't you take turns being on top? Can't you switch from time to time? Can't you enjoy being both?

Can you?

How do you move closer to the person you're supposed to be, independent in your own right, yet deeply connected to someone you love who treats you well and whom you treat well? What are the forces that drag you backward and keep you from reaching the highest manifestation of your Libra Sun? And what are the energies that can support you, guide you, enhance your positive qualities and make your Sun shine bright? The fact is you're not just a Libra. There is another energy operating, one that either cuts across your efforts and undermines them or spirits you to heights of joy and fulfillment. That energy depends not on the month you were born, but the year as well. Later on in this book the technical aspects will be explained more fully. We'll examine how you waste time chasing your own tail, why you do it, and how to pull yourself out of self-destructive obsessions and put yourself back on the road to success. But for now, check out the following table. Find your birth year and note the number beside it. Then read the section corresponding to the number.

Year–No.	Year–No.	Year–No.	Year–No.	Year–No.
1901–8	1921–7	1941–6	1960–6	1979–6
1902–7	1922–6	1942–6	1961–5	1980–5
1903–7	1923–6	1943–5	1962–5	1981–4
1904–6	1924–5	1944–4	1963–4	1982–4
1905–5	1925–5	1945–4	1964–3	1983–3
1906–5	1926–4	1946–3	1965–3	1984–3 until
1907–4	1927–3	1947–2	1966–2	10/2, then 2
1908–4 until	1928–3	1948–2	1967–1	1985–2
10/1, then 3	1929–2	1949–1	1968–1	1986–1
1909–3	1930–1	1950–12	1969–12	1987–1
1910–2	1931–1	1951–12	1970–12 until	1988–12
1911–2	1932–12	1952–11	10/17, then	1989–11
1912–1	1933–11	1953–11 until	11	1990–11
1913–12	1934–11	10/24, then	1971–11	1991–10
1914–12	1935–10	10	1972–10	1992–9
1915–11	1936–9	1954–10	1973–10	1993–9
1916–10	1937–9	1955–9	1974–9	1994–8
1917–10	1938–8	1956–9	1975–8	1995–7
1918–9	1939–8 until	1957–8	1976–8	1996–7
1919–8	10/9, then 7	1958–7	1977–7	1997–6
1920–8	1940–7	1959–7	1978–6	1998–5

Year–No.	Year–No.	Year–No.	Year–No.	Year–No.
1999–5	*2006–12*	*2013–8*	*2018–5*	*2025–12*
2000–4	*2007–12*	*2014–7*	*2019–4*	*2026–11*
2001–4	*2008–11*	*2015–7 until*	*2020–3*	*2027–11*
2002–3	*2009–10*	*10/10,*	*2021–3*	*2028–10*
2003–2	*2010–10*	*then 6*	*2022–2*	*2029–10 until*
2004–2	*2011–9*	*2016–6*	*2023–1*	*9/24, then 9*
2005–1	*2012–8*	*2017–5*	*2024–1*	*2030–9*

Libra 1

Even though your natural grace can make it look easy, you have a tough time steering your ship through the relationship waters, especially when it comes to showing anger. In fact, you can be a tough one to deal with, all right. You can be sweet and charming, but frankly, there's a very thin veneer over a lot of your old, buried anger. It doesn't mean you're a bad person. You don't want people to think you're mean and nasty and mad all the time. You want to be loving and loved. You want to want to do things for people, nice things, go out of your way, cook their favorite spaghetti sauce, and not resent them. But sometimes you just can't help it. You've got a deep streak of anger from God-knows-when that makes it pretty hard for others to know when you're really and truly smiling and when you're baring your teeth like an animal about to strike. You don't like yourself very much when you are nasty, but holding back because you're scared of what will happen if you are real is worse for you.

It takes a lifetime to get over the things that happen to us as kids, that shape our actions and responses. Your life lesson certainly involves getting over the struggle between you and an aggressive parent. It's going to come up in every relationship you have—submissive child–aggressive parent, submissive parent–aggressive child. Being born near a solar eclipse makes you a hundred times more intense than most Libras and gives you an even deeper need for better relationships, despite all your resistance. As selfless as you're supposed to be, you're fascinated, even obsessed, with yourself, big time—so much so that it can be hard for people to break the barriers you put up and get close to you. Because it's not always easy to see who is really in control—the aggressor or the victim of aggression. The aggressor beats down the victim, physically or emotionally, feels momentarily victorious, then goes on a campaign of self-hate and self-recrimination, covers it up with a thin veneer of self-justification, and on and on the cycle repeats. Offenses and apologies, splits and reconciliations, feuds and truces.

Relationships are always fraught with such control dynamics, but they only seriously disintegrate when your anger is out of control or when you are so full of angst that you hog the floor, dominate the conversation, and try to work the whole room and control everybody.

The sad thing is: Your sweetness is real. The control thing never goes away, however, and you are always seething if you are not considered in every major decision, and you are still working over rage that has its source far, far in the past. The people you seek out need to be at least as tough as you. In order to deal successfully with you and gain your respect, they have to be clear, direct, open, and self-assertive. You have to accept their strength and welcome the challenge and confrontation—not fear it or have to stamp it out.

At this point you need to probe more deeply into your obsession with being so weak that you struggle against all relationships all the time, and are seen as impossibly self-absorbed and narcissistic. In the next part, Going Deeper, reading the chapters called "Independence" and "Marriage" will give you a chance to pass through the illusion of fear of being controlled by another person, and on to a higher expression of your Libra nature that will help you create a strong sense of who you are without the constant battle, connecting on a profound level in business or personal life, and make your Sun shine bright.

Celebrities Who Share Your Issues
Barbara Walters, Richard Harris, Desmond Tutu,
Sigourney Weaver, Jimmy Breslin, Margot Kidder

Libra 2

You know the feeling—as if you woke up with a vampire's mark on your neck. You don't know where you got it or how, you just know you feel weak. That's what you feel like when you see the money in your bank account being sucked into a whirling vortex, pointlessly disappearing forever just like the $40,000 Norman Bates buried with Janet Leigh's body in *Psycho*—a silly, stupid, red-herring waste of resources. This feeling has been a recurring sensation in your life, and it could certainly cause serious panic attacks—especially for such a refined Libra like yourself. You think it's so crude even to have to deal with the gradual disappearance of your precious resources, nibbled away by a relentless rat who steals your cheese every night but somehow escapes the trap. And then you get obsessed with every nickel spent. You end up unable to enjoy your life. You don't know what's a necessity and what's a frivolous indulgence. You sit there with a loaded shotgun waiting to be robbed.

You usually engage in personal and business relationships in which your finances are intertwined and intermingled with somebody else's in very complicated ways. Separations are difficult to achieve when problems arise, because it is difficult to figure out what is whose. Life is still healthier and more profitable, however, when you join up with other people, not just because you're a Libra but because you need a steadying, stabilizing force in economic matters. Even when you have to keep bank accounts separate and carry your burdens alone, eventually there has to be some sort of fiscal union. If you want to make it in the world, you will come to see that you have to make some serious compromise between pure art and commercialism.

We haven't even touched upon the subject of sex yet. That's because this is a touchy subject. You can be sure that in your younger years there will likely be some torrid affairs, some of the even extramarital, that erode trust and confidence. And you may not even be the one involved in them. No matter who plays the injured, deceived part, bear in mind that in many cases both members of a relationship have the same capacity to get bored and restless. Both are equally capable of it. One party, however, probably has an easier time stifling the urges to play around. There is usually only one partner who actually acts it out.

Libras are tough to penetrate. It's not easy for you to admit to your darker urges, like the greedy desires that undermine your economic and personal stability. The fact is, though, that the individuals you choose to interact with often end up acting out what you yourself are totally secretly capable of. So you need to examine yourself fully and deeply, then attempt to sort out the practices and behaviors of all kinds of partners. You are certainly not to blame for the actions of others, but you owe it to yourself to think about your conscious and unconscious motives that have drawn you into the same sort of situations again, and why sex and money are so often linked.

At this point you need to probe more deeply into your obsession with who controls the money. In the next part, Going Deeper, reading the chapters called "Money" and "Sex" will give you a chance to pass through the illusion of fear of being fleeced and violated, and on to a higher expression of your Libra nature that will help you stabilize your resources while remaining true to yourself and not totally selling out, and make your Sun shine bright.

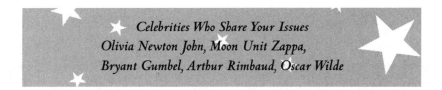

Celebrities Who Share Your Issues
Olivia Newton John, Moon Unit Zappa,
Bryant Gumbel, Arthur Rimbaud, Oscar Wilde

Libra 3

Crossing lines in relationships is your specialty. You are unlikely to marry the boy next door or that shy girl from sixth grade. Not even with twenty years of therapy. You're more likely to take up with the therapist. You're just not going to follow the gender/religious/age appropriate rules. You can't stand to stay in the psychological ghetto society would like to set up for you. Wait a minute, that's all wrong. That's upside down. You do like to stay in your own little world with people who think like you do. No, you don't. Yes, you do. Actually it's almost impossible to pin you down to just one way of thinking. You have a lot of different points of view on a lot of subjects. You can be very opinionated in your speech, especially on social, racial, or moral issues, but those views can and do change on a dime, which makes you seem to flip-flop, erodes your credibility, and opens you up to criticism for not practicing what you preach. That burns you because you loathe hypocrisy and do aim for the truth. It's just that truth has many sides, just as you have many faces.

You have been known to say one thing and do another. Haven't we all? Sure, but in your people-pleasing days when you were so desperate to have your voice heard above all others, you probably rubbed elbows with Republicans, then dissed them while hanging out with the Village People. You do talk a lot about other peoples' abuses, biases, and prejudices that really annoy you. Oh, you know how it is: Prophets are never known in their own land and all that, and eventually people will come to see that you weren't just another pretty face and weren't just talking a lot of rubbish that you didn't really believe in. But it's true. People don't always take you seriously. They do kind of tune out when they hear you start playing them that old record for the eight millionth time. So you really have to learn to speak a language everyone can understand, hear, and appreciate.

You can be a deep philosophical thinker. You're not just an angry blabbermouth with serious unresolved sibling rivalry issues. You're a thinker and a talker, and if your points of view change over time, which they will, it's not because you're a two-faced scatterbrain, exposing or disavowing the latest piece of half-baked gossip you heard on TV. Your opinions change because you have an evolving consciousness. You are curious about everything. You see all sides of issues, and you dig the Rashomon element of every story. Relationships? You've got to be engaged in a mental and philosophical dialogue or there is no match.

You need lots of different people from different ethnic and political backgrounds in your life. You have to argue to be happy, because it's the trading of ideas that makes the bond. It can break it, too, so you need to develop a common language if you want people to pay attention.

At this point you need to probe more deeply into your own issues about being controlled mentally and psychologically, to the point that it might be impossible to follow your thinking or understand the contradictions you are trying to communicate. In the next part, Going Deeper, reading the chapters called "Religion" and "Communication" will give you a chance to pass through the illusion of fear of being misunderstood on every level, and on to a higher expression of your Libra nature that will help you communicate, be taken more seriously, and make your Sun shine bright.

Celebrities Who Share Your Issues
Cheryl Tiegs, Chubby Checker, Susan Sarandon, Carole Lombard,
Roger Moore, Aimee Semple McPherson, R. D. Laing

Libra 4

Oh, where oh where is your true home? Is it where you sleep? Or will you find a better, more lasting security where you work? Such a paradox. And when you think about it, which is all the time, you probably don't even really know who your parents really are. You are most likely one of those Libras with at least two sets of parents. When you think about how many divorces there are these days, that could make you feel a little more normal. Libras like to feel normal. So many people have at least two sets of parents.

It's a little different for you, though. You could have been raised by foster or grandparents or you could have wound up with people who didn't exactly have custody. There's some sort of story in your background that causes you to feel overprotected and resentful or cut off and full of longing to reconnect. You yearn for a deep, long-lasting connection and yet you've got to leave time for periods both of escape and of yearning. Maybe you feel an overwhelming sense of responsibility to at least one parent, which, in extreme cases, can interfere with setting up your own family; you could equate family with a burden and therefore shun all aspects of having a family. But the family would satisfy your longing for the intimacy of which you were deprived.

You have to have that same passionate connection to your roots that people who haven't gotten all screwed up in childhood have. Where do you find it? How do you get over that gnawing feeling of being left—and worse, ignored—by the people who are supposed to be caring for you? Those feelings may be old and left over from a time when you were powerless, but you still have a right to those feelings. The way out: finding your security in work you are passionate about. And you will find it. Eventually, you will get the message that overattachment will lead you only to more suffering. At that point you discover your path, and even if it is not the totally blissful domestic dream you'd love to fulfill, it can be the liberating discovery of your lifetime. Will you let this old war wound, this search for the perfect mommy and daddy, mess up your professional opportunities? Will your demand for unconditional love jeopardize your success in the world? You have to come to terms with exactly whom you want to recognize and pay attention to you. This is a complicated thing to sort out, especially if you are unable or unwilling to surrender old resentments and fears. Shaking free of their hold on you will allow you to pursue your real ambitions without fearing you'll be punished if you realize them.

At this point you need to probe more deeply into your conflicts between career and personal life, to the point that you could find it difficult to pursue either one. In the next part, Going Deeper, reading the chapters called "Security" and "Recognition" will give you a chance to pass through the illusion of fear of being abandoned and ignored, and on to a higher expression of your Libra nature that will help you strike a good compromise between ambition and the need for intimate connections, and make your Sun shine bright.

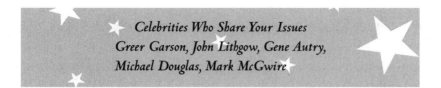

Celebrities Who Share Your Issues
Greer Garson, John Lithgow, Gene Autry,
Michael Douglas, Mark McGwire

Libra 5

You're a lover all right. That's your big thing: love. You've got to feel pang or two when you think back to high school and recall how many of the kids in your class were able to enjoy a healthy social life. They had normal crushes, they dated. Their parents kept pictures of them at the school dance on top of the TV set. Some of them even got married and are still married today. Children? Of course they have children. They are part of normal society. They're keeping the DNA chain alive. Well, how come they had such a normal life and you didn't? What's in your history or your genes that is so freaky and anomalous that you have to play out your drama in such a freaky aberrant scenario? Well, it's not freaky or aberrant to you, because it's all you've ever known. It hasn't been boring, thank God, even if it has been wickedly unpredictable. Certainly in your high school alumni magazine, if you were to tell it all, your entry would be highly over the top. Hey, you can't help it if you love danger. You're a born performer. Even though you're a Libra and would love to be just nice and sweet, you really can't hack normalcy.

Your love life is a high-wire act. You're a little flamboyant and exhibitionist about it. You love a crowd gasping as you cross that wire above a pit of lions; it gives you a rush you get no other way. As long as there's that hint of disaster—or if not disaster, then at least danger—you can remain passionate and interested. There has to be the element of the outrageous for you to maintain your excitement. Although you want to be adored forever, when you are in your obsessive mode you can easily get hooked not only love and companionship, but also on the feeling that any moment you might be whacked. Sometimes you can't tell the difference between getting smacked for no good reason and losing control to a person who comes along out of the blue and steals your heart.

Reread the sentence above. Stop right here. Read it one more time.

Therein lies the secret to your spotty love life, your ambivalent feelings about being spanked, about having children, and most of all, about what love is.

You will do best in life when you elevate your definition of love to include nonattachment, freedom for both parties, and friendship. When you can do that, you will also reduce your addiction to danger and unexpected loss, expand your ideas of what fair treatment and fidelity are all about, and develop your most unique talents best. Your special gifts may belong to humanity—not just one person.

• • •

At this point you need to probe more deeply into your obsession with being the geeky friend who isn't taken seriously as a lover. In the next part, Going Deeper, reading the chapters called "Love" and "Freedom" will give you a chance to pass through the illusion of fear of being rejected emotionally, and on to a higher expression of your Libra nature that will help you create a satisfying and fulfilling role for yourself you can be proud of without losing your sense of independence in personal relationships, and make your Sun shine bright.

★ Celebrities Who Share Your Issues
Oliver North, Giuseppe Verdi, Gandhi, Lenny Bruce, Angela Lansbury,
Penny Marshall, Johnny Carson, Margaret Thatcher

Libra 6

If you think you are lovable only if you are a totally physical specimen in perfect form, perfect health, and perfect shape, you are going to drive yourself crazy. You will spend thousands if not millions on every weird homeopathic, natural, and kooky product and device to keep you sane and healthy, including plastic surgery and the latest injections, implants, and enhancers of every kind. All your efforts will actually end up having the opposite effect. They will become a barrier between you and everybody else, which in the end could turn out to be what you may have unconsciously been actually trying to do. The fear of letting yourself go, seeing the body go, can sometimes be a healthy one. It can remind you that you can't drink excessively, do drugs for twenty years, and not expect atrophy and cellular degeneration. On the other hand, obsession with and resistance to the inevitable can lead to a fanatical attachment to the body. And it is your relationship to your body that determines not only how you treat it, but how you see yourself in all relationships.

You have to love your body, not be obsessed with it. The human machine is fueled by the nutrients we put into it. There is, however, another fuel: a spiritual component that comes from a source we cannot define or trace. Your work will somehow contribute to your knowledge of how physical and spiritual aspects combine to form a smooth, well-functioning organism. Nobody in this world is a machine, though. Nobody stays young and in perfect shape forever. There are forces and functions we can control and others we cannot.

Imagining the worst advances nothing. Neither does denying problems that are real or chronic. If you think you will be loved only if you are a god or goddess, some icon of masculinity or femininity, you're likely to miss the whole point and purpose of your life on Earth. You're a person, not a clone, but you will be a hero when you can combine magic and practicality, lyrical imagination and down-to-Earth usefulness. You can't get carried away with either one. Both need to be honored, the Earthly and the spiritual.

At this point you need to probe more deeply into your obsession with functioning, being healthy or useful, to the point that you can't tell how much is in your head and how much is in your body. In the next part, Going Deeper, reading the chapters called "Escape" and "Control" will give you a chance to pass through the illusion of fear of being considered useless, and on to a higher expression of your Libra nature that will help you stay healthy mentally and physically, keep you from letting your imagination carry you away, and make your Sun shine bright.

> *★ **Celebrities Who Share Your Issues***
> *Jesse Jackson, Jean-Claude Van Damme, Timothy Leary,*
> *Annette Funicello, Deborah Kerr, Franz Liszt, Jesse Helms*

Libra 7

It's hard to go on supporting people when they either push you away or mistreat you. Even embarrass you. It hurts even worse when they claim they're embarrassed by you. Then you've got to have a whole discussion—who's more selfish, who started the war, who pushed whom away. That's a war that could go on forever. Still, you're supposed to show up and be the backbone, the steady one. Where is it written that you are supposed to give out more than you get back and not bitch, moan, or complain about it? But that's just what happens if you don't think enough of yourself to begin with; you get exactly what you've bargained for but pretended you didn't. Oh, sure you think that you are going to "cure" the other person, or that they are going to be just a nice, quiet little mouse who puts you on a pedestal and asks nothing in return. Know this and keep it fresh in your mind: You have major issues about who's going to be on top and who's going to be on their back and receiving, to put it crudely. As we have already stated earlier, questions of dominance arise for men and women, heterosexual and homosexual and everything else in between. With Libra especially this is a particularly complicated question. Your kindness and sweetness are sincere. Your wishes to please a partner and avoid ugly confrontations and open fighting are commendable. What is clear, however, is that there is often a parent-child slant to the relationship (age differences are a big thing) in which one person is more mature than the other. You don't have to be the more openly aggressive member of the team to be the dominant one. You're certainly not as selfless as you seem. You just wiggle and wangle your way around to get what you want without a major calamity, which means sometimes you eat dirt and willingly lose the battle to win the war.

Appeasement and avoiding conflict won't save any relationship. If you live in fear that you're going to get dumped, nothing will allay that fear but actually getting dumped. This fear stems from your lack of confidence, some unrealistic choices, and conflicts about wanting to be in a relationship of any kind in the first place. You have to understand how you may be identifying too closely with your parents' relationship, either by trying too hard to copy it, or desperately attempting to avoid the pitfalls that the parent of the same sex encountered. Maybe you tend obsessively to avoid, and end up repeating patterns you saw in your parents' relationship because you mistrust your own powers to hold onto a healthy relationship. To restore equilibrium you need to understand both the positives and negatives of being alone, as well as the pluses and minuses of being with one other person. Easier said than done.

• • •

At this point you need to probe more deeply into your own issues about being so self-reliant you end up alone, or too trusting in people who don't deserve it. In the next part, Going Deeper, reading the chapters called "Independence" and "Marriage" will give you a chance to pass through the illusion of fear of being thought of as selfish, and on to a higher expression of your Libra nature that will help you participate in relationships without being engulfed by them, and make your Sun shine bright.

> ⋆ *Celebrities Who Share Your Issues*
> *Sarah Ferguson, John Lennon, Yves Montand, Ed Sullivan,*
> *Eleanor Roosevelt, Ralph Lauren*

Libra 8

The sex and money thing. Damn, but it haunts you and throws you off guard. They are forever linked, and get so many Libras into either nasty divorces or late night liaisons with shady characters. And it's so you to fall into the crocodile swamp of sex and money that usually end in life-and-death struggles. Wouldn't you rather just find one person, settle down, and not have to sully the relationship with compromising situations? It would be easier, way easier, if the society into which you are always seeking to fit (and to which you sometimes have to pander for financial reasons) would just accept your lifestyle and allow you to come and go as you wish. But it isn't just the societal conflict that wears you down.

You go back and forth inside your own head over issues of sexuality and marital fidelity. You can't really be blamed, of course. Just think of your own youth, your sex education, the notions drilled into your head about right and wrong, passion and business. Think about how much money got pissed away on things that turned out to be frivolous. Think about how much time you have spent chasing something that doesn't even end up satisfying you for more than an instant or two. While you may be at least in part responsible for these actions, who can fault you if you get tempted once in a while to fool fate, step over the line, go for that one extra bite, even cheat death now and then?

We're all flawed beings. We try to behave, but the temptations are great. Behaving is such a strain when the world is such a smorgasbord of goodies and you are as oral as you are. It's one of those human ironies that make it even tougher to be a Libra. Libras don't usually like extremes, whether it's total self-abnegation or total gluttony. You like to be honest and fair in your dealings, neither cheap and greedy nor totally stupid. When you've got a killer appetite, though, it's hard to keep that rheostat from going off the dial. You have to try extra hard not to freak out over money, or to think you're getting screwed every time, or to start acting like a crazy miser who won't take a taxi when the fares go up, not to throw away resources because you feel guilty or sexually frustrated. The link is easy to see, and none of this will come as a big surprise to you. The trick, of course, is to be able to live the intense life you have to live (some call it abnormal) and still maintain your image as a well-balanced, contributing member of society. The truth is out there.

At this point you need to probe more deeply into your obsession with being beautiful. In the next part, Going Deeper, reading the chapters called "Money" and "Sex" will give you a chance to pass through the illusion of fear of being thought of as greedy or insatiable, and on to a higher expression of your Libra nature that will help you form bonds of loyalty and intimacy, gain control of your appetites, increase prosperity, and make your Sun shine bright.

> *Celebrities Who Share Your Issues*
> Mickey Rooney, Rex Reed, Evel Knievel, Montgomery Clift,
> Walter Matthau, Bela Lugosi, Alicia Silverstone, Kate Winslet

Libra 9

Who is sane and who is crazy? If you can answer those two questions you win the trip to Hawaii and the Camaro. Plenty of Libras spend years as well as fortunes in therapy trying to solve the crossword puzzle of the mind, only to find out after they have done so that the questions are still there. If you actually do have a screw loose, then maybe no nut can ever tighten it. Besides, that loose screw could turn out to be your genius. Part of you is convinced that the family curse of madness has been passed down to you and no amount of positive thinking, headshrinking, or medication is going to do a damned bit of good. Part of you believes that they messed with your head so much, so often, and so deeply that now you have to make your fortune as the village idiot. Or in more politically correct terms, as a person with a disorder.

Is that true, though? Are you really the victim of some weird cerebral anomaly that "makes" you act in a certain way? Or are you gifted, marked, touched by the finger of destiny to change the way people think? Let the history books decide whether you were psychotic, deranged, or just a genius with iconoclastic ideas. Which one of these you turn out to be depends on your will to raise not only the consciousness of others, but your own as well, and your desire to eradicate notions of prejudice and wrong thinking.

There are no absolutes. It's a matter of perspective. Many times lies are repackaged to resemble the truth and that's a pattern that has been repeated down through the ages.

Today's crackpot often turns out to be tomorrow's genius, and unfortunately all too often, vice versa. Wherever you come from, however, ethnic and cultural differences will color all your relationships. Whatever road you choose, you cannot elect to remain silent. To live fully in this life you need to make your thoughts known. You can't just choke on loneliness. You have to learn to establish a strong mental connection that crosses national, social, religious, and racial lines.

At this point you need to probe more deeply into your own issues about being intelligent and/or sane. In the next part, Going Deeper, reading the chapters called "Communication" and "Religion" will give you a chance to pass through the illusion of fear of being thought of as out of your mind and babbling incomprehensibly, and on to a higher expression of your Libra nature that will help you straighten your head out once and for all, and make your Sun shine bright.

Celebrities Who Share Your Issues
*Carrie Fisher, Rita Hayworth, Friederich Nietszche, Thomas Wolfe,
Heinrich Himmler, Yo-Yo Ma, Chris Carter*

Libra 10

One of the most stressful situations you can imagine is being stuck in a house, stuck in a role, and chained to a family you have no real feeling for. You're not just somebody's significant other who stands in the background with a tray of hors d'oeuvres when the boss comes to dinner. Equally if you're a man. You need to make your own mark in the world. You need a relief from family responsibilities, and you need to escape from the expectations of society that you're supposed to be mom or dad and that's it, period. Sit there in the living room until they come to carry you out feet first? You can't stand the thought of rotting away like that.

Yet aren't you searching for emotional security? It must be a powerful force if it pulls you in both directions so relentlessly. First you need to be out there, known in your own right, with your place in the sun. What happens then? You pack up and run away from too much exposure. As usual with Libras, it's almost impossible to figure out what the heck it is you want. Do you want a career and a public—even political—life, or are you looking for a nice home and family? Can you really find a satisfactory balance between the two, or sooner or later does one become your true number one preoccupation? You can't be happy without some sort of career, and yet without a stable base, you don't function well. Fame is fleeting. Public tastes are totally fickle. We all know that. If you think you're going to find the happiness you seek through public adulation, you're going to be sorely disappointed, largely due to the corruption that is always there to cast a shadow upon your integrity. Yet it's so stressful to put yourself in the hands of some controlling figure who promises to take care of you, provided you surrender so much autonomy that you even forget how to write a check. Juggling home and family with career is in itself a full time job. It's a job you have to learn to respect.

• • •

At this point you need to probe more deeply into your own issues about confusing business with personal relationships. In the next part, Going Deeper, reading the chapters called "Recognition" and "Security" will give you a chance to pass through the illusion of fear of being rejected in your career and having to turn to family for help, and on to a higher expression of your Libra nature that will help you sort out where you need to persevere, when to stop clinging, and make your Sun shine bright.

⭐ *Celebrities Who Share Your Issues*
Luciano Pavarotti, C. Everett Koop, June Allison, George Gershwin, Jerry Lee Lewis, Arthur Miller, Scott Bakula, Lorraine Bracco

Libra 11

Causes: They can be your greatest contribution to the human race or your great escape from living a regular life like a regular person. You're funny about all that humanitarian stuff. Part of you knows you're unique (all right, "different"). Your uniqueness is your talent and your gift. It still bugs you, though, that you are not really now nor have you ever truly been a member of the in-crowd. Cliques are horrible. Think about what devastating things sororities and fraternities can do socially to individuals in school. Think about these exclusive clubs and organizations that exclude perfectly wonderful people from belonging for the most superficial and prejudicial reasons. It galls you that fellow human beings are discriminated against. The funny, weird thing about it is you want to belong and you don't want to belong. As a Libra your natural tendency would be to blend in, pretend, make like a chameleon, and make them think you're one of them. You are like an alien from another planet who puts on a perfect replica of a human suit to observe the ridiculous practices of Earthlings but then becomes so identified with them that you can't get the human suit off when it's time to go back to your native planet. Eventually, the novelty wears off. Your flirtation with the Good Ole Boys' Club—or whatever other cause you've identified with—gets old, and when it does, you must confront your own heart, children who need you, or your own art, any or all of which must take precedence over your social or political involvements.

There's no question that you need to be loved. It's difficult for others to see whether you want to be loved by all humanity or just one adoring person. It's hard to tell because you're not always sure yoursef. You swing back and forth from intimacy to social involvement, hoping to be caught by a commitment that totally grabs you, but always evading capture at the last minute. Until, that is, circumstances force you to find a way to make a contribution to the whole and still learn to appreciate the one.

At this point you need to probe more deeply into your own issues about romance and friendship. In the next part, Going Deeper, reading the chapters called "Love" and "Freedom" will give you a chance to pass through the illusion of fear of feeling like the fifth wheel and being left out, and on to a higher expression of your Libra nature that will help you come to understand the difference between keeping your independence and running away from love, and make your Sun shine bright.

Celebrities Who Share Your Issues
F. Scott Fitzgerald, William Faulkner, Lillian Gish,
Brigitte Bardot, Jeff Goldblum, Christopher Reeve

Libra 12

When you have a mission, it isn't work. When you allow yourself to be propelled by a force, moved by a wave that takes you forward, even though you don't know where it's going, that's faith. That's creativity.

Rare. Very rare, because you're also a dedicated control freak. You bounce back and forth between inspiration and perspiration. At first this can be the perfect blend of diligence and art, religious fervor and pragmatism. That's when you're busy and productive and not worrying about contracting some exotic fever, being assassinated, or worse, becoming a has-been. You can get very, very nuts on the subject of contamination and your own expendability. This could really make it hard for anyone to get close to you without passing through a sterilization chamber, x-ray machine, and ultraviolet shower. As open and friendly as you like to appear, you've got your share of bacteria phobia. You also can become overly concerned with being passé, over the hill, and unneeded, and that can drive you to try too hard to stay hip or relevant.

Bad idea. Of course, there has to be some nexus between the esoteric messages you get from your muse and a comprehensible, pragmatic application to those messages. Nobody in this world can say where a sense of mission will lead you. Obviously, you have a horror of becoming just another nine-to-five schmo with a lousy job you are too insecure to let go of. Dreams of glamour and greatness do lead people to glamour and greatness, but it's doubtful if the blue-collar gene can ever be successfully bred out of you.

As with all Libras you are often difficult to analyze. Part of you is right there, up front, a hard-working, simple person of the people. But you're also a slippery fish, working your deals, manipulating, always manipulating, and trying to carve out a secure place for the day when you're old and sick, which for some reason never seems to happen. Finding a middle ground between fear of ill health and denial, or faith and cynicism, will be your big achievements.

At this point you need to probe more deeply into your own issues about being committed and running away, to the point that you harm your own emotional or even physical health. In the next part, Going Deeper, reading the chapters called "Control" and "Escape" will give you a chance to pass through the illusion of fear of falling ill or being attacked just when things are going well, and on to a higher expression of your Libra nature that will help you work and play in more fulfilling ways, and make your Sun shine bright.

Celebrities Who Share Your Issues
Sting, Robert Reed, Juliet Prowse, Gwen Stefani, Matt Damon, Brett Favre

SCORPIO

October 23–November 21
Dates vary from year to year—consult your local astrologer

It's night. Somewhere an animal is howling. It's a wolf, and she's heard a twig snap in the brush near her den. Her howl lets the owner of the foot that snapped the twig know that there are wolf pups in this den. Come no closer. Warning. Come no closer. She's a Scorpio.

Scorpio is the force that protects life but can also take it away. It is the purple flower that springs up on lava-charred landscape, carried there by invisible spores. Even though he's not a Scorpio, it's Lance Armstrong's seventh win years after doctors broke the bad news to him. It's the five-month-old unharmed baby rescuers hear crying in the rubble of a collapsed building. It's whatever it was that decided existence was a darned good thing and caused the Big Bang. Not God, necessarily, but the Force that kicked God into being. Scorpio is the whole hydrogen carbon thing that scientists say makes stars happen. It's the mechanism operating behind magic—not sleight of hand that entertainers and street shysters do, but the real invisible stuff lots of people don't believe in. Nowadays they're it calling dark matter—it's all the stuff in between all other stuff. In astrology we look upon Scorpio as the energy of creativity, the yearning to break free of all limitation and bring the impossible to the real. Therefore, Scorpio rules the courage to be alone in the darkness, to fly a one-person spaceship with no companion but a computer, to circle the moons of Pluto and look back at the Earth with wonder and awe but no regrets. Scorpio is the thrill of being able to hang out fearlessly where no one else even dares to go. This is the essence of the scientist, the artist, the physician, the artisan—anyone who experiences the yearning to experience the Void. How else could a surgeon take a knife, watch the blood ooze, and courageously hold a life in their hand with the hope and knowledge that at the end of the operation the patient would be healed?

Scorpio is Picasso's ability to shatter the aesthetic senses of the Western mind. It's the ability to transform waste into usable material. It's the imagination that sees how the methane found in manure can provide a source of motor power in the future. It's the ability to look undaunted upon wreckage floating in the water after a devastating flood, move forward, and rebuild a devastated city that, once reborn, can be better than it ever was.

Now let's be real. More often than not, Scorpio is the frustration you feel when you're not getting enough nookie. Male or female, if you're a Scorpio your puberty starts not in adolescence but more likely in utero, because you are conscious of your sex organs (and everybody else's) long before you've got hair down there. If your emotional development has been healthy and relatively normal, you'll outgrow your fascination with orifices and appendages and go on to have a relatively normal life—still full of desire, but able to maintain relationships, have jobs, kids, and friends, and stay out of jail. You'll always be interested in sex, but not necessarily sex-crazed. So many Scorpios have to put on this daytime exterior, mainly because if they ever were to reveal how overinvolved they were with their own pee-pees they'd be sent to a nut house. The thing about being a Scorpio is: You are not like happy little Mr. and Mrs. Next Door who come out smiling every morning like figures in an old-time cuckoo clock. Somewhere along your DNA chain there's a gene for caffeine, or some other substance that heightens and intensifies your yearning for experience. Thirst is a good word for it, a thirst that is unquenchable. It drives you across the desert toward some distant oasis where you drink and drink and drink and then, for some unknown reason, you push on again into the desert.

Not that you can't stand to be satisfied or happy, but you seem to prefer to wander between saturation and desperation. That is why you walk away from situations that leave friends, family, and shrinks scratching their heads in puzzlement and dismay. Why would you turn your back on good, solid, stable, secure situations and slink off into the night?

As attracted as you are to material stability, it's more important for you to prove you will never be owned by money or the people who have it. In that sense you're like a bat that flies by sensors, zooming close to people's hair but never really getting caught in it. As civilized or social-climbing as you can be, you're prehistoric, primitive—brilliantly designed to live in a world full of scary predators who learn pretty quickly not to fuck with you. You're actually a peaceful sort as long as you are left alone to pursue your life of creating, earning money, getting laid, and when you have to, scavenging the couch for pennies or the garbage for the slice of rye bread you mistakenly threw away.

You are consummately seductive. Most often you use your powers to sell whatever products or services you are offering, but obviously there are a few unevolved Scorpios who devote their lives to screwing other people, cheating them, suing them, using Mafia tactics if need be, but not necessarily raping and killing and all the crazy things people think all Scorpios are mixed up in. Although you have your own idea of survival ethics that has absolutely nothing to do with the Bible or the Koran or any code other than your own, you are a highly principled individual with a pretty powerful set of moral standards.

Do parents, teachers, school, and church mess up your sexuality, or are they necessary checks and balances against a libidinous nature that compels you to pillage and forage to fulfill unfulfillable desires? That's between you, your clergy, your shrink, and your own conscience. For Scorpios there are as many types of sexual behavior as there are spermatazoa in a pint of male ejaculate. You've got everything from the celibate, austere, never-had-an-orgasm-in-recorded-memory type all the way to the I-had-six-guys (or was it seven)-yesterday-afternoon-and-it-was-great type. So it's impossible to categorize all Scorpios with regard to their sexual behavior or preference. As has already been stated, much of your sexual life depends on the emotional health of the home you grew up in and the sex education you received. If you were taught that sex is a healthy part of life, you're likely to live a relatively contented existence in a relationship; you could even be anonymous. Freudian slip—that was supposed to be monogamous. Even if you do stray once in a while and have a dalliance or two, it means nothing. It doesn't count. It didn't even happen. God forbid, however, that you even catch a whiff of suspicion with regard to the behavior of your significant other. Catch him or her even smiling too long at the person who brings your drinks at the restaurant, and you'll haunt both people for twenty years after you die. Even if you're pretty normal sexually, you still have strong surges of jealousy and suspicion that could cause you to start rifling through someone's belongings in search of incriminating evidence of their betrayal or treachery. That's something you absolutely have to grow out of if you're going to have a decent private or even public life.

If you had a totally whacked out sex education, it's going to be tougher for you to integrate your nature with society. You're either going to be very repressed, which means in a really bad mood most of the time, or carrying on in secret, away from prying eyes, away from everyone in your life, including not only your business associates, but even the people you live with—especially the people you live with. If you were raised in a home where sex didn't or wasn't supposed to exist, you'll tend to recreate the same sort of environment in the home you set up as an adult.

A controversy exists about whether or not sexual desire can be sublimated, displaced, and redirected into other channels such as creativity, research, or work. Some say yes. Others claim that the most creative individuals do not suppress their natural desires, and that is why innovators, explorers, and artists often lead such mad, intense lives. You are looking for a mad, intense high all the time. Maybe that's why you're more into pork futures than blue chip stocks, why you'll take on a job other people dump, and why your car usually has two wheels hanging over the edge of the Grand Canyon. Or you get hooked on crack, diet pills, and double espresso.

Desire, they say, is the source of attachment, and attachment leads only to sorrow. What's a poor Scorpio to do? Yours is a soul of yearning, living to die and dying to live. You bring yourself to the point of obliteration, then fight to come back. You plant flowers, tend them until they bloom, then fly over the house and unload an H-bomb on the whole shebang. Life and death—you are the third one of the triplets. Death is something you've come into contact with from an early age. You know it. You understood it at five when you saw a dog get run over by a motor-cycle. Nobody had to explain what it meant when Grandma died. For you, she didn't go bye-bye. She died. Kaput. Maybe went to Heaven or something, but you always knew Grandma wasn't at the store or on vaca-tion. You knew what death was. It didn't scare you then and it doesn't scare you now. That's why you can indulge yourself, take such business risks, go down into the Valley of the Lepers with bagels and coffee, dive into shark-infested waters just for the fun of it—not even to search for lost treasure. It's not the lost Spanish gold from a sunken galleon you're actually looking for. It's one more experience in the unknown that gives you the rush.

Only a Scorpio would get a bang out of being able to pass death and wave "hi" as casually as you would greet a neighbor you run into in the cereal aisle of your local supermarket.

Of course, that makes you powerful and magnetic. You're both attrac-tive and repulsive to many people because they perceive you as thrilling but dangerous, as irresistible as a naked model lying spread-legged on satin sheets, and as taboo as a man with TB coughing and spitting in their face. How you put these qualities into your personal crucible will deter-mine your direction, productivity, prosperity, and future. And when you look at someone with those eyes of yours, all they can do is call up their mother and say good-bye.

Your destiny is determined by how you deal with the fact that your father ran off with the lady whose washing machine he was supposed to be fixing, your mother was a total loony, or the priest messed with you when you were twelve. Scorpio is all about magic. Nobody nobody no-body can predict how you will mix the colors on the palette. Magic, real magic, is transformation that is manifested beyond anything empirical science can do. There's something in you, who knows what it is, that pos-sesses the power of healing. No bullshit. You have it. Granted, you waste half your time looking at other people's asses, but you own a power other people do not have. Your last-minute secret choices create what has never been created before and could not be copied or reproduced by anyone else. Ever.

There's an odd uniqueness in the way you combine ingredients in your recipe and no one can totally figure it out. It comes from deep within. It's a stirring. It's the "thingie" that causes an erection, surrender, union, penetration, ejaculation, the secret rendezvous of sperm and egg. Shh. We shouldn't be watching. For some it's the voyeuristic thrill of porn. For others it's that moment no one can yet explain or describe. Dark thoughts? You could be sitting down to an elegant breakfast on a terrace overlooking the Mediterranean on a beautiful morning, and right away you'll imagine what your mangled body would look like if you fell off the railing.

What causes life to arise? Fertilization, of course. But what caused fertilization? Desire.

Desire. That is Scorpio.

You've had a lot of incarnations in this one lifetime, because you live through one crisis, conquer it by totally immersing yourself in it, and then when it's over, you shed it like a snake sheds its skin. You then move on to new territory, like an explorer or a locust, depending on whether you have a thirst for experience or a raw desire to devour whatever you touch.

So how can you use your magnetism and your higher faculties to achieve your creative goal? What are the forces that drag you backward and keep you from reaching the highest manifestation of your Sun? And what are the energies that can support you, guide you, enhance your positive qualities, and make your Sun shine bright? The fact is you're not just a Scorpio. There is another energy operating, one that either cuts across your efforts and undermines them, or spirits you to heights of joy and fulfillment. That energy depends not on the month you were born, but the year as well. Later on in this book the technical aspects will be explained more fully. We'll examine how you waste time chasing your own tail, why you do it, and how to pull yourself out of self-destructive obsessions and put yourself back on the road to success. But for now, check out the following table. Find your birth year and note the number beside it. Then read the appropriate section.

Year–No.	Year–No.	Year–No.	Year–No.	Year–No.
1901–7	1928–2	1955–8	1982–3	2007–11
1902–6	1929–1	1956–8 until	1983–2	2008–10
1903–6	1930–12	10/30, then	1984–1	2009–9
1904–5	1931–12	7	1985–1	2010–9
1905–4	1932–11	1957–7	1986–12	2011–8
1906–4	1933–10	1958–6	1987–12 until	2012–7
1907–3	1934–10	1959–6	11/9,	2013–7
1908–2	1935–9	1960–5	then 11	2014–6
1909–2	1936–8	1961–4	1988–11	2015–5
1910–1	1937–8	1962–4	1989–10	2016–5
1911–1 until	1938–7	1963–3	1990–10	2017–4
11/8,	1939–6	1964–2	1991–9	2018–4 until
then 12	1940–6	1965–2	1992–8	1/16, then 3
1912–12	1941–5	1966–1	1993–8	2019–3
1913–11	1942–5 until	1967–12	1994–7	2020–2
1914–11	11/15,	1968–12	1995–6	2021–2
1915–10	then 4	1969–11	1996–6	2022–1
1916–9	1943–4	1970–10	1997–5	2023–12
1917–9	1944–3	1971–10	1998–4	2024–12
1918–8	1945–3	1972–9	1999–4	2025–11
1919–7	1946–2	1973–9	2000–3	2026–10
1920–7	1947–1	1974–8	2001–3 until	2027–10
1921–6	1948–1	1975–7	10/25,	2028–9
1922–5	1949–12	1976–7	then 2	2029–8
1923–5	1950–11	1977–6	2002–2	2030–8
1924–4	1951–11	1978–5	2003–1	
1925–3	1952–10	1979–5	2004–1	
1926–3	1953–9	1980–4	2005–12	
1927–2	1954–9	1981–3	2006–11	

Scorpio 1

If you didn't die five minutes after you were born or five minutes ago
there's a good chance you're going to be around for some time and could

have a nice life. Healthy or happy we can't say, mainly because so many Scorpios do such horrendous things to their bodies in their madcap youth that their later life is spent paying for it. Maybe it's just because you're not only a Scorpio, you're such a Scorpio that when look back on your life, it could make the Minotaur's labyrinth look like a walk through Wal-Mart on a Sunday, minus the savings. Of course, that seems normal for you, and you can't figure out why everybody around you is gasping as if they were watching some maniac with a blindfold over his eyes driving the Indy 500. As far as you're concerned, you're driving on the right side of the road, so what's the problem? Right side of the road, maybe, but you're in England, for Pete's sake. Above all people and above all Scorpios you have the power to achieve good and stamp out evil or lead Darth Vader back to the dark side, just when he was about to turn good.

You're a born sorcerer, witch, or magician—no lie. From school age you've always had more power in your little pinky than all the wands at Hogwarts. Have you abused it? Of course you have. What Scorpio in your position hasn't had to resort to manipulation of one sort or another in order to survive? And surviving in the jungle has been your big thing, seeing as how you were raised in your family's version of Jurassic Park. If you've become so hooked on survival that prosperity is an impossible concept to wrap your head around, then you will never be happy unless you are fighting, even when you don't have to. This makes it very hard on the people who want to love and support you. Biting the hand that feeds you puts a big damper on cozy closeness, and in fact there are moments when loved ones better stay away if they don't want to lose an arm. This isn't to say that you can't become socialized. It's just that it takes effort to be in society because you are so into your own survival head so much of the time. Once you learn good table manners you can definitely get dressed up and sit next to the ambassador of El Cuspador and snow the pants right off him. Deep down you're more relaxed when you're back at home where no one can see you, in your underwear and scratching your butt. Your intensely active imagination and keen senses are on 24/7, which makes you not only prolific and creative and totally driven, but completely aware of whom to trust and whom to get rid of. Once in a while the x-ray radar inside your head goes on the blink and you make a huge blunder, get yourself in a pickle that ends up costing you a near mint, but you can be happy to know that the other person will have to spend a few years picking your quills out of their hair.

People don't get over Scorpios all that easily. Bottom line: You need privacy and alone time, if for no other reason than to pick your own scabs in solitude and power down to get ready for your next encounter. You need people to anchor and ground you and demand that you emerge from your cave to participate. Relationships are your main source of revenue and prosperity. Despite issues of infidelity, which will undoubtedly interfere with marital bliss, in the end loyalty must prevail.

At this point you need to probe more deeply into your obsession with yourself, physically and emotionally, to the point that you have trouble letting anybody near you. In the next part, Going Deeper, reading the chapters called "Independence" and "Sex" will give you a chance to pass through the illusion of fear of being controlled by another person, and on to a higher expression of your Scorpio nature that will help you develop your creativity, be a better business person, open yourself up to more prosperous social relationships, and make your Sun shine bright.

> ★ *Celebrities Who Share Your Issues*
> *Kevin Kline, Emily Post, Roy Rogers, Prince Charles,*
> *Grace Kelly, Hillary Rodham Clinton, Richard Dreyfuss*

Scorpio 2

Some Scorpios are money mad. They have to sign all the checks, keep track of every cent spent, always always always control all financial arrangements, and then lose $500 out of their wallet or purse and have absolutely no idea where it went or what could have happened to it. It's the inconsistency that's so crazy-making for others. There's a huge irrational component in your attitude toward money and prosperity that can probably be traced back to a rather screwy set of values drummed into your head before you could speak. There's a whole ethos about family and money and the scariness of being poor, marrying for security reasons, and a host of other beliefs and prejudices you can't get out of your mind. They are in fact fixations that drive you to acquire more and more, which does nothing whatsoever to lessen your feeling that you don't have enough to live on. When is enough enough? How many bowls of spaghetti Bolognese can fill an empty stomach? The answer: No amount can fill a stomach that always feels empty. You're not always obsessing about the enormous wealth you could have had. On the contrary, you can certainly enjoy a glass of Perrier or fresh-squeezed OJ or Moët & Chandon Champagne. It's when there's only half a glass remaining that you start to get nuts. There's no need for you to feel put down, or inadequate just because you're not always able to do handle all your money issues alone. You weren't meant to, even if it spooks you to think you have to be dependent on your family money, mate's salary, or even federal assistance.

Financial support is a gift allowing you to develop talents or appreciate what other people can give you—learn to accept that support. You need to learn how to thank the people who make your life possible, not resent them because the financial area is one you really don't control. You're a lucky, lucky Scorpio equipped with sexiness and magnetism that needs to be more fully developed in this lifetime. Not only can you live (and should you live) as an artist, researcher, or soldier of your own fortune, but your healing and sexual powers cannot be overlooked. In fact, you will find yourself sometimes involved emotionally or sexually with individuals who are insecure about their masculinity or femininity or somehow just have issues with sex in general. Luckily you don't have those issues—once you fully acknowledge what a truly sexual being you are. In fact, sexual healing is not just the job of some dedicated prostitutes or therapists. You'd be surprised how much of it goes on, unspoken and unacknowledged, in bedrooms across the world. And though it will take guts, honest sexual communication will—must—win out in your life. So if you like to talk during sex, by all means go for it.

At this point you need to probe more deeply into your own issues about being filthy rich and retaining your moral integrity. In the next part, Going Deeper, reading the chapters called "Money" and "Religion" will give you a chance to pass through the illusion of fear of being financially dependent, and on to a higher expression of your Scorpio nature that will help you be freer emotionally and creatively, and make your Sun shine bright.

Celebrities Who Share Your Issues
Pat Sajak, Goldie Hawn, Maria Shriver, Laura Bush,
Michel Gauquelin, Charles de Gaulle

Scorpio 3

Good fences make good neighbors. Good call, but so much of the time for one reason or another you don't get to keep such strict and healthy boundaries. Because you have a yearning to get closer to siblings from whom you are alienated (even if you never had any), you get involved or overinvolved with people near you. What you think at first is going to be a wonderful opportunity turns out not only to be a bust, but to have the potential to damage your reputation. You lose perspective. You get all wound up and wrapped up with people who are actually needier than you are—more grasping, cunning, manipulative, and social climbing than you could ever be, and before you know it, you're enmeshed. Big time.

And you knew it—or at least suspected it all the time.

If you have trouble seeing that pattern in your life, just pull out your little black book, the one that lists all the names of the people you either are not talking to now or shouldn't have been talking to then and turn to pages 1982 or 2001. Anything interesting turn up? Of course it has.

You can get totally hot and heavy with people, talk to them five times a day and then, the betrayal! From that point on you never speak to them again, and you cut their faces out of the photos in your album. Happens between siblings and associates all the time. It's your old friend communication talking. Or rather not talking. Sometimes you have to move far away, not just to run away from people who refuse to recognize you or refuse to hear or accept you, but because when you make the effort to separate yourself from petty enmeshments and false relationships, your lifestyle improves. You may have to make a gigantic effort to find the home and security you want abroad, but it is there waiting for you. If you don't become a total religious convert or expatriate, you will eventually seek relationships with people of different ethnic backgrounds. It will reaffirm your faith in family togetherness, even though family togetherness, one of your dreams, also makes you nervous. You can play at it and enjoy it as long as it is in the distance.

Your dilemma is like that of the kid who takes junior year abroad, adapts to a new family, learns a new language, and finds happiness at last. The inevitable happens, though. Eventually communication problems arise, and he has to face the politics of relationships and the frustration of once again becoming involved in misunderstanding, painful silences of avoidance, and cut-off connections.

You still crave validation. Maybe that's why you are such a master of communication. Your real education won't come early. You eventually have to find your home-away-from-home, and to be fully evolved, fall for a sweaty ethnic someplace where you can't speak the language.

At this point you need to probe more deeply into your obsession with being validated and honored by people you feel have betrayed you, to the point that you get mixed up with individuals you should never have gotten mixed up with in the first place, especially if your career is involved. In the next part, Going Deeper, reading the chapters called "Recognition" and "Communication" will give you a chance to pass through the illusion of being taken advantage of and then dumped by people who won't listen to you, and on to a higher expression of your Scorpio nature that will help you connect better when you reach out, develop better boundaries, find the home you are really looking for, and make your Sun shine bright.

> *Celebrities Who Share Your Issues*
> *Marla Maples, Lorne Michaels, Danny DeVito, Rock Hudson,*
> *Robert Kennedy, Richard Burton, John Keats, Lauren Holly*

Scorpio 4

You look at a photo of the family members together and at first they all look pretty normal. Then the belching and the heartburn flare up when you look a little deeper into the picture and start remembering what really happened way back when. Just thinking of what went on there causes Vesuvius to erupt in your tummy. Despite all your efforts to the contrary, do you think that the domestic scene you have today is all that different? There may still be one parent absent, a place missing at the dinner table that everybody notices and nobody talks about. Somebody is out. It can't really be called a madhouse, exactly. In fact, you probably put a lot of energy into restoring order and sanity to the scene, just to take the edge off a deep nervousness that can sometimes be overwhelming. It's a feeling that at any minute a volcano might erupt. That's your childhood calling. How peculiar you never knew from one day to the next, or one minute to the next, what blast would go off. You would be so hooked on domestic uncertainty—yet you go to such Byzantine lengths to reproduce such a crazy scene. It's absolutely unbelievable.

But don't take it so hard. We all do similar things. We get addicted to situations to which we were introduced in early life. As full of rage as you feel toward the people who were supposed to take care of you and didn't, you're still very attached to them. So here's the thing: Since it's got to dawn on you sooner or later that on some level you are emotionally upset all the time, you can either give up your entire life and stay home with all the doors and windows locked, or you can step out into the world and meet your destiny, which is to become successful and respected in any field you choose. Actually, there's no choice involved. You have to do it. It makes you nervous to have something of your own you've become great at, because, oh my God, if you're successful you won't have a family or personal life to come home to and you'll be all alone with no one to take care of little you. Get this: That lost little kid ain't never gonna grow up. The side of you that is brilliant, creative, an excellent parent, and a born leader must always be on top right there for everyone to see. Your childhood never leaves you. Never leaves any of us. You, however, can leave it. Must leave it. Will leave it. Even if you choose to live beside Mt. Vesuvius, just to satisfy your old longing to put yourself at risk, you still have to develop a powerful coping mechanism, the one that adults are supposed to provide children to keep them from feeling unsafe.

You have to play a role of a president in midst of a personal crisis. The trick is to overcome the conflicts stemming from your rather chaotic background and be able to compete, perform, direct, and produce no matter who abandoned you thirty years ago or last Saturday night.

At this point you need to probe more deeply into your issues about being overthrown just when you're getting to the top or screwing it up yourself for personal reasons. In the next part, Going Deeper, reading the chapters called "Security" and "Freedom" will give you a chance to pass through the illusion of fear of being abandoned, and on to a higher expression of your Scorpio nature that will help you establish yourself professionally, develop your abilities as a performer and leader in your field, have healthier family values, and make your Sun shine bright.

> *Celebrities Who Share Your Issues*
> *Shere Hite, Lauren Hutton, Nadia Comaneci, Demi Moore,*
> *Billie Jean King, Martin Scorsese, Peter Jackson*

Scorpio 5

Could this be a tear-jerking soap opera or what?! And yet none of it is real. But of course it's real. Heartbreak is not just a comic-book emotion. And God knows you have had quite a dose from seventh grade right on up to your last frantic encounter. Maybe it's not all as tragic and dramatic as the last scene in *Streetcar,* but it sure has its own irony. Just think back, and you'll see how sharply the Universe slaps you in the face when you become too attached to any love object, or when you get too grandiose and think you're really hot stuff. There is something kind of royal about you, but it's more like fallen royalty—you are like someone who flaunts who they because they're not totally proud of who they are.

You're a very private person, and to have your dirty laundry dragged into public can be a crippling thing. That's the weird thing. Part of you is so desperate for attention, you can become positively exhibitionistic, and as private as you are, you could do it in the nude in Macy's window when you're high enough.

And you have gotten pretty high in your life. That's when you lose a lot of your inhibitions and carry on in the most outrageous ways. If it's on stage or you're in a sweaty artistic mood, your juices flow and the production is music sent straight to you from another place. Your "love life," however, can be insatiable, deviant, and self-destructively chaotic. Overkill with booze and drugs is bad for anybody, but you've got to be especially careful. Your mind-altering phase, when it is not directed creatively, can be pretty darned inappropriate, as off the scale as a teenager's first binge. Is it just a romantic streak you can't shake? It's that, too, but it's the four-hankie melodrama that gets tiresome as you get older.

You've got to make special efforts to cut down on your binges of romance and/or self-pity about loss, spruce yourself up, take a shower, splash some cold water on your face to stiffen your upper lip, and be sober enough to appreciate the opportunities you've been given. Then you can do something really important, and perform some special service that inspires other people, makes them laugh, or eases their burden of sorrow. There are moments when you're so angry and feeling so deprived that such a contribution seems pitifully meaningless, because your heart is still full of love and hope and seeking to fight despair. The trick is to be able to turn your heightened emotions toward some greater good.

At this point you need to probe more deeply into your obsession with being a glamorous object of everyone's attention. In the next part, Going Deeper, reading the chapters called "Love" and "Escape" will give you a chance to pass through the illusion of being mistreated and calling it love, and on to a higher expression of your Scorpio nature that will help you perform on the highest level, remember you are a servant of humanity, and make your Sun shine bright.

> **Celebrities Who Share Your Issues**
> Art Garfunkel, Christiaan Barnard, Larry Flynt, Charles Bronson, Marie Curie, Marie Antoinette, Roy Lichtenstein, Kurt Vonnegut, Ken Wahl

Scorpio 6

God help anybody who is napping on the lawn you're mowing. You're definitely a dynamo when it comes to focusing on any task you've got to complete. You and the lawn mower become one. Even the Hulk would cower in awe to see how you can gather your forces and move through any obstacle, tirelessly, eyes wide open, exhausted or sick. When you've got a job to do, you show no weakness, and project the invincibility of some futuristic machine that has no visible working parts and never wears down. That's possibly because you do have some congenital or genetic weakness that you are totally defensive about and determined to prove will *not* knock you down. Your macho affect is impressive, mainly because it's not just an act. You actually are a killer worker, especially when you're working alone and competing against yourself. And no matter how you attempt to destroy your body, which you usually try to do, you take some pleasure in repairing it shortly before it collapses completely so nobody gets even a hint of your frailty.

Your personal evolution, on the other hand, demands that you stop working and force yourself to let go of the ferocious hold you have on life, long enough to be held and enveloped in an intimate embrace, something that scares the living bejesus out of you. You need to be able to take your little secret forays and vacations into intimacy. If you insist on being all alone all the time, working to prove you don't need anyone's help, you'll be begging for someone to help you out of bed or to the hospital, because you've gone and worn yourself down to a nub. Your secret to success lies in intimacy and loving relationships, even if many of them are clandestine. It's hard for you to allow yourself to be taken away from your single life or your singular working life long enough to enjoy the ecstasy that only human contact can provide. Surrendering and submitting yourself in trust will lift you from a boring life, chained to the daily grind. This is not about religion, it's about a spiritual awakening that liberates you from all anxiety, overburdened responsibilities, and the fear of making mistakes. Putting your hands into the hands of the Infinite is the answer, although it's a tough path to follow.

At this point you need to probe more deeply into your obsession with running the whole show, to the point that it impedes your enjoyment of personal relationships. In the next part, Going Deeper, by reading the chapters called "Control" and "Independence" you'll get a chance to pass through the illusion of the fear of obsolescence, and on to a higher expression of your Scorpio nature, where you can be both professionally productive and personally happy, and make your Sun shine bright.

> ★ *Celebrities Who Share Your Issues*
> *John Cleese, Grace Slick, Roy Campanella, Rodney Dangerfield,*
> *Jamie Lee Curtis, Sam Waterston*

Scorpio 7

It's what sent the knights of old out seeking the fair damsel in distress. It's what young girls used to dream about in home economics class, finding the rich, charming prince whose every need they could meet. All fairy tales. Where have all the Lancelots gone? Have all the Cinderellas ended up in divorce court in a wicked alimony fight? The answer is no, although a lot of Scorpio Lancelots and Cinderellas think they made bad choices and ended up either alone or worse for the financial wear, especially if they made the mistake of hooking up because they thought they'd never have to worry about money again. You have to see your history of relationships as a series of lessons. What you first thought was a rare diamond (figuratively speaking) when you were young and romantic (or stupid) turned out to be something you wouldn't even buy off the TV for $19.95. But let's not forget that you weren't the innocent victim either. So you bit into a roast beef sandwich and broke a tooth. Is that a reason to become a vegetarian? You're the one who thought you needed somebody to make your life easier financially. And you probably still do.

You're probably still just as driven to find your soul mate as you are to drive them away because they'll drain you of all your resources, take you for everything you've got, and then dump you. Money again. Why does money always slip in and screw up your dreams of having a happy relationship in which money wouldn't always be a specter hanging over you? You could have a very happy relationship if for five minutes a day you would stop thinking about being cheated and focus more on the fact that you're a lucky son of a gun. You've got the benefit of freedom and good health. You're bursting with creative juices, and Lord knows you can be a hot number in the sack when you're not watching the other person's reaction.

So why do you think everybody will end up walking out on you or dying? Actually they don't. You've had your turn at rejecting people, so don't play the I'm-such-a-nice-person-why-am-I-alone bit. You're so accustomed to supporting people (and resenting them for it) that you treat everyone as if they were a gold-digging bleached-blond hussy or a hustler pool boy, which on a lonely Saturday night isn't always such a bad idea. But you don't want to live that sort of seamy, sordid life. You want a real partner, not somebody who is constantly on the verge of caving in like a sinkhole. Can you give up control, and accept and enjoy someone who is healthy, strong, and prosperous? Or do you have to carry on with a totally dependent person or swear off every relationship except those hired by the hour? Have you ever found yourself turning your back on healthy, successful individuals in order to hook up with broken people who turn to you to be fixed? You want to be able to portray good, solid, apple-pie values, but unless you can handle the kinds of people you're invariably attracted to, that's all it will be: a portrayal. Coping with your attractions means getting over a fixation on the parent of the opposite sex. This love/hate, anger/abandonment attachment thing can prejudice you and twist you around emotionally so that you turn another person into that parent and then run away from them because they are like the parent you've turned them into. Going to bed alone is no fun when you're looking for a real partner, and a real partner is always possible.

• • •

At this point you need to probe more deeply into your issues about being drained by other people. In the next part, Going Deeper, reading the chapters called "Marriage" and "Money" will give you a chance to pass through the illusion of fear of being ripped off, and on to a higher expression of your Scorpio nature that will help you develop and maintain healthier relationships without having to give up your whole life completely, and make your Sun shine bright.

> ★ *Celebrities Who Share Your Issues*
> *Reza Pahlevi, Helen Reddy, André Malraux, Lyle Lovett, Stan Musial*

Scorpio 8

As loyal and ardent as you are, you have odd notions about sex that don't always include monogamy. You have problems communicating in that area, and are very sensitive to any kink in your performance. You have to get over some really bad exposure to sex when you were younger. Very poor communication about sex could have arrested your development, even traumatized you, but let's not be so quick to blame Uncle Bernie or Father Flanagan or that weird lady you used to call Ma. Some Scorpios come into this life with a well-balanced, healthy sort of confidence about their gender, sexual orientation, and genitalia. The ones who don't, get fixated on their privates and, forget about it! that's all they can think of or talk about. Because of arrested development, their sexual activity is fetishistic, narcissistic, repetitive, and ultimately unfulfilling. They don't use sex as a form of intimate communication. It's more like a three-minute phone call.

You've got some big choices to make. You could obsessively turn yourself into a sex symbol to convince everybody (including yourself) that you are a desirable human being, or you can become a prolific artist or performer or hugely financially successful person in whatever field you choose.

Whatever wild indiscretions you perform, you still come to the same place. The most profound and consciousness-raising relationships and collaborations in your life will mostly be nonsexual. Not that you won't always on some level be a slavering red-eyed wolf breathing in the scent of a nearby little pink rabbit, because part of you will always be just that. That's why you'd better not pin any scarlet letters on any sinner you happen to be judging. You're capable of everything you accuse other people of actually doing. In fact, the source of your possessiveness is sexual insecurity, and that is where you diverge from more confident, well-balanced Scorpios. You either writhe around in the muck of prurience or renounce sex altogether and live a life of abstinence and penance. Usually you do both in an on-again-off-again sort of way.

When you get off the genital obsession kick, your life finally takes off. You produce prodigiously and begin tapping into the enormous wealth and prosperity you are destined to enjoy. What drags you down time and again is the issue of poor or nonexistent communication. You fear exposure and what will happen to you if anyone got wind of your other self. Would there be prejudice against you? Would your image be soiled? Could you lose your position? Is the minister with the stash of porn videos a hypocrite—is he just working out his issues? Is the artist who sells his work for big money just a filthy capitalist in disguise—or is he prudently blending his obsessive need to communicate to the world with a practical sense of how to live in it? Certainly a balance is preferable.

At this point you need to probe more deeply into your issues about being desirable and afraid of selling out to commercialism, to the point that you act dumb in business to your own detriment. In the next part, Going Deeper, reading the chapters called "Sex" and "Communication" will give you a chance to pass through the illusion of fear of being rejected and judged for your body or performance, and on to a higher expression of your Scorpio nature that will help you gain confidence in communicating your issues, become wealthy and prosperous without tossing it away, and make your Sun shine bright.

★ Celebrities Who Share Your Issues
Billy Graham, Bill Gates, Ethel Waters, Art Carney, Joaquin Phoenix, Margaret Mitchell, Pablo Picasso, Leonardo DiCaprio

Scorpio 9

Sometimes you're steel, sometimes you're mush. Even if you weren't born that way, you're a psychological half-breed. You are always attracted to the exotic. How can you be such a responsible, mature adult who can always be counted on to show up, and be a flight risk at the same time? Maybe it's because you are so down-to-Earth and responsible that you are always thinking that if you move to California, Rome, or Bangkok, your life will be better, happier, and safer. Your search for an ideal geographical place to call home will probably lead you far from your birthplace. Yours is a philosophical dilemma that stems from an abstract concept developed in your mind and from your attachment to a racial or ethnic ideal. You're so idealistic that you are bound to be crushed when your beliefs in laws and traditions that are supposed to protect people turn out to enslave them instead. Could this be about the Motherland? Mother church? Or could it be a more abstract idea of what a mother is supposed to be?

Mother is an abstract concept that comes down to you from generation to generation. It is taught in school, church, and the society into which you were born. You both embrace and reject those traditional values at the same time. You will most likely find someone to fall in love with whose holiday meals are totally unlike the ones you have known in childhood. At first you can embrace someone else's culture, a culture you think is perfect. It will lead you to disillusion if you idealize, ape, or adopt a way of life that is ultimately not your own. It's a sort of ethnic conversion you undertake in your relationships. You can even search for a geographical place to find your personal Shangri-la. You could even be a traitor to a culture you can no longer accept because of its fraudulent claims to protect people when it is actually starving people of what they really need.

Is this all as philosophically highfalutin as it sounds, or is it just that you're still caught between your attachment to your mother and your need to run away from an overactive sense of responsibility toward her? You've definitely got a few ethnopsychological issues and unresolved conflicts about the roles of men and women in society based largely on religious/ethnic traditions. This is a rather tough nut to crack, because as intelligent, cultured, or accomplished as you get, you are still trying to find a way to escape the humdrum grind of mundane responsibilities. Your mind is active and curious, and once you find a balance between what you have to do and what you want to do, you will be master of your own fate. You will no longer think you are being dragged down by rules that a cold, unfeeling society has set up to squash the life and sensitivity out of you. Somewhere over that famous rainbow bluebirds may be flying, and you're on a quest to find that world where candy grows on trees. Behind the sun, step behind the rainbow, you'd be in your own version of Oz where people wouldn't be hassling you every five minutes for decisions. Where could you go—your country house for the weekend with no cell phone, fax, or laptop? They'd beam you a message from a satellite to whatever spot on the globe you'd run to, because there is no escape from contact. Nor should there be. Otherwise you'd get lost in the snows of Kilimanjaro.

Whether it's an image of the Virgin Mary or Diana the Moon Goddess, or the photo of your grandmother in her babushka that sits on top of the piano, you can get very hung up on a force you think is keeping you sane, when in fact, if you're waiting for that image to smile on you, forget it. You have to return to your real life, which will always involve truth in communication.

At this point you need to probe more deeply into your issues about being in a personal setting or remaining professional, to the point that you have sometimes mixed up the two and gotten yourself into a mess. In the next part, Going Deeper, reading the chapters called "Security" and "Religion" will give you a chance to pass through the illusion of fear of abandonment and the avoidance of career, and on to a higher expression of your Scorpio nature that will help you establish a sounder psychological and emotional base, develop yourself more soundly on a career basis, and make your Sun shine bright.

Celebrities Who Share Your Issues
Walter Cronkite, Condoleezza Rice, Leon Trotsky,
Adam Ant, Toni Collette

Scorpio 10

Well, you won't go unnoticed. That's for damned sure. They'll definitely know who you are, but with your luck, some people will *not* love you at all. But you will be noticed. Don't think for a moment, however, that they're going to be running through the streets tossing palm fronds on your path or that they'll there with the laurel wreath for your coronation. Because they won't be. Oh, you'll get noticed all right, but not always the way you want to be noticed. In fact that's the weird aspect of the whole thing. You'd have to decide if you don't care what they say as long as they say something. The fact is, you can be disappointed if you maintain too high an expectation about how you are going to be received in the world. It's understandable, though. You put your whole heart into something and make scads of personal sacrifices—like a happy home life, for example. And then all your efforts are shrugged off or even ignored, if not totally put down.

So no wonder you get pissed and desperate. It's kind of crazy to think you are supposed to be treated royally when your own opinion of yourself wobbles dangerously at times toward self-deprecation. The reason: Socially, you don't relate on a completely balanced level. You were raised as a little prince or princess, maybe by one segment of the family, and then completely ignored or beaten down by another. This gives you an inconsistent idea of your social worth. While on some level you are always looking to be idolized, you also expect to be maligned or ignored.

You have to contend with factors out of your control, too. In one stroke of political luck you could lose the main structure beam of your professional support, which leaves you at square one careerwise.

But not really. You're supposed to put something out there and then forget about it. Return home and furnish your country place, nurture your family, of course! That's the solution. Have people in. Steam some clams. Reconnect with family and turn away from the dirty world. But you can't always. When you're angry or discontented, and sincerely believe you're getting a raw deal, naturally you're not going to want to go belly up and start making sandwiches for the people who have insulted you and treated you unfairly. Your pride gets you in serious trouble sometimes because it's more bruisable than a tomato. Although retreat is sometimes its own form of valor, you're not one to run away howling like a cat after somebody has stepped on its tail.

This is where your punitive, vengeful side could mess you up. This is where you have to soften your response and not spit venom. These are the moments when you should step back, get out of the picture, retire to regroup, reseed your creativity, develop a more personal and private part of your life, let the dust settle, and then come back to triumph another day.

At this point you need to probe more deeply into your issues about being honored, revered, adored, and worshiped, to the point that no amount of success would satisfy you. In the next part, Going Deeper, reading the chapters called "Love" and "Recognition" will give you a chance to pass through the illusion of fear of being a nobody or just a regular person, and on to a higher expression of your Scorpio nature that will help you make a name for yourself in the world while building deeper, more intimate bonds with family, and make your Sun shine bright.

> ⭐ *Celebrities Who Share Your Issues*
> *Carl Sagan, Lou Ferrigno, Joseph Goebbels, Auguste Rodin,*
> *Claude Monet, Indira Gandhi* ⭐

Scorpio 11

A second marriage can be much better than the first, and it can be much better than any affair with a married person. Any relationship flourishes when you're not afraid of being close to people and are able to give yourself in an intimate commitment with less resistance and acting out and running away than you're prone to when you're younger. It can be a bit complicated, too, between your kids and their kids, your ex and their exes, but by and large it's your stubborn and childish refusal to be in a committed love relationship that causes so much hassle, especially when you're younger.

You just won't give over completely. You can't. Something in you is reluctant to go into deep water. You're so terrified of drowning, metaphorically speaking. As sex-oriented and romantic (in some cases either crazed or phobic) as you can be, you sometimes hang on for dear life to nonsexual, nonemotional associations and friendships with individuals who give you advice you will eventually be unable to follow. You cling to good, sound, sensible, practical, rational prescriptions to save yourself from your need to grow up and dive into the deep end of the emotional pool, and learn to swim. Oh, you'll still do it, though. You'll sit there in the health club juice bar and go on and on about how important it is to maintain your separateness and independence, and you'll be totally clear, detached, and utterly sane about the whole thing, and grateful to be away from a crying baby or demanding lover. It's such a relief to be away from it, just to say hello to your own mind for five minutes, and hang out with people who aren't sucking at you. Your recess cannot last very long, though, because after a while even if the cell phone doesn't ring, you'll feel the pull, like the ocean tugging at you. Okay, time's up. Back into the water. You're constantly bouncing between bravely allowing yourself to be controlled by emotional needs and responses (i.e., being undone by love) and holding on to control of your sanity. Loving deeply and fully does make you feel a little sick, not just mentally, but even physically. When you're guided by your heart and not your head, you can't be truly happy until you are united with your love object. This causes nausea, dizziness, disorientation, and a state of intoxication brought on with absolutely no drugs or alcohol. This is the feeling everybody wants to have until they have it. Then they spend all their time and energy trying to recover from it or avoid it completely.

You try to cook up all sorts of global let's-clean-the-environment-let's-heal-the-world goals in an effort to reduce the time you have to be three hundred feet underwater with a cloying intimacy anybody else would love to enjoy. So your goals must eventually turn more to the creative and personal and less toward global missions. Or at least you have to face the fact that sooner or later you're going to have to deal with an adolescent's needs—your own included.

At this point you need to probe more deeply into your obsession about not getting roped in and stuck with one person or kids who keep you from living your life, to the point that you deny yourself a whole life. In the next part, Going Deeper, reading the chapters called "Freedom" and

"Control" will give you a chance to pass through the illusion of fear of missing out on something, and on to a higher expression of your Scorpio nature that will help you keep your work in the world, be able to love more fully, and make your Sun shine bright.

Celebrities Who Share Your Issues
Matthew McConaughey, Vivien Leigh, Burt Lancaster,
Jonas Salk, Albert Camus, Fyodor Dostoevsky, Teddy Roosevelt,
Nicholas Culpepper, Serenity, Sean Combs

Scorpio 12

Everybody needs a break from the grinding routine once in a while. You can't just become a hack drone with no respite from carrying your heavy load. It's healthy to step away from your work, even from your whole life for a secret rendezvous. You need that forbidden moment. You need the thrill of escaping your image as a strong, tireless hero. You get in trouble when your tendency to chase after fantasy or impossible relationships takes you too far away from the path you are really destined to follow. You are vulnerable to these little jaunts to nowhere. You can't help falling to a magic reverie and create a whole story in your head about a relationship that will not now, nor could it ever, come to fruition. People who don't know you well would never believe how fragile you are emotionally and how quickly you give yourself away, sometimes to your own detriment. Just because you're a Scorpio, people think you're impenetrable, but in intimate situations, you can be a little too submissive too quickly.

The ecstasy found in someone else's arms is indescribable. Trite though it may seem, it feels like paradise to experience warm, intimate human contact. The embrace alone releases you from enormous tensions caused by your responsibilities in the workaday world. The fruit is even sweeter and juicier in a stolen moment of bliss, a secret rendezvous, a clandestine tryst, a momentary flight away from your normal life into the magic land of a fantasy relationship—there's just nothing like it, except maybe for a psychedelic drug.

That, of course, is the problem. In professional or personal life, such behavior can become as addictive as any stimulant or substance. You can become as hooked on the forbidden fruit or bad advice as any junkie on the street, and that's no exaggeration. Nobody will ever be able to say that you don't need your moments of intimacy, because you desperately do, and you deserve them. You haven't been put here on the Earth, however, only to kiss in the shadows and hide from the Moon. You have powerful opportunities and responsibilities that demand serious sobriety and clear attention to the details of work. In fact, it is your working responsibilities that will save you from a life of sloth, self-indulgence, and indigence. Your life, of course, is split between your fine, upstanding image as a productive worker, and the need you have for secret relationships, most of which go nowhere.

The more you can balance your working sobriety with your need for running away, the better all your relationships will be. It's hard, though. It's such a strain to sit there, chipping away at a task that will never be finished when you know how profoundly you need release. It's the same with food and diet and exercise. You know you should avoid the gooey carbs and go for the green veggies. You're not a fool. You know you'll feel better, look better, be more productive, and even probably live longer if you take better care of yourself.

At this point, you need to probe more deeply your obsession with human contact, to the point that it interferes with your work or even your health. In the next part, Going Deeper, reading the chapters called "Marriage" and "Escape" will give you a chance to pass through the illusion of loneliness, and on to the higher expression of your Scorpio nature, which will help you work more productively, get a strong handle on your need for relationships, and make your Sun shine bright.

Celebrities Who Share Your Issues
Dan Rather, Whoopi Goldberg, Doris Roberts, Julia Roberts,
Owen Wilson, Ike Turner, Barbara Hutton, Martin Luther, Vanilla Ice

SAGITTARIUS

November 22–December 21
Dates vary from year to year—consult your local astrologer

When a little girl falls into a well, or miners are trapped in a mine, and somebody comes along to yank them back into safety, you can be pretty sure a Sagittarius is nearby. Whatever force embodies the nick of time, you are it. But where are you? Certainly not stuck here, wherever we are. You're off somewhere standing amid the ruins of ancient Greece. Then it's Egypt. Or is it an Aztec temple? Now you're shopping in the marketplace of Marrakech. The scene switches. It's Calcutta. No, wait. It's the bar scene from *Star Wars*. Sometimes, however, you prefer to travel by Discovery Channel only. Sagittarius is by nature anthropology, archaeology, and science fiction all rolled into one, because it rules the limitless wanderings and possibilities of the human mind. Sagittarius is the manifestation of human intelligence and the heights that it can reach. The Sadge brain is way more than ganglia and neurons firing across synapses. Something divine creates inventiveness and understanding. We're not just talking about the invention of toasters, chewing gum, and snowboards. We're talking about the search for meaning. That is the source of the ceaseless Sagittarian yearning to travel and see all worlds to imagine, and to dream—not only to dream but to realize and live out dreams. What is just a cartoon-like figment of one person's imagination, for a Sagittarius, is absolute reality. To be able to grasp the mechanism and magic of what goes on behind the human mind is the essence of Sagittarius: what we think, how we think, and most important, why we think.

Waterslides on Mars—you think that's crazy? Not only possible. It will happen. Faster than light travel? Turn over in your grave, Mr. Einstein. It's going to happen, and the reason is simple: Sagittarius. Any bright idea that has ever occurred to a fool and eventually comes true we owe to Sadge. Sagittarius is the light bulb that appears over your head when you've just figured something out and exclaim, "Eureka!" The Sagittarian mind, when fully developed, is open to seeking solutions to problems considered absolutely unsolvable by normal people. You need to spend time lying on the grass at night, looking up at the stars, and just letting your mind wander and wonder. No restrictions. No doubts. No "Don't think that way—it's crazy, it's wrong." You have been born with the ability to see a beautiful building tomorrow where a hole is today, to figure out how to find the square root of 125,798.

Sadge is the place where the buffalo roam in thunderous herds, and the deer and the antelope play and frolic and graze with no fear of wolves or hunters' arrows. Sadge is the place you go where you never hear a discouraging word and skies are blue—not a drop of rain in the forecast. There's land. Lots of land. No fences of course, because there are no limits, no trespassers, everybody's in a good mood. It's a wagon train moving west in early America, settlers waving hello to the Sioux braves and the Sioux braves waving back. It's the urge to explore the next horizon and make friends with anybody on the way. Sadge is the spark of generosity that breeds prosperity. You don't mind giving away your last farthing, sou, nickel, or crust of bread, because you don't believe there is such a thing as "last." You know without being told that there's plenty more where that came from, that the Universe is a big, plentiful, bountiful river that has been created by somebody upstairs who likes us all, loves us all, wants us all to be happy and have a ball while we're here. Of course there's a higher power! Who could even think otherwise? Just take a look at Mount Everest or the Grand Canyon or the Amazon or anything else in this magical world. Belief? Of course it's a belief. Life can't exist without belief. Belief is the trust. It engenders kindness and morality. It's what makes runners run and racers race. It's the spirit of the game, for heaven's sake. If the mind can create it, it not only can be;

it is. Well, sure there's Jehovah, and Allah, and Wakatanka, and the Moon Goddess. They're all as real as anybody wants them to be. Everybody has a right to see the High Power however they want to. It's the natural instinct of man and woman to move toward the light, to seek out what is right and good and morally true, even if sometimes their visions of morality seem to be at odds. Ultimately we are all traveling the same road toward the same brilliant light of truth.

To be born in Sagittarius is to be blessed with an extra ounce of luck other people just don't have. Is it luck? Or is it the power of an innate belief that bad things don't really happen. Everything is a learning experience and whatever happens can be turned to the good. Whether it's luck or will, there is no disaster that can ever befall you from which you do not return richer, wiser, and just as full of the same spirit of adventure and good humor as before.

It's got to be luck, though. In addition to your unflaggingly positive attitude (which drives a lot of people crazy, by the way, who think you live your life in stupid, slap-happy denial), you do have a built-in get-out-of-jail-free card that has to be pure good fortune. Not that you don't get clobbered by life. Of course you do. But somehow life doesn't ever seem to get you. If the case is not totally thrown out of court, the sentence gets reduced. You somehow are always given your millionth second chance to behave, be good, change your ways, and reform.

Now let's be real. More often than not, Sadge is in full-fledged denial of any truth that hinders their right of way in the slightest. It's not that you are necessarily out and out crooked or dishonest. Many Sadges become lawyers, judges, philosophers, ministers, writers, thinkers, teachers, publishers, and any other profession that purports to distribute knowledge. Of course, Sagittarius has a reasonably high population of scammers, counterfeiters, and phony passport makers who get their jollies beating every system known to humankind. They have to figure out ways to fool the banks into giving them mortgages, get their parking tickets rescinded even though they deserved every one of them, beat every rap, and in one way or another squeeze their way of thinking into another person's mind. So you can just imagine the level of "mind-fucking" possible for a Sadge gone wrong. You have to be very vigilant about people screwing your head up as well as you screwing up theirs.

You can be an opinionated, flag-waving fanatic when your own views are being challenged, and that is what starts wars, religious and otherwise.

That's probably where many of your problems start, of course—in your childhood religion. Human beings seem to need some sort of moral code to live by, some set of ethics to guide them on their path. It has been demonstrated that children imbued with a good sense of right and wrong from an early age tend to get into much less trouble with the law and authorities in later life. But just whose sense of right and wrong is it going to be? Your sense of justice could be rich in wisdom, compassion, and insight, and yet completely oppose that of the local church or state authorities.

You don't really like the notion of "authorities." You often see yourself as higher than most authorities. Your way is the right way, no matter what the popes or the rabbis or the imams or the other Supreme Court judges say. You make an effort to listen to the views of others. You have to think deeply about what lies at the root of religious and civil laws in order to understand the reasoning behind them. You also have to try to understand what went on in the minds of the individuals who wrote them. The last thing you want to do is spew out garbage that has no basis in fact. And that, of course, is part of the problem.

Because you tend to want to look on the brighter side of every issue, you avoid the dark side, deny it, cram it away. You end up grinning, smiling, laughing, guffawing, and howling in an effort to avoid sides of yourself that are indeed downright scarily amoral. You turn into a bleeding hypocrite. You could end up spouting what you want to believe, but can't or don't practice. You continue talking hope in the face of the most convincing evidence to the contrary. But in the end who's to say you won't turn out to be right. Obviously breast cancer patients get healed. They survive to go on and live long and happy lives. Dwelling on a potentially tragic outcome certainly doesn't help. So where does brutal honesty leave off and stupid wide-eyed cockeyed optimism begin? If the police walk in and you're standing over the body with the smoking gun still in your hands, you could conceivably get away with the mistaken intruder defense. And the bootleg CDs in your trunk—planted? Perhaps. And you were in that seedy part of town at 3 AM because you're writing a book about illicit sex? Okay. Fine.

There's a mighty thin line between truth and "truth" as you perceive it. And as many deeply sincere seekers of truth that live in the house of Sagittarius, there are just as many liars and bullshitters and puffed up grandiose exaggerators who tell you they have a place in Malibu, California, when what they mean is that four cartons of their stuff are stashed in somebody's garage on the West Coast. It's not malicious. It's never malicious. Yours is by far the most heartfelt and good-natured of all the signs of the Zodiac. The fact is half of you is not only human, but divine. Your head is in the clouds because you are always looking toward heaven, toward a brighter tomorrow, to the moment when you'll be on vacation, not just to cruise the islands, but when you will be liberated from any and all restrictions and limitations. Part of you is a mind full of hope. The other half of you, however, is very much an animal. It's horny, shits where it wants when it wants, clops through the house in wet boots knocking over the glass and good china because it never looks where the hell it's going. You are, therefore, living a life between heaven and hell, between the joy of seeking the shelter of God and the hedonistic release of giving in to temptation. Maybe that's why you are perfectly suited to be a judge. You know all too well how sexy the devil's disciples can be. You've done business with them for years. You know corruption. You've waded through a swamp full of poisonous snakes. You've been in the muck. You know how graft, extortion, and Mafia tactics can reduce right-thinking people into bawling, crawling worms. You know first-hand just how hard it is to resist a tight, beautiful ass walking down the street, wiggling at you and beckoning you into an alley. You have a complete understanding of what it means to start out with a pocketful of dreams and the Scout pledge committed to memory and then to encounter the terrible price that is usually extracted of people who want to make those dreams come true. Sagittarius is symbolized by the struggle of young Michael Corleone when he returns to New York after WWII and believes he will choose his own future.

Character is of course destiny, and it is those Sadges who choose higher over lower who rise above and beyond the bestial pull yanking them ever downward. Choosing a higher road is sometimes called right thinking. Exactly what is right thinking? In some ways it involves sportsmanship. And we say sports*man*ship because all Sadges are male. The women are never all girly and smelling of lavender goo. Even if they are gorgeous and feminine on the outside, a part of them is strictly gym teacher, so never make the mistake of thinking a Sadge woman doesn't have the capacity to work on a carburator if she has to or make varsity on the basketball team. So we don't really make a huge gender distinction here. You're all players in the great Olympic game of life. Sportsmanship is the idea of playing fair. Your vision of justice doesn't always jibe with what is written on the court documents, and a highly evolved Sagittarian identifies with a pure form of justice that often turns out to be highly personal. Things work out just the way they are supposed to, and that is a bit hard to swallow sometimes when you see that some people actually do get away with murder.

Right thinking, however, takes you in quite another direction. You have to be vigilant. Some Sadges get conflicted between their morality and their practice. They're the ones you hear the neighbors talking to reporters about on the evening news: "I can't believe it. He seemed like such a nice guy. Always friendly. Always said hello. Always helped me take in the trash cans. I just can't believe something like that could happen in this neighborhood."

You have to be a soldier of truth, but hopefully more the Salvation Army type. Otherwise you could be more the let's-kill-the-infidel Islamic jihad type. Over and over you run into the same problem, especially in a world where ideologies have created new nations that bleed across geographical boundaries.

What is right thinking for one is wrong thinking for another. Being a Sagittarius may mean you have a higher and lower self to contend with, but it doesn't necessarily mean you'll always lead two disparate and hypocritical lives, or that you keep running running running, searching searching searching, going from one town to the next, one job to the next, one relationship to the next in a mad search for some magical "next" experience. Right thinking means only that your goal to integrate the different sides of yourself has to be even more honest. While you may be prone to blurting out other people's truth, spilling the beans about your friend's abortion during the dinner when the minister is present, you're really supposed to be searching for your own truth, one not imposed upon you by church, parents, or the state, nor are you imposing your truth upon others. Truth is asymptotic. It is a place we approach and to which we hope to get ever closer.

Right thinking means that all men and women have a right to freedom of thought and a responsibility to protect each other's freedom of thought. That hope is the medicine for despair—not that you're going to put a Band-Aid on a tumor and go dancing off to the beach, but it will enable you to face each day with the conviction that it will be better than yesterday.

Your happiness will be found through right thinking.

But you're not just a Sagittarius. Other astrological factors contribute to your mind-set. You're deeply affected not only by the month you were born but by the year as well. Exactly how and why and what will be explained later, but if you want to explore the paths that keep you from falling back into animalhood or lead you to the happiness and prosperity you deserve, find your birth year and note the number beside it. Then read the section corresponding to the number.

Year–No.	Year–No.	Year–No.	Year–No.	Year–No.
1901–6	1915–9	1929–12	1945–2	1960–4
1902–5	1916–8	1930–11	1946–1	1961–3
1903–5	1917–8	1931–11	1947–12	1962–3
1904–4	1918–7	1932–10	1948–12	1963–2
1905–3	1919–6	1933–9	1949–11	1964–1
1906–3	1920–6	1934–9	1950–10	1965–1
1907–2	1921–5	1935–8	1951–10	1966–12
1908–1	1922–4	1936–7	1952–9	1967–11
1909–1	1923–4	1937–7	1953–8	1968–11
1910–12	1924–3	1938–6	1954–8	1969–10
1911–11	1925–2	1939–5	1955–7	1970–9
1912–11	1926–2	1940–5	1956–6	1971–9
1913–10	1927–1	1941–4	1957–6	1972–8
1914–10 until	1928–1 until	1942–3	1958–5	1973–7
12/15,	11/30,	1943–3	1959–5 until	1974–7
then 9	then 12	1944–2	12/8, then 4	1975–6

Year–No.	Year–No.	Year–No.	Year–No.	Year–No.
1976–6	1988–10	1998–3	2008–9	2020–1
1977–5	1989–9	1999–3	2009–8	2021–1
1978–4	1990–9 until	2000–2	2010–8	2022–12
1979–4	12/16,	2001–1	2011–7	2023–11
1980–3	then 8	2002–1	2012–6	2024–11
1981–2	1991–8	2003–12	2013–6	2025–10
1982–2	1992–7	2004–12 until	2014–5	2026–9
1983–1	1993–7	11/30,	2015–4	2027–9
1984–12	1994–6	then 11	2016–4	2028–8
1985–12	1995–5	2005–11	2017–3	2029–7
1986–11	1996–5	2006–10	2018–2	2030–7
1987–10	1997–4	2007–10	2019–2	

Sagittarius 1

You've got brains, and as long as you don't destroy your brain cells, you'll stand out and shine above your colleagues. There's no question about that. One thing, though: Do you ever need a course on listening! Listening and communication are your greatest gifts and most difficult lessons at the same time. Early relationships, often with members of different cultural or religious backgrounds, will give you plenty of practice in tolerance, religious and otherwise. The whole issue of communication is central to your success in relationships, but it will take a long time to activate your brain and elevate your consciousness. Then, in order to connect with people, you actually have to come down a few notches so that regular, normal people can understand you. Because part of you thinks that you are either smarter than everybody or have brain damage or come from morally challenged ancestors, you sometimes make too much of an effort to be brilliant or correct, setting standards for yourself no human being can meet. Feeling above everybody on the one hand and beneath them at the same time could cause you to present an image that seems to others both grandiose and defensive. You can get so heady, intellectual, super-educated, and in the clouds that nobody can understand a word you said, which would certainly give you some sort of dominant or superior position. People walk away thinking either that they would enjoy a dialogue with you much more if they were smarter, or that you are crazy. Period. Like a being from another planet landing on Earth, a being with an intelligence far greater than anything known to human beings, you land here with great wisdom to impart to Earthlings, but to do it you have to learn English, not just the grammar, but street English, the language of the people.

You're on the path to have fulfilling relationships. No matter how much you resist being in a relationship because you have to lower your level to communicate, it is the path that leads you out of loneliness and alienation, toward a more productive dialogue with your mate and all brothers and sisters with whom you think you have little or nothing in common. That is the goal—productive two-way dialogue. And that also requires listening—deeply listening to others and sharing ideas and information, teaching and learning from students. Boundaries between teachers and students can sometimes get blurred, because when you engage deeply, the personal aspect cannot be kept out of the relationship. So keeping good boundaries without being too remote and unavailable is the trick. You need to be able to step out of yourself to hear the other person without having to one-up them, and to be able to enter into full complete interaction without feeling stressed or having to constantly regain control.

At this point you need to probe more deeply into your obsession with losing control or not appearing wise or intelligent. In the next part, Going Deeper, reading the chapters called "Independence" and "Religion" will give you a chance to pass through the illusion of thinking you're smarter or dumber than everyone else, and on to a higher expression of your Sadge nature that will help you loosen up, open up, connect with other people in ways you never thought possible, and make your Sun shine bright.

Celebrities Who Share Your Issues
Steven Spielberg, Patty Duke, Robert Urich, Helen Frankenthaler,
Marisa Tomei, Robin Givens, Teri Hatcher, Katarina Witt

Sagittarius 2

Define, if you can, the term "making it." Unless you're an old hippie still living on a commune someplace, or a staunch member of some strict self-abnegating religious group, you probably struggle with the values in our modern, warped society that define an individual's accomplishments in terms of how much money he or she is making. That's totally insane, of course, because what could a person's bank account, stock portfolio, or real estate property possibly have to do with his or her value as a success-ful, productive, creative, generous, loving, sexy human being? EVERY-THING, dammit, and that's the whole problem. If you could be left alone without thinking about what other people think about where you are financially, you'd be such a happy person, but it is you who judges yourself, your accomplishments, and where you have come at any given stage of your life. You're the one who compares yourself with all the peo-ple you went to grammar school with, even if you did turn your back on money for its own sake and followed your passion. They chose what they saw as a more secure and safe path, one you couldn't take. You've tried, though. Part of you wanted so much to be strictly fiscally sound and sta-ble. Some Sadges don't get all hung up on status and money, and get all crazy measuring their contribution or the quality of their work against what somebody is willing to pay them for it, even it is sometimes unbal-anced, unfair, and even downright discriminatory.

Granted there is often a great deal of injustice and inequitable distri-bution in this world, especially in the male/female game of who gets paid more. But when you can rise above the corruption of a system that allows greedy people to get fatter, and loving, humane, evolved beings to suffer and struggle, you'll be able to work your magic on the world and be amply recognized and rewarded for it. Identification with the rich and famous is an affectation that wears thin and eventually causes a tremen-dous strain not only on your purse but on your sense of pride and confi-dence as well. Only when you actually throw it all away or lose it all in Vegas do you realize that you have resources you never knew you had. You have deeper, more creative, almost mystical powers of healing and artistic talent, and you will always be supported in those areas.

Sexual healing is a gift, one you have been given to use, develop, and enjoy, but to do so you must be able to turn away from the false belief that you should marry for financial security and not for love. You should not and cannot deny the power of sexuality in your life. This is not easy for many Sadges, mainly because sex is a spooky subject. It demands that you allow your body to take over and shut your mind and conscience down. You do it, of course—and then feel guilty.

So the answer seems to lie in finding some means of holding on to common sense and being practical, while developing a more emotionally nurturing part of yourself that permits you to be taken care of by the resources of others.

At this point you need to probe more deeply into your issues about being valuable, worthy, and realistic at the same time. In the next part, Going Deeper, reading the chapters called "Money" and "Recognition" will give you a chance to pass through the illusion of fear of poverty and loss of status, and on to a higher expression of your Sadge nature that will help you enjoy a fuller, richer, and more meaningful form of success, develop your nurturing sexual nature, and make your Sun shine bright.

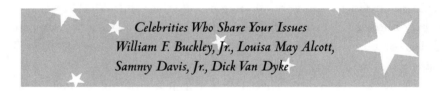

Celebrities Who Share Your Issues
William F. Buckley, Jr., Louisa May Alcott,
Sammy Davis, Jr., Dick Van Dyke

Sagittarius 3

Sometimes it's better to keep your big fat mouth shut and say nothing instead of putting a size 13 foot into it every time you feel that urge to blab. Of course, it also doesn't work if you stand there like a statue of Chief Gotchurtongue in front of an old-time cigar store, which is how some Sadges work out their problems with communication. There's no way you're going to avoid getting yourself into hot water now and then by opening your yap, so when you do, at least make it poetry. Which is exactly what many of your fellow Sadges do. They wax poetic—not always to the liking or taste or understanding of everybody who listens to it, but it's poetry nonetheless. And while your method of communication may seem unconnected, scattered, strange, wordy, or too full of your own meaning to comprehend, you definitely have a lot up there in your brain—way more than you're probably ever going to be able to reveal. It's hard to tell whether you'really a member of the rabble you seem to like to play around in, or really a patrician who's just playing the part. Certainly your relationships will show that you can't ignore the disparity between cultures, races, and religions. Class differences could present even greater issues both in personal and professional situations.

Your most frequently recurring challenge will probably be focusing your mind. It's wonderful that you can have so many things going on at once and handle them at the same time, but you could also end up with a lot of unfinished symphonies. Learning to discipline your wayward mind will be your greatest achievement and your greatest trick. You are a Sadge, after all, and that means education. It will probably take you longer to complete yours, not because you're dumb, but for the reasons just stated. There are so many courses you can take. Everything interests you for a while, but for some reason you resist that long long trip into the deep unknown and prefer to wade in shallow water. So it's the commitment to completion, that plunge into unknown territory, that both attracts you and at the same time scares you because you think it will impinge on your freedom. Completing your education doesn't narrow your choices. It widens them, but it is difficult to keep your mind from wandering. You're way too curious about everything, and you're going to go pretty far on the fact that you can converse on any subject with anyone and give them the impression you know way more than you do. That wide scope of "expertise" provides you with a broad spectrum of friends in your life. Your real success, though, is through a deeper exploration of the mind, which requires you to control it, not it you.

At this point you need to probe more deeply into your issues with communication, problems with siblings, and a scattered mind. In the next part, Going Deeper, reading the chapters called "Communication" and "Freedom" will give you a chance to pass through the illusion of fear of being laughed at when you try to say something meaningful, and on to a higher expression of your Sadge nature that will help you step into the wise role you are destined to play, understand how fulfilling intimacy can be, and make your Sun shine bright.

Sagittarius 4

Fortunately you're a Sadge and can look upon every experience as a blessing in disguise, no matter how well disguised it is—even your childhood. We could probably say that every childhood has a tragic element to it. We're all twisted and damaged, most of us by well-meaning parents who stumble through life in their own misguided daze, rarely realizing the psychological chaos they are inflicting on their young. However, there are stories and then there are stories. And yours has particularly mysterious and touching, and yes, tragic elements to it that certainly add a rich texture to your personality. Your tale makes you the deeply complex person you are emotionally. You yearn to be safe, to truly discover your parents, and to avoid the sinking feeling that gnaws at you at times when you feel all alone on a raft in the middle of the sea at night, everyone down with the ship except you; somehow you have to find your way back to shore all by yourself. This is a very deep feeling, and it drives a lot of your clingy, dependent responses in relationships. It also makes your life difficult sometimes, because as profoundly as you long for the embrace of security, you could easily go the other way and become addicted to the feelings of isolation and alienation and abandonment. Drugs and alcohol or other means of escape could erode all your efforts toward success in the world. Make no mistake about it.

Your imagination can be your fortune and probably will be. When it comes to home and family, however, your imagination can easily run away with itself. Your expectations are high and horribly low at the same time. You expect, hope, pray for, and try to create a scene of perfect stability where not a blade of grass is out of line on the front lawn, because you demand perfection and no less. At the same time you are waiting for the tsunami to take away your dream of peace. Your childhood has indeed provided you with a wealth of experiences and memories that books and movies are made of (half of which you've probably blocked out). Living in the world of make-believe is how fiction is born, but it gets a little iffy when you start to blur the lines between what is happening in the world and what is happening in the mind. Being the largely positive person you are, you try not to dwell in the past, at least consciously. And of course very few people would ever guess what goes on when you're home at night.

That's as it should be. Your day life is up and at 'em, get into the shower (bleary-eyed from a lousy night's sleep half the time), and get to work where nobody knows what's really propelling your drive and motivation.

Of course your day life, your performance life, is a strain, even if it is grounding, anchoring, and saves you time and again from sinking into a morass of entropy. It stretches you, forces you to relate, put out, be a grown-up leader in your field. You're able to handle issues, solve problems, troubleshoot, and remember details nobody else can remember. So competent, so sane, so sober. Then you go home, and it's quite another story. Is it normal to present one picture to the world and live a rather surreal existence once you are out of the eye of the public? Or is it split off and skitzy? Obviously it's nobody's business what you do in the privacy of your own home, until the police come knocking and it's in the newspapers. Then you have a lot of explaining to do. There's a thin line between upstanding citizen and alienated outlaw, and you have to figure out how to live successfully on that line.

At this point you need to probe more deeply into your issues about being left too early to survive and fend for yourself, or about having had to take care of people who were supposed to take care of you. In the next part, Going Deeper, reading the chapters called "Escape" and "Security" will give you a chance to pass through the illusion of abandonment and the fear of ending up like your parents, and on to a higher expression of your Sadge nature that will help you leave the past behind once and for all, gather the achievements and success you deserve to have, and make your Sun shine bright.

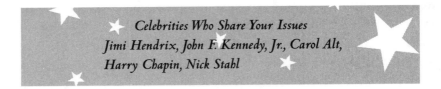

Celebrities Who Share Your Issues
Jimi Hendrix, John F. Kennedy, Jr., Carol Alt,
Harry Chapin, Nick Stahl

Sagittarius 5

When you win big in Vegas you feel like a total hero, a champ, a major player the system can't beat. When you lose, however, you're just another stupid jerk. If you could only limit your liability, you'd be able to have your fun but not have to start at square one if you do have a lousy streak. What? You say you're not a gambler?

Open your mind. Gambling has a lot of different faces. Fate has dealt you a hand in which you have a lot of freedom to form lasting associations that support you on both personal and professional levels, provided you can stay away from playing all the long shots, figuratively speaking. You've got a whopper of an issue when it comes to self-confidence, and it's what propels you to overcompensate and be more flamboyant than is necessary. In your personal life you have been known to look for impossible or un-available people who can never give you what you really need. Such adventures may be thrilling, but you've learned by now that they only hurt your ego more. In an effort to find yourself at last, you can get drawn into situations that end up making you feel rejected and more unhappy with yourself than when you started. It's not easy to stop such a pattern. Thank God you do have friends who love you and are there when you stumble back to town after another one of your emotional binges.

Sometimes the love bug opens its mouth and roars, "Feed me! Feed me!" Then off you go, or at least you did when you were younger. Hopefully you are now learning what love really is. It's not a crushing, obsessive need to be admired and worshiped above all beings. Real love has trust and allows both people to live their lives as friends as well as lovers, each giving the other space and freedom to be who they are, freed from control issues and domination and male-female game playing. Well, there will always be gender games in heterosexual or gay couples, because that's at least part of your conflict and why you're not always the cool, casual Sadge you're supposed to be. In this lifetime you have to liberate yourself from insecurity about your own lovability. Your shrink or your minister will help you figure out where this sense that you are unwanted comes from, why it's so desperately important for you to be wanted, and why you're such a ferocious gambler.

Being a gambler could pay off big time, because you're a born performer and taker of chances. Having to be the center of attention all the time gets really old as you age, and as time goes on it becomes more important for you to make a significant contribution to humanity than it is to be a big, sought-after star. Your destiny involves becoming part of a greater whole and permitting yourself to be truly loved by many people. Maybe it won't happen exactly the way you imagined it would, the way love scenes are portrayed in the movies, but you'll be loved in another way, a better way, a higher way. You have to be really grown up to see it, and even more grown up to appreciate it.

At this point you need to probe more deeply into your obsession with being a hot-shot lover, Big Man on Campus, or the most sought-after starlet in Hollywood. In the next part, Going Deeper, reading the chapters called "Independence" and "Love" will give you a chance to pass through the illusion of fear of being unworthy of being loved the way you need to be loved, and to think you're jinxed when it comes to romance, and on to a higher expression of your Sadge nature that will help you perform with all your heart, love with all your heart but still retain the distance you need to allow others the same space you need yourself, and make your Sun shine bright.

⭐ *Celebrities Who Share Your Issues*
Bruce Lee, Strom Thurmond, Lee Trevino

Sagittarius 6

As if accountants don't have sex lives! No matter how you try to stamp out or suppress the primitive drives that ultimately control us all, you're still that same double-bodied half-spiritual half-beast creature called Sadge. Although sex can gum up the works, it would be disingenuous, even unhealthy, to immerse yourself in a job for the money and to pretend to be totally analytical and void of desire. In fact sex is a huge part of everything you do, but it is hidden and subliminal. It's odd, too, because in some ways you're very up-front about everything—sex included. Maybe that is what people find sexy about you. Despite whatever other frailties you may have, or your need to play down your magnetism, you're still alluring.

You'd so love to be normal, to become an icon of normalcy—to produce work that is completely commercial and viable and sought-after by the unwashed masses. You've got to resist becoming the artist who mistakes financial security for fulfillment. You either can't give up the day job, or you make an attempt to sell out and apply your creative skills to some crass advertising or commercial gig that gives you a notion of economic stability. But even then, the work is iffy and insecure, so no matter how much money you make, you still can't shake the about-to-get-the-ax anxiety that plagues all freelancers and satisfies your unconscious need to be on the brink of unemployment.

It's ironic, of course, that despite all your efforts to find steady work with a paycheck at the end of the week or at the completion of the project, despite your wish to be useful and to put your talents to practical use, you're an artist. You probably view that as bad news. If you're an artist, how in hell are you going to make a living? What if you were told you don't have to worry about that? What if the Unemployment Fairy were to appear at your window and tell you that you have a natural ability to turn the fruits of your wildly creative imagination into very down-to-Earth, practical applications? If anything, the UF might tell you, you have to reduce your efforts to appeal to low-brow working-class beer drinkers, and move in a more artistic or even esoteric direction. The right audience will find you. The UF might tell you that worrying too much about your health or obsessing over work would only detract from your productivity, and that the source of your power is a spiritual gift you have to develop and use.

At this point you need to probe more deeply into your issues about finding steady work, to the point that you lose sight of the magical, spiritual, and creative gifts with which you have been endowed. In the next part, Going Deeper, reading the chapters called "Money" and "Control" will give you a chance to pass through the illusion of being out of work and broke, and on to a higher expression of your Sadge nature that will help you have faith in your own imagination, be proud of your sexuality, and make your Sun shine bright.

> *Celebrities Who Share Your Issues*
> *Henri de Toulouse-Lautrec, Tina Turner, Rich Little,*
> *Ludwig von Beethoven, Margaret Mead, Caroline Kennedy*

Sagittarius 7

Looking for someone to talk to? It can sure be lonely when you get up in the morning in an empty house or to have to take yourself out to a restaurant with a book and hope nobody sees you're dining alone. Again. So you pick up the phone and call someone. Ring ring. Nobody home. Even if somebody does answer, you remember how inane conversations really are most of the time and you end up wondering why you even bothered. But you try again, always reaching out in good faith, always feeling that people just aren't there. There's a vital component missing; some mental connection has been deleted you're madly searching for. That's why you'll often go for the people you end up having nothing in common with. And of course the older and more sophisticated you get, the younger they have to get. You're actually very mature and grown-up, and, when it comes to being responsible, you always have been. You've had to be because you were on your own, by yourself, and surviving without real guidance for so long. You don't know any other way. It's in relationships that you could be sharing a chromosome or two with Peter Pan.

Gaining insight into your own adolescent fantasies about relationships will help you resist the million and one distractions that threaten to victimize and ultimately disappoint you. If you didn't need to connect constantly and if you weren't so worried about being all alone, you could enjoy people when they were there and then let them go without feeling they've deceived or walked out on you. Granted, some people have profoundly disappointed you (they are actually crazy), and you, who consider yourself sane, have had the odd fortune to run into the occasional liar and even downright schizo. You've got to realize that your choices in relationships have at times tended to run from the narcissistic to the totally unbalanced, and that in itself is a form of madness.

Is it possible to find someone who is not nuts? Or do you have to either accept wackiness in others or be alone throughout life? And once you identify a pattern in your personal and business life—if your mother, say, was narcissistic, or your father was a kook, or you're always drawn to controlling or duplicitous types—how can you change that pattern? Can you? If you're an honest, forthright, truth-seeking Sadge, you obviously can't close your eyes when you see something going on in a relationship. So there has to be a way to be real and still stay connected.

At this point you need to probe more deeply into your issues about being so trusting on the one hand and cynical on the other when it comes to being in a committed relationship. In the next part, Going Deeper, reading the chapters called "Marriage" and "Communication" will give you a chance to pass through the illusion of fear of being cheated on or engulfed by another person, and on to a higher expression of your Sadge nature that will help you make good choices, accept people without thinking you have to fix them, and make your Sun shine bright.

Celebrities Who Share Your Issues
Billy Idol, Alexandr Solzhenitsyn, David Carradine, Ridley Scott

Sagittarius 8

Your need for sexual contact could provide you with great relief, but it could also get you in big trouble. That's for sure. Sex is always the catch-22 for Sadges, especially if you're trying too hard to express your sexuality or defend your masculinity or femininity. You could spend your youth proving your prowess, and in that case your youth could last a little too long. Whether you are man or woman, despite your courageous outer bravado, you suffer from deep insecurities often based how big or gorgeous you are. You have an enormous need for validation, largely due to the omnipresent quasi-absent (some would say incestuous) mother issue which has given you confidence with one hand and taken it away with the other. You'll only be considered sick if you start acting out fetishes considered unhealthy, immoral, or illegal. Attachments between parents and children may be made acceptable through rituals and practices in other cultures. In our Western society we believe that the emotional development of an individual can be seriously impaired when a child who has abandonment issues to start with is manipulated emotionally, financially, or any other way, including sexually, by a parent or guardian who is supposed to know better. The unconscious, however, exerts a tremendous undertow on even the most enlightened individuals, and when the yearning for the breast surfaces, only a breast and sucking on a nipple will satisfy.

That, however, cannot be the tail that wags your dog. Despite any unresolved feelings or unexpressed needs, you are destined to be a success, professionally and financially. Your vast resources of creativity and artistry are the assets you can use to combat any defensive and self-destructive patterns of behavior you may have. Once you take your head out from between those imaginary breasts and realize nobody is going to take care of the bills but you and that your life is about business (not monkey business), you will be hailed as a great creative artist or brilliant business person, hopefully a combination of both. Your work, however, does lean to the esoteric, and while that's intellectually pleasing to all college graduates, you must never allow yourself to become an elitist artist.

You have to conform to the society in which you live, learn to play the game, and keep your background, family problems, and sex life out of your business life, so it all depends on your level of mental evolution.

When you're aching instinctually, driven by unconscious urges, nobody can reason with you or even reach you because you're not able to reason clearly. You need to change your whole orientation from survival mode to prosperity mode. As creative and passionate as you are, you sometimes have to tear yourself away from your passion (and your search for mama) to attend to business. If you do that you'll have your reputation, money, position, and all the things you didn't think mattered—until after therapy.

At this point you need to probe more deeply into your obsession with being nurtured, either taken care of financially by someone else or searching for sexual release, to the point that you stop thinking rationally and revert to being a child. In the next part, Going Deeper, reading the chapters called "Sex" and "Security" will give you a chance to pass through the illusion of fear of being abandoned and left to survive on your own, and on to a higher expression of your Sadge nature that will help you find the comfort and safety you are looking for, feel desirable, be recognized and successful, and make your Sun shine bright.

Celebrities Who Share Your Issues
Woody Allen, Arthur C. Clarke, Tyra Banks, John Malkovich

Sagittarius 9

You're an unusual Sadge. You're not what the books say Sadge is supposed to be, because you don't come from just one culture. You've got a strange cultural history—weird, in the sense that you are some sort of half-breed (although that term is no longer used in the twenty-first century). Being a half-breed means that your parents probably came from mixed backgrounds, and it's likely that your relationships are also developed through multicultural associations. In that way you are very definitely a Sadge, because you are interested in the different ways people live their lives. You're definitely going to explore relationships with individuals who come from totally different backgrounds from yours. Unless you actually become an anthropologist, this will occur in your daily life. You could easily become an expatriate for a while, because wherever you are is not nearly as interesting as the next place you could be.

There's a glamour in the beyond, a golden sunshine you seek over that mountain. You're definitely looking for something where the Sun sets— the West—west from wherever you are, that is. You're actually on a quest for an ideal love. You may even been seeking a relationship with God, but you definitely want to achieve love on the highest level possible, possibly an ironic twist.

As a deeply thinking Sadge riddled with many idiosyncrasies of thought and behavior, you must really get angry at hypocrites. It's ironic, too, because even as you despise them, some people think you are one. There is a huge hole in your logic, a crack in the high wall of moral philosophy you've built. You're embarrassed about some hypocrisy or cultural rift in your background, and it's that embarrassment that fuels your search for higher values. You define love as being beyond all moral qualifications, restrictions, laws, and regulations. You live to search for it, and to be able to describe that search. You're not naturally a talker. You're like the PhD student who knows it all but freezes during his oral exams. Sooner or later you have to come up with the right words. You have to learn to speak what is in your heart and not just make a big fancy show of your feelings. Even though you are on a noble (if desperate) search for self-expression that will enhance your life, when it comes actually to saying it, you can appear cool and detached, it seems as if you're reading someone else's poetry. Learning to speak your truth with pride and sincerity will help you express what's in your heart.

At this point you need to probe more deeply into your issues about being honest, forthright, true, and above all sane, sometimes to the point that you don't dare open your mouth to speak. In the next part, Going Deeper, reading the chapters called "Love" and "Religion" will give you a chance to pass through the illusion of fear of being exposed as a fraud or worse, unloved, and on to a higher expression of your Sadge nature that will help you turn obsessive love into long-term friendship, develop your skills as a communicator, and make your Sun shine bright.

Sagittarius 10

People who want to contribute something to the world do something really meaningful and lasting, get all mixed up with politics. And before you know it, they get branded as bleeding heart do-gooders with jam on their faces. Or somebody is trying to put a hole in their efforts and bring them down. As hard as you try to right wrongs and keep yourself from being corrupted by those who corrupt others in this sick society, dammit! you keep finding yourself at the threshold of humiliating compromise. It is so against your Sadge nature. You're supposed to be above partisanship and dirty politics. You fight the rotten system (probably because of the view of authority figures your upbringing gave you), and yet like a boomerang returning to the hand of its thrower, you can't resist. Of course it's ironic. If you try to be St. Anybody or the gallant Sir Galahad to everyone, you're going to run into a big snag. The system you are going to change demands that you play ball with it, which will, of course, taint you and label you as part of it. The cold, unfeeling mother or the hypercritical father appears over and over in one form or another and attempts to crush your efforts. This fuels even more your determination to be in public service and send a message of healing and compassion to the world. But there's a whole group of people who don't see you as quite the angel of mercy you'd like to be. Frankly, you can't be out in public all the time.

Even if your family lets you off the hook for a time, your physical and mental health will demand privacy sooner or later. If you work all the time, you're going to dry up, and the career you think is so important to you will crumble and blow away like leaves in autumn. Although it sometimes frightens you to think that your real life needs to be lived at home in a family setting, eventually you come to appreciate what emotional refreshment is really all about. Like a person who sits broiling on the beach because they're deathly afraid of water, the time will come when you must let go of your ferocious hold on rationalism and allow yourself to bathe in the current of emotional support you were once so afraid would engulf and drown you. That's when you'll really start forgiving your parents for having ignored you.

Then you're cooking—literally and figuratively. You no longer fear the female stereotypical role of nurturing and feeding others. You will have evolved beyond the angry rebel stage, and you'll no longer be doing everything in reaction to a system you think never gives anyone a break. You'll always be a public servant, but you'll also be a whole person with a rich private life as well.

At this point you need to probe more deeply into your issues about being so pure and innocent yet deeply ambitious, to the point that your health and/or credibility will be compromised. In the next part, Going Deeper, reading the chapters called "Control" and "Recognition" will give you a chance to pass through the illusion of fear of being censured or ignored, and on to a higher expression of your Sadge nature that will help you make your public contribution, have the warm, nurturing, secure home base you so desperately need, and make your Sun shine bright.

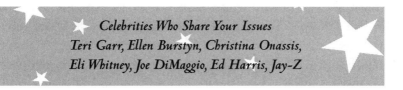

★ *Celebrities Who Share Your Issues*
Teri Garr, Ellen Burstyn, Christina Onassis,
Eli Whitney, Joe DiMaggio, Ed Harris, Jay-Z

Sagittarius 11

Well, of course you think you're a good friend. You try to be. You have a deep abiding love of humanity. It's just that individually, people are hard to take sometimes. They simply can't be counted on to return the kindness, empathy, and services you're all too willing to render. You hang out with people you can't even stand to listen to and get all involved in their problems and issues and causes, very few of which you really care about. You want to care, and you think you care, and yet, honestly, you're not really as interested as you'd like to be. In fact, half the things you get in-volved in are really a waste of your time. You'll agree to have dinner with old friends who come to town, and you'll be glad to see them. For five minutes. Before the main dish comes, you're sneaking a look at your watch and praying for the dessert and coffee moment when you can get away with saying "It's been great seeing you, but I've got to run."

One might even say that all your groups and movements and meetings that seem so important to you, all these "friendships" you work so hard at keeping up, are really distractions. Distractions? Distractions from what, you ask? From developing a healthy, grown-up personal life. From having a family, raising kids, making love—all of these activities scare the living bejesus out of you. Could it be you have an issue that comes from the old-fashioned definitions of male dominance and female submission? Very possibly there is a male/female gender story in your past, which is the source of some of the problems you may have found in long-term com-mitments. Your parents' marriage, or whatever sort of relationship they had, has left such a mark on you that you waffle and wobble in many sit-uations that require a commitment on your part, a commitment you are eager to give at first and then you back away from or out of completely.

No way are you going to march in step and follow the totally conven-tional, socially acceptable lifestyle. You want to be part of the in-crowd, but the truth is, you will never be one of the gang. You didn't totally fit into your family. No matter what kind of oddball fringe left- or right-wing gang you join, you should never allow yourself to be totally ab-sorbed by it. Can't. Shouldn't. Won't. Following your own path will mean leaving the group, not merging with it. It takes guts to deviate from the party line to express yourself freely, creatively, and honestly. You may have to risk exposure, censure, or expulsion, but you've got to stand up and fight. You have to learn to fight if you want to learn to love and not just split to avoid confrontation.

At this point you need to probe more deeply into your issues about being part of a group or relationship that doesn't really give you what you need, to the point that you stay in some relationships way too long. In the next part, Going Deeper, reading the chapters called "Marriage" and "Freedom" will give you a chance to pass through the illusion of fear of being left out or dumped by people you've given your heart and soul to, and on to a higher expression of your Sadge nature that will help you pursue your individual creativity, more easily accept your need for intimate romantic love, and make your Sun shine bright.

> *Celebrities Who Share Your Issues*
> *Sinéad O'Connor, Don Johnson, G. Gordon Liddy,*
> *Tom Waits, Anna Nicole Smith, Brendan Frasier*

Sagittarius 12

The secret life. You don't *have* to act it out, do you? A lot of people have wild fantasies, 90 percent of which are considered deviant—if not downright illegal—by 90 percent of the world. If those fantasies take over and dominate your life, you can seriously damage not only your reputation, but your health as well. As has already been stated, Sadges don't always know how to handle the animal-hormonal-instinctual part of their personalities, and if you're not careful, it could run away with you. If you try to repress those instincts, you could get really depressed and end up using drugs or alcohol as a way of easing the pain of repression and the guilt you feel for even having the feelings in the first place. It's a damned-if-you-do-and-damned-if-you-don't situation. You have to have your escapes. You cannot be chained to the job or normalcy or regularity without forays into your rich imagination. That imagination is a wealth of creativity and magic; it's not always taboo, by any means. Your imagination can provide relief and a release you need from the stresses of working for a living.

You also know that monogamy can be a strain, and if you've been brought up in any religion that equates infidelity with sin (or sex with sin, for that matter), you will definitely need oodles of therapy to come to terms with all your impure thoughts.

Of course, the antidote for escapism is practical work. You need to be so up on your finances, maybe you should become an accountant. Even if you pursued the life of a bricklayer or a doctor, or any job or profession that demands you show up on time, meet your commitments, perform a unique service, and be well-paid for it, you'd still have to escape periodically. Normal sex life? Normal orgasms? Obviously, we've all got issues about sex and sexuality. If there were no moral codes or laws we might all be running around raping, killing, and cannibalizing each other. Your path as a Sadge is to equalize the two extremes of self-indulgence and self-denial, the pure and the profane, the simple, down-to-Earth just plain folks and the dark figures who live in the forest and in your closet. You're capable of enormous wealth and an employment or productivity record nobody can match. Your private struggles are yours alone. Nobody can know or understand how tough it is for you to behave yourself, stay straight, stay sober, and produce, and still have your moments nobody is aware of. You can do it, though, through the strength of your mind.

At this point you need to probe more deeply into your obsession with being so secretive or guilty about what goes on in that mind of yours, to the point that you could have a serious split between your work life and your secret life. In the next part, Going Deeper, reading the chapters called "Sex" and "Escape" will give you a chance to pass through the illusion of feeling stifled and cramped by the boredom of business and normal life to cope with and fulfill your desires, create and maintain a successful business, and make your Sun shine bright.

Celebrities Who Share Your Issues
Dick Clark, Gregg Allman, Mark Twain, J. Paul Getty

CAPRICORN

December 22–January 19
Dates vary from year to year—consult your local astrologer

Capricorn is the stoic beauty of a Currier and Ives winter scene. People are bundled up in wool, skating around a country pond. Elegant, tall trees stand in the snow, brave sentinels indeed, bare branches reaching for the sky. All seems to be silent and dormant, but beneath the snow and the Earth, life is continuing, preparing for spring. So it is with Capricorn's quiet and understated way of preparing for the future. Capricorn rules all the Doric, Ionic, and Corinthian pillars and all the giant structures of the ancient world that housed institutions of government in the empires of old. Solid as granite and just as longlasting, Capricorn rules over everything that is the material manifestation of someone's creative vision.

Capricorn is not just the cute mouse in a black and white cartoon. It's the ability to manifest dreams to such an extent that the idea for a cartoon mouse becomes Mickey Mouse T-shirts worn all over Disney World. It is the essence of commercialism. Capricorn has an innate connection with public awareness and taste. It's not just crap, though. It's all the names—names that become icons because quality has always been their main ingredient. Crème de la crème, top drawer, main event, strictly prime time all the way. Capricorn is the solution to the Rubik's Cube, the untying of the Gordian Knot, the answer to the riddle of the Sphinx.

It represents deep thought and a profound understanding of the working of things. Capricorn is right there checking the car's transmission even before any knock or ping can be heard. The essence of Capricorn can be found in the decision handed down by the Supreme Court after long and arduous deliberation, in the just and fair conclusion to every social and moral dilemma. It's the deep freezer where peaches have already been prepared and stored for next winter, even though it's still August. It is also the reason squirrels make sure their nuts are hidden safely in their nests. Capricorn is the sentry posted at midnight watch, the acrobat's net. It is the most profound and enduring of all the signs of the Zodiac because it can tolerate pressure with unimaginable patience, the way a lump of coal becomes a diamond and grapes become Champagne.

Capricorns often get a reputation of being a bunch of dour, humorless naysayers who are too busy preparing for either their retirement or nuclear winter to grant themselves more than five minutes of quiet fun—definitely before 9 PM, the Capricorn bedtime. It's not true. Very few people know the energy drain you cope with, not to mention the morning stiffness, aches, and pains you've endured. Of course, with Saturn as your ruling planet, it's just too easy to let your fears run away with you, so that when the slightest thing goes wrong in your body, you could feel as if you're about to be put on the hospital critical list. It takes time for you to believe you're not only going to live for five more minutes, but you're actually going to be okay. If you don't feel that you're functioning at high level, if you are not at the top of your game, it wreaks havoc on your self-esteem. If you can't be the best violinist, drummer, conductor, or guy who works the lights, you get on your own case. It's the same old specter that gets you every time: the fear of not being what people (i.e., your mother) expect you to be.

When you have a goal and you're in a productive mood, you're fine. Nothing can stop you. You are fearless, tireless, and don't stop until you're standing on top of Mt. Everest and smiling while having your picture taken. However, when you crawl into the gloom, there's no sense in telling you to relax and hang loose, because talk like that usually makes you even more nervous. Certainly there is always something to fret about, first your health, then money—always something. So it may take you a while to feel totally confident about the future. After all, when you go through big physical and/or mental changes, you do look at life and death in quite a different way. And here's another thing that may not be obvious to a lot of people: Being both mother and father—doing the career thing and the home thing—is an enormous challenge for you. Unless you're a chef or involved in some other profession that permits you to act as both a hardcore business person and a nurturer, you find yourself pursuing career opportunities while always trying to spend time in the home you're working to pay the mortgage on. Even if this balancing act exhausts you and stretches you to the max, it actually affords you the opportunity to be both a traditional "man" whose job it was to go out and kill the wild animals, and the traditional "woman" whose job it was to cook them.

If you were born under the sign of Capricorn, by the time you entered first grade you were already roughly over two hundred years old. Anyone could see that, just from the bags under your eyes. Your sense of responsibility was laid down in utero, and you were delivered clutching a to-do list in your tiny little fist, along with a timetable of when each thing had to be done. It's actually quite an admirable trait, even though you think you're such a boring person. Capricorns are the sort of people who can wake up at 3 AM with three herniated discs and still show up at the office by eight o'clock. That's the key: showing up anyway no matter what. Capricorn is about living up to your word, honoring commitments, and sticking by agreements. It is the influence of Capricorn that gives you the desire to be honorable and loyal and faithful. This desire is the source of both your strengths and your conflicts. You can be absolutely Catholic about divorce, which means you may sue your ex for every penny, and take the house *and* the kids, but oddly, weirdly, and strangely, you still can consider yourself that person's best friend for life, and God help anybody who criticizes that ex or causes them grief. If anyone is going to hassle them, it's you, and beyond that you're totally loyal to the bitter end.

Capricorn is said to represent the resolution of issues with parental authority, or more specifically the stronger, bread-winning parent whom one comes to respect—after therapy, after you have gone through the anger because he or she was distant, cold, unresponsive, punitive, controlling, intrusive, and uncompromising, and rewarded you for getting good grades, grounded you for breaking curfew, and convinced you that you would certainly get killed if you dared to ride your bike on the street, with or without a helmet.

Among other things, Capricorn rules mastery over the physical world. You're not supposed to be content to be the dancer in the back line of the chorus. Capricorn has to rise to the top, like cream to the top of a quart of unhomogenized milk. Its persistence is unmatchable and from that comes your reputation for reliability, and your unflagging unflinching take-the-umbrella-to-work-just-in-case ability to forestall unforeseen contingency or catastrophe. It is the Capricorn in you that makes you want to be the best, produce the best, and be number one in anything to which or to whom you are committed. For Capricorn, the three R's are Rolex, Ralph Lauren, and Rolls Royce.

Not that you're snooty or snobby, but you can get very "What school did you go to, dear? Public school? Oh." While you can easily become label happy, you care more about the quality of excellence and your sense of achievement in a world of standards and competition. Because Capricorn is ruled by the planet Saturn, whenever Capricorn appears in a horoscope there is always an angle and a what's-in-it-for-me aspect to every deal proposed.

Can you be generous? Other than for tax write-off reasons? Sure. You can be generous, but even then, you make a little mark at the back of the your little black book under the heading What I Am Owed for This. Some people think your tit-for-tat mentality comes from what they perceive as your pettiness, but if they could look at it another way, they would see that you have a perfectly honed awareness of balanced books. You give. You take. You buy low. You sell high. It's your way. Profit is not evil. It is a natural drive of the human competitive spirit. It's the Capricorn first commandment. Be thankful for it.

You also have a deeply romantic nature you have to keep in check. If you don't put the brakes on, you can get hooked up with needy, lazy louts and have to support them until you wake up and evict them for nonpayment of rent. Although you can sympathize with liberal views and leftist politics, and even publicly espouse the Democratic Party, you're ultimately a moderate who is happier living inside the fat part of the bell curve. In fact, somewhere deep within you lies a conservative element that sometimes makes you seem like a cheapskate elitist. Here is an unfortunate but all-too-common Capricorn stereotype: The mustache-twirling landlord in a black cloak pointing outside toward the blizzard while a poor pregnant wretch begs for mercy. You've got a huge heart and can be generous to the point of stupidity, but because you've been conditioned to survive and because you had a fear of deprivation drummed into your head during your childhood, you can indeed become cynical. From an early age you were ordered to grow up, face life, recognize it's a tough world, and, if you're going to play with the Big Kids, pay your dues or get out. No whining. No crying. Act your age and stiffen that upper lip so you can stand next to the coffin at a funeral of the person you love most in the world and deliver a eulogy that will have everybody in the place screaming and sobbing. Everyone but you. You'll have your nervous breakdown later, but only for a few hours during a long coffee break. And then it's back to functioning at a high level. The moment you arrived on Earth, you heard somebody say, "Here's the contract. Oh, you didn't read the fine print? Tough titty. Next time get your eyes checked before you sign a deal."

Always remember that Capricorn is the necessary component of any business, even a personal relationship. Your love life may not always be as romantic as you make out, but the fact that you can see a relationships as an agreement with balanced books is what makes it a successful partnership. It may be love. It may be dedication. It may be hot sex (often is, Capricorns are reputed to be the horniest of all the signs), but above and beyond all other things, it is business. It thrives when there is trust and loyalty, and that's why, after they have been to therapy, people should seek out a Capricorn to marry.

Although your sign represents good breeding and culture, you have broad interests and a thirst for contact with all kinds of people. You are not content, therefore, to hang out with a bunch of blue-blood half-in-the-bag WASPs at a party with no Jews or African Americans on the guest list. Whether you were born into a dynasty of wealth or not, you've got what it takes to get those student loans and educate yourself, socialize yourself, finagle out your way into High Society, and still be able to go out and enjoy a beer with the local plumber. Capricorn has the power to start out with absolutely nothing in a roach-infested walk-up flat with a mattress on the floor, and end up in digs on the cover of *Metropolitan Home*. It is not coupon-clipping brattiness that drives you. You embody supremacy over struggle, the old-fashioned way. You want to be a star, kid? Work for it. Start out in the mail room and you can become a CEO. The can of Campbell's soup once sat on a kitchen self before it became a priceless Andy Warhol painting, and before it was a can of Campbell's soup, it was somebody's homemade recipe. Capricorn is the story of how all the Aunt Jemimas throughout history became Aunt Jemima. So maybe you're not the most emotionally expressive Sign of the Zodiac. You believe more in progress than in allowing Nature to rule. That's why you have to make sure that you do not become more interested in the production of cosmetics than in what lipstick does to test rabbits.

No matter how radical your politics or loudly you express your views for liberty and freedom, you support organized society, not rabble-rousing anarchy. Your attitudes are sometimes perceived as uptight and reactionary (especially by your kids before they realize how valuable the lessons you taught them were), mainly because Capricorn's function is to uphold the existing law. You can certainly be progressive or forward-thinking in your beliefs, attitudes, and measures, and you abhor tyranny of any kind. You do not blindly stand for an inflexible, outworn System.

You *are* the System.

So no matter how you rally for change, you will ultimately have to represent an orderly, deeply conservative method of change. When you work hard for something, eat peanut butter sandwiches and have to keep the milk out on the windowsill because you couldn't pay the electric bill, and struggled, fought, scratched and clawed, sacrificed, and worked like a damned dog to get your lousy piece of turf, naturally you're going to want to hang on to it. You're going to protect it as fiercely as a pit bull watches over its master. Your position becomes your identity after a while and you want to make sure nobody takes it away from you. (God help anybody who tries to steal your mate.) This is the backbone of the Capricorn spirit. It is one of the primal driving forces that allows you the luxury of pursuing the illusion that success is your divine right as a member of your sign. Putting aside the fact that most people in this world end up in a stinko job, hoping Saturday's lottery ticket brings in their ship, there is nothing wrong with dreaming or with thinking that you have the right to become anything you want to become. That's good. That's healthy. More power to you. You have the gift and power of self-creation, and as you get older, you can take that to the bank.

So depending on your level of evolution, insecurity, cosmic knowledge, and greed, you can either be a just, moral, loving master of the physical world or just a plain old bastard landlord. You either become the regime or you feel naked if you are not sheltered under the cloak of a strong, protective figure who will stand over you, guide you, take care of you, and provide a structure to support you. You need the security of knowing a parent is nearby. You have to have a set of rules to follow, laws to obey, and codes to live by. Either that or you become the code by which others are required to live. If people can't deal with you, out they will go.

Capricorns yearn to conform to a set of principles offered by a long tradition, backed up by cultural heritage. Your desire for a comfortable, orderly life does not mean you have to end up married to a control freak, working for one, or being one. Obviously there is something you find psychologically or emotionally fulfilling in receiving protection or offering it. The string attached, however, is a big, long, heavy, unbreakable one. Capricorns have a choice to make: They can be staunchly loving and loyal protectors, or they can treat relationships as if they were running a protection racket just exactly the way the mob offers "protection" to a neighborhood candy store. You can be someone's rock of Gibraltar or you can force your way upon them. "You're not going to be protected by anybody else, so don't try anything funny. These are the rules. Live by them and live." The approach you take depends solely on how confident you are about being a person who can be loved and trusted. If you lack that confidence, you may constantly issue an unspoken threat that can be horrendously anxiety-producing.

Because you are such a strong and stable figure, your strength can turn people on—at first. They get the notion that their hero and savior has arrived. Nothing more to fear. No poverty, starvation, sickness. Thank God for the cavalry, Superman, Big Mama, and all the other characters who have ever promised to take care of anybody else. It's all so wonderful. Olive Oyl screams, Popeye pops his spinach, and in a moment or two, he arrives. They've found their rock, someone to stabilize them, ground them, hose them down when they go off, and drag them back to shore when they swim too far out and get caught in a rip current. At its highest evolution, Capricorn truly is as brave and heroic as a lifeguard at the beach, when sharks are sighted swimmers are screaming.

You have to be aware of the dark side. Power often gets carried away with itself, and if the person you are protecting starts getting the idea that he or she doesn't need your protection any longer, that's when you get insecure. That's when somebody could get their knees broken or wake up in bed some morning with a horse's head next to them on the pillow. When you're grown up and sure of yourself, you don't cling or punish. Capricorn can get lethally defensive, however, and when that happens, *Capricorn will not be disobeyed.* It is capable of crippling someone emotionally, attacking them mentally, paralyzing them financially, and, if all else fails, obliterating them entirely. Capricorn's purpose depends on another individual's need for protection. What starts out as heroics can either lead to a lasting bond or to a cycle of reward and punishment—reward for dog-like loyalty, punishment for even the slightest question of disobedience.

While times are rough and the strains of living in society are growing, it is still difficult for you to decide which side to take in the fight between your belief in liberty and your belief in order. Whether you have an authority problem or not, your prefer not to be identified with the rousing rabble, even when you chafe under the yoke of government restrictions. The worst thing you can do when times are tough is to fall apart and go crazy and drop into chaos. It undermines the sense of security you need to be able to live in peace and harmony. To be secure you have to be strong, and for that you need organization. While you believe in individual freedom, part of you is nauseated by all the people who run around and have abortions and let men marry men and let lesbians raise kids, while we in the West are all about to be overrun by a horde of "barbarians," who cut off your head at the drop of your hat! Are these liberals kidding, or what? They go on and on about human rights abuses, but they will be the first to blame the government the next time a hurricane hits or some pit bull craps on their lawn. Some people feel left out and disenfranchised by and from everything the government does, unless it feeds them chicken soup every day and tucks them into bed under eiderdown quilts every night. They hate taxes. They hate prices. They hate everything the government does to keep an economy strong. And by God, you are not going to knuckle under to the whims of a whining fickle mob, comprised largely of people who want to be taken care of but can't face being governed by the people taking care of them.

The strange thing is, another part of you is totally with the people, for the people, by the people, and of the people. So exactly how are you supposed to live in this world now and where exactly do you stand? How do you move more with right action toward achieving your goal of mastery with sensitivity? What are the forces that drag you backward and keep you from reaching the highest manifestation of your Sun? And what are the energies that can support you, guide you, enhance your positive qualities and make your Sun shine bright?

The fact is you're not just a Capricorn. There is another energy operating, one that either cuts across your efforts and undermines them or spirits you to heights of joy and fulfillment. That energy depends not on the month you were born, but the year as well. Later on in this book the technical aspects will be explained more fully. We'll examine how you waste time chasing your own tail, why you do it, and how to pull yourself out of self-destructive obsessions and put yourself back on the road to success. But for now, check out the following table. Find your birth year and note the number beside it. Then read the section corresponding to the number.

Year–No.	Year–No.	Year–No.	Year–No.	Year–No.
1901–5	1912–10	1923–3	1932–9	1943–2
1902–4	1913–9	1924–2	1933–8	1944–1
1903–4	1914–8	1925–1	1934–8	1945–12
1904–3	1915–8	1926–1	1935–7	1946–12
1905–2	1916–7	1927–12	1936–6	1947–11
1906–2	1917–7	1928–11	1937–6	1948–11
1907–1	1918–6	1929–11	1938–5	1949–10
1908–12	1919–5	1930–10	1939–4	1950–9
1909–12	1920–5	1931–10 until	1940–4	1951–9
1910–11	1921–4	1/7/32,	1941–3	1952–8
1911–10	1922–3	then 9	1942–2	1953–7

Year–No.	Year–No.	Year–No.	Year–No.	Year–No.
1954–7	1969–9	1984–11	2001–12	2016–3
1955–6	1970–8	1985–11	2002–12	2017–2
1956–5	1971–8	1986–10	2003–11	2018–1
1957–5	1972–7	1987–9	2004–10	2019–1
1958–4	1973–6	1988–9	2005–10	2020–12
1959–3	1974–6	1989–8	2006–9	2021–12
1960–3	1975–5	1990–7	2007–9 until	until 12/23,
1961–2	1976–5 until	1991–7	1/7/2008,	then 11
1962–2 until	12/30,	1992–6	then 8	2022–11
1/14/63,	then 4	1993–6	2008–8	2023–10
then 1	1977–4	1994–5	2009–7	2024–10
1963–1	1978–3	1995–4	2010–7	2025–9
1964–12	1979–3	1996–4	2011–6	2026–8
1965–12	1980–2	1997–3	2012–5	2027–8
1966–11	1981–1	1998–2	2013–5	2028–7
1967–10	1982–1	1999–2	2014–4	2029–6
1968–10	1983–12	2000–1	2015–3	2030–6

Capricorn 1

It's got to hurt when you try so hard to be caring and nurturing to other people and they tell you that Josef Stalin or Old Mother Hubbard could have taken a lesson from you. You certainly know how to get to the top, and what to do to stay on top, but that doesn't mean that you have to close yourself off to warmth and security and live by the God-help-anyone-who-gets-in-the-way rule. You're not like that. You have a totally sweet and loving and sensitive side which, unfortunately, you don't always get a chance to show. You've got a few male/female issues about who gets to be on top, and they are so deeply ingrained in your genes that you can't just toss them off and be all trusting and vulnerable. This gender-authority stuff probably goes way back to a time when your ancestors simply accepted the fact that men made the laws. Period. The patriarchy has influenced your behavior and to this day continues to do so. Male or female, it's really hard for you to relinquish your spot of turf.

You're a tough cookie all right, but then you've had to be. So it's nuts to tell you to hang loose, just sit around with a cup of mint tea and a muffin, although that's exactly what you need to do. You're wound pretty tight, because you are so scared to relinquish your post for five minutes. While it is wonderful to be a household name that everyone recognizes instantly, you may have to learn the difference between fame and contentment. There is a big difference. Your life gets really out of whack when you get obsessed with who you are in a desperate diva, Norma Desmond–like way. That's exactly when you should move off the dime you're sitting on and allow yourself to be nurtured and cared for by somebody who knows how to make pasta al dente. You need the warmth and intimacy a relationship can provide, despite the fact that you tend to freeze and stiffen when somebody goes to hug you. You've been conditioned to be cool and polite, like a well brought up preppie, but what you really need to round you out is a little old-fashioned ethnic screaming out an open window from which freshly washed underwear is hanging. Your diligence is commendable, but you periodically need to be reminded that without someone around to lubricate your machinery, you run the risk of becoming a rusty old relic, hanging on to an image that has gotten old, tired, worn out, and antiquated.

At this point you need to probe more deeply into your issues about being so desperate to be self-reliant and considered successful, to the point that you push away the very people who can comfort you. In the next part, Going Deeper, reading the chapters called "Independence" and "Recogntion" will give you a chance to pass through the illusion of fear of losing control, and on to a higher expression of your Capricorn nature that will help you maintain your reputation and position while also developing more lasting relationships in business and personal life, and make your Sun shine bright.

Celebrities Who Share Your Issues
Ethel Merman, Carlos Santana, Cab Calloway, Simone de Beauvoir, Rod Stewart, Robert Bly, Soupy Sales, Stephen Stills

Capricorn 2

If you were a true dyed-in-the-wool, card-carrying Capricorn's Capricorn, you'd be into safely saving money. Period. No risks. Plenty of Plans B, C, D through Z. Odd thing is, all Capricorns are concerned with financial security, because they know there is no security in that area. Even though you are often freaked about money, for sure, you're not really all just about business. You probably think that's your curse, but it's actually your blessing. God knows you've had your share of financial disasters, which is already rather un-Capricorn. Real, true, fundamentalist Capricorns babysat or mowed lawns, and from those piggy bank savings they made their first investment, which by now has grown into at least six apartment buildings. They wouldn't take crazy, insane risks the way you do. But then, the higher the risk-to-reward ratio, the greater reward. So when you win, you laugh all the way to the bank.

It's inaccurate to say you're into money or not into money. It's not that simple. Being nuts on the subject is not the same thing as having your idiosyncratic conflicts about it. Fundamentalist Capricorns are consistent in their attitudes toward business and finances. You, however, are not. And there's a good reason for that. You're not supposed to be in total control of your own economic well-being every minute, all the time. It may turn out that you are not obliged to support yourself financially. You're definitely going to come into money, but it will most probably not be because you came up with the new gadget absolutely everybody has to have in their kitchen. Your security is going to come through others, and that will take the control right out of your hands. Of course you'll interpret this as bad news, the way you interpret everything.

That's not to say that sooner or later one of your off the wall dreams might not score, but if that happens, it won't be because you schemed to get financial control. It will be because your creative ingenuity was operating with no thought of what could come of it financially. Your destiny is to reap rewards for pouring your heart into something or someone. Genuinely caring for someone (not just because you want to be mentioned in the will) will make you rich in ways you can't imagine.

Whether it goes against what your mother told you or not, sexual honesty will eventually win out. You'll probably twist yourself into the world's most twisted cruller trying to avoid that, mainly because it horrifies you to think you would turn away from financial security for sexual reasons. But eventually you will, at which point they may ask you to turn in your Capricorn club card. Let them. You're on Earth to find success through your own fertile creativity, and not just by doing what other people think you should do. But you won't have this epiphany when you're young and trying to break away from your family's control, and think that economic independence alone will make you happy. You have to learn as you get older that that kind of security blows out as fast as it blows in. Liberation from an enslavement to poverty consciousness will be your greatest achievement.

At this point you need to probe more deeply into your obsession with being so vulnerable to financial disaster that you organize all your efforts around commercialism to the exclusion of your more creative or emotional needs. In the next part, Going Deeper, reading the chapters called "Money" and "Freedom" will give you a chance to pass through the illusion of fear of loss of independence and stability, and on to a higher expression of your Capricorn nature that will help you feel more confident about your fiscal future, open your creative channels, enjoy sexual relationships without fear, and make your Sun shine bright.

Celebrities Who Share Your Issues
Ben Kingsley, Howard Hughes, Ava Gardner, Joe Frazier,
Aristotle Onassis, Janis Joplin, Maggie Smith

Capricorn 3

Your life could be a hundred times simpler if you were one of those Capricorns who simply did really well in school, knew exactly what they wanted to do, went to graduate school straight through, and by the time they were thirty were all set up. Well, it is unlikely that you followed such a path, due to your restless curious mind. You have followed countless tributaries off the Capricorn river. It takes you longer to focus. It is difficult for you to stop looking at the clock and feeling itchy to move on to the next place, project, or person. Who's to say why you get as antsy as you do?

Though it's not at all stereotypical of the anally retentive Capricorn, you have an odd streak of cat-killing curiosity. That straight and narrow road just isn't for you. Something forces you to veer off the eight-lane freeway onto a road that isn't even on the map. This provides your thirsty mind with mini experiences nobody knows about. They are periodic lapses and forays into nowhere, mentally or geographically. While you can't resist these deviations, mainly because they satisfy your urge to explore and provide you a necessary escape from the rigors of work, they could also land you in a heap of trouble when, in your urge to get away for a quickie, you go off the main road during a driving rainstorm and lose your way entirely.

You have these little lapses of behavior for good reason. It's a strain to be mentally present under the best of circumstances, not to mention when some teacher is droning on about algebra when you've got your eye on the cute person sitting next to you in class. It's hard to blindly accept what other people lay down as absolute truth, so when you see a sign that says "DANGER, NO TRESPASSING" you just have to see for yourself what's so wrong with violating a little taboo. You have trust issues, because you've experienced tragic deception and sorrow, brought on by the people closest to you whom you were supposed to trust. Sometimes it's hard for you to separate fact from fiction. Facts are boring, and truth is relative, so this is exactly why, when you open your mouth to speak, music comes out.

It's a cliché to say that some people have to get drunk to be real, but for some folks in vino veritas is the only way. They can't speak without the help of intoxicants of some kind. You are going to step into your own shoes and experience self-realization when you overcome your desperate need to constantly change direction like a rabbit running from the hunter's rifle. Sober up and acknowledge your love of education and the law. In order to do that, you need to find teachers you respect and laws you respect, and you have to understand your role in a higher service capacity. Bottom line: You are way more intelligent than you sound.

At this point you need to probe more deeply into your obsession with needing to get away, to the point that you could become scattered and fragmented, lose credibility, and not be taken seriously. In the next part, Going Deeper, reading the chapters called "Escape" and "Communication" will give you a chance to pass through the illusion of fear of being trapped and forced to narrow your interests, and on to a higher expression of your Capricorn nature that will help you focus your mind, travel to places you might never see otherwise, enjoy relationships with people from other ethnic, social, or racial backgrounds, and make your Sun shine bright.

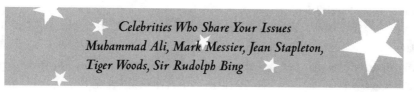

Celebrities Who Share Your Issues
Muhammad Ali, Mark Messier, Jean Stapleton,
Tiger Woods, Sir Rudolph Bing

Capricorn 4

Whether you had a loving, wonderful father who worshiped you or you had to hide him from your schoolmates, there's something about one or both of your parents you were terribly ashamed of, embarrassed about, or totally pissed off at. Who "wore the pants" in your house is not really easy to determine, because there was possibly an effort to protect the man's masculinity on the one hand and to destroy it on the other. You've emerged from your past with a strong belief in family life, but there is something, if not totally fraudulent, somewhat false about your childhood—a story you concocted, an identity you assumed, stories you've told or been told about events that didn't happen, or about a background you really didn't have. Success depends upon your overcoming feelings of inferiority or shame about where you come from. In fact, you've got to make it your badge of courage.

Capricorn that you are, it is important for your sense of self-esteem and sense of normalcy that you marry. You must marry in a traditional way and make public your bond. You must connect with and be part of a public life, even if you still fear the exposure of whatever memories linger from your past. Because you know how to deal with professional situations in a sophisticated way, you'll never lack opportunities in the career sphere. Despite any odd feelings you may have about where you came from, people of great position and power will offer you chances to move up in the world. You're bound to rise like cream to the top of the bottle of milk. In fact, the partnerships and bonds you form in business will be more supportive than the family ever was, or is. Still, you are bugged by having to work sometimes, mainly because career takes you away from the privacy of the world you seem to need so deeply. And that's kooky, because when you are home for too long, you feel out of it and empty and have to find something to do to get you back into life and out into the public.

No matter how cozy you get, you have a job to do in the world. You have been born with fortunate constellations that allow you to make major connections and develop a public image that brings you rewards and recognition. It takes a lot of maturity to begin to appreciate those gifts and not focus on the family you don't or didn't have. It's just too easy to think of all the ways life has denied some of the personal joys you think you would like to have had. It's a lot more difficult to see your life as full of opportunities to make your mark upon a world you'd be so relieved to run away from. Nothing doing. You're a born pro. You just have to step up to the plate, not act like a diva, and learn to deal with people proudly and with sensitivity and a sense of compromise.

At this point you need to probe more deeply into your obsession with being both embarrassed about but overly attached to your childhood and the whole issue of family, to the point that you could miss all the great opportunities available to you on a professional basis. In the next part, Going Deeper, reading the chapters called "Independence" and "Security" will give you a chance to pass through the illusion of fear of being thought of as a fraud because of what you come from, and on to a higher expression of your Capricorn nature that will help you come out of your shell long enough to take advantage of the career and public recognition you're destined to enjoy, and make your Sun shine bright.

Celebrities Who Share Your Issues
Cary Grant, Steve Allen, Tracey Ullman, Val Kilmer,
Kit Carson, Jim Bakker, Sally Rand, Phil Spector

Capricorn 5

You could win the lottery. It's always possible. Don't they always say that if you don't play, you can't win? You'd be surprised how many poor suckers there are, however, hanging around the track and betting on the long-shot nag. People do win. Statistically, there have to be winners. Plenty of them. You have to have compassion for the losers, though, who unfortunately do number among them certain unevolved Capricorns. They are so scared to get stuck in a nowhere job that they move all their chips onto the table—in more ways than one. They pick the most speculative high-risk professions like showbiz, that pay off one in sixteen gazillion. Sometimes there is a big payoff. More often than not there isn't, however, and that's why there's a light for every broken heart on Broadway. If you're one of those Capricorns you might consider Debtors Anonymous, unless you've got generous rich friends who don't mind bailing you out, or a nice big fat inheritance you could conceivably lose in an all-night poker game.

It's not that you're purposefully self-destructive. You are a Capricorn, after all, and are always worrying about your old age, even when you're eighteen. It's just that until you figure it out, you're going to be equating money with love in a very complicated arrangement. Because you don't feel loved or lovable, you'll tend to throw money away, gamble, win it, and lose it again. If you can get beyond this feeling, you will see that you have a contribution to make and you will find that you can be handsomely rewarded in material terms for that contribution—not for sure-fire hits-that-can't-possibly-miss-type schemes.

Yes, it is all about love and your belief in what you are worth. It could get all twisted and end up coloring your choice of job, personal life, everything. You could become so desperate that you attempt to swallow your love object whole, like a python. Your yawning hunger for attention could inspire an abnormal attempt to be normal with "normal" love life, "normal" family, "normal" kids—because as much as you may hate to admit it, you care what people think. Sometimes too much. Your salvation comes when you can actually be proud to deviate from a norm you'd never really enjoy anyway, embrace a more liberating sexuality, and overthrow the tyranny of equating love with material wealth. There are people like you, you know. Creative, liberated people with progressive ideas about how people can live together without eating each other up. You're one of the fortunate people who, as they gain in wisdom and get older, care less and less about what people think. You can enjoy a more sexually liberated existence when most other people are thinking about cashing in their 401(k)s. Your idea of sexual liberation, freed from the stereotypes and prejudices of old-fashioned stodgy, conservative thinking, makes you an unusual Capricorn, a more open-minded, progressive-thinking, futuristic kind of Capricorn who has no intention of going along with the program if repression is part of it. All you have to do is break free from the System.

At this point you need to probe more deeply into your issues about equating being a loving, lovable person with the idea of wealth and prosperity, to the point that it hinders your creativity and ability to grant as much freedom to others as you need for yourself. In the next part, Going Deeper, reading the chapters called "Love" and "Money" will give you a chance to pass through the illusion of fear of poverty and loneliness, and on to a higher expression of your Capricorn nature that will help you be freer creatively and emotionally, have more social confidence, develop a healthier sense of prosperity, and make your Sun shine bright.

Celebrities Who Share Your Issues
Marlene Dietrich, Jon Voight, J. D. Salinger, Sun Myung Moon, John Cardinal O'Connor, Matt Lauer, Paul Revere, Bebe Neuwirth

Capricorn 6

Because work always has bumps, blips, and a million distractions and interruptions, one would think it would be impossible for you ever to get bored. You do, though. Often. And yet it's possible for you to glom onto the dullest routine and refuse to give it up. It can be hideously, repetitively dull and you still won't give it up. Then, boom! You switch channels, you're gone, and in that case it's difficult for you to hold a job at all. Such extremes. You probably prefer to live the life of a freelancer, which can cause extreme shortness of breath and colon spasms in Capricorns, most of whom require a regular mind-numbing schedule. On the other hand, it's quite possible that, in spite of your terminal restlessness and need for constant stimulation and change, you could go for the repetitive job you could do for thirty years with your eyes closed, just to avoid that empty, no-job feeling. It's hard not to jump around from identity to identity, though, and even if you're an actor, a successful one, you'll be cuckoo between gigs.

It's not easy for many Capricorns to let go, because they believe if they leave everything to God, the repo man will get the Volvo. That, however, is precisely what you have to do. Let go. If you must rush out and get another turtle the minute poor Harry gets run over by the vacuum cleaner, by all means do, but you need to find a way to live in between jobs or pets, which is hard for you to do. As you get older, you must come to understand that just because nobody was driving the bus in your early life, you do not have to treat your life as if you were a security guard at a 24-hour convenience store. Rationality is good. Critical ability is good. Detail orientation is also good. But you have to go beyond the obsession with noticing and pointing out the dandruff on a shirt collar worn by a man two blocks away. You have to learn how to step back and see the whole galaxy in which the Earth itself is less significant than that speck of dandruff. It's vital for your mental health that you be physically fit, mainly because you have to function all the time at your top level of performance. At least that is what you think. You are hurt when your pure efforts of help, counsel, criticism, or advice are not taken seriously, and at that point you can try way too hard to make yourself heard and understood. You need silent meditation. You need to focus your mind on higher issues and bigger pictures, and try not to be too aware of who believes or listens when you speak.

Your path is learning, and to do that, sometimes you have to keep your mouth shut and your mind open. It's not really the money or the fame and notoriety that drive and motivate you. You have a mission you are trying to pursue. You see yourself in a service profession. You would like to integrate your particular belief system and morality into your daily life without being thought of as a total hypocrite, or worse, a total kook. To succeed in public life you may periodically have to retreat from public life.

At this point you need to probe more deeply into your obsession with being heard, listened to, and understood, to the point that you can defeat your purpose of proving your integrity and intelligence and just appear nuts. In the next part, Going Deeper, reading the chapters called "Control" and "Communication" will give you a chance to pass through the illusion of fear of being thought of as stupid or foolish and onto a higher expression of your Capricorn nature that will help you come out of your shell long enough to be fulfilled in work, seek the spiritual peace you are destined to find, and make your Sun shine bright.

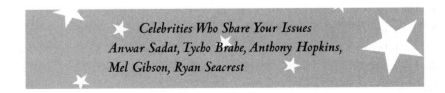

Celebrities Who Share Your Issues
Anwar Sadat, Tycho Brahe, Anthony Hopkins,
Mel Gibson, Ryan Seacrest

Capricorn 7

As ridiculous as traditional gender roles are, they come up again and again in relationships, even between the most enlightened couples. Who is going to be the more dependent one, who's the boss, who is "the man" and who is "the woman"—they are all maddening issues that never seem to go away, even in the twenty-first century when so many of those worn-out identities are beginning to seem totally preposterous. Just a few short years ago, a man didn't have to know where the forks were kept in the kitchen, much less feel comfortable creating a ratatouille for the one he loved. And a woman out there in the market place, competing for an account and showing up a man? Forget it. The sexes are not totally equal yet, and for you these issues are still a drag. You've certainly seen that it doesn't work when you act as ditzy as Lucy Ricardo.

You've also seen that it doesn't work when you become the spineless caretaker and end up catering to someone's endless, needy insecurity. You don't want to end up alone, God forbid, but you sure have a hell of a time taking care of people who can't take care of themselves. Has it ever occurred to you that you feel most alone when you are in a relationship you are afraid to lose? You know how you get roped and hog-tied when somebody is down or in need—if they're homeless, it makes them ten times more attractive. You've simply got to see it's your own fear of abandonment and your anger at not being cared for that makes you resent your partners. Your resentment eventually drives them to act out so you can confirm your loneliness.

Don't forget you are very mad at your parents, especially the one of the opposite sex who failed to provide the security you feel you deserved and made you grow up way too damned fast and become responsible long before it was fair or appropriate. And what happens? No matter how you try to pick people who are considerate and warm and caring, you have to be careful not to end up being their parent. That could make you damned sick of all relationships.

You don't have to live either by shunning people or caving in to their insecurities or problems and having to give up your whole life to take care of them because you feel guilty. We could say you're a Bodhisattva Capricorn, which means you're a highly evolved soul who has come here to Earth for the benefit of all sentient beings, and you refuse to be happy until everyone is happy. It's either that or you have a hell of an attachment to the notion of saving one of your parents.

At this point you need to probe more deeply into your obsession with being so damned responsible that you have to fight people off to get a minute's peace. In the next part, Going Deeper, reading the chapters called "Marriage" and "Security" will give you a chance to pass through the illusion of fear of either being left or overrun by dependencies, yours and other peoples, and on to a higher expression of your Capricorn nature that will help you free yourself from guilt if you have your own life, and make your Sun shine bright.

Celebrities Who Share Your Issues
Sandy Koufax, Jude Law, Annie Lennox, Denzel Washington, Kevin Costner, Howard Stern, Al Capone

Capricorn 8

As sedate and loyal as you try to be in your highest Capricorn moments, deep down you could be one of those horny Capricorns who will do God-knows-what to meet insatiable desire and to create and maintain an image of seductive glamour. It doesn't always have to be so intense. If you want to do anything creative or daring in this life, you have to be able to deal with rejection. You may need to learn this lesson because of something as "harmless" as losing in a child beauty contest or getting no valentines when you were in the third grade. It could also be as serious as being exposed to sexuality either too early or in a negative way. It takes years to understand and accept the conflicts we all have between our earthly desires and what society considers appropriate behavior.

You have to understand also that many Capricorns see themselves as drab and uninteresting. On some level maybe you do, too, and that's why you're super-conscious of your image, of what is appealing, and of making sure you are always noticed. You have a need to be admired and desired, hence that hint of being risqué, that glimpse of stocking, that bulge in the blue jeans, that open blouse. That's not wrong or crazy. It's just an idiosyncrasy of having been born when you were born. You're the proper Bostonian with the streak of taboo—you can be naughty, but usually in a very chic context. As monogamous as Capricorns are reputed to be, you've got huge issues with the confinement implied in being with one person all your life, one person and one person only, all the long, long days of your life. Although you may not act on all your fetishes and fantasies, you've got 'em.

Another thing: Your creative talents are laudable, but in order to be fully realized as an artist and a Capricorn, you have to get over thinking that money is bad. Money can always make a Capricorn nuts, but whatever you want to do in this life, you have to be mature enough to know that if you turn to business, money will not corrupt you. You are not betraying yourself to be commercial. You're a Capricorn. Until you unite art and business, you'll be floundering and denying your true destiny.

Don't forget that sex sells. There's no denying that seductive parents can screw a kid's head up just as badly as a prudish don't-touch-your-body-type repressed fundamentalists. But your pursuit of glamour can easily become an obsession with your image, either as a sexual figure or pure artist. While this can create great mystique and quite a snappy image, it could get kind of scary as you get older.

Capricorns are supposed to age with grace and natural beauty, and it will take lots of therapy for you to resist some of the more drastic measures some folks take to appear youthful, alluring, and desirable. Your attractiveness comes from the whole package of you—your inner wisdom, your interest in people, your business sense—everything that makes you the person others can count on. That has very little to do with the hootchy-kootchy stuff you're automatically prone to.

At this point you need to probe more deeply into your obsession with being artsy and gorgeous, to the point that you turn away from prosperity. In the next part, Going Deeper, reading the chapters called "Sex" and "Love" will give you a chance to pass through the illusion of fear of having the whole financial burden on your shoulders and not being loved, and on to a higher expression of your Capricorn nature that will help you unite your creativity with practicality, deal with sex in a healthy way, and make your Sun shine bright.

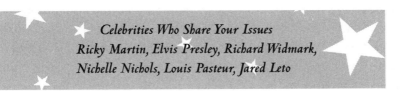

Celebrities Who Share Your Issues
Ricky Martin, Elvis Presley, Richard Widmark,
Nichelle Nichols, Louis Pasteur, Jared Leto

Capricorn 9

Some Capricorns get so uptight when they have to get up in front of an audience and speak, they have to have a stiff belt of scotch before they step up to the podium. Maybe you don't have to go that far, but it's not easy for you. Other members of your sign go the other way. They are utterly pedantic. They cover up their nervousness or feelings of intellectual inferiority by becoming death-defyingly boring.

It's perfectly understandable why it would be a challenge for you to shut down your rational, scientific mind and let the poetry and music flow out of you. You're among the many people who pursue rational explanations for everything, only to end up having to fill in the gaps with your own broad interpretations of what you perceive to be the truth. That won't always win you friends and influence people, because despite your protestations to the contrary, your views and visions are strictly not scientifically provable—or even repeatable. Your ultimate path is like that of the honor student who, once she gets her PhD, dumps it all and moves to Tahiti. You might as well, because sooner or later you have to abandon any rigid positions you've taken for a much more plastic, pliable, open-to-interpretation version of reality. This is not easy for a Capricorn for whom sanity is such an issue. You will find it impossible, however, to cling to what is strictly sane and rational, because of your own point of view relative to the acceptable dogma and party lines of the times you inhabit. You'll cling to it and you'll reject it at the same time, like a fallen Catholic who cannot tear himself or herself away from his or her rage toward Catholic school and an irrational defense of the parochial educational system at the same time. Try to be sane and scientific all you want for as long as you want, but when it comes right down to it, you're a poetic genius, wearing a touch of lunatic fringe. At worst you could be perceived as a total nut, which would be horrible because you're always terrified of your brain going one way or another.

Allowing your "poetic" voice to speak takes time, effort, practice, and maturity, because it is difficult for you to allow your deviant stream of consciousness to drown out your knee-jerk parroting of traditional doctrine. Even if you are deeply critical of the accepted doctrine, you can become as controlling as the voices you are seeking to criticize or even silence. You have to either become disillusioned enough or exposed as a fraud before your wiser, more compassionate voice can be heard. Because of your rebellious curiosity, all your relationships will reflect this need for a mental connection and dialogue, and they will almost always cross religious, racial, educational, or other cultural boundaries.

Yours is a soul torn between science and art. It is vital for you to develop talents, hobbies, and pursuits that periodically take you away from the routines and mental ruts you could easily burrow into. Like that honor student covered in chalk dust and hypnotized by the mystery of quadratic equations who slips away once in a blue moon to a winter escape on a tropical island and becomes somebody else, so do you have to allow your other, more magical, self to emerge, even if it is a little cuckoo.

At this point you need to probe more deeply into your obsession with being sane, to the point that you could be perceived as a hypocrite. In the next part, Going Deeper, reading the chapters called "Control" and "Religion" will give you a chance to pass through the illusion of fear of losing your mental or physical health, and on to a higher expression of your Capricorn nature that will help you develop the skill you are destined to find in poetic communication, and make your Sun shine bright.

> ★ *Celebrities Who Share Your Issues*
> *George Reeves, Rush Limbaugh, Nostradamus, Susan Lucci,*
> *Paul Cezanne, Kirstie Alley, Joan of Arc, J. Edgar Hoover*

Capricorn 10

You are one of the unusual Capricorns, mainly because you are unusually ambivalent about success and fame—being publicly recognized and having to juggle your position in the world with a need to nurture your family life. Oh, you want success, all right, and will sometimes scratch and claw your way to the top. If, however, you get involved in messy relationships and dirty politics and you haven't been kosher in your efforts to get there, you can be sure your Capricorn conscience will get you, even if the lawyers and the tabloids don't. You'll knock yourself right off your own pedestal. You won't be ignored, that's for sure, and despite your confounded ambivalence about being exposed in public, it's unlikely you'll spend your life squeezing homemade linguini out of a pasta maker in your country kitchen—although ironically, that's where you can actually be yourself, where you don't have to put on some mask and play to the crowd, and where you will be restored to normalcy, away from the fraudulence and madness of public taste.

It's a drag to be typecast and for people to remember you for just one thing—perhaps a scandal—and that's why you don't follow the traditional, Capricorn go-up-the-corporate-ladder-dress-for-success-play-the-game-suck-up-to-the-boss-type behavior. When you do engage in that sort of ass-kissing politics, the results will be disastrous. Your choice of relationships, partners, and allies is sometimes an embarrassment and in some cases really infantile. Until you gain inner strength and personal confidence, and can figure out who the hell you are, you'll tend to hook up with people or corporations you think will help you create and establish a secure and stable public identity and position. It backfires, though, when you try to find too much security under the protective wing of any regime, and you find yourself once again plunked down alone with your pasta machine. Your public identity is usually going to turn out to be a drag show, designed to help you avoid the awful feeling of being home alone, exiled, forgotten, passed over, and out of the game.

You're more of a producer than a performer. In fact, that's the irony of your genius. Your greatest achievements may be private, personal, and even anonymous, not because at times you're going to be cheated out of getting the credit, but because you're actually happier creating the star than being it.

The lure of fame, power, and position is, however, irresistible, and it could take years before it dawns on you that you aren't really who the world thinks you are, or rather, who you *want* the world to think you are. You're not just the wayward rebel, madly and blindly searching for acceptance and/or companionship at the expense of sound judgment. You're actually a powerful force and inspiration for others whether the world gets the joke or not.

• • •

At this point you need to probe more deeply into your obsession with what success is all about, to the point that you lose sight of the intimate connections you really need for sustenance. In the next part, Going Deeper, reading the chapters called "Marriage" and "Recogntion" will give you a chance to pass through the illusion that somebody else is going to finally make you feel successful, and on to a higher expression of your Capricorn nature that will help you stand on your own two feet, redefine success, develop the family ties you so desperately need to feel fulfilled, and make your Sun shine bright.

Celebrities Who Share Your Issues
Marilyn Manson, Cuba Gooding, Jr., Sissy Spacek, Albert Schweitzer,
Richard Nixon, Andy Kaufman, James Earl Jones, Chairman Mao

Capricorn 11

It would be cool to be thought of as some gorgeous bimbo or hot stud both sexes drool over. When you're young and look the part, it *is* kind of cool. Sexual freedom can be truly liberating, especially if you need outlets you don't find at home. If you were part of the sexual revolution of the 1960s & '70s, you know how much fun it can be. All that, of course, was before AIDS. Genital herpes notwithstanding, such an existence proves to be energy-expensive after a while, and keeps you from your true path in life, which is actually about intimacy, loyalty, and creativity. You'll certainly never totally behave, even if you renounce the flesh utterly. A person must have the latitude to go and come as he or she wishes. You don't want to go to the other extreme and get preachy and judgmental about other people's behavior, just because you've seen the light and have reformed. You'll always have to keep something going on the side (not necessarily sexual) just to maintain your options, in case "the real thing" comes along—which of course you are still waiting for, hoping for, praying for, harder than the Jews are waiting, hoping, and praying for the real Messiah.

If you have a Utopian dream of perfect freedom, even if it seems unrealistic or smacks of degenerate anarchy to some, you're not about to abandon it just because it doesn't make money. Money, however, always enters the picture, and without it you can kiss your dream of liberty goodbye. Turning your dreams into reality (i.e., cash) means buckling down, committing yourself deeply, and being able to stay long enough in one place emotionally and creatively to allow the roots you put down to sprout and eventually bear fruit. Your restless urge to pull out and move on is partly normal, partly nuts. It's normal in the sense that no one likes to have their butt stuck in a bucket of cement for ninety years. It's nuts because your neurotic death anxiety leads you away from the security you seek and closer to dangerous, on-the-edge situations that only increase your worry about the future.

A healthy balance between profligate self-indulgence and practical creative discipline will allow you the latitude you need for your forays into rebellion and naughtiness. But this balance will anchor you deeply in a truly fulfilling creative expression and satisfying love, things you fear will choke you but which in the end will nourish and protect you and bring you greater prosperity than your freedom alone could ever promote. It's a gamble you have to be grown up enough to take.

At this point you need to probe more deeply into your issues about not knowing where you are going or what you are going to be when you grow up, to the point that you have trouble making any long-term commitments at all. In the next part, Going Deeper, reading the chapters called "Freedom" and "Sex" will give you a chance to pass through the illusion of fear of thinking you're not desirable and thus fearing love itself, and on to a higher expression of your Capricorn nature that will help you develop the enormous talents you have and even better make money from them, deal more healthily with intimacy, and make your Sun shine bright.

Celebrities Who Share Your Issues
J. R. R. Tolkien, Paramahansa Yogananda,
Martin Luther King, Jr., Henry Miller, Dave Matthews

Capricorn 12

Some people can be horribly narrow-minded or unfair. Just because your lifestyle doesn't exactly jibe with what Her Royal Majesty thinks is cricket, that doesn't have to brand you as a total goofball. If you're not in line with what the mind-bending administrators think is appropriate, you get knocked out of the running. Oh, perhaps in your youth you will be seduced by the party line, and in a childish effort to be acceptable, be tempted to sell out, blend in, and silently suffer injustice, mistreatment, or abuse.

Eventually, however, you will clear your throat, cough one or two times, clear your throat again, and if you are not heard yet, eventually do the unthinkable: Come out of the closet and speak up. It could take years of therapy, of course, before you can even tell your shrink what's really on your mind, mainly because you've got masochistic silence drummed into you. And the anger at being talked down to, perceived as stupid or crazy, often impedes your discovery of the true life of great service that awaits you. It's easier to be thought of as big, dumb, stupid, and crazy, than to have to organize your thoughts just to placate a twisted society you don't even really care to belong to. Mental chaos is fun. It lets you go on playing a role that allows you to be the butt of jokes, and it keeps you in a state of protective coloration and ambiguous identity. Like an autistic child who is never expected to hold down a job, it is way less stressful to be the Harpo stooge than the voice of reason and actually root out abuse and wrongdoing. Acting on your perceptions will defrock the priests of the culture, but may also force you to give up your own comfortable fantasies of belonging and acceptance, as well as the prospect of fitting into a society whose madness, hypocrisy, and injustice you can tolerate silently no longer.

Some people would swear that we are all born with the tendency to be narrow-minded and prejudiced. Others believe that our early experiences teach us to be fearful and mistrusting. Whatever the root cause, it is debatable how much we can ever free ourselves from wrong thinking. In an effort to liberate ourselves from teachings and doctrines we believe are poisoning our minds, it is too easy to go to the other extreme and be seduced by the childish wish to find a quick fix, some magic potion that would lead us straight to liberation. You can attend a weekend workshop, find a new guru, or do hallucinogenic substances. None of that stuff works if it doesn't resonate with something deep inside you. Temporarily, it might provide you respite and release from a life of daily exercise, work that tires you out, the grind of commuting, and all the other trappings of life. You need your vacations from all of it. Eventually, however, you see that there is no escape from your own mind and you have to deal with all the goblins, ghosts, and phantasms that lure you into nowhereland. The answer is to be found somewhere between your love of fiction and the pursuit of fact.

Developing your powers of communication, perception, and analysis may seem drab at first look, but together with your imagination, they will make you the successful Capricorn communicator you are destined to be.

At this point you need to probe more deeply into your issues about being smart or dumb, to the point that you've been afraid at times to open your mouth. In the next part, Going Deeper, reading the chapters called "Escape" and "Religion" will give you a chance to pass through the illusion of fear of being undermined or attacked from behind, and on to a higher expression of your Capricorn nature that will help you find your true calling, and make your Sun shine bright.

Celebrities Who Share Your Issues
Vidal Sassoon, Diane Keaton, Larry Csonka, Simon Wiesenthal,
David Bowie, Dolly Parton, Barry Goldwater, Nicholas Cage

AQUARIUS

January 20–February 18
Dates vary from year to year—consult your local astrologer

It's pouring down rain. Can't see two feet in front of you. And wouldn't you know it? Of all days. Something in the damned engine got wet that isn't supposed to get wet. Kerplunk. The car goes dead. Right there on the freeway. And of course the cell phone is out of range so no way can AAA be contacted at this hour. You're sunk. But wait a sec! A car comes down the road, blinks its lights, pulls over, and the guy is a master mechanic. In five minutes you're rolling toward home crooning "Singin' In the Rain," at the top of your lungs and feeling happier than Gene Kelly ever did. This is Aquarius at work.

Everything that pops into your life at 11:59 to save the day means you've got Aquarius in your life. If you want to delve deeply into the essence of Aquarius, read the *Guinness Book of World Records* cover to cover and you'll have it knocked. It's Aquarius when you get a call from the doctor's office telling you they read the wrong x-rays. You're not only not dying, you have an extra kidney. It's even more Aquarius when you're so relieved that not only do you not sue, you take the doctor out to lunch.

Aquarius is any crazy, ridiculous, wacky, can't-ever-happen thing that happens. If it turns out that UFOs are parked in front of the supermarket and inside aliens are wheeling their carts around looking for bargains, or if scholars decide that Jesus was actually a woman who had to pretend she was a man to get her ideas across in a time of patriarchy, that's Aquarius. How does the toaster make toast? It's a special blend of simple physics, witchcraft, and Aquarius. How does Aquarius work in our lives? Some klutzy lab assistant knocks a beaker of some unknown substance into a vat of deadly poison, and the next thing you know you've got the cure for the common cold.

Aquarius is the magic and miracle of accident, but are there really any accidents? Is that just a pile of leaves on the ground in your front yard? Or if you took a step back and looked at that pile of leaves from a different perspective, could you see a certain design there? If so, you're probably an Aquarius. Granted, not even the most evolved Aquarius can predict the next turn of the kaleidoscope. Scientists will tell you right out that the exact same experiment conducted under the exact same conditions at different times will often yield completely different results. This is why it is insane for anyone to say that he or she knows exactly what will happen in world politics, music, art, or especially the economy. It's the x factor. The chocolate in chili, the twelve-fingered pianist, the mutation that disobeys all of Mendel's laws of heredity, but works anyway. And maybe that's one of the great gifts of Aquarius: It can break with tradition, break the family curse, operate on brand new principles, and solve the previously insolvable equations.

If life is like a computer game that comes with no rules and no instructions, then Aquarius has a special genius for finding the prize and meaning in a series of random choices. You enter the game at any random point and are immediately presented with choices, none of which are explained. At the first turn you enter a corridor where a group of strange-looking men are singing a song in a language you've never heard. A woman steps up and offers you the CD. You take it, and you find yourself standing before a great cathedral, then you're in a garden full of morning glories and night-blooming jasmine. You don't know if you're in California or Transylvania. An old man grabs at you from the shadows, you turn onto yet another corridor and, where are you? Is it the General Assembly of the United Nations? Can't be, because there's a large-what-looks-like-a-beetle making crackling noises into a microphone. A giant squid answers in English from a tank of liquid. It claims to be Jewish and is requesting citizenship in the state of Israel. All beings in this bizarre universe seem to be of one accord on all issues. You've come upon some ideal society, it seems, where the common goal is peace. So this is what they've been singing about. All the false turns, dead ends, bad choices—they've all led you here to this wonderful place. Harmony and understanding. Revelation. The moon must be in the seventh house at last. And Jupiter must have finally aligned with Mars. Peace is guiding the planets and love is ruling the stars.

It's Aquarius in its highest vibration. It's the Aquarian reward for open-mindedness, for taking a chance and trying different routes, and fearlessly moving from seemingly random encounter to random encounter. Aquarius is experimentation, surprise.

Now let's be real. So many members of your sign are so sick of the craziness and insecurity in their lives that they're more than thrilled to get a job, get a relationship, and get a place to live. Period. Forget the joy of adventure. You're still nauseated from the roller coaster ride you came in on. Make no mistake about it. Your parents may tell you that you were planned for, but if you are an Aquarius, you were an accident. They may have wanted a child and loved you to death when you got here, but you definitely were a surprise and changed their master plan. And on some level, without willing it or wanting it or consciously causing it, you do the same to others you encounter. You enter their lives, and, in some ways you definitely screw them up, but in other ways force them to be spontaneous.

That's funny, because if there is one thing you hate it's to have people pull surprises on you. Considering that your sign rules serendipity, it's amazing how rigid you can be—rigid and controlling and so weirdly conservative. That's the big myth about Aquarians. You're supposed to be holding hands with blacks, yellows, reds, browns, and whites, singing "We Are the World." Forget it. You can be wickedly clannish and exclusionary. How can that be? You just don't like people on top of you, breathing down your neck, expecting you to be chummy. For all your love of humanity and your desire to help turn the Great Wheel of Dharma, people on an individual basis annoy you to no end. Even if you don't openly confront them, their behavior makes your flesh crawl half the time. Sometimes you seem downright absent and disconnected when a person is speaking to you. You give them a certain look that makes them shiver and they can't tell if you have stopped listening to what you perceive to be their foolishness and stupidity, or if you're having some sort of mild seizure, or if you're not human at all. Maybe you are an alligator alien or something, dressed up in a human suit, studying us while simultaneously listening to instructions from the mother ship. You have a terrific ability to make a person feel absolutely ridiculous without saying one solitary word. It's not that you're cold and unfeeling. You just don't get all gooey and gushy and hysterical, and you have an ability to shrug your shoulders and say "That's life" even when your '67 Mustang rolls over a cliff or somebody hands you a brand new Rolls. The reason you react with such cool sangfroid to everything is not because you are necessarily a cold-blooded reptoid from another planet (although not all the evidence is in), it's just that you don't get all nuts even in the face of the most heinous disaster or fabulous turn of events in your favor. You have had to deal with the most impossible and unexpected twists of fate so many million times. When you react like a cold bitch or an unfeeling bastard, it's just that you are not going to be thrown, not going to let yourself appear to be thrown by anyone or anything. Actually you are a very humane and gentle being, and you'd rather just change your phone number than get into a hair-pulling kick-and-scratch fight with anybody. You can be loving and passionate, of course, although when one looks at many Aquarians, their legs and arms don't exactly fit their bodies and you wonder how they manage in bed. But to each his own—you find Virgos sexy, and you get the hottest when you're in a motel room at the airport when one or the other of you is about to take off.

You are ruled by the planet Uranus, which is tipped eighty-four degrees on its axis, so you can never see the world the way everybody else does—hence your unpredictable demeanor and contradictory behavior. For example, you're a bit torn between a very conservative, tight, church-family-money-oriented family background and your desire to freak them all out by moving to the heart of Africa. You're able to have lunch with Michael Moore and dinner with Bill O'Reilly with no sacrificial blood shed at either meal, other than that of the lamb chops on the plate. This is not hypocrisy. Your liberal leanings are honest. It's your lifestyle that is conservative. If you live in America you're a split ticket. No matter how you attempt to be strictly left or strictly right, you can't be. One reason you can't completely agree with anybody is that your political and personal views are privately, profoundly anomalous. Deep down you are an anarchist in the true sense of the word, and that's how and why you rise to the top so often. Both ends of the political spectrum are attracted to you and could swear you were on their side.

Habits, tics, allergies, modes of behavior, phobias, and fetishes that seem totally bizarre to people who consider themselves normal are totally normal for you. Either you are allergic to dust or peanuts, or live on Diet Coke and Dunkin' Donuts. It's impossible to describe the infinite possibilities of absolute kookiness that comprise your life. You could have the straightest job in the world, working in the post office or selling Fruit of the Loom underwear and do it all for thirty years, your home could be Ethan Allen early-American—nobody would ever guess what crazy stunts you're really into. That's because you seek security and stability from the straight society you don't really belong to, just as you probably never really and truly fit into your family. Talk about "ET phone home."

At this point a comment on the use of the word "straight" is necessary. In your case it is not necessarily the opposite of gay. It refers to the Establishment that always holds some perverse appeal for you. Gender? Aquarius isn't big on gender differences, and as times goes on Aquarian men can look like older women and the women like teenage boys.

In relationships, you're the moth dancing toward and away from the flame. You go for the controlling types, even though you can't take them all the time. You're attracted to dominant individuals, but it won't be too long into the relationship before you let them know who's boss. You maintain control by keeping the other person at arm's length, or otherwise on edge. You're at your most ardent, though, the night before you're going off to war, or more like just on vacation. It's not that you're not into sex and love and romance. Well, you're not really. Your feelings can be deep and long-lasting, but you don't want to be caught dead or alive appearing saccharine or needy. If you get word while you're on the tennis court that your mother just died, you could stay right there and finish the game, not because you don't care that your mother died, but because that's your way of coping with situations which for most people would be emotionally traumatic. You come from and live in a world normal humans can never inhabit. You live among us but you are not of us. That could make you either the greatest screw-up in the village or the fool on the hill who just so happens to have invented a time machine. Good thing, too, because you live half the time in the French Revolution and half in the year 3572, when people don't sleep at night, they just plug themselves in to get recharged.

You're a deviant, not a pervert. Some people think you're crazy. Let them. You have to ride this bronco called life in your own way. Unless someone has walked in your Birkenstocks (or attended a formal wedding wearing them) they can't imagine the time warp that is your life, and how many reversals of fortune make up your picaresque history. Despite all your quirky notions, you are happiest among like-minded friends— people who turned left off the main highway and wandered into the computer game. People who will not, cannot knuckle under to the Man's program. You do crave intimacy and warmth, but not on a steady diet. You prefer the member-at-large role, where you can relate freely and warmly. Somehow you've got to find your band of on-the-edge intellectuals, half of whom probably didn't go past eighth grade but are better-educated in the things that matter than all the PhDs at Harvard and Oxford combined. But your destiny is not just about hanging out with misfits who hate whoever is running things. It's finding people like yourself who are willing to put their differences aside and check their egos at the door in order to bring about a more perfect union for everybody concerned. Kind of like what democracy is supposed to do. As an evolved Aquarius you have to be able to live and work with people you absolutely cannot stand.

Money? You may be a big movie star, a filthy rich oil baron, or the world's greatest orthodontist, but when it comes to money, you're in the same leaky boat as the social worker handing out soup over on skid row. It comes in, it goes out, it comes in, it goes out. If you try to find a sense of permanent security in money, you'll be smoking Havana cigars one day and running your hands through your hair and screaming the next.

Your material stability could come from music, from drugs and pharmaceuticals, legal and otherwise, or your grandpappy's will. You will find, however, that your life here on Earth is ultimately not going to be about the accumulation of wealth for its own sake. Not by a long shot.

You're really here to contribute to the common good, and you'll be most fulfilled when you are part of some greater cause. You gotta watch out, though. Aquarius rules street gangs like the Jets, the Sharks, the Crips, and the Bloods—any all-for-one-one-for-all, womb-to-tomb-type thing, misguided or not. At its worst, Aquarius is just a lot of Leos getting together making noise. The higher purpose of Aquarius protects the rights and freedom of everyone to pursue their own version of the bluebird of happiness.

Your contribution doesn't have to be fancy or grandiose. Whether it's drawing up the new by-laws for the group or inventing a no-rinse mop, helping the tsunami victims or selling no-shrink underpants, your goal is improvement of humanity.

So how do you move more with right action to make your special contribution? What are the forces that drag you backward and keep you from reaching the highest manifestation of your Sun? And what are the energies that can support you, guide you, enhance your positive qualities, and make your Sun shine bright?

The fact is you're not just an Aquarius. There is another energy operating, one that either cuts across your efforts and undermines them or spirits you to heights of joy and fulfillment. That energy depends not on the month you were born, but the year as well. Later on in this book the technical aspects will be explained more fully. We'll examine how you waste time chasing your own tail, why you do it, and how to pull yourself out of self-destructive obsessions and put yourself back on the road to success. But for now, check out the following table. Find your birth year and note the number beside it. Then read the section corresponding to the number.

Year–No.	Year–No.	Year–No.	Year–No.	Year–No.
1901–4	1904–3 until	1906–1	1909–11	1912–9
1902–4	2/5, then 2	1907–1	1910–11	1913–9
1903–3	1905–2	1908–12	1911–10	1914–8

Year–No.	Year–No.	Year–No.	Year–No.	Year–No.
1915–7	1939–4	1963–12	1987–9	2011–6 until
1916–7	1940–3	1964–12	1988–8	2/14, then 5
1917–6	1941–3	1965–11	1989–8	2012–5
1918–5	1942–2	1966–11	1990–7	2013–4
1919–5	1943–1	1967–10	1991–6	2014–4
1920–4	1944–1	1968–10	1992–6	2015–3
1921–4	1945–12	1969–9	1993–5	2016–2
1922–3	1946–11	1970–8	1994–5 until	2017–2
1923–2	1947–11	1971–7	1/22, then 4	2018–1
1924–2	1948–10	1972–7	1995–4	2019–12
1925–1	1949–10 until	1973–6	1996–3	2020–12
1926–12	1/28, then 9	1974–5	1997–3	2021–11
1927–12	1950–9	1975–5	1998–2	2022–10
1928–11	1951–8	1976–4	1999–1	2023–10
1929–10	1952–8	1977–3	2000–1	2024–9
1930–10	1953–7	1978–3	2001–12	2025–9 until
1931–9	1954–6	1979–2	2002–11	1/29, then 8
1932–8	1955–6	1980–2 until	2003–11	2026–8
1933–8	1956–5	2/6, then 1	2004–10	2027–7
1934–7	1957–4	1981–1	2005–9	2028–7
1935–7 until	1958–4	1982–12	2006–9	2029–6
2/13, then 6	1959–3	1983–12	2007–8	2030–5
1936–6	1960–2	1984–11	2008–7	
1937–5	1961–2	1985–10	2009–7	
1938–5	1962–1	1986–10	2010–6	

Aquarius 1

A strong relationship will strengthen you, stabilize you, and bring you joy. As loving as you try to be toward other people now that you're grown up, you were no easy kid to raise. You needed direction but couldn't take it. You yearned for warmth and affection, probably pushed people away, then yanked them back when they'd had just about enough of you. You still need direction, and you probably still have trouble taking it. Hopefully the older you get the more you can understand and accept love without thinking it's a synonym for submission. You are attracted to strong egos, and strong egos like to control, so naturally you're going to have to change your rebellious behavior if you want to have somebody around. And you do. But being the eternal rebel without a cause isn't going to attract your soulmate or make you a star, especially if you constantly seek out people to disagree with who are going to fall into the role of the dad who is always about to spank you for your naughtiness.

You get a kick out of playing the bad, mad child nobody can control. You can't settle for the bourgeois life. Settle down and get married and be normal? You may get married but you'll never really be normal. You're way too identified with yourself as a rumbler to move out to suburbia without causing some political ruckus up there that embarrasses the partner you've chosen to keep you in line. You need that partner you constantly run away from. And even if you don't actually run, you pull capers now and then just to assert your singularity. You wait for the jerk of the chain to remind you you're not a free bird able to fly in and out whenever you feel like taking off. It's annoying to have that kind of constant surveillance. You hate it. But you love it, too. You need a long leash so you can forget (or pretend to forget) that you're not a completely free agent. You also need your boss to seize back control when you've gone too far over the line, which you will do forever and ever if somebody tries to censor your thoughts or limit your actions. Funny how you may do everything to be unlike your parent of the same sex, yet sooner or later you have to face the fact that you are more like him or her than you ever wanted to be. As you get older you understand more about your parents' marriage and how tough it is to fit that square peg into a round hole.

If you can team up with someone who is not subject to the same turbulent, torturous fears of giving up independence, you will discover what it means to be a grown up and have an adult relationship. It will be a strain sometimes. Part of you would always rather be the child than the parent. Equality in a relationship is what you have to seek. Making a connection with someone more able to handle intimacy will show you how to have a relationship, and what your real contribution is going to be.

• • •

At this point you need to probe more deeply into your obsession with being so self-reliant that you would rather be alone than deal with the responsibilities of a grown-up love relationship. In the next part, Going Deeper, reading the chapters called "Independence" and "Freedom" will give you a chance to pass through the illusion of fear of being controlled by another person, and on to a higher expression of your Aquarian nature that will help you remain a free agent while connecting on a profound and intimate level in business or personal life, and make your Sun shine bright.

Celebrities Who Share Your Issues
Paul Newman, Lewis Carroll, Garth Brooks, Joe Pesci,
Justin Timberlake, Jerry Springer, Christina Ricci,
Paris Hilton, Clint Black, Elijah Wood

Aquarius 2

If all you had to do was click your heels together three times and make a wish, you could have everything you would ever need. Without those damned ruby slippers, though, you have to find another way to generate income. At times you may feel frustrated because you'll think you can't make much of a contribution without money. But you can. You can donate time and energy to the breast cancer benefit, walk for AIDS, bicycle for the tsunami victims, or perform all sorts of charitable acts. Frankly, though, it's not enough for you. Try not to go too nuts when many of your efforts to create financial stability go down the drain along with all the assets you've tried to accumulate. Isn't it maddening and infuriating when people tell you to have faith and be more spiritual, and you see all these morons raking it in while the slow leak in your pipeline leads you ever closer to screaming, if not entirely into madness?

It's true that you can't control or predict which direction that infernal current of fortune is flowing in. Sure things often turn out to be dead ends or scams. The more seductive and glamorous the opportunity, the more foolish you feel when you end up with a worthless stock certificate in your bank vault, or your latest foray into a Broadway musical closes after three performances, or your most recent inspiration isn't flying off the shelves and selling a million copies. Fortunately, your fortunes reverse in your favor just as unpredictably. Your dog digs a hole in the backyard and it turns out to be an oil well. There's just no predicting it. It's such a mistake for you to measure your contribution in money. Don't laugh. You're an artist, a person whose path was chosen for you, a path of service and enlightenment. Of course, very few people will even know the boiling tar pit you have thrown yourself into over money. Your glamorous image and even icon status in your field or community belie how agonized you are half the time, or how much you could spend on booze and other substances to distract you from your fears of drowning financially.

You really don't have to worry who makes more money, since you can almost always get backing for whatever you want to do. People believe you are bankable no matter how many ups and downs you've had financially. While you may think money is your main issue, it really isn't. The whole notion of material prosperity beckons you like a hooker at the edge of an alley, only to disappear when you follow her into the darkness. Your real deal is your integrity as a performer, an innovator, and a reformer. You're going to be able to break ground, set new records, raise the bar if you can resist your anger or disappointment or expectations about the financial returns on the investment of your time, energy, efforts, and love. It's the work you choose to do, not what it's going to pay you.

And here's a weird twist. If you can be completely open and honest about the way relationships between men and women and finances have impacted your sexuality, then you can eliminate any hang-ups you may have about opening yourself up sexually. You may think this comes from left field and has nothing to do with your life, but to be a completely productive and creative person you have to deal with what makes some people uptight sexually and why they get phobic about disease and cleanliness. Does it make sense to be monogamous or are your ideas about sexuality inherited from others who also feared what it meant to be sexual? Answering that question leads to happiness.

• • •

At this point you need to probe more deeply into your obsession with being financially dependent, to the point that you can waste too much time thinking you should be more practical and commercial instead of following your passion. In the next part, Going Deeper, reading the chapters called "Money" and "Escape" will give you a chance to pass through the illusion of being without resources, and on to a higher expression of your Aquarian nature that will help you enjoy prosperity, become emotionally freer, and make your Sun shine bright.

> *Celebrities Who Share Your Issues*
> *Wayne Gretzky, Norman Mailer, Christian Dior, Placido Domingo, Franco Zeffirelli, George Stephanopoulos, Chuck Yeager*

Aquarius 3

Good God, the things that come out of that mouth of yours sometimes. People have to wonder what planet you came from or who raised you. Communication can be either your source of strength or the bane of your existence. What about all your nervous energy? It could drive anybody crazy. It's a shame, too, because, Aquarian innocent that you are, you're trying to get people to pay attention to you, see things your way, and connect. You're a progressive thinker no matter how crazy or out of step you may be perceived. It's not you who is out of touch. It's all the people who can't or won't hear or understand you. They may not know that, in your own way, you are doing your bit to fight the forces of evil and repression in the name of truth, justice, and the American way. You want to improve communication among human beings. It's ironic, because people don't understand you very well. And it's not just your weird voice. You will not be silenced. There happens to be a little thing called freedom of speech that says you have the right and duty to speak freely and dammit! you're going to.

Of course as you become more seasoned and mature, you put more thought put into your speech, and that's one way to get people to take you more seriously. It takes a lot of effort to resist mouthing off whatever comes into your head. There is such a thing as diplomacy—it's what keeps people from mauling each other. You can feel compelled to assert your dominance verbally in ways that can be considered abusive. You call it staying connected and in communication. Someone else could consider it stalking. Calling someone names in private is one thing, but if it's caught on tape and repeated, it doesn't do a lot for your image as a dispassionate observer of humankind. Your big lesson is learning to understand the point of view of others, especially if they aren't "your" people. Especially if they belong to that other group, the bunch you have problems with, have been rejected by, are angry with, jealous of, or simply can't stand, even if they are your siblings. Especially if they are your siblings.

Sometimes it's scary for you to verbalize your feelings toward people closest to you, especially siblings, and you may never know where you stand with them. But if you'd like to be remembered for having come to this freaky planet and done some good here, you need to evolve beyond just spouting some empty, pious words you don't believe in but think somebody else wants to hear. You have to master the art of how to be in relationships with people whose lifestyle completely bugs you and makes you uneasy, because it is so indirect—more like guerilla tactics. Your sincere urge to unite with people who are at a distance geographically, politically, or intellectually can be fulfilled only if you learn to connect on a bigger level, see a bigger picture, and communicate with wisdom, understanding, and compassion.

So why isn't your true voice listened to or heard, or understood better? Do you embody the old adage that a prophet is not known in his own land? Your true voice is not just a trail of vile oaths. Nor does it make saccharine rationalization for all bad behavior. Your true voice will be heard when you expand your sphere of awareness and develop an understanding of intercultural relations. You'll definitely marry out of your class or religion. You have to. You will. You can't avoid it. And even if you try to avoid Jews or Muslims or Catholics or lesbians, pal, you're in for the education of your life. You must listen to what people have to teach you and not avoid education because learning takes too long. Education is your path to liberation and happiness in relationships.

At this point you need to probe more deeply into your obsession with being an independent thinker, to the point that you resist relationships with people who have a lot to teach you. In the next part, Going Deeper, reading the chapters called "Independence" and "Communication" will give you a chance to pass through the illusion of being angry but afraid to express it, and on to a higher expression of your Aquarian nature that will help you gain insight into behavior (yours and others) that will lead you to happier relationships, and make your Sun shine bright.

> *Celebrities Who Share Your Issues*
> *Linda Blair, Tom Brokaw, Helen Gurley Brown, Dick Cheney,*
> *Ashton Kutcher, Nick Nolte, Thomas Edison, John McEnroe, Jim Orso*

Aquarius 4

Domestic stability is everything, or so you would like to think. Think back to your childhood. You call what you came from a traditional family? You probably do. Of course, when you're a kid you don't know any better. You think everybody lives under the same regime you do. The fact that money or the lack of it ruled the entire family has colored your view of what makes people secure in life. The Golden Calf was right outside the door to remind you every time you came in or went out just how much meat cost. Rich or poor, you have a fear of being kicked out of your apartment for nonpayment of rent, or of foreclosure on the property. It comes up all the time. It probably even came up this morning again for the 800 millionth time. Almost everything you do is motivated by an irrational need to make sure you have a place to live—not only a place to live, but a showcase, a house full of items you're afraid will someday have to be auctioned off on the lawn—and a houseful of happy people.

Wait just a minute. Where are those happy people? Peeking in the window do we see people who are really happy? Or are they playing at being happy? The fact is, we do not see a Norman Rockwell scene anywhere but maybe on the cover of that old *Saturday Evening Post* you're keeping with everything else you won't throw away. You so want that rose-colored life. But it may turn out that you haven't been put on Earth to dig in the garden wearing a big straw hat, although that's exactly what you want to do every chance you get. You've got a job to do in this world, and if the fear of eviction or homelessness or alimony—or worse, financial dependence—drives you from your house and out to work, so much the better. No matter how neurotic or unrealistic, whatever gets you to accept a more public life will propel you upward and outward toward a destiny you cannot and should not escape. There has possibly been separation or tragedy in the family, one that creates feelings of emptiness. Being afraid to leave your palatial home or step away from financial control by your parents can be such a waste of precious time. If you come to the end of your life in a modest apartment with someone who shares your family karma, it will be a lot more authentic than a castle filled with servants but no real people, no real love.

You can never completely satisfy that ravenous hunger for a personal life if you insist on feeding it with some fantasy that wealth equals emotional security. Nor will those fantasies fill a hole that was dug years ago in your childhood and has eroded you sense of well being and safety. All these old fears and memories that motivate you and force you to take on a public image based on sex appeal can create a stressful set of circumstances for you to cope with and live up to, even if you gain icon status in your field. No matter what tail is wagging the dog, success in the world will pursue you. You can't get away from it. Gender issues, questions of money vs. sex, you against impossible odds—all these forces will conspire to keep you from falling too far back into old patterns of trying to be more conventional than an Aquarian such as you should ever be. Success out in the world, however, is assured.

At this point you need to probe more deeply into your obsession with equating wealth with emotional well-being, to the point that you would turn down great professional opportunities because you mixed business and personal feelings. In the next part, Going Deeper, reading the chapters called "Money" and "Security" will give you a chance to pass through the illusion of poverty and abandonment, and on to a higher expression of your Aquarian nature that will help you worry less about your future, enjoy success, and make your Sun shine bright.

> ★ *Celebrities Who Share Your Issues*
> *Geena Davis, Federico Fellini, Germaine Greer, Clark Gable,*
> *Charles Lindbergh, Betty Friedan, Lana Turner, Abraham Lincoln,*
> *Charles Darwin, Princess Caroline of Monaco, Ice T, Ellen DeGeneres*

Aquarius 5

A life without love or the joy of children? Impossible. Gotta have 'em both. But what if your ideas about love and romance are skewed and even arrested at a certain stage of your development? If you have trouble accepting the fact that you are getting older, the objects of your affection will keep getting younger and younger until you have to start checking IDs to be sure they've reached the age of consent. Although you may never outgrow your love for romantic quickies, you'll eventually find a more intellectually edifying environment among peers who stimulate you mentally and help you—force you—to think about something somewhere other than being loved. Creatively you are likely to be astonishingly prolific, because on the subject of love and/or kids, you will always probably be a damned fool.

If you are surrounded by the right people your thoughts remain more rational, even profound. You won't lose your adolescent propensity for telling a joke at a very serious moment. This is a comic gift, even if it is your way of getting control of conversation, bringing it down a notch or two, and putting yourself at the center of attention. But you can't be blamed for doing what comes naturally. That's the way your mind works, although some would say it's self-destructive, or question why you can't stay on one thought without sliding into another. It could be poetic genius, although these days they call it something else and shove Ritalin down your throat. All kinds of racial and religious issues will enter your life personally as well as professionally, and although you're probably going to be loved by many, it will bug you that you can't be loved the way you want by one.

Well of course you could, if you'd only stop there. Some distinctive feature of your image makes you overcompensate and interferes with normal social interaction. In fact, your overwhelming desire to express freely who you are emotionally or intellectually could put you at odds with the thinking of your day, and make you a total icon or do you in, or both. You have to realize that it's just as important to love freely and understand as it is to be loved and understood. This is the key to all your relationships. It's why your love affairs go wrong and your children hurt you. You really must grow out of your romantic fantasy about what personal happiness is. If you are truly a citizen of the world, then you will never really belong to just one person, no matter how you long for it. You belong to the world. You're a lot more fortunate than you may realize when you're trying too hard to be loved. You've been put in the situation in which you find yourself to be an activist, to put aside personal gratification for a contribution to the collective good.

At this point you need to probe more deeply into your obsession with love and novelty, to the point that you stopped developing at sixteen. In the next part, Going Deeper, reading the chapters called "Love" and "Communication" will give you a chance to pass through the illusion of fear of having to think before you plunge, and on to a higher expression of your Aquarian nature that will help you communicate creatively without worrying you won't have an audience, develop a greater perspective allowing healthier, anxiety-free space and freedom in relationships, and make your Sun shine bright.

> *Celebrities Who Share Your issues*
> *Lord Byron, Humphrey Bogart, Virginia Woolf, Vanessa Redgrave, Jackie Robinson, Queen Beatrix of the Netherlands, James Joyce, Big Boi, Nathan Lane, Paula Zahn*

Aquarius 6

The sunglasses are cool if you want to be a star, but it's not just about sunglasses. This is not a life of leisure you are leading. For you it's either work or working vacations. When you're working you're crazy, but when you're not working you're even crazier. You could probably say it's a calling. You didn't choose it. It chose you. Vacation? Are we kidding? Even a day off doesn't exist. Rarely in recorded memory has there been one completely consecutive period of twenty-four hours during which, if you were not actually working, you weren't ruminating, cogitating, or stewing about work. Work probably gives you a good feeling because when you are performing some sort of useful service, you get a sense of belonging and, pardon the expression, "family" that you seem to need, often desperately. Working, although it can be such a dead end, does make you feel safe and connected.

Sometimes, however, you can become too chummy or messily involved with subordinates and coworkers. If they refuse to be the mommy-daddy-baby-makes-three fantasy you've constructed to give yourself that sense of family you miss deep down, you'll charge them with abandoning you. You know how it is. You try to turn the cleaning lady into your mother. No matter how you try to personalize professional relationships, the career path is the path you need to follow. It pursues you. You chase recognition but flee the public thing at the same time. You have to be known, honored, and admired, but you're reluctant to give up your privacy. Given your work life, you can never totally hide your identity with sunglasses and a hat pulled down over your ears.

For you, name recognition is a double-edged sword. You want people to know who you are but you want to remain anonymous at the same time. It's kind of cute. On the one hand there's your "How dare you, don't you know who I am?" way of relating to strangers. On the other hand you see yourself as a worker bee, the behind-the-scenes leprechaun whose purpose is to serve and disappear. It's tough to be an international icon and conduct an Ozzie and Harriet existence. In plain English, ain't gonna happen. The American family, as portrayed in old movies and sitcoms, is gone, if it ever did exist. As much as you may long for the safety of old memories that may have never actually happened, you have to create a new reality based on your reality, which frankly means you cannot stay home as much as you'd like.

It's weird. When you tear yourself away from the family and do get to work, there's the family right there at work. And when you do finally pull out and take time to get away, it's work that still chases after you. When duty calls, you're front and center, soldier. That's the identity you know best: hard-working nobody. And yet you'll never escape being somebody. You have to find the balance between being somebody and refusing to be a nobody.

At this point you need to probe more deeply into your obsession with successful and anonymous at the same time, to the point that you don't know where to find your true family. In the next part, Going Deeper, reading chapters called "Control" and "Security" will give you a chance to pass through the illusion of fear of being useless, and on to a higher expression of your Aquarian nature that will help you pursue a fulfilling career, be able to sustain intimate bonds, and make your Sun shine bright.

> *Celebrities Who Share Your Issues*
> *Douglas MacArthur, Oprah Winfrey, Sonny Bono,*
> *Charles Schwab, Burt Reynolds, Galileo Galilei,*
> *Matt Groening, John Travolta, Oscar de la Hoya*

Aquarius 7

You are definitely the marrying kind. That is an understatement. It's the splashy wedding followed by an absolutely unloving marriage that frightens the living daylights out of you, and why not. As a young person your greatest dream is to fall madly in love with someone who's even more madly in love with you. The two of you get married and are the envy of the entire world. But in order for that to happen, you have to have some decent role models to follow, especially when seeking a member of the opposite sex to marry. Even if you're gay, you need a role model for a successful relationship. If you're desperate and love-starved, you're going to throw yourself into a relationship with verve, gusto, and glitz, only to find you've given yourself away too quickly, and surrendered up almost all of who you really are. In hope of making a happy long-term marriage stick, you cover up your secret prediction that it can't last, that either they'll get tired of you or you them. Playing married is not the same as being married. It's not such a long drop from the honeymoon breakfast on the Mediterranean terrace to the scene in divorce court where people are screaming at each other.

It doesn't have to be that way. Not at all. And as you get older you come to realize that it's a hell of a lot wiser to hold on to a large part of yourself, get over the teenage marriage thing, and be able to be alone and enjoy your freedom without being bitter or thinking you're a totally unloved and unlovable loser. Marrying for image is dangerous; you could trap yourself, but good. Control freaks are drawn to you because you are an independent free bird, but for God's sake, don't fly smack into the lion's mouth. It's a joke that could take you years to get, but when you do, you look back at the million times you made a fool of yourself over what you thought was love, and you'll think "What the hell was I thinking?"

Baby and bathwater–wise you don't have to throw romance totally out the window and be all cynical. You do, however, have to connect with a grown-up you find attractive, instead of just getting custody of another child with an ego the size of Minnesota. Glamour is alluring, but you have to learn to value what you are bringing to the table. Undervaluing yourself can undermine a relationship as much as finding fault in another person as a way of getting out of a commitment that doesn't feed you the adoration you want. Giving out and not getting back infuriates you. If you start out worshiping somebody and pretending things about them rather than relating to them like a grown-up, then of course you're going to feel cheated on. The trick is to keep some distance and never give up all your independence.

At this point you need to probe more deeply into your issues about being more in love with someone than they are with you, to the point that you get mixed up with the wrong person and call it romance. In the next part, Going Deeper, reading the chapters called "Love" and "Marriage" will give you a chance to pass through the illusion of fear of being emotionally enslaved, and on to a higher expression of your Aquarian nature that will help you remain a free agent while connecting on a profound and intimate level in business or personal life, and make your Sun shine bright.

Aquarius 8

It's sexual, but it's not. It's innocent, but it's not. Allure mixed with repression can certainly be titillating. Aquarians get the reputation of being nonsexual, and that's got to bug the hell out of you, as much as sex scares the hell out of you when you're younger. From an early age you're curious about it, however, and whatever craziness was put into your head about sex and disease has made you act in all kinds of strange ways.

It's true that sex and disease can be linked, and probably will be for a long time to come. So it doesn't matter whether Aquarians are normally sexy or not. You have to come to terms with issues of sex and health so prevalent today, which makes you either freakily phobic about getting near anybody's precious bodily fluids, or the contrary. You could take stupid risks just to overcompensate for repressive or ignorant or nonexistent sex education.

Perhaps you are here as an observer, rather than a participant, in the odd rites and practices of human fertility. Yet you are as full of yearning for intimate contact as the rest of us. Or are you? It's possible that your hormones run more like chilled Perrier than hot mulled wine. Maybe that's why you work so much, why you throw yourself into your "art" with the dedication of a priest or priestess. Could work be a way to take the edge off a nature that is both desperately yearning for celestial orgasm and bored with the whole damned thing? The trouble is, you can't work all the time, and you can't go on forever thinking that starving yourself is noble. You can make plenty of money despite your horror of being corrupted by materialism. You have to love what you do, but here's the news you've been both waiting and dreading to hear: You will also have to do it for money.

Purity and innocence may get you into Heaven, but they won't pay the airfare to Florida in the winter. You must depart, at least temporarily, from your holy mission to tell the world how repressed it is—and make some real money and take a break, wet your whistle, add a little lube to the machine. Starving yourself silly either financially or emotionally would be cool if you were a cloistered monk in 906 AD, but in this twenty-first century you have to come to terms with whatever guilt you have for enjoying yourself and dare to let the prosperity flow. If you allow yourself to love prosperity as much as you love getting into debt, you'll be in fat city. The trick is to understand that you are here to support yourself and also have the faith in yourself that you can generate income, enjoy everything this life has to offer, and not go to hell for it.

At this point you need to probe more deeply into your obsession with purity and chastity, to the point that you don't take a weekend off to walk on the beach. In the next part, Going Deeper, reading the chapters called "Sex" and "Control" will give you a chance to pass through the illusion of fear of letting down your guard, and on to a higher expression of your Aquarian nature that will help you stay focused, loosen up, make some money, have faith in life, and make your Sun shine bright.

> *Celebrities Who Share Your Issues*
> *Yoko Ono, Stendhal, Sir Francis Bacon, Babe Ruth, Gypsy Rose Lee*

Aquarius 9

Is it a ventriloquist doing the speaking? Or is it the dummy? Hard to tell sometimes just who's really and truly talking instead of having the string at the back of their neck yanked and mouthing somebody else's words, doing someone else's bidding. When you took tests in school (you hated those), was it difficult to figure out whether the teacher wanted you to write down what you thought or to just parrot some crap that was in the book you were supposed to have read? It will probably take longer for you to learn how to speak for yourself. In some cases it never happens. Some Aquarians spout the party line and take all their cues from on high. Either that or they think they're too dumb or too scared to say what they think and so they say little or nothing at all. It's really a shame, too, because you've got some amazing observations to share with the world about what's really been going on. You just have to open your yap and stop worrying what will happen if you do.

Let's hope you're one of those wise Aquarians who isn't scared of what people will think, and is willing to talk. Of course you worry about what people will say or think of you. That's one of your biggest issues—whether or not you'll be considered intelligent, or educated, or suffer rejection or persecution because of your religious or ethnic background. That is one reason why race or religion will always enter into your relationships and you will be seduced by and attracted to people who come from completely different backgrounds. You will allow yourself to be swallowed whole by those backgrounds the way a boa swallows a pig until you eventually have to fight your way out or disappear entirely. You certainly wouldn't want disasppear, now, would you? Nor would you want to go to the other extreme and start bending other people's minds and influencing the way they think, except of course if you believe you are doing right.

It's all a matter of communication in relationships, and in some unevolved Aquarians, it's wrapped around the bid for dominance and tactics of intimidation. That's the trick. One person doesn't have to beat another one down and brainwash them, do they? Teachers don't have to screw up the ability of their students to learn. Ministers aren't necessarily going to lead their flock astray. Oh, but when students fall for their teachers and members of the congregation fall under the spell of their spiritual guides, anything can happen. Anything. And the great thing is, you'll live to tell about it.

At this point you need to probe more deeply into your obsession with being sane and smart enough not to follow people blindly, to the point that you lose your own ability to trust your own eyes and ears. In the next part, Going Deeper, reading the chapters called "Marriage" and "Religion" will give you a chance to pass through the illusion of fear of rejection if you don't allow yourself to be controlled by another person, and on to a higher expression of your Aquarian nature that will help you speak more freely, and make your Sun shine bright.

> *Celebrities Who Share Your Issues*
> *D. W. Griffith, Jackson Pollock, Rip Torn, Eva Braun, Mark Spitz,*
> *James Dean, James Hoffa, Rosa Parks, Jennifer Anniston, Axl Rose*

Aquarius 10

What a scandal. What a shocker. It's outrageous. Unheard of. And to think that you of all people . . . Why it's absolutely something you might never expect to read in the tabloids. And that's just the place for some story about you to end up. In the tabloids. In your younger days, before you grow up and buy property, you're likely to act in pretty scandalous ways, at least in ways your parents would consider scandalous. But so much of youthful behavior is motivated by wanting to do exactly the opposite of what your parents would expect of you—trying not to be anything like your mother whom you consider nuts, if she wasn't a total witch.

You have an innate mistrust of doctors, shrinks, anybody with absolute power, and you'll go to great lengths to bring them down. You're actually torn between the ultraradical and the archconservative. The conflict between sexual rebel and God-fearing churchgoer will show up one way or another in your work and personal relationships. Some of the wacko stuff you'll pull, especially when you're younger, just to get attention, could come back to haunt you later. You hate to be passed over or ignored, and yet when you are dragged into the limelight it's rarely to enhance your golden image. Funny, too, but the more you try to flee the grip you believe your family background has you squeezed in, the tighter you feel the grip. Only later in life do you come to understand the value of family ties and the importance of intimate trustworthy associations.

Trust is a gigundous issue, mainly because you were so betrayed so early by a regime you knew was a corrupt plutocracy you'd never respect. At least somebody in your childhood gave you sound principles about finance, which, until you're more mature, you will also reject in favor of a more Bohemian lifestyle, and that's putting it mildly.

Let's just say people should be able to do what they want to do in the privacy of their bedroom, no matter how cracked it may seem to others, and not have to see it plastered all over the newspapers. So if you want your own dirty laundry to remain your own business, you can't make it your business to squeal on others.

Society is a satire all on its own. What is taboo in one generation is legislation in the next. As long as you understand your own deeply conservative streak and eventually come to terms with it, you'll be able to sit in both houses of congress.

At this point you need to probe more deeply into your obsession with being recognized for naughty behavior, to the point that you behave solely for shock value. In the next part, Going Deeper, reading the chapters called "Sex" and "Recognition" will give you a chance to pass through the illusion of fear of being trapped in a bourgeois family setting that represses your sexuality, and on to a higher expression of your Aquarian nature that will help you develop your professional life but not allow it to mask your need for intimacy, love, and prosperity, and make your Sun shine bright.

> ### Celebrities Who Share Your Issues
> Ronald Reagan, Alice Cooper, Gertrude Stein, Mikhail Baryshnikov, Gene Hackman, Christopher Guest, Laura Dern

Aquarius 11

You're one of those Aquarians who love humanity but can't stand people. Like everything else about you, you are definitely weird in your tastes and attitudes; your political views and moral stances are completely unpredictable and indescribable. On the one hand, you're a freethinking peaceful anarchist, open to all, loving all the wonderful square peg misfits who can't fit into round-hole society. Then you can turn around and get a bug up your nose about Eric So-and-So or Freda-What's-Her-Face and exclude them for reasons you consider valid and excellent, but reflect your inbred exclusionary prejudices. You might have a really tough time acknowledging that you've still got a touch of prejudicial unfair thinking, the stuff you loathed as a youngster because of its narrow-minded, hateful, unjust, effect on you. It's actually great you're the kook that you are. You break the mold, all right. You're certainly going to create controversy during your lifetime. You'll follow a path whether it brings you high financial awards or not, because when you believe in something, get out of the way world, the opinionated tank is coming through.

You are not able to follow any map or conform to what anybody expects of you. Never did. Never will. It's not in your nature to give up your fierce hold on your independence and even if you're not as great in group activities as you'd like to be, you still love the common cause. You'll fight for human rights, to worship as you choose, even though organized religion has almost done you in. In fact, the whole issue of education as social pressure is one you could actually become rabid about.

With maturity you should be able to accept a more personal, intimate sort of communication without escaping quite so often, back to your constituents who shelter you from having to be a lover or a parent.

Whether you admit it or not, you're a born politician who sooner or later has to show that you're made of a lot more than strategy and manipulation. There's actually a heart under all that. The path of highest development will lead you to a much more personal involvement, with lasting intimate ties, and greater communication. All you have to do is say "I love you" and mean it.

At this point you need to probe more deeply into your obsession with being so rebellious and restless, to the point that you pretend it is friendship when it is really love. In the next part, Going Deeper, reading the chapters called "Religion" and "Freedom" will give you a chance to pass through the illusion of fear of losing your independence, and on to a higher expression of your Aquarian nature that will help you communicate better, not just on global issues, but with your own children and everybody else you hold dear, and make your Sun shine bright.

Celebrities Who Share Your Issues
Carmen Miranda, Eartha Kitt, Dan Quayle, Chris Rock,
Dr. Laura Schlessinger

Aquarius 12

So many Aquarians become hugely famous, and many of them share an odd phenomenon. They burn brightly for a while, then vanish and go into obscurity, only to return again to popularity and notoriety in a different incarnation. They tend to like to drop out and disappear periodically, often by choice. In fact when it's not by choice, they freak out and think life has passed them by and they're just forgotten has-beens. They go ballistic if they're ignored, and yet they're always running from the light like cockroaches when you come into the kitchen. They are always seeking greater privacy and seclusion. So if you're that type, we're going to have to send you out to work, get you out of the house, and away from your constant obsessing about how nobody appreciates how much you've done for them, how you've sacrificed, and on and on. You feel totally secure when you are given a job to do. Although you may consider regular, steady, consistent habits a drag, that is pretty much the only way you're going to stay sane.

Although scrubbing the kitchen counter and commercial soap-selling stuff may in some ways be beneath the star you are, work is work. So many actors end up winning awards for bit parts they had to take for no other reason than they needed a job immediately.

It's the love-hate thing you have with obscurity that is interesting. You can't be an A-list celebrity and hope to keep your personal life from being discussed and evaluated by people who have no idea what is driving you to act or perform in a way that probably does seem totally wacky (to some people). If it's self-destructive, which, okay, it has turned out to be sometimes, then so be it. It's your life and it hasn't interfered too much with your ability to do your job, has it? Or has it?

Your private life made public? What a horror. Yet the public version of you can be so skewed so that it's not really you at all. Are you the buttoned-up, efficient, showing-up-on-time, well-trained soldier—disciplined, well honed, and in charge of your craft? Or are you in bed with the pillow over your head reaching for the snooze button? Oh, if they only knew.

And if it slips out. If they find out. Then what? If they ever knew how down you can get when you feel like a used rag. You need your escapes. You need your time off. You need your forays into the obscurity of your private little world to seek ecstasy and to grieve in secret. But you have to learn how to balance that need with the ability to come back and work productively and live healthily enough to escape once again.

At this point you need to probe more deeply into your obsession with being so secretive, to the point that you give in to every temptation, seduction, and distraction that allows you to flee the grind of life. In the next part, Going Deeper, reading the chapters called "Escape" and "Recognition" will give you a chance to pass through the illusion of fear of being controlled by another person, and on to a higher expression of your Aquarian nature that will help you battle a System whose taste you deplore even while contributing to it, maintaining your integrity, and make your Sun shine bright.

Celebrities Who Share Your Issues
Buzz Aldrin, Tom Selleck, Franz Schubert, Mia Farrow, Leontyne Price, Alfred Adler, Leslie Nielsen, Michael Jordan, Bridget Fonda

PISCES

February 19–March 20
Dates vary from year to year—consult your local astrologer

Monet's *Water Lilies.* Debussy's *La Mer. Ports of Call* by Ibert. Spielberg's DreamWorks logo. Pine Lake on a full moon evening with only the call of a distant loon to break the silence. Bursting into tears uncontrollably when Lassie comes home. The Dalai Lama's gratitude to the Chinese. The belief that R2D2 really speaks to C3PO. Pisces is fireflies that you'd swear were pixies in the night forest. Pisces is the faint aroma of lemon verbena that tells you an elegant woman recently passed your way. It's the darkened movie theater where you're transported to 1920s Chicago or ancient Rome or Tibet, and where you sometimes steal a kiss in the back row. It's the ability to put on your headphones and shut out the most annoying toothy chatter of the morons sitting next to you on the plane. It is union with the Universe, communion with God and Goddess. Pisces is the changeling, the magical capacity to transform from one state to another: ice to water to mist to water to ice to water to mist and back again, subtly. Pisces is the tinkle of the bell during Communion when worshipers are silently sharing the mystery of transubstantiation. It is the undescribably blissful experience of liberation from all attachment while being open to the love of all beings everywhere in all worlds, as well as the happiness you feel when you look into the eyes of someone you know loves you totally, completely, without question and whom you love the same way.

Now let's be real. Pisces is also the ability to pass gas on the bus and actually convince yourself it was the lady sitting next to you. It's the starry-eyed feeling you get from the first sip of your second martini that makes you fall in love with everyone in the bar. It's not only art and the artist who embodies it, but it's also the failed artist who wouldn't sell out to a corrupt and tasteless world but who now has a civil service job by day and boozes it up at night. It's the nature-worshiping vegetarian in nonleather sandals with his own generator and solar panel house in the woods, as well as the conspiracy-obsessed nut, holed up and scanning the Internet for more clues into the government's plot to control our minds and poison our bodies. Oddly enough, if you're a Pisces, you could make it on Wall Street and get away with convincing everyone you're a tough, hard-boiled business person. Even if you're a raging hot pop sensation, most likely you had nothing to do with it. That happens a lot to members of your sign mainly because you're dripping with talent and no matter how much you try to hide, eventually you're noticed and brought to the front of the line.

You're a funny mixture of a child's enthusiasm and an old widow's cynicism—not bitter, though. While you can get totally excited and full of joy and laughter at the simplest things, you also expect to be disappointed by just about everything, with good reason. You have been there and done that at least a zillion times. Maybe because your imaginary world is so much better than the shabby excuse for existence ours is, nothing on a tangible level can compare with the fabulous experiences that go on in your head. Wondering what the Mona Lisa must be like is a hell of a lot more exciting than standing in a mob line for two hours at the Louvre to see a tiny picture behind glass of what looks like a fat guy in drag. So while part of you is always hoping for that transcendental experience, every experience falls just a little bit short of ecstasy. You're always hoping, though. Disguise it all you want to, but you're an incurable romantic, and no matter how many times you've been dashed against the rocks of despair, you're always hoping. Your yearning for transcendance is probably why Pisceans are often thought of as a bunch of coked-up addicts. You usually have to go through your trashy period, which could come at any time, before or after you've married and had kids. Eventually, though, you stagger out of the haze, pull up the shades, and, squinting through a whopping hangover headache, start your life all over again.

You shouldn't think negatively about these observations, because you're definitely the wisest of all the signs. As timid as you can be in childhood, you're the one who is ultimately open to all experience and thus afraid of none. You could walk down the runway sporting Vera Wang's latest creation and immerse yourself in the Champagne bubbles of glamour, but if you end up barefoot picking apples, that would be fine, too. Paradoxically, although you're at home nowhere on Earth, and as much as you savor ease and luxury, anywhere will do, because your real life is lived somewhere in the interior far from the city's maddening noise, the destruction of the rain forest, or the glitzy beaches of the Hamptons.

Sometimes you seem faithless and irresponsible, switching allegiances, twisting stories and changing positions you've sworn to uphold. The last thing you want to do is hurt people. But if anyone thinks they're going to throw you in a cage for life, they're a fool, even if you beg to be incarcerated. Ain't going to happen. Your life here is a series of states and experiences, a whole gamut of identities that cannot be captured in one snapshot. Here you are holding the baby. There you are in a topless bar. And that's you in a bar-mitzvah suit. Or leaving rehab. Receiving an award at a banquet. The essence of you inside, however, remains the same, dedicated to love, acceptance, and forgiveness.

Some distant day the world will finally end—and rest assured it sure as hell eventually will—by some stupid human blunder or computer glitch or maybe the Sun will swell up and engulf the Earth. However it happens, there will be some Pisces lying in a hammock in some lush, green backyard, sipping a tall, cool drink, looking up and uttering, "This is exactly why I never felt like doing anything!" Some people say that you're a lazy, shiftless good-for-nothing bum who uses every excuse imaginable to call in sick. Far from it. Pisceans are motivated toward money and success, but not consistently, of course, because your real life is lived on another plane. Some people think you're just plain paranoid and nuts because you can see, feel, and sense the undercurrents that pervade everything. Nobody should think you can't tell diamonds from zircons, because you've got a deep streak of practicality and street savvy. You'll let people think they've made a fool of you, but in the end, you come up the winner. You don't really live down here in the nonfiction world with the rest of us, though. For you fantasy is reality and reality is fantasy. That's really good news for the homeless Piscean schizo who believes aliens and the Republican senators in Congress are listening to his thoughts through the fillings in his teeth. For you, it's a struggle to stay grounded without help. It's so hard sometimes to distinguish fact from fancy. Just think of trying to figure out what happened in Chappaquiddick. Global warming is probably real, but if you think about it too much, you'll start recycling your own toilet paper.

That's the weird thing about being a Pisces. You're ruled by the planet Neptune, which means there are a whole assortment of little fishies swimming around in your brain. Some are cute; others are downright unbearably beautiful. You've got the dolphins—highly evolved, spiritually magical—guiding shipwrecked sailors to land. And then there are the toothy predators who can swill a person down with a couple of hundred gallons of seawater and not even get the hiccups. You've got at least a hundred thousand identities and by golly you're going to live 'em all out before your life is over.

You can be amazingly grounded and organized when you're inspired, though, and that's the thing with you. When you're inspired you don't need food, drink, or sleep to accomplish any task. And you certainly don't need diet pills or coke or crack to keep you up and functioning. That stuff is usually hauled out when you're in one of your "this-whole-world-sucks-and-I've-got-to-get-pumped-up-or-I-may-just-end-it-all" moods.

But suicide? Pisceans are probably the least likely to go the car-in-the-closed-garage-with-the-engine-running route. For all your self-destructive thoughts and threats, by the time you are ready to do the deed, you already feel much better and see how ridiculous you were even to contemplate such a foolish act. Besides the fact that you love life way too much—you're fundamentally a true hedonist. You love your comforts too much, and you'd never want to give people the chance to say you were weak. Even though in your own mind, you're falling down like a rag doll every five minutes, you're going to be the last pin standing when all the bowling balls have come rolling down the alley.

Achieving a state of ideal security, pure emotion, and spiritual communion is possible due to your natural inborn largeness of spirit. It's way too easy to simply lower all your standards and permit yourself to be violated so you can retaliate by violating the standards, practices, rules, and laws of others—and then call it universal love, acceptance, and forgiveness. How can you totally open up and believe, when time and again you've seen how when the lights go up, the whole experience was a show, a dream, a mock-up, a stage set with cardboard figures reading a script full of empty words? How can you live fully and totally in the world and remain above the clouds where you're really happiest?

You need to live at least two lives, often simultaneously, while you are passing through this plane of existence. When we look at you we see tears in your eyes and we can't tell if you've been laughing hysterically at some side-splitting joke, or you've just been crying over some pain and heartache you're trying to shield us from. You get furious at the thought of sacrifice, and yet you've made a few gigundous ones already.

Is that love? Does love mean giving up something or someone you want more than anything in the world for some greater moral or spiritual good? Is it self-indulgent to go after your heart's desire or are you programmed for renunciation and self-denial? Are you being generous when you allow people their transgressions, trespasses, crimes, and misdemeanors and take them into your arms again without bitterness or rancor? Or is that what they call codependence these days? Are you truly the personification of compassion or just a stupid jerk caught up in a tawdry cycle of sadomasochistic foreplay?

You are the freshness of innocence and the cynicism that comes from living too hard. You are Liz Taylor in *National Velvet* and Liz Taylor in *Who's Afraid of Virginia Woolf?* Pisces is the rainbow that can never be separated from the storm that precedes it. Since you are ruled by the planet Neptune, you are impossible to figure out. Was it really an alien abduction or just a silly nightmare? You are quality and trash—Verdi's *Gilda* as sung by Joan Sutherland as well as lip-synched crapola as performed by Milli Vanilli.

You're the purple heather of the misty moors of Scotland. A father's tears when he beholds his first-born child and a mother's pain producing that child. The miracle on Thirty-Fourth Street. The Virgin's appearance to Bernadette. Disney's *Fantasia*. Ron Howard's *Cocoon* (as well as the baseball cap he wears to hide his baldness). Messages from your dead uncle. Peace restored to the entire Middle East. The history of the African American race from ancient Africa to 50 Cent. Healing hands and shyster's scams. Christ's last words: "Into thy hands I commend my spirit," or "What a total schmuck I've been!" The line between truth and falsehood, love and foolishness. How to achieve the higher manifestations of love, acceptance, and forgiveness, if you are not just going to sit in a monastery in the Himalayas and never have to have a relationship again with the exception of an avalanche now and then?

How do you move more with right action as a way to achieve your goal of union with the Universe? What are the forces that drag you backward and keep you from reaching the highest manifestation of your Sun? And what are the energies that can support you, guide you, enhance your positive qualities and make your Sun shine bright? The fact is you're not just a Pisces. There is another energy operating, one that either cuts across your efforts and undermines them, or spirits you to heights of joy and fulfillment. That energy depends not on the month you were born, but the year as well. Later on in this book the technical aspects will be explained more fully. We'll examine how you waste time chasing your own tail, why you do it, and how to pull yourself out of self-destructive obsessions and put yourself back on the road to success. But for now, check out the following table. Find your birth year and note the number beside it. Then read the section corresponding to the number.

Year–No.	Year–No.	Year–No.	Year–No.	Year–No.
1901–3	1908–11	1917–5	1925–12	1934–6
1902–3	1909–10	1918–4	1926–11	1935–5
1903–2	1910–10	1919–4	1927–11	1936–5
1904–1	1911–9	1920–3	1928–10	1937–4
1905–1	1912–8	1921–3 *until*	1929–9	1938–3
1906–12	1913–8	2/27, *then* 2	1930–9	1939–3
1907–12 *until*	1914–7	1922–2	1931–8	1940–2
3/13,	1915–6	1923–1	1932–7	1941–2
then 11	1916–6	1924–1	1933–7	1942–1

Year–No.	Year–No.	Year–No.	Year–No.	Year–No.
1943–12	*1961–1*	*1980–12*	*1997–2 until*	*2015–2*
1944–12	*1962–12*	*1981–12*	*2/27, then 1*	*2016–1*
1945–11	*1963–11*	*1982–11*	*1998–1*	*2017–1*
1946–10	*1964–11*	*1983–11 until*	*1999–12*	*2018–12*
1947–10	*1965–10*	*3/15, then*	*2000–12*	*2019–11*
1948–9	*1966–9*	*10*	*2001–11*	*2020–11*
1949–8	*1967–9*	*1984–10*	*2002–10*	*2021–10*
1950–8	*1968–8*	*1985–9*	*2003–10*	*2022–9*
1951–7	*1969–8*	*1986–9*	*2004–9*	*2023–9*
1952–7 until	*1970–7*	*1987–8*	*2005–8*	*2024–8*
3/6, then 6	*1971–6*	*1988–7*	*2006–8*	*2025–7*
1953–6	*1972–6*	*1989–7*	*2007–7*	*2026–7*
1954–5	*1973–5*	*1990–6*	*2008–6*	*2027–6*
1955–5	*1974–4*	*1991–5*	*2009–6*	*2028–6 until*
1956–4	*1975–4*	*1992–5*	*2010–5*	*3/7, then 5*
1957–3	*1976–3*	*1993–4*	*2011–4*	*2029–5*
1958–3	*1977–2*	*1994–3*	*2012–4*	*2030–4*
1959–2	*1978–2*	*1995–3*	*2013–3*	
1960–1	*1979–1*	*1996–2*	*2014–3*	

Pisces 1

Oh you're a slippery one, all right. The term "greased pig" might be a little crude, because your heart is in the right place. In fact it's probably in too many places, at least when you're younger and full of the seductive allure most Pisceans are dripping with. And for a long time you can't help it. When you're left too much on your own, half the time you're a lost little lamb, madly searching for yourself and seeking meaning and purpose, the other half of the time not giving a good goddamn about anything. It shows in your body, your face, your clothing. You can go from the super-exotic glamorous to the homeless look and vice versa in a matter of hours. Or minutes. Sometimes it just depends on the lighting in the room. Half the time you see with utter clarity, and then you can drift into a blithering haze you have to be snapped out of. You can be utterly self-absorbed and selfless at the same time, and even the people who think you're a total nut will have to concede that you're attractive, interesting, even hypnotic and irresistible—almost the way a sign that says "Don't Skate Here" is irresistible to kids about to take a dangerous step onto thin ice.

So it all depends on where you're at on the evolutionary ladder of Pisces. If you're one of the really self-indulgent self-destructive ones you'll wear out your body and look a total wreck before you clean up at thirty. If you're the messianic "I-must-save-this-rotten-world" type, nothing will stop or impede your missionary zeal for very long. One thing is certain: You cannot focus on yourself, depressed or otherwise, in self-pity or disillusion without swirling away into nothingness.

Connecting with people, making contact, sweeps you immediately out of your reverie or morass of cosmic misery. It forces you to clean up your act and start taking better care of yourself. You need someone to bring you back to Earth from the la-la galaxy you live in. That person can hose you down and remind you about the practicalities of the boring daily grind we all have to deal with down here on this planet. As much as you have a desire to serve mankind, it's a strain to relate to people much of the time. Their needs and demands are so banal. And yet those petty menial annoying details are exactly what will bring your blurry image into focus. It is relationships with people and your desire to connect with them that unites inspiration with perspiration to bring dreams into physical manifestation.

Prayer is good for digestion, but so is granola. So mix a little organic orange juice in with the vodka and you'll be on your way.

At this point you need to probe more deeply into your obsession with being the mysterious, sad victim, to the point that you get really self-destructive and lose credibility. In the next part, Going Deeper, reading the chapters called "Independence" and "Escape" will give you a chance to pass through the illusion of fear of losing your edge and being controlled by another person, and on to a higher expression of your Piscean nature that will help you remain an exotic figure, have healthier relationships, resist them less, and make your Sun shine bright.

Pisces 2

You don't want to be driven bananas worrying about money, or get into a crazy head about whether men or women are making more. God knows if you're a Pisces it's easy enough to go bananas over everything else, not to mention your antics trying to get into Heaven and Hell at the same time. Anybody who's ever had to skip a meal or dodge a landlord knows darned well how demeaning it is to be without resources. It can be just as embarrassing to be supported by a parent or a mate or some sponsor you have to appear before, hat in hand, looking at your shoes and acting grateful. Anybody who thinks those people on welfare don't hate themselves really is cuckoo, because when you don't have economic independence, you almost feel like you don't exist. Being beholden to somebody else for your daily bread is not a feeling of security at all. Oh, that burns you. So naturally you want to scratch out some scratch for yourself. Damn, though. It seems as if the devil is always right there to snatch it away. Yes, you're a Pisces and should be thinking only of the next world. But you're enough in this world to know that the one who controls the money calls the shots, and you absolutely loathe being put in such a dependent submissive position, even if you are a Pisces.

Of course, if you're so evolved that you have no interest in living what some people call "la dolce vita" you are never bothered by such annoying details as banks, or wills, or stipends of any kind. You're probably not that evolved yet.

You are a full-fledged flask-carrying Pisces. You still want a nice, big taste of the good life and that puts you in a quandary. Should you remain true to your wild nature or sell out and go totally commercial? If you allow nature to take its course, you will eventually find your way back to where you are supposed to be in the first place. You are the embodiment of talent, sexuality, and creativity, and if surrendering to all three makes you completely submissive, so be it. Of course, that's easy for somebody else to say, but when you're right there in the thick of a relationship, money and the person who controls it are very much factors in how you perform—in bed and out. Money is the carrot that gets the donkey to stand up and pull the wagon, but 500 years from now when they look at your history, let's hope they see that you were able to overcome your fierce anger about men, women, and money and transcend your fear of loss of control and your fear of being known. Sounds great.

At this point you need to probe more deeply into your obsession with being so self-reliant, to the point that you don't dare accept the good luck that is handed to you. In the next part, Going Deeper, reading the chapters called "Independence" and "Money" will give you a chance to pass through the illusion of fear of being on the dole, and on to a higher expression of your Piscean nature that will help you earn your way, enjoy the resources of others, develop deeply fulfilling sexual relationships, and make your Sun shine bright.

> *Celebrities Who Share Your Issues*
> *Mario Andretti, Anaïs Nin, Michelangelo, Vincente Minnelli, James Van Der Beek, Aidan Quinn, Gabriel Horn*

Pisces 3

You're obviously a lot hipper than most of the people who think you're either crazy, wrong, or just plain annoying. It's not that you set out to shake people up. It's just that you do have a thing about narrow-minded fat cats who have all the money and won't listen to anything that threatens their position in the slightest. When they say it's not the money, it usually is.

Or is it? Sometimes in personal relationship crises, when people start fighting over money, more likely they are fighting over deeper, more painful issues that are difficult to face—like sex, or racial or religious differences. Such issues are very hard to acknowledge; it is easier to identify the problems of who's not getting enough as a problem about money, when more delicate issues are really causing the strife.

So you have to learn how to talk to people and present yourself and your ideas in nonthreatening ways. Sometimes you may have an actual language problem, because you're definitely going to be in foreign territory, whether you're just a visitor or an actual expatriate. Truthfully, you're always a visitor in whatever culture you've been plopped down in. It's clear you have an intelligence far greater than most of the clods you run into, especially in business. You're not crazy and you're not stupid, even if you can't spell "oxymoron" or do math or think inside the box or even be totally monogamous or even 100 percent hetero. And it may take a lot of growing up before you can accept the fact that you are a stranger in a strange land, with ideas, views, notions, philosophies, and especially appetites that aren't exactly considered kosher in anybody's language.

Oh, you'll scream until you're hoarse, thinking that maybe if you scream loud enough, somebody will finally listen. That may happen, but until it does, you're likely to be more like the voice of truth crying in the wilderness. Without compassion for and understanding of the ignorance of others, life will seem like a recurring dream in which you are trying to tell people something vital for their survival, but when you open your mouth to speak, nothing comes out. The wisdom and art with which you have been blessed don't necessarily have to be contaminated by commercialism. They have to be united with it.

At this point you need to probe more deeply into your obsession with being financially secure and listened to by people who don't think you're smart enough to handle your own affairs. In the next part, Going Deeper, reading the chapters called "Communication" and "Money" will give you a chance to pass through the illusion of fear of not being considered competent, and on to a higher expression of your Piscean nature that will help you make better connections, raise your ability to relate to people from all backgrounds, and make your Sun shine bright.

Pisces 4

You may wonder how in the name of all that is holy you ever landed in that family. Did the stork just open its beak to burp and accidentally drop you down that particular chimney, or was there some cosmic plan involved? One way or another you must come to terms with having been raised by people ill-equipped to take proper care of a child. It makes you think sometimes that individuals should have to fill out forms or submit to mental examinations and tests before they're allowed to have kids in the first place. Maybe that's a bit harsh, but if you haven't totally blocked out or distorted memories from your school and preschool days, you'll see exactly how fragmented and inconsistently handled the whole era was. That nervous, restless, capricious, anything-goes style of nurturing still haunts you from time to time. Of course, it's probably become very important for you to be sane and nurturing to your own kids, if you have any. Ironically, you may even have to take care of the nuts you call your folks when they get old (the ones who were supposed to be taking care of you when you were young).

Anyway, it doesn't matter, really, because you're a Pisces with an enormous capacity to understand that life on Earth is just a crazy trip anyway that demands a lot of acceptance and forgiveness on your part. If you were the type to show anger and seek revenge you'd have grounds to do so. What's the point, though? All that was in the past, and you're way past it. At least most of the time.

You still have problems in communication when the subject of family comes up, and being cut off from them has its plusses and minuses. On the plus side, you are free to pursue a wonderful fruitful career full of support, admiration, recognition, and public support from people of all races, creeds, and colors. Such independence from family can be a minus when the old feelings of abandonment, guilt, anger, and isolation come back to haunt you, at times so severely that you can almost find it difficult to step out of the house. Even when you're at the top of your game, you still feel that shallow emptiness, like a man performing on stilts at a circus who feels that at any moment he could be toppled. Funny thing is, when you focus on what you're doing, your intelligence, the message you are trying to send to the world, you will be heard, whether the family was deaf to you or not.

At this point you need to probe more deeply into your issues about putting yourself emotionally in the hands of people who will periodically drop you off with someone else or drop you on your head entirely, to the point that improper relationships could leak into your career. In the next part, Going Deeper, reading the chapters called "Communication" and "Security" will give you a chance to pass through the illusion of fear of being professionally undermined, and on to a higher expression of your Piscean nature that will help you feel safer, guard the great professional standing you are destined to achieve, and make your Sun shine bright.

Celebrities Who Share Your Issues
Nat King Cole, Arthur Schopenhauer, Nikolay Rimsky-Korsakov, Kurt Weill

Pisces 5

It's your Piscean vulnerability that makes you so attractive to others. It's also what has gotten you whacked so many times. You're attractive, yes, but you're not exactly right for the usual leading romantic roles. There usually has to be some tragic, ironic, weird, or science fiction twist to your love story, because no matter how many breast implants or hair plugs you get, you're just not the old-fashioned traditional guy-meets-girl-girl-kisses-guy-fade-out type of person. You'd like to be. You try to be, but you are not. You have an enormous yearning need to be loved and to have the security of a family. Maybe, probably, definitely, you didn't feel wanted, loved, nourished, and secure early enough, and it could well have impeded normal social development.

In high school it has to be awful to feel "different," but as you get older those same differences become your talent and your trademark. They can bring admiration and recognition from a world that appreciates and reveres your special talent and uniqueness. Of course, that other thing still lurks somewhere between your heart and your stomach. You're so sensitive to rejection and obsessed with having a "normal" love relationship. Yet you can be so un-Piscean in your efforts to find love. Instead of being open and understanding and allowing the Universe to provide you with what you need, you can be moody, clinging, possessive, demanding, overattached, jealous, and dependent. Major turnoff. Instead of getting the love you need, you could actually destroy the moment. It's certainly not out of malice. It's out of the desire to protect and nurture those you love. It's just that dependency is such a touchy issue and you are still so sensitive about the mothering thing.

Sometimes you have to tear yourself away and go do your thing out in the world. You do have a significant contribution you have to make. Your responsibilities to the world are on a bigger, more global scale, and will not permit you to indulge in as much intimate ecstasy or personal grief as you may think you need. If allowed, you'd be swallowed up by either or both. Success awaits you, provided you can spend less time in self-indulgent searches for a mommy you never had.

At this point you need to probe more deeply into your obsession with being properly cared for, to the point that you could become fiercely clinging and overattached to lovers or kids. In the next part, Going Deeper, reading the chapters called "Love" and "Security" will give you a chance to pass through the illusion of fear of being unceremoniously dumped, and on to a higher expression of your Piscean nature that will help you develop your performance abilities, reduce your dependence on people you want to take care of you as if they were your parents, step into the professional role you must accept in order to make your contribution to the world, and make your Sun shine bright.

Pisces 6

Selfless service is a key phrase often used when referring to Pisces. As if any of us can totally dedicate ourselves to some cause or path or person without getting some ego gratification out of it. You're no exception. Your ego is very much invested in the work that you do. In a way, your work is you. You put your whole self into it, so how could your ego not be a part of it? But to say you do what you do just for the attention or applause or self-aggrandizement is totally unfair, especially since you've given up so much personal happiness to do what you do. Your work is your personal happiness. It's your way of loving and being loved, and if anybody thinks you've been able to avoid personal heartbreak by working as much as you do, they're crazy, because as much as you love your work, it's caused you plenty of personal heartbreak. Let no one make any mistake about that. Sure, ego is involved, sometimes too much. The ego gets in the way when you feel rejected. Then you tend to push, sometimes too hard, at which point you wind up behind the eight ball.

As grand and grandiose as you can be, you're really the sort of individual who identifies with the poor, downtrodden, mistreated, ignored, disenfranchised beings whom society looks upon as a dispensable species, a lower form of life, whose needs have little or no importance in the great scheme of things. Somehow, on some level, you were probably treated as such and that is where your anger comes in, as well as your need to be adored and treated like royalty. Not going to happen. Besides, that's the childish part of you that is just trying to get notice for yourself and gather personal power. It's not really your highest motive. Not by a long shot.

You're actually on a mission in this life. It's a mission to restore dignity to all beings of this Earth. Is it crazy? It's only crazy if you start deciding which beings are worthy and which are not. It's only crazy if you become so entrenched in your beliefs and philosophy that the work itself is drained of the humanity it is setting out to preserve. What if you are presented with a hugely ironic situation in which you are asked, for the betterment of the common good and the welfare of a majority of beings, to give up what you are doing? Could you do it?

At this point you need to probe more deeply into your obsession with being valuable and wanted, to the point that you cheat yourself of a whole dimension of intimacy and personal liberty. In the next part, Going Deeper, reading the chapters called "Control" and "Love" will give you a chance to pass through the illusion of fear of being a useless piece of archaic machinery, and on to a higher expression of your Piscean nature that will help you continue your meaningful work, liberate you from enslavement to old ego insecurities, and make your Sun shine bright.

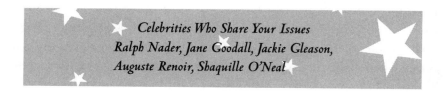

Celebrities Who Share Your Issues
Ralph Nader, Jane Goodall, Jackie Gleason,
Auguste Renoir, Shaquille O'Neal

Pisces 7

When you feel out of balance and out of control, you think you need your personal zookeeper and parole officer, and you go chasing after control freaks you eventually have to dump because they're on your case every five minutes. Would you like to get to a point where you don't think you're going to go off the deep end, you're more stable, and can have a more stable relationship that's not so full of extremes that it eats itself up? Here's a strange irony: The people you think are going to anchor and stabilize you have often turned out to be way crazier, compulsive, and more unstable than you are. Different, but still crazy.

By nature half the time you're a clean freak—the other half you're a major slob. It's usually in relationships that your slob self emerges after a while, as if to drive the other person mad. But you let yourself go only when the other person starts to pick pick pick pick at you like a canary at a hunk of bird seed. You want to be with someone. You need them there—until that moment that always seems to come when you look at them as if they're some inferior being who somehow got a key to your house. You get so totally smitten at first, like a dog that falls instantly in love with the prospective master who has just walked into the pound.

You give them that Pisces oh-you-probably-wouldn't-want-a-beat-up-mutt-like-me look, and the next thing you know you wake up in their bed the next morning, happy at last. Then they start rubbing your nose in your own doo-doo and making you sleep outside in the rain because you did a no-no on the couch while they were away at work. Then one of you is out.

Your relationships are bound to center around "in sickness and in health" with the definitions of those words becoming blurrier and blurrier all the time. So are you happier and more secure getting your nose hit with a rolled-up newspaper time after time to keep you behaving just so you don't have to be alone? Or are you better off giving up the idea of togetherness and allowing yourself to drift in and out of functioning just to find some peace in life? The best alternative is to find a happy spot to curl up in between.

At this point you need to probe more deeply into your obsession with being stabilized by someone more sober than you are, to the point that you totally lose faith in your own abilities to cope on your own. In the next part, Going Deeper, reading the chapters called "Marriage" and "Control" will give you a chance to pass through the illusion of fear of going nuts on your own, and on to a higher expression of your Piscean nature that will help you remember the gifts you bring to a relationship, form stable ones, and make your Sun shine bright.

Celebrities Who Share Your Issues
Johnny Cash, Ted Kennedy, Elizabeth Taylor, Kurt Russell,
John Updike, William Westmoreland, Ruth Bader Ginsburg

Pisces 8

What do you think would have happened to Cinderella's marriage if, soon after the wedding, there was a revolution in the kingdom, Prince Charming found himself in a financial mess, and Cinderella had to go back to work and support him? What would that have done to their sex life? Or what if the Prince finds out that after all those years of being locked up and forced to wear rags, Cinderella expects him to keep shelling out big bucks for a little nookie? Crass as it is, the issue of sexual equilibrium and financial dominance must not be avoided if you are ever to find long-term happiness in a relationship.

Your dreams of "how it will be after we're together for fifty years" rarely include the very difficult subjects of monogamy and gender roles. There's no sense in playing dumb and saying you don't relate to it, because you do. Money interferes with intimacy—heterosexual or not—after a while, because one person will resent not being taken care of, financially or emotionally.

It's so complicated. Companionship and passion rarely sleep in the same bed. On the one hand you are looking for the compatible mate you fit together with like a plug in a socket. The minute your bodies come together and you make the magic of electricity, you also require a challenge. You like to prove you're desirable. Novelty and long-term compatibility don't exist together without games, constant challenges, or fights. Fights are normally so un-Pisces. They upset you. They disrupt the harmony, the music, the unity you are always seeking to create.

But you're also about business. You have to be. You cannot, must not, should not allow this fantasy of intimacy to blind you to the fact that you have to support yourself (and often the other person), even if it makes you angry to still find yourself fending for yourself when you were supposed to be able to relax and not have to think about your financial future. Uh-uh. You've got to be both the financial boss and the sexually submissive partner and/or vice versa. You could give up sex entirely, but what fun is that?

At this point you need to probe more deeply into your issues about having to carry the burden financially and not being sexually desirable, to the point that you get into messy emotional and fiscal relationships you can't get out of without a major hassle. In the next part, Going Deeper, reading the chapters called "Sex" and "Marriage" will give you a chance to pass through the illusion of fear of being used but unappreciated, and on to a higher expression of your Piscean nature that will help you stick to business, worry less about your desirability as a sex object or your performance, and make your Sun shine bright.

> ★ *Celebrities Who Share Your Issues*
> *Ivana Trump, Tom Wolfe, Chastity Bono, Rupert Murdoch,*
> *Jack Kerouac, Meher Baba, William H. Macy, Chris Klein*

Pisces 9

You don't have to have been raised Catholic, fundamentalist Muslim, or Orthodox Jew to be slapping your forehead and shouting "No surprise to me!" to anyone in earshot, when you see the scandal that has rocked the Catholic Church in the last few years. Nothing, absolutely nothing burns your butt more than evangelists with their seedy private lives, teachers who mess with their students, and shrinks who jump their patients on the couch. For you it's a blood boiler. No contest. And with damned good reason. It's part of your experience, a page in your history you'd prefer to tear up and burn but can't.

And yet, you've got to have compassion for the lost souls who take advantage of the innocent. Part of you, wise Pisces that you are, part of you knows that nobody is really totally completely 100 percent innocent. And while it may sound like blaming the victim, you know that on some level, victims and perpetrators are sometimes brought together for reasons we don't understand. Of course, you could conceivably make it your life's work to be an undercover cop, seducing and exposing these wolves in sheeps' clothing. Taken to an extreme, this could make you extremely sexually paranoid. You could perceive anybody who finds you attractive as dangerous.

You can be pretty seductive and misleading yourself. Despite your issues, you have a message to pass on and a beautiful voice to communicate that message in a more loving way. Artist, researcher, or academic, you've got an excellent head for business, if you'll just get up the courage to speak up and make sure you get what's due you.

You have played the dumb blonde more often than is good for you in this life and you've gotten screwed. You're a Pisces. The search for the big high has led you into more dark twisted dead-end alleys than anybody should be in after dark. Mentally you'll always be a lot healthier if you can stay rooted, right down here in the world where people know how to negotiate financial deals, talk about the weather, and hold hands on a spring afternoon. That's maturity and fulfillment. Although you'll probably think it's boring, you'll live a longer and more prosperous life.

At this point you need to probe more deeply into your obsession with being cheated on and lied to, to the point that you don't believe anything or anybody and could become faithless yourself because of it. In the next part, Going Deeper, reading the chapters called "Religion" and "Sex" will give you a chance to pass through the illusion of fear of being sexually controlled or psychologically dominated, and on to a higher expression of your Piscean nature that will help you focus on healthier communication, reap more financial rewards from your efforts, and make your Sun shine bright.

> *Celebrities Who Share Your Issues*
> *James Taylor, Bernadette Peters, Jean Harlow, Percival Lowell*

Pisces 10

Suing the tabloids may not sound like a good way to spend time, but believe this: There are a few major celebrities, who shall remain nameless, who would rather have sordid lies and distortions of all sorts appear in the headlines than not to see their name at all. Not everybody is that obsessed with being talked about. Some celebs have been known to make sure their publicists tip off the press about how they are going to show up at such and such a restaurant at 10 PM—then the star arrives in sunglasses and fights off the paparazzi, violently—and whaddaya know, it's tomorrow morning's scoop.

What does all this have to do with you? It's a metaphor for your ambivalence about being "discovered." Don't forget, the Pisces part of you is the invisible artist, the angel who comes and goes, does its miracle thing and departs unnoticed and unthanked, happy to have spread a little love around the night.

But you are not the selfless little hoofer at the back of the chorus line. Maybe it's all because of the crazy mother you had, but you're not going to be content making baked potatoes in the microwave. Even that takes too long if it means you have to stay in the kitchen. You need your public fix. And that's just what it is. A fix. A rush. A major high. To be somebody else for a while, to be known, recognized, talked about. To be the subject of buzz. And there's hell to pay if God forbid there is no buzz. And yet, you don't want it, either. You are still a Pisces. You know how stupid fame is—and hypocritical and full of cheap politics and sexual discrimination (to say nothing about the racial issues).

You can't help wanting to act out your fantasies. It's dangerous only when you're afraid to acknowledge your roots, when you're afraid that the family is going to impede your worldly progress, that you'll have to go home to Nowheresville to look after your sister or hang out with cousins you once pretended not to recognize. Fame versus family is not an either/or situation. You only get robbed of your position if you flee your family. And with the upbringing you had, it's no wonder you are tempted to deny your roots but are deeply attached to them at the same time. You only appreciate the home as you get older and realize how fruitless it is to want to be known as the person who knows everything and is afraid to talk to their own family. It's not career or family. It's career *and* family.

At this point you need to probe more deeply into your issues about being too invisible or too visible. In the next part, Going Deeper, reading the chapters called "Recognition" and "Religion" will give you a chance to pass through the illusion of fear of being controlled by another person, and on to a higher expression of your Piscean nature that will help you to make your mark in the world, retain your integrity, bond in better communication with the family, and make your Sun shine bright.

Pisces 11

It is certainly easy for people to tell you to settle down, get married, have kids, and give up all your ideas of helping humanity evolve. You can't help it, though. You're an idealist, and no matter how many times you've been disappointed, and no matter how often your dream of finding a society of evolved beings has been shattered, you still go on searching. It's been a tough trip, even since high school, mainly because you're really not the groupy type. People love you. But it seems that they always want to tie you down. You certainly already know what it feels like to stand on your head to do something for people, and then have them barely thank you for all your efforts.

You have to wonder why you go on working and struggling to make their lives easier. As altruistic as you are, there's also a political bent to your motives. You're hooked on being accepted and recognized. You do genuinely believe in freedom from oppression for all. It's just that you are tied to a desire for acceptance. For some crazy reason you are still hoping the world will recognize the sacrifices you've made. Like it matters. Like it really cooks your eggs when they say "Thank you very much, you're a great person," and then turn around and walk out and you're stuck doing the dishes.

You chase after these goals that seem to mean so much to you and then, in the end, when you do get it—the attention—it doesn't mean nearly as much as it did before you had it. The reason: What you are looking for is the security and happiness that can be found only through a deep, intimate love bond with another person. It's not easy for you to own up to, however. You have been known to use your professional commitments as a way of avoiding what you perceive as cloying dependencies.

Because Pisceans are forever getting sucked in emotionally, members of your sign usually have to make special efforts not to end up with six kids and no life. You keep your commitments open and tentative until, after a while, your life starts feeling empty. Not that you have to go the six-kids route, but you find sooner or later that intimate contacts and relationships that involve some semblance of love and family are not going to swallow you up, take away your freedom, and impede your worldly success. They will in fact add depth and meaning to an existence that could otherwise give you back a lot less than you put in. All you have to do is open yourself to love and it will come flowing toward you.

At this point you need to probe more deeply into your obsession with being part of a group you don't even want to belong to, to the point that you miss out on intimate love. In the next part, Going Deeper, reading the chapters called "Recognition" and "Freedom" will give you a chance to pass through the illusion of fear of being left out, and on to a higher expression of your Piscean nature that will help you do your political, social thing, have love and a family at the same time, and make your Sun shine bright.

Celebrities Who Share Your Issues
Prince Edward, Rex Harrison, Rob Lowe, Roger Daltry,
Rob Reiner, Alan Greenspan, Juliette Binoche

Pisces 12

So you're a dreamer—what's wrong with that? Let them laugh. Let them all laugh. If you have a vision you have to pursue it. You have a particular notion of how people are supposed to live, or could live if they would put aside their petty differences and egos. One big happy human family. Anarchy? Well, yes, but only in the highest sense. Not everybody running around looting and shouting and eating each other. (Although there are always going to be jerks and naysayers and even assassins who come up behind you and whack you just because they don't like your haircut or the way you voted.) But you know that in the highest sense, freedom—creative, spiritual, and emotional—makes a better world for all. Is that too much to ask? Shouldn't be. That's not magical thinking, is it? Just because you have a philosophy of life that may seem unrealistic to others, that doesn't make it wrong or childish. The only problem is that you can go pretty far down the hole looking for Wonderland, Shangri-La, or Munchkinland.

But here's the thing: Your innocent, altruistic dream could make you a great visionary, a great missionary, or a total nut. It's great for poetry and fiction, but will it play in Middle America? That's the question, and don't say you don't care because you have to care. Everyone has to have access to Shangri-La, including the members of that other party. You could become obsessively paranoid and end up being alienated, secluded, and antisocial—the very antithesis of the goal you were trying to achieve. Then you would be excluded from the world you have created, done in by the people you thought were your soulmates.

At what point this great inspired mission of yours becomes a dangerous escape from reality no one can say. In your eyes it is an escape into reality—and therein lies the rub. What you consider reality, others consider foolish fantasy. And what the world looks upon as right, normal, and true seems completely crazy and mad to you. Outlaws, misfits, weirdos, nerds, and dweebs could also just as easily become psychics, mystics, poets, and prophets. That can happen when you channel your visions, focus your creativity, and allow yourself to be captured. It's service, but not boring. It's a service that permits you to channel all your creativity into a comprehensible, palatable form.

You may have to be able to translate your esoteric message of universal love so that other people can understand it. You will not, however, be able to suppress your competitive spirit forever. Although you may have to suppress your urge to be alone on the stage, and stay within a chorus, your mission is ultimately not a group thing. It's a solo act—you could end up doing your thing alone. And in the end it's not magic or mysticism that you will have to pay attention to. It will be simple rules of health and hygiene.

• • •

At this point you need to probe more deeply into your obsession with your own interior visions, to the point that your inner life affects your ability to work and function on a daily basis. In the next part, Going Deeper, reading the chapters called "Escape" and "Freedom" will give you a chance to pass through the illusion of fear of being attacked from behind, and on to a higher expression of your Piscean nature that will help you pursue your dreams, develop healthy self-expression in work, and make your Sun shine bright.

Celebrities Who Share Your Issues
George Harrison, Bobby Fischer, Chelsea Clinton,
Vanessa Williams, Jon Bon Jovi, Bugsy Siegel,
Neville Chamberlain, Jonathan Demme, Mary Wilson

PART TWO

Going Deeper

THE PATHS TO HAPPINESS

Where Your Obsessions Tend to Make Your Life Go South
and
How Your Innate Powers Can Help You Find Your True North

In the first part you saw that you were not just an Aries or a Cancer or a Sagittarius. You've seen how complicated a person you really are. And now that you have briefly identified your strengths and weaknesses, conflicts and paradoxes—now what? It's so easy to simply say, "Well, that's me. That's the way I am. It's my karma," and leave it at that. But that isn't going to lead you to wealth, health, and happiness. Far from it. Knowing the issues is just the first step. Going deeper is the next step. And that is the next task at hand.

You're about to discover the cosmic way to cope with the desires that undo us all. The secret lies in the effect of the Moon. We've always known the Moon was powerful. You hear about it in love songs and see it in the changing tides of the ocean. Astrology tells us it's that shining circle in the night sky that holds a clue to what makes our hot buttons hot and what keeps cool heads cool. The path of the Moon around the Earth cuts across the Earth's path around the Sun—the Zodiac—at two points we call the Lunar Nodes. Often underplayed, but vital components of astrological interpretation, the Nodes describe the source of our unquenchable thirsts, insatiable hungers, and unshakeable addictions, as well as the means we all have to overcome those addictions and achieve our goals. We're going to use these Nodes of the Moon to help you realize your potential, resolve your conflicts, and get back on the road to ful-fillment.

When you get in touch with your real self—your higher self—your potential is realized and your future assured. No need to worry or ob-sess. And no matter how evolved we are, we all worry and obsess. When we worry and obsess, our lower, unconscious self takes over. We act out like babies and try to cover up our feelings by seeking comfort and grat-ification in ways that end up being self-destructive, preventing our Sun from shining and obscuring its brilliant light.

If there are ten people in a room we will inevitably be drawn to the one person who, it always turns out later, brings us face to face with our deepest issues, struggles, wishes, conflicts, and desires—the ones we en-counter again and again, over and over. If you're over fourteen years of age, you've got to know exactly what I'm talking about. And the weird thing is, it isn't even conscious. Far from it. What are the mysterious forces that have us twisting ourselves into pretzels, turning ourselves into something we're not, just for the sake of a relationship? Those forces stir us from somewhere way down in the basement of our souls, and be-fore we know it, we're locked into an old pattern, singing an old song, dancing a very old dance. It's normal, natural, and very, very human. We all do it. Motivated by primitive needs and wishes, we are drawn by cer-tain inexorable forces into situations we've experienced a thousand times before, but we can't seem to do a damn thing about it. How does it hap-pen? Where does that behavior come from?

This part of *SunShines* is about all those sweet, delicious, magnificent, naughty, wickedly self-destructive obsessions that get us every time. We all have them. In fact, you're going to discover how many people born under other Signs and in other years share the same issues you have and are coping with them in much the same way. It's just that each person uses those issues differently according to the Sun Sign path he or she is on. We all have issues, even the nice little old grandma who puts only eight thousand miles on her Pontiac in fourteen years. She has her obses-sions, too. Things she absolutely can't get along without. People she seeks out who are still bad for her. Her own little ways of acting desperately. Obsessions are not always visible, like smoking three packs of Camels a day. Some are quite subtle. In fact, obsessions with cigarettes, booze, food, or even other people aren't really the only obsessions we're talking about at all. They are merely symbols, symptoms of our irrational attempt to fill an unfillable hole that goes much much deeper. Five bucks will get you that ten right now, there's a little voice inside you, begging for satisfaction, pleading for gratification. Whoever or whatever belongs to that voice is down on one knee at this very minute, singing you a ditty more plaintive than Al Jolson's "Mammy." That tune could be about the money you're after, or sex, or fame—anything you're obsessed with having more of because you're furious you didn't get enough of it when you were younger. We get hooked into situations that end up disappointing us and hurting us when we think that another person can give us what we think our heart desires.

In order to fully realize all the potential that lies within you, you need to see some of your out-of-control patterns of behavior, while at the same time getting cosmic about it all. We are going on a search-and-destroy mission for some of the deeper causes of your obsessions—all those things we absolutely "love to do," the people, places, and things we glue ourselves onto, all in the name of love and the search for happiness. Many of the things we do in the name of love and happiness actually exclude other people, because they're not about grown-up giving and sharing. They're based on something personal and private we're hooked on, be it an old hurt, a string of memories, anger we can't let go of—any number of a host of things we end up "loving" more than we love other people. Without complicating the discussion with a lot of clinical or technical clichés, for the moment let's say only that we're going to define in hard-core detail some of those naughty obsessions that make human beings out of even the most pious of saints.

We all have many of these mad, mad obsessions, born out of a thirst or a desire for something we either are running after or from. We all get ensnared in relationships that turn out to be no damned good for us. We have all wrecked perfectly good situations just because of those dumb movies we play in our heads. We all glom onto things that interfere with other, healthier aspects of our lives. You know how it feels when you find yourself in a gooey relationship, bonded by a glue that usually turns out to be the same stupid set of issues that goofed you up in the past, made you think it was love, made you swear to yourself it was love—when it was really something else entirely. It was that driving need you have that must be satisfied (we'll see how it's a losing battle because it's so unsatisfiable). These thirsts, hungers, and addictions form the foundation of the hidden agendas and obsessive behavior we all exhibit in relationships time and again. These ever-recurring issues are always embedded in every connection we have, personal or business. In fact, if there is someone important to your life right now, especially someone who is driving you crazy, you can be sure your thirst, hunger, or addiction is playing an important part in everything you do and say to that person, morning, noon, and night, seven days a week.

We go after happiness in one of two ways. We steal it. Or we earn it. Stolen happiness is fleeting; we never get to keep it. The earned kind we can never lose. Your obsessions are the key issues about which you have little confidence and where you expect to be rejected or defeated, so you tend to steal gratification, not earn it. They could be a part of your personality where you felt so cheated and deprived somewhere back in the past, you are now obsessed with grabbing your five minutes of bliss. They are the points at which you sell yourself down the river, overcompensate for your inadequacies, do absolutely anything to get what you think you really want, and because of them, of course, you eventually lose your way.

Why do we keep going after what is bad for us?

We don't?

Oh, but we do.

There's a part of all of us that's addicted to something we've never had enough of, never had the joy of experiencing fully. A place where we feel we weren't encouraged enough, where we still tend to cave in, crumble, collapse. Where we are made of paper and we know it. Where we have to bluff our behinds off because we can't back up our promises. Where we lack credibility within ourselves. Where all we need is a little negative tap from life and we go plummeting down a hundred and two stories onto the pavement below. And so, when we get a lick of the thing, whatever it is, we're hooked.

Read the sections that were assigned to you in the previous part. Because of certain complicated astrological factors, they may be others that apply to you as well, but the ones we gave you are the big ones. You will find that other people born under different Signs share your issues. For the moment, though, stick with the ones you have been directed to, according to the month and year of your birth. Read the material. Be honest. Don't worry—nobody is looking.

Remember that *SunShines* is a book is about happiness, two kinds of happiness—stolen or earned—how to identify them and hopefully shift our energies toward the more lasting kind. If we cannot or will not shift those energies, we get stuck in our obsessions, and even the best relationships are crushed under the weight of our own enormous needs, infantile wishes, and frustrated desires. At that point we end up at Betty Ford Center.

First, we're going to take a hard look at your particular thirsts, hungers, and addictions. They are your hot buttons. We're going to hit some of those hot buttons that have harmed—even destroyed—many good relationships and lured you into some lousy ones in the past. We'll examine the kinds of people you tend to get hung up on and why (probably because they're strongest in areas where you believe you are weakest). We'll discuss how you may have inherited certain obsessions from events in your childhood (and maybe even before) and look at how the suppression or overemphasis of certain issues is still affecting you today. Remember that your obsessions are your points of greatest vulnerability, the spots where, because of so much past deprivation or rejection, you have become as intricately involved with pain and anger as with pleasure; where you deeply want to believe that at last, this or that person could give you what you want, make you sublimely happy and complete. It's a fantasy you are looking for, a dream, your compulsive search for the impossible, achieved at the expense of good, solid relationships. It's not that you can't be happy with all your obsessions. Au contraire. But because of the enormous sense of deprivation you have been nurturing there since you were two, you keep going feverishly back over the same material, repeating the same patterns, hoping the impossible, that there will be something in it *this* time. Only to feel empty afterward—again.

Don't despair, though, We're not just going to hold up your x-rays and sing, "It's malignant!" We are going to propose some very real and very practical ways to unhook yourself from what you're hooked on. We will search for and create some real methods to pull you out of the darkness and toward the light, and lead you to the lessons, practices, and meditations to ensure healing in all relationships. You will find new key words to help you keep from going too far south and get back on the right path, find your "true north" and realize all the potential stored up in your Sun Sign so that you can actually be happy in your business and personal life.

But hey! This isn't religion and we're no angels, none of us. The purpose of this book is not to turn everybody into little goodie-goodies who wouldn't dare get a grass stain on a pair of white shorts. You're definitely not going to get to the end of this book and bam! hang your crutches up on the altar and dance away to a castle built by Disney, filmed by Spielberg, and blessed by God. Our obsessions are precious to us all. We need the release they provide from the realities and pressures of our lives. We love our obsessions. We probably couldn't live without them, even if it killed us. But we are going to give you some real, live, powerful ammunition to improve every relationship you have today. When you finish this book you will be freer than when you began. That is a promise.

INDEPENDENCE

What Gives You Great Pleasure

Coming and going as you please

What You Tell Yourself, Your Shrink, Your Guardian Angel, but Nobody Else

Yeah, I guess you could say I'm a lone wolf. I mean, I can be very social, I like people. I really do. It's just that I have to be alone to do my thing, whatever it is. When I see couples holding hands, you know, like old people in their eighties ambling along together on their shaky pins, holding each other up and helping each other up the curb, I think, wow—that's nice. That is a really nice thing to have in your old age. I always have people in my life I'm close to. Some are very close. But I've got to say it, part of me is just not the marrying type. I've been married, well, sort of, but that was too much pressure for me. Even though sometimes I'm lonely (nothing like when I was younger and used to get so depressed), even though I'm lonely sometimes, I'm really not. I really like to come home from work, eat my dinner, and not be hassled, not have to talk to somebody, be nice, or even have sex if I just want to watch the news by myself and go to sleep. Alone. You can't imagine how nice it is a lot of the time to pull those covers up to my neck, snap out the light, and know nobody's going to bother me until the morning.

What is my own thing? I don't know. Being on my own, I guess. As much as I bitch about having to do everything by myself, I also like it. I can go to restaurants alone, go to the movies alone. In fact, I like to go to the movies by myself. I can sit where I want, and if I want to cry I can cry alone and not have to be embarrassed that I'm making a fool of myself in front of somebody else.

Frankly, I don't like to have to answer to somebody else about my whereabouts or my whatabouts. Sometimes I feel like cooking dinner, sometimes I like to be curl up and eat cereal or a PB&J. I don't like to be obliged to think about what somebody else wants to eat. And don't think I'm selfish, because I'm not. I'm a very giving person, and maybe that's why I need so much time alone.

Where You Go South

Of course you enjoy being alone. You're alone now. You were alone yesterday, you were alone five years ago and that's all you've ever known. Hey, right from the get-go you felt like an uninvited guest. They grumbled when they had to set an extra place at the table for you, and from that moment on you've been invisible. Except you haven't.

You can become totally obsessed with yourself. Who you are. What you are. How you look. Your body. Your nose. Your face (facial hair, too). Not in the I'm-so-gorgeous-and-wonderful way, either. Just the opposite. You've said so many horrible things to yourself when you've looked in the mirror, you'd never insult other people that way and you'd never let them insult you that way either. So for all your talk about how you enjoy being alone, you're not all that nice to yourself when you are by yourself. You can be downright cruel, in fact. One has to wonder what kind of jollies you get from hanging out with yourself if half the time you're hanging yourself. We're not talking literally. You are way more interested in more glamorous types of self-destructiveness that get you into trouble.

Make no mistake about it. You are a glamorous figure. Of course you think you're totally ugly and unattractive and just a piece of crap nobody in their right mind could ever want, and if they do want you what's wrong with them. Actually, you're very glamorous and magnetic and someone a lot of people would like to get closer to, but before they do, they should know that they are playing with fire.

"Me?" you say, "Dangerous? Hardly." But you are dangerous. It's because you're dangerous that people are intrigued. People can't resist the pouty, misunderstood outcast. They are fascinated, hypnotized by your spell. It's sometimes a witchy dance; you dare them to approach, you beckon them into the shadows. Isn't it wacky? You consider yourself so unappealing and yet you have such enormous power to attract people. That's the paradox and the truly treacherous aspect of your cosmic black side. You can get so swept away with your bad boy/bad girl image that you swirl downward in it and can actually put yourself out of commission, temporarily or otherwise, if you don't pull out of the turn fast enough. Of course, the crowd is always breathless to behold the daredevil, the acrobat who flies without a net.

In you, what appears to be self-effacing and humble can actually be a murderous vengeance on the self, an unyielding self-loathing that will be satisfied with nothing less than total annihilation. When you start ragging on yourself the cruelty is unmatched. You'll either eat yourself into cardiac arrest, or starve yourself so you're as skinny as a fashion model's pinky finger. Before you realize how great an asset you are in a relationship, you get really down on yourself and push people away. You'll try every possible way to prove to yourself and everyone else that you're a mean, miserable, worthless piece of garbage they'd be better off without. You cover it up so well. Everybody would think you thought you were the greatest. They'd never know you had such a low opinion of yourself. The aim of spiritual evolution may indeed be the transcendence of self. It is not achieved, however, by tearing yourself apart and calling yourself names when you're alone.

Your kind of aloneness is unique. You could be married with three kids and have been working since you were fifteen, but you still feel alone in that world you live in. Even if you are one of triplets conjoined at the hip, your separateness will always be the issue. You always want to be "different," and it is your differentness that makes you appealing to people, draws them to you, but keeps you apart from them at the same time.

You push yourself beyond all human endurance and take on pressures, projects, and responsibilities no one but you can handle, wearing yourself down to a nub, pretending to be what everyone thinks you are—a being with super powers. Of course, this serves to only exhaust you. Then you have to run away, escape the very people who want to support, love, and adore you, because the stress of being everything to everyone is just too much. You have to get off by yourself. Alone again. There you are. This kind of aloneness is deep, private, and inexpressible, and before you realize how much you need people around you, it can culminate in a swirl downward into self-pity and anger. You get angry because you have to live for others, do for others, please others, serve others, take care of others, and it's damned exhausting.

You wouldn't have to go through any of this pain if you didn't have such an obsession with independence. It's your mad need to control control control that inhibits you from fully relating to others. Even if you stay hitched for forty years, part of you has difficulty fully entering the relationship. Your higher self has no desire to tyrannize other people. You do, however, try to control them. In your effort to become indispensable, you feel you have to meet their demands and answer their needs, and the performance drains you. Still, you feel compelled to serve others so that you have the upper hand, you're in control of the supply of love, and you can turn it on and off when you want to. You stress yourself out to the max to maintain even a shred of independence, because your greatest horror is to become a burden on other people. You dread such dependence. It terrifies you to be thought of as somebody who has to be carried, and for this reason you always remain a little apart, and lonely. Deep down you probably do feel weak, paralyzed, unable to hack it on your own. You seem to equate human need with weakness, and, man or woman, you're afraid of being a "little girl." This will manifest itself differently depending on your gender. The result, however, is the same. You insist on your maleness, on a certain macho image you have created that has nothing whatever to do with whether you are sexually oriented to the same or opposite gender. You're the typical Joe Guy who does everything, tackles life, and doesn't ask for help. No matter how much you do for people, you've got a deep, narcissistic streak. It's actually very narcissistic. It's all about you, no matter how much you do for other people. It still puts you in the primary position and no matter how many people are around you, you're a solo act.

There's a secret behind your strong image. Behind your super competence lie fragility and need, protected by an impenetrable wall of well-crafted defense that has been built up since you were five, and even before. Your more vulnerable feminine side is revealed only in the most intimate situations, and even then you allow only part of it to show and for brief periods only. Your wall of defense has a male persona, but unlike Marlene Dietrich in a tux, your need to be "male" is more than a drag act. It's the part of your personality that gives you peace and pleasure, and releases you from the strain of revealing a more submissive, curvaceous, beveled, and civilized aspect of relating. You are more comfortable being the lone animal, gnawing on a bone in a cave than you are sitting at a State dinner between the secretary of state and the queen of Lambada, but as you will see on the following pages, being socialized is the path you have to go in.

You may have felt unwanted, even hated by one of your parents, or you could have been the subject of early beatings. Some event or situation eroded your confidence in yourself and damaged your self-image. It is also very likely that you have (or have had) a serious problem identifying with the parent of the same sex. You were either ashamed of that parent, or desperately determined that you would never end up like or act like that parent, or have to play the same role that parent played in their marriage. That is always why you tried so hard to be something else, and the attempt was largely successful. The prosthetic self you have created is a pastiche of identities you've admired, all contributing to your image of independence.

A Key Relationship Issue

It bugs you to think you are not really independent or that you have to live your life through other people. As much as you need connection, and thrive best when you overcome your anger long enough to have relationships, it still irritates you to think that you might not be able to function on your own without support. This is exactly the conflict with which you are presented, and once you can master the art of negotiation, you will feel a heck of a lot happier. There are moments when you are up, joyful, confident, and filled with hope for the future. Then a pin pricks the balloon and you can be easily deflated. Your confidence dissipates and your strength collapses. That's when you need people the most, but that's when you push them away. You need comfort, support, and help to do whatever you want to do, yet you insist on handling everything alone. You need your space and your autonomy, because people do make demnds and exert pressure. Their needs keep you from taking care of your own needs and you resent it. It's a paradox, because when you do get rid of them and curl up in your own little ball of solitude, you're not happy. In fact, you can feel pretty lousy about yourself when you are not in a relationship.

Issues to Resolve

Depression arising from inability to express anger appropriately
Low self-esteem
Fear of not being able to make it on your own
.Crushed gender identification
Weak identification with same-sex parent
Abuse or having been put down in childhood
Overattachment to Self

Your Past Life (If There Is Such a Thing)

In one of your past lives you were an animal that never traveled in packs. It hunted alone, ate alone, slept alone, and came together for mating only. In another life you evolved into a kind of Aryan Superman. Or someone a lot like him. A champion for the downtrodden, or a pain in the ass. Probably both. Definitely a man. A highly respected and feared man. You were generous but crude and volatile. No one dared cross you or awaken your anger because your rages were known throughout the land. You lived alone with many concubines and had countless people fawning over you and rushing around to satisfy your many needs, which changed from moment to moment. You trusted no one. Depended on no one. Needed no one. Whatever whim struck, you pursued. It was a wonderful life, being able to say and do whatever came into your head, having no commitments or responsibilities, wandering the globe or being considered the town crazy or a revered leader—it was a blast. You were a good person, but you were interested in only yourself.

You got way too into it, though. You did ride roughshod over a lot of people. You snapped at them impatiently, and everything they did annoyed you. You needed constant attention and blew people off for little or no reason at all. You grew bored easily and restless from lack of boundaries. Your life was full of exploration and wonder, but it was rootless, and you resented any form of commitment that you considered entrapping and castrating. Most important, you did not attach enough importance to women and their role in society. They were incidental to your needs, dispensable commodities which, when they got on your nerves or in your way, were discarded. All people were mere bumps in a road along that you wanted to speed. For your personal growth, since you were so perfect in every way, you needed only one thing to complete you. And that's where this life comes in.

Finding Your True North

The supreme irony of your life: You don't like to be alone. You don't want to be alone. You actually don't do all that well when you are alone. When you are released from the pressure of being with others, it doesn't take long before you start to feel lost, alienated, and sorry for yourself. Then you pick up the phone or go out looking for people, or you shout into the next room to the mate you just barked at, "Hey, hon. What's on TV? Want some cookies?" Marriage helps, of course, if you can stand it. For a woman with your key word of "independence" it would be a major step forward in you personal evolution if you took your husband or partner's name. Not a very politically correct thing to do today, of course. If you're a man, you might consider hyphenating your name. Even though it's difficult to relinquish the ferocious hold you have on your singular identity.

The whole idea of marriage is one you have to explore deeply, and the result could turn out to be one of your greatest contributions to society and to yourself. You're interested in relationships, and even if you resist the whole shebang, you'll probably turn out to be a marriage counselor, or a minister who performs at weddings, or a piano player who performs at them. Marriage is the path. Don't vomit. You might be one of the lucky ones, the ones who make it last. Marriage, when it's good, is not one person running the show with the other person pitter-pattering behind like a little duck. A successful resolution of your independence issue leads you into the arms of a life companion who lets you be strong (because otherwise you'd go completely mental) and still understands your deep vulnerabilities. That other person doesn't take any of your crap, either. That person has to be strong, too. Otherwise you'd mop the floor with them. He or she has to make certain demands. You have to be present in the relationship, fully and totally committed, no waffling. You need to be grabbed by the hair and held to your word. You should probably get married in a Catholic church because those guys don't fool around. Not only would you have legal fees to deal with if you decided to ditch the relationship, you'd have Hell to contend with if you ever wanted to have sex again. Legal commitments and contracts are also vital to your development. You need binding agreements, partly to overcome your horror of them, but mainly to ensure that you will honor promises and not wiggle out.

That's why gay marriage has become such a big deal lately. It's one thing to share a cappuccino and then say "Okay, we're married. Now let's go to Ikea and buy a futon." You need society behind you. You need a person to bevel your edges, socialize you, make sure you sit at a table for your meals and not just stand at the counter, shoving it in and swallowing without chewing.

In business it's the same story. You're a solo act. You like it that way. If you are left alone to do what you have to do, everybody's happy, especially you. But unless you make a real connection, a deep one, you'll be toiling away in your little cottage making trinkets the tourists will never see. In fact, your greatest successes will come when you are swallowed up by, or work in conjunction with, something greater than yourself. Even then, of course, your dissonance will eventually stand out and you will always be noticed for your anomalous behavior, good or bad.

Cooperation is the key. There's no sense pretending to be selfless and submerging yourself in another, sublimating all your needs in exchange for validation. One thing is sure. You bring out the best in people and you're able to do more for them than you can ever do for yourself. Sometimes that gets to you, but it's really a gift you've been given in this lifetime. It actually does work both ways, because when you are with people, you have no problems. Being together erases your issues, so the more you improve the life of another person, the more your life moves up a notch.

Your success in finding happiness will depend on your ability to relate deeply and fully to other human beings. Your opportunities in life will be directly affect by your ability to join with people and be sensitive to their thoughts, wishes, and needs. That's not natural for you. You don't easily surrender to the truth that you are not an island, a 100 percent autonomous being. It's not a shame to need people. It's no shame to acknowledge you're not a one-man band playing the harmonica, drums, tambourine, and trumpet. You're part of a greater whole, and there's something beautiful and cosmic in coming to terms with your interdependence.

Wow! So you're not alone. You're not the only person in the world at all. You're an important piece in the puzzle of the lives of everyone you touch. Not the only piece, but an important piece. On good days that feels good. On bad days you probably don't believe it. You are part of this great Universe. You came here to develop your sense of connection to other human beings. Although you started out alone as an alien, you have come here to be civilized and socialized. Like Tarzan, who found polite society difficult, you too have to wear shoes, learn manners, eat with a fork, and remain as much as possible in the company of people.

How to Get Your Power Back

That, of course is the total key to success: the ability to be in a relationship without resorting to subtle manipulation or out-and-out despotic control. The trick is to be able to validate others without losing yourself, or pleasing them insincerely for fear that truthfulness will result in abandonment. You have to shed your own negativity and childish behavior that drives people away. To gain your power you have to open up and allow people to be there for you. No matter how difficult it is for you to be present, and keep your eyes from glazing over and drifting back into your own head when someone is talking to you, the effort it takes to remain bonded and present in a relationship will, paradoxically, strengthen you, restore your connection with the world, open you up, wake you up, plug you back into the people you love, and reduce the power of the inner critical voice that keeps telling you that you're a worthless loser. At that point you cease resisting your destiny, which is to have fulfilling relationships after all, and you rise to the challenge of being a grown-up, able to listen to others and receive the wisdom and strength they can provide. At that point something clicks in. You're able to encourage others without needing to control them. You return to life. You're happy.

Paths to Healing

Remaining bonded and always in communication
Cooperation and compromise
Pride in collaboration
Giving credit and thanks to others
Learning to listen and be sensitive to the needs of others
Discovering what lies beyond the paper door of Self

A Final Word to Send You on Your Way

Being strong gives you a sense of control over your life, makes you a survivor, and provides you with an identity people will never forget once they meet you. There is, however, another ingredient to your happiness: You have to give up your habit of thinking you have to do it all alone. To bevel your sharp primitive edges, you have to relinquish the fierce hold you have on yourself. You must learn how to connect more deeply and more sensitively to people. Once you develop honest empathy toward and interest in other people, you will meet success. You have to believe that other people have a vital contribution to make to your life. You have to appreciate them, bring out the best in them, and most of all believe that they have come into your life for the purpose of making you whole.

Your Weird Image to Contemplate
A confirmed bachelor buys a diamond ring

Your Song to Sing in the Shower
"Goin' to the Chapel"

Your Magic Words for Happiness
Trust in others

MONEY

What Gives You Great Pleasure

Feeling permanent and marketable

What You Tell Yourself, Your Shrink, Your Guardian Angel, but Nobody Else

I don't want to be poor. I know what it's like and I don't like it. I'm not cheap, no matter what anybody says, and I'm not greedy either. But there's got to be some conspiracy or something, because no matter how much money I have, sooner or later the devil comes and tries to take it away. I'm not being paranoid either. I could tell you a long story about what it's like to have nothing, to be hungry, and to have to go without, and it's not fun, okay? There are two kinds of people in this world, and you know who they are: the ones who've got it and the ones who don't. End of story. The things rich people have done to be rich have to disgust anybody who has any sense of morality. While I have no intention of becoming like them, I'm not going to be some stupid idiot who smiles politely and ends up with nothing. And believe me, if I don't take care of business I will end up on Section 8 or whatever they're calling charity cases these days.

Don't tell me prosperity is a flow from the bountiful Universe unless you know firsthand how it feels when they turn off your phone or your lights and you have to break your neck running to the bank to cover a check. A lousy check. Or how it feels to have to take a damned bus to the airport after scrounging a cheap ticket off the Internet, and have to pretend to be happy in the middle seat! No, it's not a sin to want to walk into a first-class lounge and have the attendant call you by your name and offer you a glass of Champagne. It's just a great feeling to walk up ahead of the proletariat when they say "First-class passengers can board now." It makes you feel like a million bucks and I love it. It's a kick to be able to go by a store and see a flat-screen TV or a state-of-the-art stereo—doesn't have to be diamonds or rubies—just to be able to walk in and plunk down my plastic and not have to get the heebie jeebies when the first of the month comes around.

I don't really require a whole lot: just a nice life without the hassles of worrying what will happen to me if I allow myself a luxury once in a while. I will not let the bastards screw me out of what is rightfully mine. I won't, and that's what people will do if you let them. *If* you let them. That's why I stay up nights figuring things down to the penny. Not because I'm a miser, but because I'm going to beat those pigs at their own game.

And, of course, every time I think I've got it figured out, I wind up behind the goddamned eight-ball, fiscally speaking. If I made a million dollars, I bet I'd owe the government two. It happens to me. It does. And the minute I think that maybe I do have a creative idea or two, maybe I have a value dollar-wise, maybe I do rate a prime-time TV show or actually have commercial possibilities, the whole thing falls apart. Either somebody beats me to the patent, I price myself out of the market, or some other curse befalls me somewhere between concept and production. Sometimes I actually do think I'm cursed. The up and down of it all. The insanity. It's like a roller coaster. You think I'm being negative? Try being me.

Sure, I love the idea of living in the lap of luxury, but who can afford it unless you win the lottery or you come from big money, which, believe me, doesn't do you a damn bit of good, the way they control you. And sure it burns me to see the trash that's on TV and in the movies. And those singers raking it in. For what? For putting out crap that the people eat right up. So I figure, that's the deal, take the money and run, crap or no crap.

Am I wrong?

Life is about business. If you can't take care of business, you're up the creek. I'm good at it. I love it. Well, I hate it when I'm the bottom, but I love figuring out the money and bargaining. So you want to think I'm just a hack who sells out for the money? Fine. Wonderful. I'm not a fool and I know what this world is all about—the proverbial pie, and dammit I want my piece.

Where You Go South

It probably would cause you to have a nervous breakdown, but the best exercise for your spiritual development would be to take a few $100 bills, slowly tear them piece by piece into little shreds, and flush them down the toilet. It's wonderful to be cool and sharp in business. It's a gift. It also happens to be your curse. It's your curse because you can't get off it. It's your damaged CD that keeps repeating "What's it going to cost? What's it going to cost? What's it going to cost? How much? How much? How much?" You must know there's a good reason for your—shall we say—talent for calculating. It's the hole in your pocket. Actually it's your personal black hole. Let's take a little trip there. The destination? We could call it the Bank Vault in Hell. There you will be surrounded by $842 thousand trillion (when the dollar again has value in that future time) where the time lock will click and you and the money are together. There you will be richer than your wildest dreams. And then what?

Maybe that's a little exaggerated. But you know you already feel that way sometimes. Either you don't have enough or you have so much and you're trapped by it.

You could say that everybody's a little crazy on the subject of money, and you'd probably be right. It has such nutty value in our society. When you see people lining up all the way down the street and around the block to see a van Gogh exhibition, when you think of the millions of dollars that have been made by those who sell trinkets with his prints on them, and then you remember that the guy drove himself to death because he couldn't pay his rent, it makes you see how screwed up the whole money thing is. Or think about the Hollywood icon who ends up on Social Security in the Actor's Home, barely able to afford a Blockbuster video of her own movies, and you gotta just wonder. You really do.

And yet there you are still slugging it out trying to, what you call, "survive" but always on the edge or falling into what is an amalgam of fantasies of abject poverty and fabulous wealth. Poverty and wealth are glued together like day and night, locked forever in an unholy embrace.

The fear of being without drives you hungrily onward. You have the sense that something is going to be taken away from you, stolen, absconded with—that your talents or services or wisdom or kindness will be undervalued. You are afraid that your sincerity and loyalty will be summarily betrayed and that you will be mocked for your stupid innocence. That your gifts will be exploited by unscrupulous individuals. And, brother, have you run into unscrupulous individuals. Have you gotten royally screwed. Not that you haven't given the old heave-ho to a few other people in your life because—don't deny it—you have been so deathly afraid of being taken advantage of, you haven't been totally 100 percent aboveboard yourself. You've resorted to bean counting and penny-pinching and out-and-out cheapness. Oh, you say it's not cheapness, it's thrift. Call it what you want, but it's cheapness. No offense, but you're just not clear on the money issue.

You'd help anybody paint the entire outside of their house and refuse to take a penny for it because, "Hey, we're friends." But if somebody were really to hire you to paint a house, you'd think "Hey, you know what painters get for a job like this?"

The reason? You do not have a consistent idea of your value, not only as a performer or provider of services, but as a human being. Part of you thinks Fort Knox and all the countries in the world don't have enough money to pay you what you're worth. On the other hand, you'll beg on your knees for a chance to be of use to someone and forget the cost. If it's for love, you don't want a cut. So you see how weird you are about money? You think everybody's out to rob you. You've got money stashed in places burglars would never think to look. You cry constant poverty.

You live close to the edge, but somehow, some damned way, guess what, you pull it out at the last minute.

Why? Who devalued you?

Who or what got you to think that survival depends on financial independence, that whatever happens you need to squeeze the juice out of every last nickel, make the egg salad last to the day before the day the mayonnaise expires. Who turned you into such a hoarder that your place looks like an antique shop? The answers vary from family to family. If poverty in early life made you fixate on financial security, or rather financial independence, your big horror is having to go to some Big Daddy or Big Mamma and ask for an allowance. Maybe your family has so much money that you're already defeated before you start, because you will never make as much money as you will inherit.

Most of us would love to have a problem like a huge trust fund. The fact is, however, that it many heirs feel infantilized and in some cases paralyzed by their money, and they spend—no, *waste,*—huge amounts of energy and time trying to prove they don't need their family's goddamned money.

There's another reason you could feel defeated, especially if you are a woman. It's the old, outdated belief that women do not need financial independence on their own. All they need is a man to take care of them, and they don't have to worry their pretty little heads another minute. The idea that women shouldn't make the same money as men—or more—could drive you to obsessive attempts to keep the bank accounts separate, compete instead of cooperate, and bite the hand that would feed you if you would only let it. You resent support rather than feel grateful for it, and you do everything you can to remain financially separate, which in the end provides you with only half of what you could have. If you're a man, you're constantly burdened with the issue of financial support, and you struggle constantly in competition with anyone you see who makes more money than you do.

Ironically and paradoxically, wealth becomes an asymptotic ideal you can never achieve.

So you either live like a pack rat, buy yesterday's bread, shop at thrift stores, and hoard every last dime and every empty cottage cheese container you ever bought. Or in extreme cases this childish competitiveness results in absurdly lavish, Liberace-like ostentation. Your inconsistencies are glaring to anyone who can look deep enough into the infantile rages you can get into when money is involved. For all your crying "Foul!" you know you have fudged and twisted the truth in money matters and have not been completely forthright—although your honor is always the big issue.

A Key Relationship Issue

It's got to burn you when you hear that some no-talent jerk in town just made a fortune producing a pile of junk the public is eating up like candy, while you, who are loaded with talent, love, and oodles of spiritual awareness, are hobbling along, barely able to make your monthly nut. You could just as easily go wild when you are stuck in some goofy job because of the paycheck, and you hear that some old friend from high school took a creative chance and made it big. If it satisfies some sick need you have to torture yourself, you can easily find people who are doing twice as well as you are, financially speaking, and expending half the effort. Or you can rail against the fact that, in this day and age, for political or sexual reasons, there is still a hideous inequality in the wages people are paid. It will do you in if your focus too much on what you are getting, or rather, what you are *not* getting. You want to bolster your creative momentum and foster a sense of drive and motivation. Don't undermine it with self-deprecating criticism and unproductive rage—against yourself for not making more money, or somebody else for making more, even if that somebody is willing to support you while you are finding your way and doing your thing. It's self-destructive to feel like the poor relative at the dinner party, especially if you are denying the special gifts that you actually bring to the gathering, some of them not material gifts at all.

Issues to Resolve

Economic drains
Horror of the bottom dropping out of your life
Guilt over money

Sexism and finance
Lack of fiscal responsibility
Impaired ability to generate your own income

Your Past Life (If There Is Such a Thing)

Maybe in your last life you were a money-hungry merchant in a market-place in Marrakech or some exotic land. Maybe you were somebody who lived only to build a financial empire, sacrificing all personal and creative happiness. You were rich. Very rich. You would spend your evenings sit-ting alone at a dinner table, eating only onions and cold potatoes and por-ing over your bank statements and stock certificates. You never lived to enjoy the fruits of your labors. You knew no other way of life.

You counted your coins. You weighed your gold. The reflection of it glittered in your eyes. You were like the old Disney character, Scrooge McDuck, who splashed around in a pool of money. You were a victim of your own appetites. It was a lavish life, but you were enslaved to the acquisition of wealth. You had no time for frivolity or love. You were too busy collecting rents. So the Universe said that in your next life you will not miss out on life. The slavish dedication to the earning of vast for-tunes will not be the road you must take. In your next life you will be a magician.

And so you are—or potentially could be.

Finding Your True North

You must overcome your fear of your own creativity, thinking that the artist's life is foolish, self-indulgent, and worst of all, impractical. In the old days there was no shame in having a patron to support you while you tapped away at your sculptures and paintings. Today it's hard because agents, art dealers, and publishers have been known to exploit the naive, and artist or not, everyone needs some business savvy. Your path, how-ever, must always involve some form of art or creativity. You may never have the guts to quit your day job and take up basket-weaving, mainly be-cause the financial dependence would drive you nuts. If that's the case—and it probably is—you need something else in your life that fulfills this other need, one that has nothing to do with how much money you're getting for it. Either you plunge yourself into the creative life, or you act as a catalyst, a tool of creativity, and become the bridge between art and communication. It takes enormous courage to turn your back on values society believes are the "smart values." It takes guts to follow your passion and pursue a heart's desire your parents would hate to hear about. The money part is easy, although you're tortured by it. Torture over money is your addiction. You're as turned on by the thought it might be taken away as you are by the notion of making a mint. Just notice the mini heart attack you have when you misplace your wallet for five minutes.

You'll be liberated from this obsession when you understand your fear that the rug will be pulled out from under you. The ground under your feet is not solid. It's like living on a fault. You don't trust material reality. Even your body seems fragile.

For all your furnishing and hoarding, if the place ever does burn down, here's your great gift: You're the first one out there serving coffee to the firemen and saying, "Hey, no worries. It's just things. At least nobody was hurt." When the crisis happens, you actually don't give a damn about money and possessions. When you develop your creative potential, you come to understand that life is short. Then a transformation occurs, and you become immune to all fears.

In addition to your creative talents, you have the gift of magic and healing. Whether you've been to medical school or not, you possess and exude a healing power. You can make cripples walk and blind men see (metaphorically speaking). As long as you love what you are doing, and you are doing what the Universe has ordained for you to do, you will always have what you need and will want for nothing. You just can't start thinking, "This is great. I should turn this into a commercial venture. I'd make a million."

Wrong. Do the thing you're passionate about, forget the money, and you'll have plenty.

Life on Earth can be very seductively sweet. Everything has sugar in it. When it comes to the baubles, bangles, and beads of this material life, pretend you're a diabetic. You don't have to cut out all goodies. Just get control of your appetite.

Developing a mature and profound philosophy concerning death will lead you away from all your insecurities, because dealing with death and the dying will provide you with insight into the meaning of life and perspective on all the issues you spend so much time fretting over—not to mention the hours of every day you have wasted haggling over money and pinching pennies until Abraham Lincoln gets skin cancer. So you must and will be confronted with death and the dying. Don't shrink from it. You will gain gifts you couldn't possibly imagine, including the big inheritance. This doesn't mean you have to hurry over to visit the old aunt you haven't seen in twenty years because she's dying and may give you her grandmother's jewels. Meeting the challenges and responsibilities of dealing with death and the dying for the sake of the mature experience will lead you to untold wealth in ways you cannot predict or expect.

Your life has another healing aspect as well. It involves sex. You can't just say, "That was the best sex I've had in years." You have to mean it. You have to develop your sexuality honestly so that there is love, trust, and a desire to satisfy each other with no inhibitions. You have to reach a point where you are honest, totally, 100 percent honest about what turns you on, and what you deeply and profoundly need for satisfaction on the most intimate level.

You have been given the gift of sexual healing. When you are wholly within your body and without fear, your potential for intimacy has no limit. Tantric union is the goal here. You can achieve ecstasy on the deepest level if you can divest yourself of gender issues, competitiveness, and fear of your dependence on another.

It's complicated, the sex and money issue, but even if you marry for strictly financial reasons, the day will come when you find that you are turning out to be the sexual doctor for your mate. Because in your earlier life you may want to sacrifice your passion for practicality, you end up having to give in to your desires and have affair with your pool boy or your French maid.

You have the power to heal people sexually through your own honesty. Becoming the sexual creature you are destined to be, you can achieve a tantric union, one that creates a bond on a physical, mental, and spiritual level no man or woman can ever break. This unites your soul with your body, which because of too much interest in money and the things of this world, risk being tragically split apart.

How to Get Your Power Back

First of all, concentrate on the creative outpouring being granted to you by the Universe at this time. You have a magical power, and it's nothing to ignore or look down your nose at. This is a mystical life you are supposed to be leading. You can create a masterpiece of your life and leave a legacy that will last long after you've gone in search of the great bank loan in the sky. Your talents are unique, profound, full of insight, and imbued with a life force that may not be able to raise the dead, but sure as hell can heal the living. Second, your sexual powers have a healing effect on those whose confidence has been shaken emotionally or sexually. In olden times you would have been highly revered for these sexual endowments, because people would have come to you for your particularly singular abilities in the emotional area.

This talent does not merely involve unusual physical endowments, sexual prowess, or gymnastics. You have the ability to restore life and joy to others whose sexual attitudes, educations, or behaviors have made it difficult for them to express adequately the regenerative qualities of a deep physical union. At the moment, you can. Be grateful. Be very grateful.

Paths to Healing

Accepting the generosity of others
Knowing what wealth really is
Shedding the burdens of acquisitiveness
Following your passion
Being honest about sexual needs
Achieving Tantric union

A Final Word to Send You on Your Way

Life is so tenuous. Tsunamis and hurricanes and terrorist bombs have shown us that. We still have car payments to make, kids' running shoes to buy, and school tuitions to meet, not to mention health coverage, the IRS, and all our other endless financial responsibilities. Plus, it's nice to have nice things, live well, be surrounded by beauty and take trips once in a while. Best of all, it's comforting to know that your feet are on solid ground.

Except they are not. Life is a mystery. Earth is hurtling through space at an ungodly speed in the wake of comets, meteors, asteroids, and who knows—maybe even hostile aliens in spaceships. You need to learn how to proceed toward the future with faith in your own instincts for survival, creation, and generation. You need to learn to see your life as one piece of a big puzzle you fit into perfectly. You must not be terrorized by the void that surrounds us all. If you have courage, it will support your artistic urge and the give you the power to leave the comfort and warmth of what people call security and explore what lies far from the firelight around which society sits huddled together.

The animal in you needs to be heard. It needs to howl in ecstasy in the moonlight, calling out to Nature in gratitude for its powers of fertility and creation. Regeneration and reproduction are the miracles given to you to practice. Your path to immortality demands you search the cycles of life and death for wisdom and insight without misgivings or fear of the consequences. You need to pierce the illusion of material reality and see straight through into the beyond. For you, that is happiness.

> ### *Your Weird Image to Contemplate*
> *A rich country doctor accepts cranberry muffins as payment from a grateful patient on whom he has performed miraculous brain surgery*
>
> ### *Your Song to Sing in the Shower*
> *"Whatever Lola Wants"*
>
> ### *Your Magic Words for Happiness*
> *Fearlessness of the dark*

COMMUNICATION

What Gives You Great Pleasure

Casual contact and familiar territory

What You Tell Yourself, Your Shrink, Your Guardian Angel, but Nobody Else

Misunderstood? Misunderstood? Try to imagine what it would feel like for a Chinese person who didn't speak one word of English to be plunked down on a back road in rural Georgia. You still wouldn't get it. I didn't even know there was anything wrong with me. Maybe they were trying to protect me, but I didn't know there was anything wrong with me until I went to kindergarten. I don't remember a whole lot of things from my childhood, but I'll never forget that day. It was early September. School started right after Labor Day. It was a beautiful early autumn day. I was only five, but I remember it clearly. They both got out of the car and took me by the hand and opened the school door and told me to have a nice day and turned around and walked away and got into the car and drove away and left me there to walk into the school all by myself. And then the principal came out of her office and looked down at me and said hello and when I opened my mouth to say hello she kept saying "What? What? What? What?" Probably today Child Family Services would get after any parents who did that, and today they've got programs for kids with "learning disabilities." I didn't even know there was such a thing as another language. At home we spoke only Turkish. I think the therapist probably thought he was doing a good thing, although he didn't know his ass from a hole in the ground. It was he who told my parents if I was ever going to live a normal life the time to start was immediately. Can you believe that? You think that sort of thing doesn't leave one hell of a scar? So you know I'm proud of the fact that at 52 years of age I got an MBA from Harvard. My parents always pushed me to have an education, but what an introduction to school! So you want to talk about being misunderstood!

Where You Go South

It doesn't help much to hear the old saw about how prophets are not known in their own land, but in your case it's true. You have a communication issue that started way back and persists to this day. You've certainly had the embarrassing experience of trying to tell somebody something really important—like some big huge revelation or discovery or invention you know could really change the way people look at life or live— and they either look at you as if you were crazy, or their eyes glaze over and they just tune out as if you were babbling on in ancient Egyptian. You've got to have had that maddening feeling that something happens on the way from your brain to your mouth that nobody can or wants to hear. Something vital gets lost in translation and the loss separates you from loved ones. Even in business. You're not always listened to. You're not heard. You're not understood. Of course that makes you crazy and makes you more determined to make yourself understood, but the more you push, the more people tune out. That only makes you more determined to get your ideas and points across, and before you know it you actually are running off at the mouth and repeating the same thing over sixty times, which makes people think you're just plain stupid. So of course you lose patience and give up and let them think you're dumb in order to get their attention.

You're right about one thing. Your message gets scrambled on its way down from your head to your mouth. You actually do get the feeling sometimes that you're a Chinese person parachuting down into rural Georgia. The natives don't understand that you want to know where the nearest bathroom is until you actually act it out and take a whiz right in front of them. That's how you feel. That's how you've always felt. You're frustrated and angry because of the fact that you have a long-standing difficulty in communicating. As a result you make the simplest ideas more complicated than they have to be by going on and on and on and on to the point that people want to scream "Shut up!" It's awful to feel isolated like that, to feel like an alien from Jupiter with so much to share and give. When you tell a joke nobody, but nobody, laughs. Do you actually, honestly have a screw loose?

The bad news? Yes. Part of you is a bit off your rocker. Could be a couple of pistons misfiring in your brain. That's possible. Could be chemical. Of course, you never know. A hundred years after your death the world could hail you as an epic poet, but it's not easy here and now to feel that people really get you.

Part of you is infantile and rebellious, stamping its foot like a two-year-old having a tantrum because its parents are demanding it behave like a grown-up and refusing to gratify its childish, narcissistic needs. Part of you is restless, impatient, scattered. You jump up from the table before the meal is eaten. You have trouble finishing things. You absolutely refuse to be weighed down and held. You insist on flying from thing to thing, project to project, job to job, or relationship to relationship, and always because deep down you get bored. Something comes over you—the urge to move on, surf channels, flip out, indulge yourself, act like a fourteen-year-old, act in direct opposition to what you know to be mature, adult, wise, moral, and even legal. There's a rebellious—even deviant and crooked—streak in you that is so foolish and self-destructive, that you could discover the link between lung cancer and cigarettes and then run out and buy a pack of unfiltered Camels. You could write an impassioned essay on the tragedy of AIDS in Africa, then go out and have unprotected sex with a stranger. Maybe it's not that drastic, but you do need a break from the strain of grown-up thinking. As a result it's your great irony that you cannot 100 percent practice what you preach. You know what's right, but you just can't always listen to your higher self.

How does this translate to serious problems with siblings? Again, it's the communication issue that causes splits and rifts, and separates people. Same thing with school. You'd rather be thought of as stupid than get locked into formal education. Even when you do make it to college, it's hard to pick a major, mainly because you're interested in everything.

Is this a bad thing? Of course not. It makes you the classic Renaissance person. It reveals your curiosity, your thirst for variety, and your ability to be several people at once. You have more than one identity. At best this allows you to show up at a business meeting and give people the impression you went to a fancy boarding school, even if you got your GED while working part-time at the local supermarket. Then you can go home, change clothes, and flip into a creature of the night. At worst? Sybil on her worst days.

Your childhood was disruptive. Problems in education turned you off. Somebody convinced you you were "abnormal." The language they spoke at home was foreign to you and you were left out of the loop. People spoke down to you, if they spoke to you at all. Your intelligence was impugned could have been a million things. The disparity between your potential and your ability to communicate adequately what was going on inside your head practice made it increasingly difficult for you to want to pursue your education. Like a Catholic kid who can't reconcile puberty with abstinence, your behavior drifted away from your sense of morality, and it became harder to unite the two sides of your personality. It became easier to let people think you were stupid or crazy.

A Key Relationship Issue

Variety? You probably think you are the great communicator, but in fact, you are not. At least you haven't been. You've tried, though. In some ways you've tried too much, even made some promises out of hope and enthusiasm that you might not be able to keep. You've made snap decisions and said things off the top of your head that have gotten you into major soup. There are possibly people you are on the outs with, relatives or neighbors or siblings you can neither get along with nor shake out of your life completely. You may have fallen into a rut of everyday living that may be comfortable and familiar but colossally boring, with all resources and topics of conversation exhausted long ago. Apart from the dreary details of errands or discussing children or sick aunts, there is nothing more to say that is worth saying. You may even be too dependent on empty chatter that skirts real issues, and avoid painful subjects that have taken over your inner life. You've gotten lost in the simplicity and comfort of drivel as an alternative to empty silence.

Issues to Resolve

Frustration at not being heard or understood
Language barriers
Speech impediments
Addiction to immature behavior
Instincts that are stronger than conscience

Your Past Life (If There Is Such a Thing)

Maybe in your last life there was way too much talking without thinking. Somebody shot off their mouth without contemplating the consequences of their words.

Words lost their meaning. There was a parochial, small-town, small-minded attitude. Rural Georgia. There may even have been incestuous relationships—not necessarily sexual ones, but there could indeed have been genetic disorders or mental attitudes and ways of communicating that were handed down from parent to child. Metaphorically, you lived in rural Georgia. Everybody knew everybody. All the relatives lived in walking distance. They were into each others' business. They had no need for anybody else. Conversations were endless but empty. Exhausted. There was nothing to talk about but they kept talking about the weather, the cows, or Amber's latest pregnancy. They just kept talking. You were the vox populi. You mastered the art of small talk in this little nowhere town. In fact you were the town gossip, the information center, repeating over and over the same information. The town hall is on Main Street. The gas station is closed on Sunday. Caleb's daughter Amber is carryin' again. You mastered the dialect. Maybe it wasn't rural Georgia. Maybe it was rural Sicily or the steppes of eastern Russia. It was someplace where nobody strayed more than thirty kilometers from the church square. You didn't have to think. It had all been thought out for you years before. All you had to do was spit out the script the way a bored rabbi drones on in Hebrew having long since forgotten the meaning of the words.

That was then. In this life you're given a whole new set of opportunities, opportunities that involve expanding your mind, and leaving your zip code.

Finding Your True North

In your younger days you could never have dreamed how far you would travel, how far you would be forced to travel to discover your true self. The great revelation of your life, however, will be to discover your own intelligence. This revelation will not come slowly, and it may or may not involve formal education, because teachers and school will always present anxieties for you.

Overcoming all communication obstacles will allow you the greatest revelation of your incarnation. Brilliance—the brilliant, shining, thrilling, blissful purity of mind. You want to call it God? You probably don't, but there is a "thing," a something you never tapped into as a kid. You couldn't, didn't believe in it. Didn't know it is existed. The power to know is magic, thrilling, blissful. The ability to think, the joy of exploring and learning. It has absolutely nothing to do with communication. Although you're always jazzed at the thought of sharing your great wisdom, being ignored is likely to be a great disappointment in your life. Moses gets the Ten Commandments on Mount Sinai, rushes down and tells the people, and they all scream "Go fly a kite! We're too busy slaughtering animals and having sex!" Or Jesus, with his message of truth, love, and forgiveness, gets strung up on a cross for his zeal to spread the word. So you won't ever be able to resist the temptation to blab the secret of life. How many people know what the hell you are talking about is another story.

The path is learning itself. Exploration. At some point in your life you must put yourself in a culture that speaks a language you do not understand. You should probably marry out of your birth religion, nationality, or race at least once.

Your development depends upon the expansion of your consciousness to the point that you find yourself surrounded by people, customs, laws, morals, and even food completely foreign to what you have always found familiar, safe, and comfortable. You will need to experience the stress and strain of cultural, socioeconomic, or moral differences.

Your path is education in any of its forms. You've been put here on Earth not to yak and yammer like a minister speaking in tongues to a stupefied crowd, but to discover the power of your own mind to think for itself. This will require a fearless effort. No one can lay out the curriculum for you, cut a swath through the jungle of the mind, or provide the map. That is the point. God, or Goddess, or the Universe, or whatever you want to call the Great Intelligence that rules all things, actually does exist.

Even if you've been made to think you can't think, you can not only think, but you are actually here to develop a philosophy that encompasses the origin, purpose, and ultimate soul of what it means to be a human being. You have to find it. Enlightenment comes in many forms. There are as many paths as there are people. Could be a PhD. Could be a GED. You have to find your own version of morality, break through the prejudice of ignorance, false belief, and stupidity, and poke through into the light of your own perception of truth and knowledge.

It's not about who listens to you, who believes you, who shares your vision, or who understands and applauds your version of higher human purpose. Silence is difficult, of course, when you are bursting with awareness and the elation of the discovery of your own mind. It can be painfully frustrating to reach a pinnacle of understanding and still have problems communicating it, but the real thrill is the awakening. How could anyone ever express in a million words what it felt like to step on the moon, or take that first peek into the mystery of bacteria, or witness that magical mystical moment when Helen Keller realized she could think? Intelligence is happiness.

May the Force be with you.

How to Get Your Power Back

Stop hanging on to people you have nothing to say to. Get rid of your shadow and get out and travel. Do something you've never done before. Go someplace you've never been, where you don't know the language, the customs, the geography, the culture, the terrain, and even the weather. Challenge yourself in subjects you thought were beyond you in school. Study something nobody—including yourself—thinks you can master. Stop talking and start doing. Quit obsessing over the people in your life, especially relatives who you cannot or will not talk to, and move into a state of higher consciousness. You do have one. Break all rules. Make discoveries. Challenge teachers and clerics. Cut your way through a new jungle and be a brave pioneer. Do not go along with the Program. Be the first to break new ground against all odds, against all logic, and especially against all advice.

The most rewarding relationships will be with those individuals of completely different ethnic and social backgrounds. Overcoming preconceived notions and prejudices will be your path to growth and happiness from here on.

Paths to Healing

Continuing education
Thinking in bigger terms
Developing mental faculties that heal splits
Shedding the drone of meaningless chatter
Developing respect for your own mind
Telling the whole truth and nothing but the truth
Searching for wisdom, not an audience

A Final Word to Send You on Your Way

How easy it is to lose one's self in the dithering, blithering routines, errands, and comings and goings of existence. Take the kids to school, call your mother and say nothing in an endless, pointless mission of trivial pursuits. You must expand your mind and raise your consciousness if you are to provide yourself with the perspective you desperately need to see life as a joyful experience. This doesn't mean you have to quit your job and go around the Cape of Good Hope on a blow-up raft. You must always, however, be open to learning on every level. You don't have to risk your neck on a rocky ledge to prove your joy in discovery, but you must always be open to new experience. Putting your nose to the wind toward whatever lies in the future gives you a limitless capacity to imagine and manifest your own life. It will give you the ability to view your whole life as a passage of learning.

Your Weird Image to Contemplate
Fifty years after quitting school at fifteen
to have her first baby, Grandma gets a PhD

Your Song to Sing in the Shower
"From a Distance"

Your Magic Words for Happiness
Relish the adventure

SECURITY

What Gives You Great Pleasure

Hiding out

What You Tell Yourself, Your Shrink, Your Guardian Angel, but Nobody Else

Yeah it's great I guess. I got the nomination and everybody's telling me I'm probably going to win. Like I give a damn at this point in my life. I would so rather spend the time working on the house. The place needs work and I don't have a second to devote to it. I don't even care that I'm the one who has to go slogging down into the basement in hip boots trying to find the leaky pipe. To me, that's fun. My little hut (some people would call it a mansion), the one spot on this Earth I can find peace in— when I'm here. I've got this beautiful home, except for the leak, a son who's in college I never see, a teenage daughter I never see, a wife I never see because I'm out working. And now I have this awards dinner speech I'm supposed to write by Saturday night. It doesn't give me any thrill that my clients think I'm God just because I can give them a little help with their lives. They swarm all over the office, and sometimes I have to pull down the shades and pretend I'm not there. I don't know how I even got here. I wanted to have a little farm someplace. And now with everything going on here, I'm hardly ever home. On top of everything I'm supposed to be taking care of both my parents—*both,* mind you. If you don't think that galls me . . . but that's life. When I think of how I had to fix my own lunch at age seven! When is somebody going to take care of little me?

Where You Go South

Once upon a time there was a guy named Alex. All his life he wanted to go live on a beach in Hawaii. Then he figured he could live out his dream, get married and have children, and they would all live in peace and harmony in tropical paradise. Not too much to ask, he thought.

One day Alex turned forty, he couldn't take it anymore. He packed up and moved to Hawaii. He left his job, just walked out with the clothes on his back and a few hundred bucks in his pocket, and took off. He had a big job, too. He was the head of a huge division of his company. Big job. Perks. Insurance coverage. Company car. First-class airfare. The whole kaboodle. He just couldn't take it. So get this, he moves to one of the remote islands off Huau or someplace and sleeps on the beach. Some guy comes along one morning and says "Hey, buddy, you can't sleep in front of my house." Alex notices there are coconut shells all over the beach in front of this guy's house. So he offers to clean up all the palm leaves and the coconut shells and whatever from the beach if the guy will let him sleep on the beach. He does it and the guy is pleased and lets him sleep in this little grass hut in front of his house. After a couple of weeks the guy tells him the next-door neighbor needs the same service, and they'll lend him a wheelbarrow or a cart or some little thing to carry the shells away in and give him a few dollars for his effort.

Before Alex knows it, all the neighbors notice what a great job he's doing. He earns enough money to buy a pick-up truck to do the jobs and, of course you can guess, blah blah blah he now owns not only one of the biggest carting services on the islands, but he's the busiest upscale landscaper in all the Hawaiian Islands, and here's the kicker, *he's never home.*

Get the joke?

In case you don't, you're searching for privacy and peace. You want it. You need it. You're desperately trying either to create it or keep it together, and that is perfectly understandable. Why shouldn't you want to create a refuge, a home base so you can feel safe and comfortable where you live? Isn't that one of the most primitive needs of all primates? Food, shelter. And surrounding yourself with others of your kind whom you trust not to eat you while you're asleep.

It may not be easy to connect the dots and understand how clinging to a dream of home and family could be related to a weight problem or food fetish, but you'd better believe there's a connection, and a damned deep one.

And the reason you often find it hard to leave the house on even the simplest errand? "Where are my keys? Where are my glasses? Did I lock the door? Did I leave the gas on?" It's related to the fact that you feel an emptiness down in the pit of your stomach you'll do anything to relieve. It has nothing to do with Prilosec or Nexium, either. Well, of course, after a while it might, because one's sense of security does indeed harken back to our most primitive needs: food and shelter. Why, then, should such a primitive drive cause you to be obsessed with starvation and homelessness? No matter how big your freezer is or how many acres of land you own, you've still got a thing about both those issues buried somewhere deep in the pit of your soul's tummy. This primitive drive to be safe and comfortable becomes an obsession, with good reason, of course. If time after time you make your nest in a tree that is cut down for lumber just when you get cozy, you're likely to be ferociously attached to the place you live in, just to prove this time it's for keeps. Permanence is everything to you, probably because something deep within you feels so damned temporary, as if you were huddled against the north wind in a makeshift lean-to that's always about to give way.

It's got to have already occurred to you that your constant need to get home is not just because you've got a million things to do there. Maybe you haven't figured out that your love of home borders now and then on agoraphobia. You do get obsessed with your place. It's normal to need a house of refuge and a place to run when the world gets to be too much. But do you realize how many opportunities you've messed up or missed over the years because of that personal life of yours? Maybe that's a little strong. You've made honest efforts to create a happy home, so it's not fair to say you have a screwed-up personal life. It's just that it usually takes time away from your career path. As much as you revel in your private life, it drains you. You'll have to admit that almost each and every time you were about to make a big advancement in career, something came up at home that demanded your attention and your loyalty and life energy. Family is fulfilling when it is not vampirically sucking at you.

Nobody would ever guess you can be as infantile and insecure as you feel sometimes. People think you're totally together and professional, and it's only when you start playing emotional games and allow your feelings to gum up the works that people see you're a steel exterior around a vat of goo. Few people get to see that your skyscraper was built upon four toothpicks and that you're not the stalwart tower of strength you appear to be. When you let old insecurities erode your confidence and leak into your business, you weaken and become family-dominated, which brings you back to square one: your childhood. Abandoned by your parents? You bet, more than once. All you have to do is think back to the most recent holiday. Or when you were five. Or, how about the minute your mother got pregnant with you? We've all got tales to tell, but yours is particularly poignant because your parents really did abandon you. It was real, although in most cases completely denied. And it was not all your imagintion.

That's why you can get so touchy on the subject of family. Even if you come from a *Father Knows Best—I Remember Mama* sort of perfectly normal home, it is very likely that there wasn't a whole lot of honest-to-goodness emotional support and tender nurturing. In fact, even reading this passage has got to make you feel kind of queasy to think of all the half-buried memories it brings up—if you haven't suppressed it all, which who could blame you if you did. But even though it's easy for many people to say their parents weren't there for them, in your case, they weren't. And maybe not because they were cruel and inhumane. Situations could have arisen that made it impossible for them to be Mamma and Papa Bear the way you would have liked. They didn't have to be alcoholics or crack addicts, maybe they were just uptight Puritans who didn't show love. In any case, they were emotionally absent. What drives a person buggy is having to pretend nothing is wrong, everything is wonderful, be nice, go home for holidays, send Mother's Day and Father's Day gifts and cards, never ever acknowledge that you feel and have always felt a yawning cavernous emptiness and a deep unexpressed anger for having to deny the times they demanded allegiance and made you lie and go on as if these were your God-given parents. Maybe that's why it was so important for you to have a family. The problem arises when you are so spooked by the thought of living in an empty house and ending up with the same feelings of emptiness you dreaded as a child, that you'll go to great lengths to create an scene of domesticity. When the feelings aren't there, you still want to prop up mannequins and place them around your living room.

A Key Relationship Issue

No matter how independent we think we are, at the end of a long, arduous day dealing with the cold, cruel world, when we slip off our shoes, snap off the light, and crawl into bed, there's no point in even trying to pretend we all don't long to fall into the embrace of someone who's waiting for a kiss, someone with arms to enfold and comfort us and let us know that it's all going to be all right after all. It's that pair of arms with its intimate embrace that lets us know we are not alone to fight this wicked world all by ourselves. The danger lies, of course, in our being sucked in by that need. Everybody needs a sense of belonging. That's totally natural and healthy. We all need connections with relatives. We all need to establish and preserve a sense of roots and develop deep, long-lasting bonds. It gets weird, however, when we are willing to stretch ourselves beyond the limits of all endurance, put up with bad behavior and even abuse, blind ourselves to other people's weaknesses and addictions, and allow ourselves to be dragged down by them—just to maintain some prosthetic version of a family. We can become so obsessed with not being all alone in the world that we create dependencies that eventually drag us down and keep us from moving ahead. We hang on and we hang on, populating the house with nine actors, just to preserve the illusion of normalcy.

Issues to Resolve

Obsession with personal safety
Clinging and overprotective attitude toward family
Inability to detach
Constant retreat from worldly responsibilities
Having experienced trails of abandonment
Living with fear of impending eviction
Dealing with agoraphobia
Getting stuck with sick parents
Overinvesting in traditional family
Feeling as if the nipple was yanked from your mouth
Curling up by a fire that went out

Your Past Life (If There Is Such a Thing)

Maybe in your last life you had a lot of kids. A *lot* of kids. It was the cultural way. Birth control? Forget it, you just popped 'em out like popcorn. Housebound for years, you were totally identified as a parent, probably a mother. Family was everything. Whether it was the Waltons or the Munsters, blood was everything. Genetics ruled. Maybe you come from a long line of ethnic families who never trusted anyone outside, or some tight-knit sect who lived apart from the world someplace up in the mountains where "nobody knew nuttin" about what was going on in the outside world and didn't care to. The outside world was shut out. Your own world was all that mattered. You puttered around the house, walked around the house in slippers and a robe, and flipped a lot of pancakes. You took naps, even hibernated when the season warranted. You never read the newspapers, except the obituaries to see when Cousin Henry was being buried. The news bored you, unless some dignitary was coming to town or your property taxes were going up. If your child threatened to marry outside the religion, you tried to hang yourself.

Whatever the situation, you remained in the womb of family too long.

You were happiest when you were pregnant, which was all the time. As if soldiers has suddenly barged into your country cottage, the moment came, though, when you had to learn about the world outside the house.

And so it is today.

Finding Your True North

The world is now your oyster. Everything and anything you have ever wanted to pursue as a career path is possible. Many roads lie before you. People in high positions recognize your talent and potential. You'll be dancing in the back row of the chorus, and from the darkened theater the producer's voice will shout "That one," meaning you, and the next thing you know you've got the lead. Whatever the gift is, you've got it. As long as you don't start messing around and trying to make a boss give you what you didn't get at home, your professional life will be filled with limitless prosperity. In fact, that's your destiny. Whether it coincides or conflicts with your dream of what your life was supposed to be doesn't matter. Your purpose here is to leave home, move out, separate from your birth mother and father, and set out upon the highway toward earthly fulfillment. As difficult as it may be to shun emotional enmeshment, you need to try to keep it at a minimum. Your job is not to hold a collapsing excuse for a family together, but to turn your back on genetics and the long line of historical blessings and curses that have been handed down. You must break the chain. You need to be out in the world, experiencing the headaches and ecstasies of corporate management. You need to develop your political skills of negotiation. Dealing with people in power, heads of companies, even heads of state, will mature you and give you the stature you deserve. Fame may not be your goal, but you will never be able to escape (nor should you) becoming recognized for your special gifts and abilities. At times this will annoy you, because each time an opportunity is presented, you'll be torn between it and home. Just as you're stepping up to the podium to address an auditorium filled with people looking to you for guidance, someone whispers in your ear "You have a call. Your father's in the hospital," and you've got to walk out there with grace and polish and not buckle. It will be just another test of your ability to move ahead. There will always always always be times when your professional demands will interfere with your personal needs or domestic responsibilities. Just know that your escape into family is a necessary release from a very demanding schedule. Moments of retreat and repose in the woods or by the sea or just with your cat, the fireplace, and a good book will refresh your soul enormously. It can't be your life, however. Retirement is not for you. You'd wither away in a month, and the release you thought you wanted would never bring you true happiness.

Your path is the world. You need to become known as a leader in some field of expertise, kicking and screaming all the way. You will reach your potential and find fulfillment only when you have shed the outworn attachments and achieved a position of respect in your community. Obviously, the attachments you have to your parents, relatives, and kids are deep and complex. Nobody is telling you to cut yourself off from them and never speak to them again. You need to gain distance and objectivity, and for that reason you've been cast in a role that breaks with cultural tradition.

It's a tough balance to achieve, no question about that. You obviously have issues detaching and separating for all the reasons we've been discussing. What you will find, however, and this is a promise, is that when you do find the courage to walk away from the swamp of emotional entanglements where there are no boundaries or rules, toward relationships where boundaries are secure, you'll feel like a grown-up at last. You'll be able to meet challenges, take on leadership roles, and be much better at coping with a world that at first seems cold, unfeeling, and unsympathetic. Professional relationships that expect you to perform will reward you for performing, not failing. Success is a gift, not a burden.

How to Get Your Power Back

There is nothing to be gained from getting angry because you don't have exactly the right kind of support from the family you are wishing for and craving. In fact, leaning too heavily on that support is actually a danger. Naturally you'd like to go somewhere for the rest of the summer (or even the rest of your life) where you could be safe, cozy, and surrounded by loved ones and little animals. The real power comes not from trying to recreate idyllic scenes in the present as an antidote to deprivation you felt in the past. Success comes when you force yourself to drag yourself out of the house. Make your contribution to the world.

Work. Force yourself to remain in a professional position, even if you think it takes you away too often from the thing you really love to do—especially if it keeps you away from the thing you really love to do. Which is nothing.

Paths to Healing

Finding pride in making your own way
Resisting the urge to turn everyone into your parents
Maintaining professional distance
Setting limits and boundaries
Shedding inappropriate bonds of intimacy
Saying good-bye to conventional bloodlines
Rising above origins
Appreciating the career that sustains you
Pursuing success despite lack of inner tranquility

A Final Word to Send You on Your Way

You need to step with both feet into the world and prove your superiority and expertise in any field you choose. Although it would be more comfortable to remain behind tall bushes and closed doors, under a down comforter and living cozily in your own head, you cannot realize your potential without achieving excellence in the matters of this world. Such an achievement demands determination, perseverance, time, effort, and focus on a goal. This kind of diligence requires that you try to avoid personal distractions. You have to learn how to be a professional in professional surroundings.

Personal feelings must not hinder your course or harm your business relationships along the way. You need to develop cautious and conservative optimism, based on the confidence that only a track record of dependability and competence can provide. You need not only to be able to relate to top executives and celebrities, but to be one as well.

Whatever is going on in your private life must not influence your decisions or public behavior. Then you will gain a reputation for being a blue-chip stock. It's not about chasing fame or fortune. It's about the pursuit of excellence, which is the result of profiting from opportunities and logging in thousands of hours of practice. You will earn the esteem and admiration of your peers. This will shape your talent into a marketable commodity or service that will support you financially and earn you a place in your community.

Your Weird Image to Contemplate
Vietnamese orphan wins an Oscar

Your Song to Sing in the Shower
"Fame"

Your Magic Word for Happiness
Mastery

LOVE

What Gives You Great Pleasure

Performing

What You Tell Yourself, Your Shrink, Your Guardian Angel, but Nobody Else

Just another heartbreak. I should be used to it by now. I wonder what they'd find if they actually x-rayed my heart, or CAT scanned me, or whatever they do. I wonder if there would be actual scars there.

People tell me I bring these things on myself. I've been called a Drama Queen more than once, and it really hurts. It hurts because it's not as if I enjoy the pain. I don't. There's so much love in me, it's not funny. I'm such a loving, affectionate person it isn't funny. I'm really a kid at heart, I guess. Just a kid who needs a lotta lotta lovin'.

I've had my dangerous love affairs. That much I'll admit, but it's not as if I go chasing that sort of thing. And I don't know why I'm so attracted to impossible people. Am I angry right now? You bet I am. Sometimes when I drive along the street and see a couple kissing, I feel like rolling down the window and screaming at them, "Ha! Ha! It'll never work out!" I know that's terrible, but I get pissed when I think of the kick in the teeth I get whenever I show how much I really need love. You want to talk about rejection? I've made a goddamned fool of myself more times than I'd care to admit. I can't believe all those times when I've bared my soul and let somebody rip it right out of me—and then want to be friends again. What do people think I'm made of? Do they think they can do whatever they damned well please and get away with it?

At least now I am trying harder not to get so wiped out every time I fall in love. Each time I say I'm not going to let it happen, but I'm so damned romantic. It's always a fresh slap in the face with a dead fish. How does anyone ever get over that? Do I freeze up, turn off, harden the shell around my heart so nobody can ever hurt me again? I've tried that, but it doesn't work. It's not me. I'm too loving, I guess. That's my problem."

Where You Go South

No one would dispute the fact that you are sensitive. Anybody who ever tried to satisfy you emotionally would also say that they've walked away exhausted by your bottomless demands. You may see them as reasonable and normal, but other people see them as tasks and tests and challenges impossible to meet.

That might surprise you, since you're always the one who feels you give more than you get back. Romantic love, you need to acknowledge, is the most complex and fleeting illusion of all. The term "limerence" refers to the state of being in which your feelings for another human being cause the actual chemistry in your body to change, and frankly, you've got it bad. The term "lovesick" is actually very real. Although it's the "sickness" everybody wants, it's also the sickness nobody wants once they get it. You can't eat right, or sleep right, and the nausea goes away only when you're in the presence of the person who you think is going to fill the hole in your heart. Your life doesn't belong to you anymore.

This is normal. This is natural. This is how everybody feels.

Here's where you're different, though: You are addicted to living in the state of limerence. The condition of limerence lasts only for a few months; possibly, if you're lucky, it lasts up to a couple of years. It's nature's way of getting people to come together and bond. It's the rare moment in a couple's encounter when bliss blinds them both. It's actually Cupid's little joke, because by the time the anaesthetic wears off, you're left with two real and flawed people.

You, however, refuse to leave that state of limerence. Your needs for love are so enormous and your demands so high that you don't do well in the afterglow. You have such a fantasy about what it means to be loved, such a cockeyed notion about intimacy, that nobody on this Earth is going to be able to fulfill such a fantasy or live up to such a notion.

Your adolescent idealizing and the romantic dreams around which you organize your relationships blind you to the fact that you are setting up a scenario that can lead to hurt. In fact, some would say that you are attracted to emotional entanglements only if they are impossibly complex and have within them the seeds of destruction. The ideal love you think you are seeking is focused upon an object that can never be realized in the way you imagine it. Someone is distant. Someone is unattainable. Someone is destructive. Someone is dangerous. You tend to become overinvested in and overidentified with your love object, and that is why you will either have or become a child who will never grow up. Part of you clings fiercely to the need for thrill. While it satisfies your adolescent need for drama, it can easily interfere with the development of normal, mature adult relationships. You can idealize the potential of your children (if you have any) in the same way. The bond between parent and child can easily be twisted into an incestuous attachment, in which the child substitutes for the mate. If a parent feels a loss of love in a marriage, it is all to easy to "marry" the child, causing the child to be overburdened emotionally and sexually confused. The child will have to hurt and reject the parent later in life, acting out in destructive or infantile ways in an effort to sever a bond he or she felt forced to experience.

While you perceive yourself to be open-hearted and loving, these feelings can be self-involved and narcissistic, and rarely include the reality of the person you are attempting to swallow whole. You can be such a fiend for attention that you demand center stage in every performance, hogging the spotlight in your bigger-than-life one-person show that is a dark, picaresque adventure of romantic and personal tragedy. You cannot be loved enough. You don't merely cuddle with the teddy bear, you tear the stuffing out of it.

Appropriate? Appropriate? Well, if we are to be kind, let us say simply that your approach to socializing, dating, and love has always been a bit on the unconventional side. If, however, we are to be raw and real, we'd have to consider your attitudes toward romance as deeply distorted. Nobody's blaming you. Look at your home life—not exactly the most loving or supportive environment for what could be considered a normal lifestyle. As a child you had to cope early on with rejection and nonlove, and if you don't think that had repercussions for you right up to last Saturday night, you're nuts. Here's what nonlove is: Because of an early rejection or a feeling of being unwanted and/or ugly, people in a nonlove situation will chase after impossibly unavailable people, or get stuck with one who will give five minutes of love and affection, punctuated by days, weeks, or months of—if not abuse, then some form of emotional absence. If you happen to be on the receiving end of this lovely situation, what you think is five minutes of bliss is actually the addiction to the long periods of emptiness that precede and follow that brief and shabby respite.

Your childhood home may have failed to provide you with an adequate role model for socializing, dating, and meeting members of the opposite or same sex on a healthy, wholesome, acceptable, and socially accepted basis. What constitutes a normal, healthy loving home? Whatever it is, you've probably never seen it. To brand any form of personal expression as perverted is dangerous, because what passes for perversion in one culture may be standard practice in another. What can be said about your early life, however, is that you felt love-starved. Whatever circumstances prevailed in the household, you were somehow relegated to the role of emotional scavenger, raiding the metaphorical fridge or trash can for scraps of affection wherever you could find them. And what passed for affection was wrapped in an odd mantle of rejection, so you learned really early how to sing for your supper, perform like a dolphin for one slurp of dead mackerel.

Of course it's your parents' fault, but you can't really forgive your parents until you ruin your own children's lives. If you don't have kids, or even a parakeet, it may be hard to see how just existing or trying to survive based on your own emotional training can screw up the people you live with.

To get rid of what you see as a curse in your love life, you need to get back on course and find out what love is really all about—for you.

A Key Relationship Issue

On the subject of finding love in your life—not next year, next week, or tomorrow, but right now: The need is real. The urgency is real. And when it's time to party, you've got to party. More power to you. Obviously you experience an enormous and profound, yawning, cavernous need to be loved and validated and recognized and admired. There is absolutely nothing wrong with such a need when expressed appropriately. There is such a thing as healthy narcissism. Narcissism is natural, and if it expressed wholesomely and without overattachment, there is no need to avoid or deny it. What is wholesome and what is not? Just look at your own behavior and question yourself when your affections are directed toward individuals who, because of realities, circumstances, and situations beyond anyone's control, cannot fulfill your dreams and wishes. Clinging insecurely, dishonoring boundaries of propriety, making unreasonable demands in an effort to have proof that you are loved will not bring the results you so deeply desire. So it's not a question of finding someone to love you. The question is: How can you find the love you deserve to have?

Issues to Resolve

Addiction to passion without affection
Unrequited love
Insatiable urge to pursue impossible love
Affairs that go nowhere
Infantile need for attention
Propensity for romantic tragedy
Feeling unwanted as a child

Your Past Life (If There Is Such a Thing)

Maybe in your last life you were a master at the game of love. Perhaps you were a Casanova, a Lothario, Rudolph Valentino, or some hot Latin lover who romanced all the wives, deflowered the virgins, and did it all with smooth aplomb and slithery skill but without real heart. Your life didn't contain deep love, but it was a never-ending romance, and definitely a lot of fun. Or maybe you were a famous courtesan who drove others wild, but who would never let herself be really touched. You could also have been an innocent and loving wife who kept getting pregnant, year after year. Every time you ovulated you were ripe for the picking. You had no time actually to love and nurture all the children that came from the lovemaking. You had kids, scads of them, and never had a chance to live in the world. Your world was your kids, and although they surrounded you, they didn't truly touch your heart. You lived to please the selfish, seductive man who was also never really there to provide a decent role model for the thirteen kids who were left pretty much to fend for themselves.

In any case, you were alone on your stage, a solo performer completely attached to your image, which you considered glamorous. Even when it had that *Death in Venice* or *Sunset Boulevard* tinge to it, you were attached to an image that had long since faded. Like the old rooster who chases chicks or the way Mae West acted at the end, your attachment to your image as a buck or an ingenue inspired your desperate efforts to retain the starring role in your one-person show, oblivious to the world around you. A greater perspective was now needed.

Finding Your True North

It's no use to tell someone who's desperate to be loved that attachment brings sorrow and that the path to happiness can be found only when you stop looking for romance. When you're walking those streets at 5 AM like a hooker with blisters on her feet and warts on her whatchamacallit, determined to make that last ten bucks from a fat, drunken john, reason is not operating. True happiness, however, lies in the opposite direction from the sort of imagined intimacy that Hollywood always used to plant in your head when the movie ended with a kiss and the guy got the girl.

You are a citizen of the world, no, the galaxy, even the Universe. Don't laugh or groan or think this is some pathetic attempt to cheer you up because your love life stinks. You've been given a gift, even if you don't know it or appreciate it. You are loved and have always been loved. And what's more, you will always be loved, probably long after you're gone.

Although perhaps you've rarely—if ever—experienced what you consider a truly successful romance, from the time you were in kindergarten you had friends; people liked you. Loved you. You had a natural ability to meet strangers and talk to them, put them at ease, and make them feel welcome. You have always been able to provide a sense of belonging to those who felt out of it, alienated, not part of the group. You may not have noticed this gift or thought of it as particularly important. You certainly didn't think of it as anything cosmic.

Even as a child you were probably a little friend to siblings or to one of the parents. Friendship has always pursued you. Even when you wanted something else, people offered you friendship. Love comes in all shapes and sizes, and as you grow older and become more mature, you come to appreciate the kinds of bonds that don't involve clinging and overattachment. In fact, freedom is another gift you've been granted in this incarnation. Of course, when you're in an insecure, obsessive mode, freedom is the last thing you want. You can't take your eyes off your latest projection of nonlove. And you certainly can't permit the other person to have freedom, because if he or she has any interest in a relationship with anything or anyone other than you, you're plunged into loneliness and despair. However, when you're back on the path and headed toward your True North, you don't sit there grappling with rejection and lusting after movie stars. You love your life and thank your lucky stars that in this life you are not tied down to a sick child or roped into a twisted relationship that starves you instead of feeding you. Your job is to turn around and walk away from that sick child, tear yourself away from any relationship that keeps you in a tortured, hungry state. The mature goal is to move away from anyone who toys with you, preys on your emotional vulnerability, or strips you of your dignity with the promise of love they can't or won't fulfill.

Your freedom is not a penance. It's a reward for all the time you gave up your freedom to take care of others. It is for this reason that you sometimes have had to be reminded not to collapse into a scene that erodes your liberty.

Nonattached love is different from the sick version of nonlove to which you were introduced long ago. Love without attachment means someone you love can tell you who they slept with last night and you think it's funny. And vice versa. Is that an "open relationship"? Yes, but you probably have many of them, especially with people you have never slept with. The minute you start harping on the intimate love thing, you tend to lose perspective, not to mention your grip on reality. So your greatest and happiest relationships will be liberated from your childish needs to be the center of attention at every gathering, wedding, birthday party, communion, or bar-mitzvah. In fact, when you truly enter the human race, you will forego this narcissistic compulsion to be the star. You will participate in an organization or group, not dominate it.

Obviously you can't help the fact that you're a natural performer and tend to shine in any crowd. Your creative talents and reputation precede you. It is when you turn those talents to serving the common good that you will be on track and coming back into the light of the Sun.

It's not grandiose to think you have a real contribution to make to the human race, to all beings everywhere in the galaxy. To do this you have to pay the price of foregoing intimacy in the traditional sense. When you use all the love in your heart to shower all beings, making no distinctions, revering all, clinging to none, you're in your zone.

When you can close your eyes in a crowded train or bus and wish for the happiness of all the strangers around you, your own being will be filled with an energy that cannot be described. It has to be experienced directly. "Hearts full of passion, jealousy, and hate," as the song goes, present a glamorous image of what is really the wretched human condition of misery and longing, topped off with intoxicating bliss. You don't think you've had enough of all that? It may be fun, but the evolutionary road on which you are traveling is really headed in quite a different direction, despite all your efforts to the contrary. As far as children are concerned, you're better off with other people's children than your own. With them you have humor, perspective, and mature detachment, and are not at all judgmental or invested in their actions as a reflection of your insecure self. You are the godparent to the human race. Think of it. If that isn't a gift, then who knows what is?

How to Get Your Power Back

You will find fulfillment in freedom from attachment. Love does not have to be roped in and tied up like a poor, defenseless calf at a rodeo. Keeping your freedom and allowing others theirs will not only liberate you from the torturous agony of jealousy and insecurity, but will also draw people to you. They will be attracted to your own sense of independence and appreciate your progressive ability to accept them as they are. This doesn't always put you in the position of the romantic lead, and it demands that you resist getting sucked into a complicated emotional scene that will lead nowhere. Don't turn up your nose at friendship.

Friendship may turn out to be the most rewarding type of relationship you form. That does not mean you won't be loved. It does mean that when it comes to emotional expression, you need distance, perspective, and most of all, humor. Then you'll be fine.

Paths to Healing

Allowing freedom and space to others
Relating more fully to another person
Letting children go
Giving up personal love for greater cause
Outgrowing the thrill of high-risk gambling
Appreciating the vast resources of people at your disposal
Loving all beings, freed from traditional bonds
and conventional attachments

A Final Word to Send You on Your Way

Fate may enter your life without warning to remind you that you belong to a human community of which you are a vital part and to which you must contribute. Instead of narrowing your sphere of influence and flattening you into a one-dimensional cardboard image of a person, this discovery will lift you up to meet a greater destiny. For that reason you may be asked to forego glamourous illusions of intimacy and open yourself up to experiences that are out of the box. This will widen your view, broaden your perspective, and allow you to bring others to new heights of awareness. You'll be able to teach by example when you allow others the freedom to explore their potential as you are exploring yours. You need to transcend your notions of what love really is, as well as the cultural conditioning and social trappings that affect us all. You need not only to appreciate your greater role in society but to open your heart to all kinds of people, all races and creeds, tall and short, fat and thin. You need to cultivate a sense that all human beings are your children and under your protection. Being genuinely concerned with the welfare of beings everywhere is the path to freedom and happiness. You will become a more empathic lover and friend to all those whom you encounter. It is the true practice of altruism, even if it is born out of personal tragedy, and leads you to become a citizen of the world.

Your Weird Image to Contemplate
The Phantom of the Opera volunteers for the Red Cross

Your Song to Sing in the Shower
"With a Little Help From My Friends"

Your Magic Words for Happiness
Generosity of spirit

CONTROL

What Gives You Great Pleasure
Working

What You Tell Yourself, Your Shrink, Your Guardian Angel, but Nobody Else

Can I relax? Of course I can relax. Didn't I just go to Florida for a couple of days last spring? Besides, I get a kick out of it when people tell me to relax. Nobody has any idea that all my ten fingers and ten toes are plugging up a dike that is just about to give way, and that dike is my life. I'm glad I love what I do, because otherwise I'd really be up the creek. I love when they tell me to have faith in the flow, but in the meantime who is going to change the cat litter and walk the dog and empty the dishwasher and bring the clothes to the laundry and make sure there's juice in the house and go online and get the plane reservations for my business trip and prepare for Monday's workday and everything else I have to do? It's a good thing I keep busy, because I'm basically lazy and could probably turn into a bum if I didn't have responsibilities. I'd probably end up a junkie or an alcoholic, wasting away in Margaritaville.

Besides, I like to work. It feels good to be working and doing something. I'd love to be one of those people who take vacations every other week. My life is like a 7-11. Somebody always wants something and when I'm not waiting on people, I'm washing the floor and getting ready for the next customer. Who else is going to do it? The elves while I sleep? Even they leave messages on my answering machine about stuff they want done. I'm not complaining. It actually keeps me going. Of course it would be nice to get to the country more often and live like a human being and not a robot in an automobile factory. When I do get the chance I enjoy it, but to tell you the truth, even those little getaways are working vacations. There's nothing that makes me crazier than to see some able-bodied young person on the street begging for loose change when I'm busting my butt to make ends meet all the time, to tell you the truth. I hate to be idle. I can't stand it. It makes me nervous. I like to be doing something, and I also hate the insecurity of being out of a job. That is the worst. Maybe that's why I work so hard.

And that's another thing that drives me crazy. No matter how hard I work I'm always thinking I'm about to be canned and tossed out on my butt. I'm a bit of a health nut, too, but I think today you have to be, what with all the chemicals floating around in the air and the ozone layer and all the rest of the garbage poisoning us every minute. I mean I'm not obsessed with germs or anything, but you've just gotta keep after it or your whole system is going to run down, which it always does, dammit.

Where You Go South

You've certainly heard the term "workaholic" whispered behind your back by people who say you're hiding behind your work, and avoiding life. What they don't understand is that work *is* your life. It's not just a job or a day job. It's what you do, what you have to do. Sure, it's repetitive. Some people would consider it colossally boring, the day-in, day-out aspect of it. But while some people would go mad from the humdrumness of it, you find a strange comfort in it. Like the clickety clack of the train passing by on the tracks every morning at 6:31, the regularity is calming. It makes you feel secure. Life is safe. Life is regular. Like the chant of a town crier in olden days, "Eight o'clock and all is well, Eight o'clock and all is well." That's how you find peace. In the tick-tock of a watch. Precision. Focus. Consistency. Amen.

Nobody can step away from emotions as deftly as you. You can handle the three hundred guests at a wedding and do your grandma's funeral with the same attention to detail, and you never confuse where the flowers are going. And you don't cry at either function. At least not in public. You wait until you are alone in the bathroom. God forbid anyone should ever see you crying. Nobody can touch you. Your power is to zoom in and reduce a situation to its simplest form, fractions to their lowest common denominator. You discover order in the greatest chaos—if they ever really need to find that needle in a haystack, they know whom to call.

Simplicity and elegance are one thing; myopia is another. You're a fiend for reduction and are often obsessed with refusing to see the cubist version of life. For you this is it. Boom. When you formulate a hypothesis, boom! the gavel comes down and you refuse to see that life is complicated. But people *are* complicated. They're not just good or bad.

That's your cosmic black hole, the rut: the black-and-white picture that rejects color, the two-dimensional view of existence that can't or won't accommodate depth and the complexity of human experience. It's as if you lived in a flat world, running your little course up and down the same streets like Pac-Man. You dare not deviate from the routine. You risk becoming like the inside of an old watch that ticks until its mechanism dries up and stops. When you get on a critical kick, nothing can please or satisfy you. You're worse than your Great Aunt Mary Catherine who almost fell in love once until she came to her senses and became a nun in a Catholic school who spent her whole life making sure couples didn't dance too close but stayed far enough apart to leave room for the Holy Ghost.

Cold. Untouched and untouchable. Unable to be pleased. The dehumanized cyborg with seemingly no feeling or compassion. That is your false self. You start identifying with your ability to see things as they really are, with no magic, no subtlety. You become a machine, or rather, you pretend to be a machine. Nothing will seduce you. Pot does nothing for you. You're definitely not a drinker, possibly because you know how you can get after one glass of wine. People admire your stoic ability to stay sober and get up and go to work—Seven Dwarfs style. You may be feeling lousy and bitching to yourself, but the minute somebody's around, you're the perky nurse, the attentive teacher who never takes a sick day, the cop who will never retire.

You can also drive yourself wacky with your health. You run yourself ragged without a break, and when your resistance is low enough and you catch a little cold you start rewriting your will. You don't merely get a cold, you get lung cancer. And you don't have a speck of dirt in your eye. It's an inoperable cataract. But if you do get a really serious disease, you deny it.

It's an automatic response; you have to stay busy, with even the most trivial or menial detail. Even though you claim your hygiene habits are impeccable, you skip showers now and then and once in a while forget to change your underwear. Sick or well, you can't help spreading yourself thin and keeping yourself in a state of frazzled tension, trying to play out every option in your head and control all results and consequences— most of the time imagining the worst, of course.

That sort of troubleshooting ability isn't always a liability. While it gives you a cautious edge to your personality that borders on the hysterical, it also permits you to size up and diagnose a situation with eerie accuracy. On the other hand, it gives you a dire, dour, and dark view of everything and everyone. The cynicism, although humorous sometimes—you usually have to have the last word, which is usually biting, critical but hysterically funny—gets old because you're always seeing either rain or AIDS on the horizon.

You hang that "Keep Away: Danger" sign around your own neck because you are scared of contamination, terrified that your rational mind is going to be infected with a virus of emotion, or that some predisposition or genetic weakness will finally come up and grab you just when your life is starting to get a little easier. No wonder. For one thing, very early childhood illnesses or exposure to sickness in the family can easily rob you of the belief that the human body is a divine instrument that runs mysteriously to a beat of life that is and of the Universe. You get it into your head that health, good health, may be taken away at any time; the body is fragile, untrustworthy, and can break down at any time. Perhaps a parent actually was ill, or experienced illness in their own childhood, and thus never trusted good health. Because of this, nutrition was and continues to be an enormous issue in your life. That's why you go from trans fats to raw veggies and back again. You fundamentally distrust your body's power to regenerate, and as a result, your imagination can run wild.

The control factor also can be traced back to your youth. Something or someone so spooked you into fearing intoxication (actual or emotional) that you resolved to stay sober and awake and not allow nature to take its course. You were told, or rather you saw for yourself, the disastrous and pathetic life that could result when people had dreams, followed those dreams, and ended up stuck in drab, monotonous, routine jobs until the day they died. So on the one hand you do everything you can to make every scrap of an idea you have useful, but you can also get horribly gummed up on the details, because you dread becoming an obsolete piece of machinery in a changing world.

While your will to control gives you the talent to be an expert in anything you choose to do, you risk falling into a drab and monotonous routine. The irony is magnificent. In your effort to be uniquely useful and exhibit the brilliant rational powers you were born with, you can dry up inside, use your same lesson plan for the next ten years, and hope the students don't figure it out.

You can't help yourself sometimes. You can't stop working. You've been in such a blue-collar slave mode for so long you can't stop.

Even in the most intimate moments, you're still making decisions about whether or not you've had enough and it's time for an orgasm. You devote your life to the elimination of chaos. Your attention to detail is excellent thanks to your strong memory, and as a result you could always beat anybody in debate with your unassailable logic and lightning-fast wit. And sometimes you can be quite annoying about it, too.

A Key Relationship Issue

Burying yourself in your work may be deeply fulfilling. You get a tremendous amount of joy not only from the work you're dedicated to, but from your relationships with the people you work with. They provide healthy outlets both on the job and socially. They help you relieve tensions and get you away from whatever stresses and strains you find at home. Apart from the usual swampy quicksand of politics and nest of reptiles always hidden within any office or company or institution, you find a great deal of support and comfort in the embrace of fellow employees. You eat right, you stay off the hard stuff for the most part, you exercise, you work out, you try to be diligent and dutiful and pure. But something is missing. There's a void, a rip, or tear in the very coat that is supposed to keep you warm. No matter how much effort you put into it, no matter how much carousing you do and what a good time you have, no matter how often you tell yourself you're having a good time and this is what you want to do, you know you are losing yourself in the process. There's an emptiness that follows the promise, a dejection that lies under the optimism, a disappointment that the job that promised fulfillment is falling far short of paying off. What seemed to be the fabulous new opportunity of a lifetime seems rather shallow. You try to cover it up. You try to deny it. But it's there and it won't go away.

Issues to Resolve

Fear of obsolescence or dispensability
Congenital or hereditary risk factors
Inconsistent health habits
Illness as submission to parent figure
Illness as attention-getting device
Handicaps excluding you from normal competition
Terror of contamination in relationships
Fear of making a mistake

Your Past Life (If There Is Such a Thing)

Maybe in your last life you were a craftsman on the Ponte Vecchio in Florence, carving your little boxes for tourists until you went blind from the close work. Or perhaps you were a nun who never married, did your duties, performed your ablutions every morning and every evening, said your prayers, did your rosary, cleaned your cell, worked for the poor every day of your life . . . and never once ever touched or saw God. In fact, you forgot God existed. So convinced were you that evil temptations lurked everywhere, you lived a vigilant, exemplary life. The supreme irony: Your vigilance against intoxication and addiction became your addiction and intoxication. You removed yourself from the path of all temptation and in the end were kept from the spirituality you sought by the fear of temptation itself. You were good and clean and pure, but had no frame of reference to provide you with compassion for all the fallen souls whom you were serving. Like the minister who preaches and has cut himself off from knowing first-hand what it feels like to be a real, flawed, flesh-and-blood human being, you tried to save souls without knowing what sin was all about. The mind had overtaken the heart. You need to live another, more juicy and complicated existence. In order to solve the mysterious puzzles of human existence, you would need to discard the one thing you thought was holding you together—logic.

Finding Your True North

Discipline and hard work are major ingredients to any success in whatever you want to do in life. There's another factor, though, that cannot be denied. Order lives only if chaos is present. This is a world full of entropy. Machines run down. Nothing lasts forever. This world is finite. Some day the Sun will swallow it and every living being will be swallowed with it. Nothing we do will ever perpetuate forever the fleeting and fragile illusion we think of as reality. There is a rhythm we cannot hear and a vision we cannot see when we are married to life as we are taught to fear it.

The control you think you have is a dream. You are contributing to the human condition in all the wonderful services you perform, but you are a mere drop in the ocean of consciousness. You help to turn the wheel of the Dharma; you are of it but you are not it. The wheel of the Dharma is the path of human beings on their evolutionary journey upward to a place we cannot even comprehend. You are a cog in the wheel of a gigantic machine, the perpetuation of which you are destined to help maintain. But you are not in charge of it. The subservient position you need to take is not in some lousy stinking day job you hate but don't dare quit.

You are serving a much higher master, and for that reason the jobs you have, the services you perform, must have a higher meaning for you. It is hard for you to be out of a job for five minutes without feeling threatened or useless. It is hard for you to surrender control or to understand that while you may be rowing diligently in the river, the river has a current you must obey.

Surrendering control demands faith. Your fear that faith will put you straight out of a job is groundless. Faith is the foundation of your success. As you grow older, you'll see that it is not childish, foolish, or silly to believe in the plan of the Universe, or God's wish, health and love, or however else you come to perceive the bigger picture, of which we are all an integral part. For this reason you definitely need to step out of work periodically, to cease your tasks, to retire from the world to meditate, pray, or in some other way achieve a holy communion and a direct contact with the Force itself.

This will not detract from your life. It needs to become a greater part of your life. It's hard to sit there and meditate on the Oneness and the Light when there are dishes in the sink, but if you don't do it in some way, your life will dry up and you'll cease to be effective in any way.

You don't have to wear a burlap tunic and rush to a cloistered monastery or the Himalayas. You could take a day trip to the beach or share a glass of something with a friend in a café. It must be away from work. It must be rest. It must in some way reconnect you with the enormous rhythm and harmony, which is what is really keeping this world going.

You try so hard to be good and sinless, but to tell the truth, you need your moments of sin now and then. Sin? Sin? It's so hard for you to allow yourself joy and pleasure, but they are not sins at all. The idea of allowing yourself to be taken by love may scare the daylights out of you. It *will* scare the daylights out of you. After all, achieving emotional and spiritual intimacy means being intoxicated, out of control, not rational. Anything can happen. You might get swept away. You wouldn't be in charge. You'd be at the mercy of events, situations, and circumstances, the outcomes of which you couldn't predict.

Oh my God. What would happen if you let nature into your life? What would happen if you had faith in a future you couldn't manipulate?

What happens to a leaf when it goes swirling away in the tide? Exploring those very experiences will never lead you away from your Sun's promise, but will help you fulfill it.

The same thing is true about your health. Granted, the Ebola virus can strike anyone at any time, any place, and if there is a genetic predisposition to illness of any kind in your family, all you can do is try to avoid behaviors and habits that can bring it on—not do things you know will actually attract certain diseases, just so the other shoe can drop and your worst fears can be confirmed.

Again the magic lies in faith. Miracles happen. They are real. A girl wakes up from a coma; a blind guy gets struck by lightning and can suddenly see; a fetus predicted to be severely disabled turns out to be the most beautiful baby in the hospital nursery.

Most often, however, miracles occur on another level. Certainly psychic health plays an important role in determining physical well-being. This is a tricky subject; does praying over a terminally ill patient ensure he or she will rise from the bed and be healed? The number one task you must take on in this incarnation is to put your mind in a spiritually healthy condition, rich in an abiding faith in the Universal Force. Your challenge is to challenge science. You must take up the gauntlet and follow a more spiritual and artistic path in life.

How to Get Your Power Back

You should not, cannot, must not work all the time. Period. You'll run dry. Your creativity will wither. Your zeal and enthusiasm will vanish, not just because the job doesn't deliver what it originally promised, but because you have invested way too much in thinking that the job could answer all the problems of your life. It can't. No job can. You need privacy. You need quiet. You need to get away. And above all, you need intimacy not just with another person, but a kind of spiritual intimacy that you can only find in communing with the Infinite. Even in matters of health, you can't think you're going to control all the machinery. You can live on green grass juice and jog a hundred kilometers every week, but there is a point at which you have to realize that you need to develop strength on the inner plane. You need a certain touch of intoxication that lets you feel deeply. You need to be able to trust your creative instincts and go on hunches and intuition. It's not always easy to turn away from the hustle and bustle of hard-core material life, pull back from all worldly distractions, and allow yourself to close your eyes, turn off your mind, relax, and float downstream. No fair peeking.

Paths to Healing

Finding spiritually fulfilling work
Surrendering to the protective power of the Universe
Discovering your version of "God"
Forgiving
Accepting imperfections and chaos
Being able to accept criticism
Living for spirit, not flesh

A Final Word to Send You on Your Way

There comes a time in each person's spiritual evolution when he or she must awaken to the fact that there is such a thing as spiritual evolution. Once you are aware that we control almost nothing, you begin to gain your freedom. Awareness of the cosmic chaos that surrounds us all could drive anyone to order three more martinis. With stillness of mind, however, comes an inner calm and a deep, abiding sense of trust in the greater order that exists within the random chaos. This sort of liberation is not necessarily linked to organized religion, unless some form of orthodoxy conforms to your needs, but brings you the understanding of the impermanence of all phenomena. How fleeting and instantaneous all of life really is. How pointless it is to fight and hold grudges and be petty. How silly it is to get lost in ecstasy or grief. Far from being cold cynicism, this sort of knowledge permits you to enjoy fully the pleasures of your life, immerse yourself in your work and relationships, but never become so attached to them that you are not able to let them go. You feel deeply, you are committed to the betterment of loved ones, associates, and family, you feel what they feel, are happy when they are happy, sad when they are sad. You are always aware, however, of the movie, the fiction, the flickering shadow show we call life on Earth. You can be content as a world famous movie star or a as hairdresser over there on Third Street. You personify an old soul who has seen it all, done it all, had it all, lost it all, and has not been distracted from the one unifying truth that binds all living beings in all worlds—the force of love, goodness, mercy, and compassion.

Your Weird Image to Contemplate
After walking away from a plane crash without a scratch, a prosecuting attorney becomes a Buddhist

Your Song to Sing in the Shower
"When You Wish Upon a Star"

Your Magic Words for Happiness
Wisdom in impermanence

MARRIAGE

What Gives You Great Pleasure

Hanging out with somebody

What You Tell Yourself, Your Shrink, Your Guardian Angel, but Nobody Else

You're damned right I get depressed at weddings. Here it is a cold night, and I have to make dinner for myself, curl up with my cat, and get ready for another day. Excuse me. I've neglected to mention the eight hours I'm going to be in bed with my goddamned self. It was all so close. Right there for me. And now I'm here, another night, another day. Alone, alone, alone. Just once in a while, not every night, but just once in a while, I'd like to have someone to sleep with. Not the married ones. I'm sick of them. Out-of-towners, maybe, here for a night or two. How cool would that be? I could have the passion, sex, tenderness, and companionship, and still keep my life. No hassles. No commitment issues.

Yeah, but knowing me, I wake up and right away I'm their slave. Pathetic. And I never seem to learn. I guess I just don't know how to do it.

There has to be a way. I can't always just be "either hassled or lonely," can I? Wouldn't it be great to have someone? Maybe they'd watch TV and then we could make love and sleep together. I could continue working, of course. And then maybe they'd leave tomorrow or the next day and I wouldn't freak out. Yeah. Sure. Right.

I have never been able to figure it out. Either I'm all alone or on top of someone and totally afraid they're going to leave me. And here's the kicker: I'm never really relaxed until they do. I'm like the guy who's been crawling across the desert, and finally somebody gives the poor slob a drink of water, but just as he's about to take a drink that somebody snatches it out of his hands and says, "Hey, go slow! It's bad for your stomach!"

So you see, I'm afraid to reach for the water. I'm afraid to enjoy my happiness or even remember it. Isn't it perfectly natural to want someone in your life, a companion? Not a slave. Not a master. Just a companion. Someone to come home to. Someone to walk the dog and carry the bundles and go with me to my mother's. Sexy, too, yes, what I consider sexy. And turned on to me, of course. Money? It could be a problem, but a person with their own life path, yes, and making money, too, that would help.

It's really the companionship I want, to share my life with someone who listens to me, cares what is happening to me, and isn't all about them. I want to know there's someone who can say, "No, honey. You sit there. *I'll* get the coffee." That's normal, isn't it? That's not crazy or nuts or selfish.

So what goes wrong all the time? Why do I have to be the one who has to handle everything, the one other people depend on? Will somebody tell me what's up with that?

Where You Go South

Why do you give all your power away so fast and then have to wrestle it back from someone you've gone and enslaved yourself to? You're an active, social, independent, motivated person, but the minute you get into a relationship, boom! paralysis of the brain. You don't see friends. You don't dare go anywhere without your honey. You rearrange your whole schedule (and life) around that other person, and before you know it, you have no life. Your entire existence is built around solving that person's problems, curing them, healing them, caring for them, meeting their needs, making sure their martini is dry and the carrots are organic, and if need be, lying to yourself to protect them from their own truth.

You lose a vital part of your brain—the decision-making part. Suddenly it's, "Honey, should I tie my shoes? Sweetie, should I wind my watch?" You can't even budge without your sugarbunch. The poor soul can't even get up in the middle of the night to go to the bathroom because you've wrapped your body around them. If they are longer than five minutes in the john, you start yelping into the darkness, "Don't take too long. I miss you already!"

After a while, though, the king-size bed big enough to hold the two of you hasn't been built yet, because you feel smothered. You feel choked. You need your space. It suddenly dawns on you that you've ceased to exist. And all those stupid, tiny, meaningless decisions you couldn't make without consulting sweetikins? The poor sap comes home one night to find a note from you on the door of the fridge: "Moved to Alaska. Will get in touch. Love ya." You ask what's up with that?

Here's the deal: Deep down if you don't think you deserve a happy marriage, if you feel you are going to get cheated on in the end, you will steal a partner you shouldn't have in the first place. You'll play at being married, fool around, manipulate circumstances so you can put one over on the Universe and enjoy togetherness on the fly until you get caught and found out. That's the crazy part.

So you see, it's not nearly as simple as you made it in the beginning. First of all, you're not really as casual about striking up a conversation and building a real relationship as you say, or even imagine you are. And you are not just interested in finding a companion to hang out with the way you say you are. In fact, you are possessed by the idea that it is a horrible fate to be alone, and the urge to have someone in your life, especially in your younger days, drives you to take up with a completely inappropriate person who, you hope, is going to fulfill your fantasy of normalcy. Because you are so deeply invested in hooking someone, you often do not wait to find out what kind of fish you've hooked on the line.

You project a million and one fantasies on them, invest them with magical powers they couldn't possibly have, in the hopes that they are going to rescue you from an empty, lonely, nonexistence.

Naturally, this god/goddess-like image is a fantasy, because no person can possibly live up to your hopes, wishes, prayers, and dreams, and, when the pedestal cracks—and baby, you can count on it—the statue falls and you are crushed under the debris of your own imaginary construction. Why would you be so devastated?

People are people. They're human, flawed, silly creatures, full of absurd contradictions. They say one thing and do another. They rarely practice what they preach. They'll pick up a check for a party of ten in the restaurant, then buy day-old bread for themselves. They'll scrub the sink ten times a day, then forget to change their underwear. We're all complex, unpredictably silly organisms. So why do you get so disappointed?

When you dress another person up in imaginary clothes, paint a picture of them that has little or nothing to do with who they are, when their true reality peeks through—as it inevitably will—you are shocked, horrified, and disgusted. The disappointment shatters your faith in people, your own instincts, everything. You cannot believe how, after everything you've done for that person, they could let you down. How could he? How dare she?

You make a colossal error when you think people are going to act or respond the way you say *you* would. Trying to make someone over into a version of yourself is nuts. And why you insist on testing people at their weakest point is a big mystery as well. It's almost as if you look for that aha! moment. You know that somewhere, somehow, someday, when you least expect it, you are going to be stood up, walked out on, abandoned, cheated on, and in general left holding the bag.

Despite all the compliments and accolades you heap upon someone, you don't expect anything but a sorry conclusion to the drama, if that is exactly what you will wait for. In fact, you could live happily with someone until you are both one hundred and two, and then when the old codger dies in his or her sleep, you would scream "Dammit! I knew this was going to happen!"

You think you want to be cared for, when in reality it terrifies you. It scares the living hell out of you to actually express need, or worse, to be in a position where you have to accept help, because of the string attached. You are afraid to "owe" anybody anything. You have as much of a horror of being dependent on someone as you do of being alone, shopping for one lousy lamb chop, and eating dinner in front of the tube.

What you sometimes fail to understand, especially when you're younger, is that you, too, extract a price for your generosity to others, a price you yourself would never want to pay. No one can really satisfy or fulfill you as long as you insist on being the one in control, the one who gives. Maybe that's why you have been drawn to dependent people, children, and those in need. You know that in your earlier days you committed yourself blindly to some pretty destructive people, people for whom you could play both mommy and daddy, people who would need you, people you could guide and mold—or so you thought. In the end, though, when they reverted to their more primitive selves, didn't it seem like a slap in the face after all the effort you put in to tame them, civilize them, and make them as grown-up and responsible as you?

You know it did.

And then you probably swore off all relationships for a while, until that gnawing feeling and that awful voice came back: "You're a loser. You can't get a relationship going." You may have everything a person could have, job, house, money, health, a car—but you have no one to share it with.

So the cycle begins again. The hunt is on. A new fantasy appears. This one won't bring you down. This one won't end up as an embarrassment. This one is different. This one is more real, more possible, *more appropriate.*

Then, as we drill a little deeper, we find the nerve at last: It is the institution of marriage that is your great madness. It makes you weep with longing and gag at the same time.

Hmmm. Where could that kind of conflict come from? Somewhere deep down you have a dread of the fate that awaits people who marry or commit themselves totally to another person. Tragedy follows union— that's the madness that propels you toward impossible bonding situations on the one hand and compels you to flee from commitment on the other. It can't all be madness, however. Such a fear can't have sprung from nothing. The frantic search for a companion must have its roots in some early perception that twisted your vision of marriage.

And so it does.

Ask yourself this question: Was the parent of the opposite sex, in your opinion, a loyal, loving, supportive mate to the parent of your same sex? Absolutely not. If you are female, the picture you got was that men are self-destructive, controlling infants who crush women's potential and sense of independence to support their own fragile egos, and then end up leaving them. If you are male, then you think weak, dependent, narcissistic but controlling women drag men down, dominate them with their weakness, and destroy all men's dreams of greatness.

You had a parent who never grew up, remained a child. You felt alone at age six but were told to "act your age" meaning act as if you were thirty. You never had a really "normal" childhood, mainly because you had to protect your parents from your needs for love and attention. One or both of them were even more needy than you were. You had to take care of them, often literally, because of illness, or some other infirmity. Maybe you even had to substitute for a parent. Years before you could really cope with being an adult, you had to be an adult.

You saw how unstable or untrustworthy or controlling or selfish or just plain absent the parent of the opposite sex was, and you were never going to let that happen to you.

Except, guess what?

Before your enlightenment, you are doomed to seek dependent, controlling sickos who need you so you can go on taking care of them and hiding your needs from them, and then be angry and disappointed—just the way you felt toward the parents you dared not confront because they were too fragile or selfish to be there for you. Got it?

What a conundrum. You know you can't really have a life companion until you know someone inside and out, but once you know them inside and out, the glow is gone. Their flaws and failings become too much for you to cope with, and you can't go to the next step of intimacy. So you either plunge into the marriage thing too quickly and then repent, or you wait until you've been disappointed and don't even want to marry them. The old warning light flashes. Get the hell out of there. Don't get too close. Leave them before they leave you. The moment you need them they won't be there for you. Grab it while you can because it can be taken away at any moment. That's where the stolen happiness comes in. Hurry up and get married. Marry them quickly before you see what they are really like.

A Key Relationship Issue

Being rescued. Who wouldn't like somebody to ride in on a white horse, armed with a sword and shield, scare away all the bogeymen who threaten you, and with one wave of the hand alleviate your fears and frustrations, troubles and cares, so you wouldn't have to worry about another thing as long as Sir Lancelot was around. Maybe you don't have that kind of fantasy. Maybe you are merely making a reasonable request for a soul mate to shoulder the burden and be a true "other half." That's not an unreasonable need. No matter how helpful, loving, loyal, or sexy someone is, you are waiting to discover his or her fatal flaw—that one piece of personality, that one previously unnoticed trait, that tiny little sliver of truth you missed the first time around—likely to burst your bubble big time. It is at that point that you realize that maybe, without being aware of it, you have given up too much of your own strength too quickly. In your wish for an ideal companion, maybe you surrendered yourself and everything and everyone that had been important to you for the sake of a relationship you had put way too much investment in. It's not that the person wasn't worth it. It's just that you have lost yourself in the process.

Issues to Resolve

Obsession with having somebody
Disappointment in one you've leaned on
Commitment to a self-destructive person
Embarrassment for what your mate is
Poor role model from opposite sex parent
Men draining women, women dominating men
Someone not being there when you need them

Testing people at their weakest point
Expecting to be dumped

Your Past Life (If There Is Such a Thing)

Maybe all your relationship issues come from your last reincarnated life. What if in your last life you were a woman? No matter what your plumbing is in this life, you were a woman then. You lived in a much more conservative time. Gender roles were very clearly defined. As a woman, you followed the man's lead. His word was law. And there was hell to pay if you broke it. You were a woman of high intelligence and skill, born with much potential. Even if you were not obliged to walk a few steps behind him, silently serve him, and actually kneel when he came into the room, you were never to outshine the man, compete with him, buck him, or injure his pride in any way. In fact, you gave up a lot to soothe his ego, serve his needs, and build up his confidence. Forsaking all your own goals, your potential languished and died on the vine. You never developed yourself fully—and as a reward, he took care of you.

Of course that's all made up about your last life in ancient Sumeria or Africa or Norway, but the shoe probably fits. In another life you were too obedient, too eager to please, and too submissive. You got really fed up with that role and needed a big push in another direction. Now you've got that push. Time to develop your male side.

Finding Your True North

You do not have to roll up into a tight little ball of defensive bitterness. Having autonomy doesn't mean living a lonely life of solitude. Just the opposite. You bring so much to a relationship, and frankly, you can be alone only so much of the time without going batty. You know how you are. You only spend as much time alone as you have to before you start thinking of people you can call up on the phone.

Having a healthy sense of autonomy means knowing who you are, being comfortable with yourself—proud of your achievements and able to take full responsibility for your choices and actions. If you made a stupid investment in Internet stocks or you screwed up the beef Wellington so royally you end up taking everyone out to dinner, you cop to it and go on. Being autonomous doesn't mean you have to blame yourself for everything that happens. It does mean you always have to remember that you are a strong, capable survivor, and that in the end you can always handle whatever comes up. It is a challenge to attain a state of individuality that totally doesn't hinge on another person's plans or state of being. When holidays or weekends come around, naturally you want to take the other person's needs and wishes into consideration, but it is all too easy to let their insanity (or whatever else you want to call their behavior) dictate how you are going to spend Thanksgiving. And after you've found yourself running around on Thanksgiving morning looking for the last turkey in town because your "other half" never got around to letting you know what the plan was, you know you have to take things into your own hands.

It's quite a delicate balance, for sure, but it becomes the achievement of a lifetime to have a life, have a path, be somebody in your own right, married or single. It's especially difficult in the beginning, especially to have the courage to keep your friends, maintain your bowling night, still visit your grandmother, or just sit there at your computer and do what you have to do even if inside, you are all worked up because You-Know-Who will dump you if you're not standing there at attention front and center the minute they call on the phone.

People will try to play with your head, scare the daylights out of you, and retaliate with threats of running around with someone cooler or sexier than you, if you don't give up your life immediately. Self-reliance is not your penance. It is your achievement. Transforming your concept of marriage and relationships will bring everything you've ever wanted in terms of a good, healthy, honest relationship into manifestation, even if it takes a divorce to do it. A relationship need not be the trap that swallows you whole and spits you back out in pieces. A relationship, a real one, is composed of two people, not one person and one vegetable. It need not be just the bride and groom on top of the cake or a couple of brawling exes in a courtroom. A wedding is not a marriage. When you're alone and don't have the joy of companionship, you see happy couples wherever you go. Couples dancing. Couples dining. Couples kissing. But when you're in a bad relationship and drowning, you envy all those lucky sons of guns out there who can go to a movie after work without having to report to somebody else, or worse, worry what that someone is going to do to you or to themselves when you dare to take five minutes for yourself.

It is natural, when you crave a connection, to think that somebody is going to rescue you, and easier still to cover up your own very hidden belief that in the end, it won't work out or that the person will turn out to be a jerk or a crackhead. To hide your own pessimism, you see them bathed in a divine glow. You have met another human being, both divine and flawed—just like yourself. A real person with strengths you admire and weaknesses which, once you find them out, will be very hard to live with. If you remember that from the outset, then you won't be so likely to test people and wait for them to fail. You also won't be tempted to think you have to fix them.

One of the greatest gifts the Universe has bestowed upon you is your vitality and Life Force. People feel your juice. It enlivens and enriches them. You can inspire people just by being around them. Many people will want to suck you dry, and you have to guard against being drained by those who take but do not give. Just because you want to please someone and be accepted and loved by them is no reason to allow your healthy boundaries to be eroded, as much by your own fear of being alone as the seductiveness of other people.

It is not easy for you to ask for help or accept it, not because there are not competent or generous folks out there, but because you have seen first-hand the power of the strings that are attached. Good boundaries will help to let go of your fear of what may happen if you accept kindness and caring. To overcome this fear you have to let go of your expectation of what you owe them for this kindness.

Boundaries are hard to maintain because you are fundamentally a kind and compassionate person. You don't like to see anyone in pain. True love, however, has nothing to do with curing someone or tolerating and rewarding bad treatment from them. Being present for someone's pain without being engulfed by it is achieved only one way: maintaining your separateness and not merging entirely. You don't have to buy anyone's love or loyalty. You have to remember that you are enough. Whatever wicked treatment or rejection you suffered in the past makes you bend over way too far backward to please others. You do not have to sell yourself down the river to the lowest bidder.

You don't have to close down and be selfish. Well, in a way you do. Your natural instinct to reach out and help someone is one of our finest qualities. No matter where it comes from and no matter how you often kick yourself for being a fool, be grateful that you have been blessed with a generous and mature spirit. You feel out of whack when you pass by a soul in trouble and don't stop to ask if you can help. That quality sets you apart from all the hogs and slobs who care only for their own big, fat lives. Your desire and ability to be there for people, no matter how lousy you are feeling, is a great gift and asset.

What you need to do, though, is to also think of your own needs. You need to develop a compassionate understanding so that you are not tortured by the neurotic compulsion that it is your job to remove everyone's pain. In some cases, compassionate understanding is all that is required. When you encounter individuals whose physical, mental, or spiritual illness goes deep, then you have to recognize your limitations as a healing human being. Some problems need more time and patience than exists in one lifetime. No matter how beautiful, handsome, sexy, rich, or wonderful someone is, there will always come a denuding action, word, or deed that bursts the bubble and ends the idyll.

And ain't that a kick in the head. There will always be a fatal flaw, the one thing you can't tolerate. If you are waiting for that to appear, then your expectation of that fatal flaw is *your* fatal flaw.

No one knows exactly where the line between compassion and masochistic abuse lies. That is a point every person must find or himself or herself.

We come into this life on a journey. Along the way we encounter many different beings and souls, each one mirroring our own strengths and weakness. If we had nothing to learn from them we wouldn't meet them in the first place. You have a lot to give, and for that, God bless you. Because you live in a world full of people, you cannot avoid encountering foolish or wounded beings. Each and every one of us has a weak spot, a place where the timber is rotting. Stand on it and you're sure to fall through. Looking for the good in people does not mean blinding yourself to their problems.

Know this. Man or woman, you have entered this human realm to develop your masculine side. It is not a punishment to be given the opportunity to live a more independent lifestyle, freed from the bonds of traditional relationships. You are here to remain a whole person in your own right, proud of your singular achievements and bearing your idiosyncrasies with good humor. Go forward on your own and others will follow.

How to Get Your Power Back

You get your power back by being strong and independent. You can't expect people to play the role you have to play now. You have to take on what has traditionally been considered to be the masculine role. This simply means that you need to take initiative, be more assertive, and not wait for the miracle to occur. Being independent and having your own life doesn't in any way preclude having happy, fulfilling, prosperous relationships. It does mean, though, that you cannot fall into an unhealthy dependency, rewarding bad behavior and putting up with someone's improper treatment of you just because you don't want to be alone. While it is always prudent to consider the impact your actions will have on people with whom you are having a relationship, major decisions need to be based on what you believe to be the right course to take. There is no way to take your power back other than to realize you tend to give it away prematurely. Then you have to overcome your fear of being abandoned if you do dare exhibit strength. Your Life Force is tremendous. Don't sell it short. Don't be afraid of your male side. It's not your curse. It's your blessing.

Paths to Healing

Learning that we are all alone
Maintaining your identity in a couple
Relating without guilt
Allowing people their pain and weakness
without thinking you have to cure it
Not idealizing people and then being crushed
when they turn out to be human
Shedding false notions about marriage
Retaining individuality and autonomy

A Final Word to Send You on Your Way

There is a defining moment in every life when a man or woman must choose whether to follow the lead of another person or to step into his or her own shoes and take another road. People will always try to sway and influence you, guide, advise, and manipulate you into doing what they think you should be doing, and it is a lot easier to give in than to fight. When you have overcome all the urges to put yourself first above everyone else, or to suppress your needs to please others, you rise to another level. You are in another zone, beyond the personal struggle for dominance, fear of being trapped or abandoned, or even the desire to beat someone else up. It is not personal at all. You are not drawn in or involved in any unhealthy way. You see a situation in which your strength, talent, and courage can save a life, or add to a life, or enhance the life of another, and you enter the burning building with total knowledge that everything will turn out fine if you stay focused on the job you have to do. No sense of doom or danger. No messy involvement. You are there because you can do what others cannot do. You are not acting out of childish grandiosity or feelings of superiority. You are following a path you yourself have cut out. You are at the head of the wagon train, not because you have killed off the competition, but because of your singular devotion to become the best individual you can be. The courage you demonstrate is not ego-driven. It gives you the ability to hack through the jungle, kill the poisonous snakes, and take the hostile arrows because it paves the way for others to follow. You are the leader when you think not of yourself, not of your position, but only of the obstacle in front of you that must be removed.

Your Weird Image to Contemplate
Without even mussing her apron,
a fifties housewife starts pumping her own gas

Your Song to Sing in the Shower
"My Way"

Your Magic Word for Happiness
Heroism

SEX

What Gives You Great Pleasure
Being creative and persuasive

What You Tell Yourself, Your Shrink, Your Guardian Angel, but Nobody Else

Whatever you do, don't tell me to raise my level of consciousness and not to have desires and needs and longings like everybody else. And I don't want to hear that desire causes suffering or any of claptrap that's supposed to make me feel good about my frustration. I'm a normal person. I'm not a sex fiend. I just need to be held and touched and desired, same as everybody else, and I resent it when people tell me I'm the one with problems. I'm not some weird perv who has to be contained because I can't control myself. I'm actually a very creative person, and my desire to be creative has always meant more to me than the money, and I don't think that's weird either.

I should just go with my feelings. I've seen what happens to people who don't "go with their feelings." If you think I'm bad now, I'm wonder-

420

ful compared with the way I was back, say, a while ago. At least now I'm not throwing all my money down a rat hole.

I am actually a lot better. I realized it myself a while ago when I came home from one of my "nights out" and realized I was living like some crazy alcoholic or drug addict. I was letting everything go. Everything and everyone. My place looked like a murderer's hideout. I realized then I wasn't really living in my house. All my energy was going into a mad pursuit. But still, please, don't start with the sexual addiction thing. I know I can go over the line now and then, but considering all the hideous sexual repression I was raised under, if I had sex six times a day between now and the year 3000, it wouldn't be enough to make up for all the times I've had to pretend I didn't have feelings, sexual or otherwise. In my house money was all that was happening. Love and sex, forget it.

Where You Go South

These days there's an awful lot of talk about "sex addiction." Celebrities check into rehab for it and it gives the media reporters something delicious to chew on. The actress Elizabeth Taylor once said that in her day if you wanted to have sex with somebody you married them. Times have changed. AIDS has put quite a damper on the sexual revolution of the 1960s and '70s, although not, it seems, for everybody.

It's a tough call: Are you just a lusty, life-affirming healthy human being? You do have an inordinate desire to be desired and to be desirable. Sexual rejection can plunge you into an abyss of depression and self-deprecation, and it is for this reason that you could go to the most absurd lengths to make yourself desirable. On the other hand, because you are also hung up on being rejected, there will probably be times when you do things to make yourself look unattractive. [Note to plastic surgeons: Find all those prospective patients with this particular astrological trait and exploit the hell out of them. They will be total suckers.]

Sex can be a healthy outlet, one that should be available to all those who want it. If, however, you are told you can't have it, you shouldn't want it, it's wrong, it's evil, you'll go to hell, you'll get a disease, your hair will fall out, you'll go blind and die—that's not going to foster normal sexual relations. It's like everything else, really. When you are denied something for reasons you don't understand, you're going to want it all the more. You're going to want to rebel. And that rebellion will never cease, even if it is childish or destructive. Never stops. The rage built up within you because you feel you are denied what every other human being is born to deserve is going to simmer, simmer, simmer, and when it boils, brother, look out.

No, you're not necessarily a sex offender or a molester. Their problems are a lot more complex and involve impulse control. You think about sex almost every time you encounter someone. What do they look like naked? How would they be in the sack? Do they think you're hot? You wonder about all sorts of prurient and XXX-rated thing better left to your imagination for the moment. Do you have a dirty mind? Some people would think so. You do get that old-man-in-a-raincoat gleam in your eye, and you sometimes peer into strangers' eyes as if to see if they are relating to you as sexually as you are relating to them.

The sexual taboo is so profound and so deeply instilled in you that you may not even be that sexual. You may swear you are not a sexual player at all. If that is the case, then you're probably a sex therapist, gynecologist, proctologist, or a porn director. The obsession is there, and depending upon how the taboo was drilled in your head, you will either practice or not. Either way you're an expert on the subject (although some would say total freak). This is complicated, of course, by the fact that in certain instances you are repelled by sexual advances. At the core of you there is also disgust and revulsion and a twisted sense of what sexual relationships should be all about. This has nothing whatever to do with your sexual orientation or gender. Whatever the dysfunction is, it began long ago. Its origins could be no more serious than a poor sex education. Many families live a nonsexual life, so when the children experience the birth and development of their sexual curiosity, it is either ignored or squashed. The child then feels guilty and attempts to hide his or her drives in order to be acceptable to the parent(s) and other members of the family. It then becomes more and more difficult to integrate sexual feelings into any other relationship appropriately. If you saw one of your parents sexually rejecting the other and you saw that early enough and often enough, it's going to turn your head around 180 degrees.

Sometimes the story is darker. If, as a little boy, your mother dressed you up in her nightgown and high heels when nobody else was home, or, if you're a girl, your father went poking around where he had no business, or Uncle Bernie took you out for one hell of an ice cream cone or Father Patrick gave you the soprano solo, and if it happened often enough, it's going to screw you up. It just will. Many people get diddled with as kids. We experiment, we fool around. People fool around with us.

If, as a kid, you have too many experiences in an atmosphere that is verboten, or if your natural curiosity was branded as sick or evil, you can easily get fixated on the forbidden aspects of sexuality, finding excitement in what is condemned or forbidden, seeking thrill after thrill until it finally does you in. In fact, it becomes the only kind of sexual experience you can enjoy. Everything else seems boring and commonplace. Monogamy seems like just another trap, prohibiting you from exploring sexual feelings to their fullest. You pursue dangerous or unavailable sexual partners. Those who are safe, secure, and available are, sadly enough, the ones from whom you hide your darker desires.

You can achieve sexual fulfillment—the thing you are wishing, hoping, and praying for—just as soon as you cease your endless search for immediate gratification. There's nothing wrong with gratification. It's a kick. It's a blast. You need it. You can't take too much safety, security, boring practicality, monogamy, and, most of all, the business end of Life on Earth.

Is it a death wish? Hmm—is it a death wish? That most definitely is an issue for contemplation. Perhaps an early near-death experience or a trauma scarred you and compels you to look over the edge of the abyss. Some people believe that infant circumcision could sexually traumatize boys for life. Some threat to your safety as an infant could be the cause of your need to expose yourself to danger, to try to seduce everyone, to live in a shadowy world that society shuns and fears, and to frequent places and associate with people no fine, nice, church-going, God-fearing person would go near. But you feel comfortable around the sexual outcasts of the world. If you are posing as a fine, nice, church-going, God-fearing person, you know what will happen to you if you are recognized some dark and shadowy night in the wrong place.

For this reason your life often gets split off between security found in stable business practices and fiscal desperation. It starts out harmless. A glimmer. A twitch. A little tickle down where the legs meet the rest of you. But before it gets anywhere a voice you can't bear says "Not now! Not now!" You react. You get angry. You insist, you get even more determined, even more aggressive, until you feel you must prove that satisfying your sexual desire is not only right but heavenly ordained.

The result unfortunately fails to unite the upper and lower parts of you. Au contraire. Body, mind, and soul split even further apart. What could develop into a healthy relationship becomes a fetish, a fixation on a body part, or a certain exact, ever-repeating exercise or practice that gets you off.

The ultimate orgasm you are looking for never brings you the ecstasy you are looking for. It leaves you alone, empty, and forlorn because it didn't involve the union of two bodies and souls. It was a personal, private, narcissistic release from your own tension. This hampers relationships because in extreme cases, it is not union, it is masturbation. You either go on a wolf hunt for the ultimate orgasm, or you can't even get one. Sometimes you will hurry up and have it and get it over with because you know you're going to feel lousy afterward. You could even go so far as to put yourself in death's way just for momentary gratification, which in the end doesn't even do the trick. You'll go to such extremes in search of some experience that is ultimate ecstasy, ultimate Enlightenment, ultimate release from a world that chains you to it.

Before you run out and either join a monastery or jump off the nearest bridge, let's go a little deeper into the mystery of your cosmic black hole to see how it affects not just your love life, but how it affects your personal income and business abilities and how to get back your power.

Your life is often divided between material prosperity and financial desperation. You've got to wonder why you've thrown so much money away and wasted so many golden opportunities to make your life permanently prosperous. Whatever early experience you had—either a near-death experience or negative sexual one—oral/anal fixations have kept your attention down at the base of your spine, if you get the picture. Your anger toward society, your parents, the church, etc. is so profound that you prefer to live on the edge in every way. Part of you would rather be a starving artist than sell out to the big, repressive machine of society. You abhor commercialism, because it smacks of superficiality and hypocrisy, and no matter how many big dumps of money you get, sooner or later you're fighting to stay afloat or running away from the IRS. If you had today one-half the money you've spent on your "exploration" of sex, you could probably retire tomorrow.

A Key Relationship Issue

Can you imagine the crazy lengths some people will go to simply to remain attractive—especially if they think they are getting older and starting to feel invisible when they walk down the street? You can get a face-lift, a tummy tuck, a boob job, you can tattoo on your makeup and Botox yourself right to oblivion, but if your head is in a desperate place, you will go nuts trying to hide wrinkles or dye out the one strand of gray that dares to appear in your roots, just to make sure you remain alluring. Good looks always matter, of course; it's hard to feel good about yourself if you know you don't look decent. Some people actually tell themselves they are rewarding themselves with ice cream or pasta, when they are in effect punishing themselves for their sexual frustration. The more weight they gain, the worse the situation gets. Obsession with being skinny is the same deal.

Behind all this overattachment to your looks is the fear of just dropping off the face of the Earth with nobody even noticing. This sort of insecurity undermines the success of long-term relationships, and you can become suspicious and jealous. You can start listening in on someone's phone conversations, and poking around in an address book that doesn't belong to you. You can sexualize every possible relationship, appropriately or not, until you end up destroying even a potentially great bond. Sex is a necessary and even holy outlet for emotions. It's when you feel it's being denied you that you act out.

Issues to Resolve

Search for the ultimate orgasm
Sexual rejection
Lack of magnetism

Emptiness after sex
Poor sex education
Early abuse
Irrational fear of as well as attraction to death
Insistence on proving sexual desirability or prowess
Dreams of being financially cared for

Your Past Life (If There Is Such a Thing)

Who knows? Maybe in your past life you were a very accomplished sexual acrobat. Maybe you were a brilliant artist who lived only for his craft and preferred to die, rather than subject his masterpiece to crass, commercial exploitation. He remained faithful to his art, then died in his attic apartment, leaving behind only his magnificent work and a few crumbs of stale bread on his table. Maybe you led the prosperous life of a concubine whose sole task it was to perform to please your master, and live in the lap of luxury. You could have been a prostitute in Paris at the time of Toulouse-Lautrec. For all you know you could have been immortalized in one of his paintings. You never considered it work, because for you, sex was everything, and you totally excelled at it. You never thought about money because all your Earthly needs were met. You were completely supported financially and never had to earn a cent. Then, something happened, and you were cut off from your source of money. You had no other skill other than seduction and sexual acrobatics. Your business dried up. You wandered through the streets stubbornly refusing to recognize that the world you lived in no longer existed. You sank lower. You performed sex acts for a glass of cheap wine. Anything they wanted you would do, just so you wouldn't be left alone with no money, no food, no place to live, and no way to earn your keep.

In this life you've got a fresh opportunity to test your skills, develop your genius, and earn true prosperity, but to take advantage of it you have to turn your back on your old habits and your shady past.

Finding Your True North

First of all, you have to get over your anger toward people who are either more repressed than you are, or more sexually liberated. Part of you is definitely conservative Republican in the sense that your values are a heck of a lot more conservative than anybody would ever think. In fact, you're a born businessperson, or you will be, just as soon as you grow up and figure out that you and you alone have to shoulder the financial responsibility. Nobody is there to pick up the tab anymore. The buck stops at you. Even if you are more gifted than Michelangelo, this isn't the Renaissance, and the Medicis and popes who anted up for artists are long gone. You must become the bridge between esoteric art and hard-core commercialism. You're a born salesman or woman as well, mainly because you're still an expert in seduction. Even if you don't wiggle your fanny or show your thigh, there's still that look in your eye that says it all. It says, "If you want to buy my wares, follow me and climb the stairs," as Cole Porter said. So when you start using your head, money will spring into your hands.

The petty jealousies that have burned your soul, the rage at the world for not supporting your needs, the scheming and the deceit and the manipulation have all brought you naught. The hours and hours you've wasted walking dark corridors and dungeons in search of the elusive bliss led you nowhere but to poverty, loneliness, and despair.

Joy comes from prosperity, not hunger; fulfillment, not yearning; having, not wanting. Emotional contentment leads to financial security and vice versa. They are one. They both depend on the the taming of desire.

There's nothing wrong with desire. It drives us to improve the quality of life and the demands for satisfaction and release. What you need to do to find peace is to turn down the volume on your desire button. It's up way too loud, for all the reasons you have read on the previous pages. You have become too accustomed to wanting and not having. You have tossed assets away so that you could continue your life of privation and struggle, partly because you want to distance yourself from what you consider to be the hypocritical values of a repressive society, and partly because you still want someone to foot the bill for your projects and/or your antics. You no longer have the luxury of considering mainstream commercialism crass and shallow. Nor can you guard your creative projects in an ivory tower, unwilling to allow them to be touched by the filthy hands of those who have the money to buy them. To find success, you must welcome and not alienate those who could conceivably help secure you a more stable future. You may never love business, but you have to attend to it, even if it takes your mind off your exploration of sex. Because you don't really want to perpetuate poverty, you need to be businesslike and professional.

How to achieve more sound business practices? Business school could help if you promise not to try to sleep with the teacher. It's not really necessary for anyone to tell you how to conduct your business, because you have it all right at your fingertips. You have a brilliantly commercial mind. When you're not staring at somebody's you-know-what, you know exactly what will sell and how to sell it. Even though half the time you're pretending to not be able to add two and two.

One thing does need to be mentioned, though: impulse buying. That out-of-the-blue urge that comes over you to run into a store, drop your plastic, and go home with a big-ticket item you really don't need. That is not prosperity. That is manic spending, and believe it or not, its cause is often sexual frustration. You figure if you're going to feel lousy about your sex life, you're going to do it in a Porsche. Not smart. Prosperity comes from a combination of business savvy, creative ideas, and prudent restraint, something you can achieve only when you have a tighter rein on your desires—which, when you're out of control, are a team of wild horses on crack pulling your wagon toward the cliff of destruction.

In sexual matters, it's the same issue. Nobody can dictate how you should conduct your personal life. Many people have a stable, upright, upstanding life partner on the day side of their lives, while handling the dark side secretly. They get caught, confess, and promise to change, but they rarely do. Then they get divorced and are free to pursue their lascivious fantasies, only to begin at once searching once more for a loyal life partner.

How can you deal with your need for a loyal mate and handle your taboo fantasies as well? You need to grow in your appreciation of the magnificent world you live in. It is a world full of tulips and lilacs and irises and stately architecture and gracious fountains. Being in and of this world roots you in beauty and permanence, so don't have to live like a bat flying off in the night. The green of trees, everything that springtime has to offer can connect you with the Earth and the cycles of life. Don't snicker because it sounds too gay to appreciate a pink tulip or the emerald head or snowy tail of a duck splashing in a fountain.

This is the key in relationships as well. The most fulfilling, long-lasting, life-affirming relationships you have will likely be with those people with whom you never have sex at all. Just think that one through. Monogamy is tough for you, although some people open up and are more able to handle intimacy when they are in a monogamous relationship. You will find that either you stray or you attract people who stray until you learn that the thrill of the chase and the smell of the hunt lead nowhere. Once you have them in bed, unless you share a deeper connection such as values in common, the bond is thin and breaks easily. Although you may, in early life, consider shared values less important than a couple of huge you-know-whats, your most profound and enduring relationships will be built over long periods of time and survive the deviations and detours of all your sexual fantasies and dalliances.

You have to come to this on your own. Your own life experience has to show you that what you consider boring in youth, you appreciate in later years. It takes practice and it takes discipline to stay above ground, enjoy the sky, and resist the underground passages where the worms live.

Only you can determine what is of enduring value in life. The path back to the Sun is away from prurient, desperate longing and obsessive sex. The way to your power comes through the bonds of loyalty. They free you from your wish to speed toward oblivion, both emotionally and financially. Uniting art with commercialism without losing your integrity will bring you fulfillment and prosperity.

How to Get Your Power Back

You shouldn't be surprised to hear how much power money has in bedrooms of even the nicest, most proper homes in the loveliest neighborhoods. That's a scary thing to hold over someone's head, but if you have one shred of power, sometimes you have to use it, whether it's noble or not. The real power you wield, though is that you are the rock in other people's lives, the indestructible gem other people come to value over time. It's not about how irresistibly sexy you are, or how many people fall over their feet to get you into bed. Collecting specimens is not the goal now. Or shouldn't be. Your power is in your loyalty, your ability to outlast all the fantasies, and your capacity to endure, unscratched and unscathed. Living totally in the present on a practical, buy-bread-today level will reduce all your dread of the future and reduce your fear of rejection. So then, in the end, it does come back to money.

Paths to Healing

Appreciating closeness for its own sake
Learning to give pleasure as well as receive it
Overcoming desire for instant gratification
Handling money properly
Conquering the urge for unnecessary spending
Loving security and loyalty
Rising above animal instincts and desires
Making assets grow
Following good business practices
Resisting dark intrigue and taboos

A Final Word to Send You on Your Way

Pursuing thrills and chasing danger, living by your wits, and getting a bang out of hanging off the edge is fun, but when you come to an awareness of who you can really be, you put aside your primitive urges. We know that eventually all that is material will pass away, and yet there are values that last beyond time. Your Oriental rugs will get stained when the cat throws up on them. Your TV will eventually go on the blink, and someday, even you will simply wear out. What will remain, however, is one of your greatest gifts: the loyalty and steadfastness you exhibit in your relationships, both business and personal. While sexual contacts can produce almost unbelievable highs and release from tension, it is your task to be present after fleeting and ephemeral ecstasy. For you it is not about the chance encounter, the shady deal, the mad seduction that enslaves another human being under your magnetic gaze. It is the enduring trait you have that makes up in quality and longevity what it lacks in immediacy. People know that you were there, you are there, and you will be there.

You are not a flash in the pan. You are not a fad. You're the clothes that never wear out or go out of fashion. You're a classic. It is your solid presence people come to appreciate. It is the power of your anchoring, down-to-Earth existence that appreciates in value over the years in the eyes of other people. This enables you to gather more prosperity and draw more material wealth to you as time goes on. Your business practices reflect your honesty, fair play, healthy boundaries, and dependability, so people are willing to reach into their pockets and share their resources with you in trade for the creative and healing gifts you have developed by following your steady course.

Your Weird Image to Contemplate
At the opening of her show, a dedicated artist sells every painting

Your Song to Sing in the Shower
"Diamonds Are a Girl's Best Friend"

Your Magic Word for Happiness
Forever

RELIGION

What Gives You Great Pleasure

Being considered knowledgeable

What You Tell Yourself, Your Shrink, Your Guardian Angel, but Nobody Else

Truth? What a joke. I can't tell you how disappointed I've been in my life, just because I've believed in things. Call me a cockeyed optimist. And yes, I'm an incurable idealist, but that's not a bad thing, is it? It's a good thing to have a positive attitude and to have dreams. You know where we'd all be if there had never been anyone with vision? We'd all still think the Sun went around a flat Earth. Nobody would have ever challenged anything and we'd all be obedient gorillas, blindly following the most dominant male. So yes, I've been whacked and disillusioned over the years. Don't think it still doesn't burn me when I do let down my guard and have faith that my dreams for a better world are at long last about to come true, and whammo! once again I'm tossed off into yet another grand canyon.

I'm not stupid or crazy. I've got a few brain cells that didn't get fried way back when, and I can still string a few thoughts together. Okay, so maybe I'm not Einstein but I resent the hell out of these people who get up there and spout off preachy crapola, and I'm supposed to sit there and listen when I know I know at least as much as these knuckleheads do and frankly probably a lot more. It's just that they don't care what anybody thinks and I do. They will say just about anything, feed the public any horseshit they want, because they think people are dumb and will swallow anything. Of course, they are right. People are dumb and will swallow just about anything if they hear it from somebody who seems knowledgeable or is in some kind of position of authority. There is one guy I've heard on TV, though—I've even sent donations to his church. But most of these phonies? Don't get me started.

Where You Go South

I don't think you can decide what to believe. If you were really an independent thinker, you wouldn't be such a sucker for some of this New Age baloney that frankly has sometimes turned out to be just as much of a crock as you insist the Bible is. You can be either a rabid fundamentalist Bible thumper or a rabid fundamentalist Bible trasher. You claim to be an independent researcher, but you have hung your star more often than not on what serious scholars and investigators have determined is just a lot of hooey.

So your claim to be a profound thinker has huge Swiss-cheese holes in it, mainly because you tend to substitute one dogmatic belief for another. Your loathing for the posturing of clerics is probably well founded. There are plenty of false prophets, evangelists, and "men of God" (and plenty of women, too) who are indeed wolves in sheeps' clothing, preying on their docile, half-asleep flocks. But in your case it's impossible to tell whether you're going to be picketing the church because you want it to sanction gay marriage or, in Opus Dei fashion, clamoring for a return to Latin.

You get carried away with your anger at some people's ability to convince others of their point of view, but you can be just as much of an extremist wacko as all the people you condemn. You don't always seem able to grant them their right to think what they want, because you think that they are aiming directly at your mind. Demagogues are dangerous only if people believe them. So why do you get so red-faced enraged at certain people's narrow-minded, prejudiced efforts to control mass thinking when your prejudice against them can be just as narrow or dangerous?

Whether you're a xenophobic isolationist or a progressive ecumenist, you lack the ability to allow other people's lifestyle to exist without thinking it endangers your own. Racial, religious, national, ethnic, sociological, or any other form of prejudice works in many ways, and you will inevitably come in contact with it and be strung up by the heels by it as long as you continue to deny you can be just as bigoted as the worst bigot in Redneck Woods.

If you weren't so drawn to people your grandmother would think you had no business consorting with, these problems wouldn't keep coming up. But it's like a dog whistle in your ear. You can't resist putting yourself smack in the middle of situations where some form of moronic prejudice is going to come up. And then you're off and running. Talk about a dog on a bone!

When you get on that subject, there's no stopping you. It's a one-way trip to no place. You're not even conscious of the fact that you are always bringing yourself into close contact (and even marriage) with people of different racial, religious, or ethnic origins. Your curiosity and interest in other lifestyles is healthy, and especially in the twenty-first century, there isn't the stigma attached to intermarriage that there was in much of the twentieth century. In spite of the change in society's thinking, however, you are still looking for a belief system that will not mislead or disappoint you. Unfortunately, social or educational differences between individuals eventually surface, along with the prejudices that are invariably attached to them. So no matter how high your consciousness attempts to be, some beliefs are ingrained and pop up again in moments of crisis.

Your ideas about education also stem from your social insecurities. You have an intense fear of being thought of as dumb or uninformed, and as a result you could tend to overeducate yourself, only to end up hiding the diplomas because for one reason or another you lose respect for the institutions that issued them. You give the whole intelligence issue way too much power, and if you're not scared of stupidity, you have an intense terror of going mad or losing your faculties of higher reason. It's proba-

bly one of the reasons there are moments when you bore people to absolute death. They especially want to fall on their swords when you start
going on one of your endless political diatribes against the wave of mind
control currently being perpetrated against the masses by IBM or Disney
or the Machiavellian puppeteers hiding behind piety in Rome, Tehran, Tel
Aviv, or Washington, D.C.

What does any of this have to do with the fact that your hopes are
draped in grandiose hyperbole and that you're doomed to be crushed and
disappointed if things don't turn out exactly the way you dream?

Maybe it all started with your parents, whether they were either card-
carrying Communists, Klansmen, or members of some other subversive
group. Prejudice or radical liberalism played a part in your upbringing;
politics, religion, and education became for you fanatical outlets for your
intellectual frustration. At the base of it all is a painful moment when
your parents, teachers, and/or ministers were stripped of the heroic idealism with which you looked upon them. The hypocrisy that lay behind
the doctrine was damaging. The people you believed turned out to be either wrong or out-and-out liars. You were cast adrift, disillusioned, a
piece of your mind broke off—and you felt alone and deserted, an idealist in the midst of exploitative cynics.

The fact that certain people failed to practice what they preached left
you in an intellectual and political void. If priests are liars and hypocrites,
and teachers are blind dogmatists, and parents are just plain crazy on certain subjects, then you can trust nobody who tells you anything that is
touted as true.

Rather than remaining in this empty state of longing for truth, you go
on a sincere if obsessive search for it. You become the learned scholar. In
a vain attempt to dissociate from the deceptive racial, ethnic, or religious
doctrines of your past, you seek a life outside the parameters of your
own cultural heritage. You live abroad. You marry "out." The most twisted
aspect of this reaction to childhood disillusion and your anger at your
own gullibility is the addiction you have to repeat it. You still look for the
angel, the savior, the silver lining, the blessing in disguise, the person
who (this time), is going to give you the answer of answers to life's burning questions. You take workshops then drop them. You defrock priests
and expose frauds, after getting hooked on their message. All this be-

cause the stories they told you were the absolute truth turned out to be no more than rumors, tales, myths, or even lies.

In your attempt to free yourself from childhood disillusions, you could put too much stock in new ideas, new hopes, new people, and new situations. Instead of liberating yourself from mental manipulation, ironically you fall victim to it. You need a voice of your own and this is the lifetime to develop it.

A Key Relationship Issue

Who can resist the lure of the arms of an exotic stranger? It's just a fantasy, and there's no law against thinking, is there? At least not yet. But, hey, while you're at it, why not design the person of your dreams? It's almost impossible to resist the temptation to stray into a fantasy, because whether you're in a good relationship or not, there is still the desire to find a soulmate who thinks like you, vibrates with you, and connects with you mentally, sexually, and spiritually—especially mentally. When you're traveling abroad, you are bound to run into individuals who are unbelievably attractive and who promise so much. They appear to be exactly what you would have ordered if you had called Central Casting. That's the secret. So you go to another culture. Italy, perhaps. France, maybe. Or the States. You travel somewhere far away from your life in the hopes of finding someone who can open new doors for you, treat you to new delights and foods. Or maybe you'd like some college professor with glasses wearing a sweater full of chalk dust—some egghead, a really brainy type. If you don't watch out you could fall for your psychiatrist. Now there's a rich fantasy. Perfect, too. Then when you get too crazy you'll have someone right there to talk you down. Perfect. Go for it. None of these fantasies will come true, unless the other person is a real person. It can't be just someone you listen to with a starry-eyed look in your eye. You have to talk, too.

Issues to Resolve

Looking for answers
Praying to a deaf God

Absurdity of a college degree
Pain of education
Brain damage
Irrelevance of religion
Restlessness
Racial, ethnic prejudice

Your Past Life (If There Is Such a Thing)

Maybe in your past life you knew everything there was to know. You had read every book ever written. You studied politics, literature, science, and mathematics, mastering those disciplines from your mountain-top retreat. You were an accomplished astronomer, understood celestial mechanics, and were able to grasp the laws of physics and electricity long before the discovery of the atom. You knew that bacteria and viruses were the causes of most of the diseases that afflict human beings, even when physicians of the day believed evil spirits were to blame. You were wise but refused to share your knowledge. Everything was a big secret. Everything was in your head. Nobody knew anything but you. In fact, you started thinking that maybe you were the only person you knew with a direct line to God. You had no boundaries. The world was your oyster. You saw the forest but you missed the trees. Your thirst for knowledge was at first admirable but then it became an obsession. You lost touch with the people around you. You lived in your mind and had little regard for what anyone else thought. You had all the answers to life's questions. Your wisdom was boundless.

That's where you got carried away. You thought that knowledge was to be found only in books. You filled your head with a pastiche of beliefs that you accepted without question, and you even sought to impose those beliefs on others. Your intent was far from malicious. Your convictions were deep and your faith profound. Your zeal, however, bordered on fanaticism and persecution. Dogma precluded dialogue. Belief left no room for discussion. You wandered into a distant nebula, beyond the maps, off the charts, and you got lost. No one could reach you. You could reach no one. No one could find you, connect with you. You were happier alone with your thoughts, alone on the ultimate LSD trip, inverting yourself into your own mind. You were like an astronaut adrift in a tiny capsule, blissfully masturbating mentally with no interference, no static, and especially no challenge to your view of life. Isolated and as blissfully happy as a mystic high up in the Himalayas and as firm in your resolve as a terrorist. What began as a mind-broadening experience became closed and narrow. You lost touch with people. You needed to reconnect.

Finding Your True North

No matter how long it takes to find your voice, find your voice you must. Your voice. Your point of view. What you think. What you see, hear, smell, and taste. Eventually you will have to stop worrying whether people think you are crazy or stupid. It's not about what Moses said, or Buddha thought, or Mohammed did, or Jesus believed. It's what *you* believe. On the other hand, not all priests, imams, ministers, and rabbis are hypocrites, pedophiles, and liars. Just because you've been led astray and disappointed by your own gullible search for someone to guide you, you don't have to snoop around to get the dirt on the pious, or expose all lawyers and teachers for the shysters and frauds you're convinced they are. You will waste too much energy in the present taking revenge for disillusion in the past. That hobby is not your real path and will not help you develop your true voice.

The mastery of language is your true path, mastery that goes way beyond knowing about nouns and verbs, although that is part of it. Understanding the construction of language and the mechanisms that connect thought with speech must become a fundamental aspect of your life's work.

When one human being cannot connect with another, you can feel such an awful kind of loneliness. Your efforts to make yourself understood or your failure to do so will impact every business or personal relationship you have. An alien visiting Earth would have no meaningful experience to report if it could not find a suitable way to tap into the way we think. Your interest in foreign cultures is admirable and could be rewarding, if you can overcome the language barrier as well as your infatuation with the exotic. The communication factor arises in every interaction you have, from the most superficial message left on voice mail to the heated discussions surrounding issues of liberty, patriotism, and racial bigotry. Although religious or cultural differences are sexy in the beginning, lifestyles eventually clash, and the older you get, the more easily you connect and communicate with people of similar backgrounds and common socioeconomic and ethnic references.

Such a statement horrifies you in your younger days, when you'll do anything and everything to get yourself excommunicated, expatriated, and exfoliated from a culture by taking on the religion or political affiliations or even adopting an entirely foreign language as your own. As time goes on, you will find yourself more connected and in touch with your own kind than you ever dreamed you would.

To do that you must not be afraid to speak your mind. Organizing your thoughts into a coherent body of speech is not second nature, familiar, or comfortable for you. It will probably take years for you to develop confidence in your own observations, which will usually be radical and revolutionary, mainly because your rage at early gospel teachings will most likely never go away completely. Your heresy will come from personal experience.

You have to think of yourself as a caveman whose yearning to make himself heard helps him blast through his lonely silence. His first grunts are indications of his need to satisfy some primitive need for food or shelter or sex. His first utterances are unintelligible cries of fear or pain, a mindless yelping that issues from his lungs and chest, as lonely and strange a sound as a baby's first cry.

You start out there, and from there you begin to overcome the silence, the fear of what people will think of you. You start out small and slowly master a new language, becoming a universal translator seeking a mode of communication everyone can understand.

You may never think you know enough. You may never feel ready. Try to avoid filling your mind with everybody else's knowledge, points of view, and opinions. Accept nothing that you have not observed to be true. You are a scientist in the lab of human experience.

Siblings? If you have any they are your opportunity to maintain open channels of communication with individuals on totally different and incomprehensible paths. In youth your paths will diverge. Your lifestyles will be different, and your politics will be incompatible. The older you get, the more tolerance you need to develop. Just think how far we've come from those first chaotic grunts of human beings contemplating themselves in a vast incomprehensible world, to the treatises on life and death written in hieroglyphics, classical Greek philosophy, the writings of Ovid and Cicero, the printing press, the telephone, radio, TV, and now the Internet.

Your path is to further the development of human communication, to cut through the babble that passes for understanding, and to establish a new mode of linking individuals to the unconscious drives that both move them forward and alienate them from each other.

Find that link.

How to Get Your Power Back

After you've had your fling on the cruise ship, then what? Integrating fantasy into daily life becomes the challenge of every relationship. Whether you meet someone online, at the church supper, or in a smoky bar in Hong Kong, there are communication issues that must be overcome. You'd be surprised at how many times the problems arise after individuals of different backgrounds come together in the frenzy and passion of first encounters. To keep yourself in check and to stay sane and grounded, you need someone nearby, even an annoying relative or nosy neighbor, to remind you who you are so you won't totally lose yourself. This is not someone you particularly want to hear from or speak to, because your mundane daily life can seem so humdrum and boring compared with living in Paris or sweeping along the streets of New York, on the arm of someone who doesn't participate in your life at home. Maybe you can't pick up and move to another country now. Maybe you need your little pied à terre, fine. But to rush off on yet another tangent, uh-uh. You've got too much to handle right where you are. Besides, it will be refreshing to take just a few short trips. That you can live in two places and still be one traveler. Just be sure you speak the language.

Paths to Healing

Respecting your mind and its limitations
Making connections and reaching out

Communicating clearly, not in abstractions
Learning by doing
Overcoming ethnic prejudices
Renouncing archaic systems you once believed in
Being humble in knowledge
Coping with ostracism of church and state
Trusting your own perceptions
Shedding cultural bias
Exposing hypocrisy compassionately

A Final Word to Send You on Your Way

The genius who understands the theory of relativity but who falls over his own feet while stuttering goofily in personal situations may be an endearing image when you are younger, but it does nothing for your credibility in relationships as you get older. Whether you have two PhDs and are smarter than everyone else in the world or are struggling to ask for tea after a stroke, you cannot, must not live alone in your own mind. You have a yawning need to reach out to your brothers and sisters. That need must be fulfilled. Once you have overcome the insecurities and restless urges that stem from nervousness or anxiety, you begin to sharpen all your senses, intuitions, and natural gifts of observation. For you then, life is not just about dreams or vague theories or dogmatic beliefs based in fantasy, but the acuity of your own empirical abilities. You must share your thoughts with those close to you. You live in the present, moving about with the speed of an electron, drinking in every bit of information conveyed to your senses. Mental connections will always be more lasting than momentary pleasures of the flesh, and you get infinitely more mileage out of any relationship that supports the sharing of thoughts than one where silence creates a void.

Your ceaseless curiosity makes you the center of information, the nexus between ignorance and knowledge. You become an inflection point on the graph of human awareness, trading data, relating facts, recounting tales in an oral tradition. You become a way station for travelers in consciousness. People come to you when they want to be connected on one of the thousand levels on which you can communicate. You can speak many languages, move easily from one environment to another, and find common threads with individuals from infinitely disparate social levels. You move in and out of social and professional environments with the ease and skill of an ambassador. You have the power to trade ideas and connect people from all walks of life, put them at ease, and put them in contact with whatever they need.

Your Weird Image to Contemplate
Patty Duke's stunning performance as
Helen Keller in the play The Miracle Worker

Your Song to Sing in the Shower
"A Boy Like That" from West Side Story

Your Magic Words for Happiness
Speak now

RECOGNITION

What Gives You Great Pleasure

Being on the A list

What You Tell Yourself, Your Shrink, Your Guardian Angel, but Nobody Else

I did it because I wanted to do it whether my name was attached to it or not. And, sure, sometimes it gets to me when I work behind the scenes and everything goes smoothly and nobody knows or cares how much effort I put into everything. But you know what? In the end, I know what I did and that's what counts. Although, sure, it's nice to be appreciated.

Am I going home for Christmas? Do you know what a trip that would be? I'd love to, except I'm too busy right now. Way too busy. I don't mean to toot my own horn, but I just have to say it. I did all the work, I mean *all* the work, for the gala dinner. I got the place, the caterer, the tables, the speaker. I organized the entire blasted event with absolutely no help from Evelyn or Todd or anyone else on the board. In fact, just the opposite. It was a fight all the way, every step. And then, don't you know, the whole event is a total success. We raised over $40,000 for the hospital. At the end the president gets up—the president, who does squat I might add—the president gets up to deafening applause and thanks Evelyn and Todd and Betsy for the flowers (which I had to remind her to order, by the way) and everyone else and completely leaves me out. Not that I care, because that's not why I did any of it, but it's not right. So then, while everybody is getting up to leave, as an afterthought, the president screams out, "Oh my God, how could we forget blah blah blah," mentions my name, and everybody turns to me. By then I'm totally embarrassed, and it's way too late. The night was ruined for me, but the hell with it, we raised the money. People enjoyed themselves. But of course Evelyn, and Todd, too, in bed with the president. That whole thing doesn't interest me. I didn't vote for her, and I didn't want her to get in. In fact, when I told Evelyn what I told her, I never thought she'd repeat it to the president, but the hell with it. The night was a success. The food? Fabulous, of course. Guess who supplied the dessert? Me, of course.

Where You Go South

It's not just you. Any sane person contemplating the millions upon millions of dollars thrown away on lousy movies, moronic sitcoms, or humiliatingly crass commercials would naturally want to tear the hair out of their head. The world is full of corruption, and the shameless behavior people have to indulge in to get to the top is enough to turn anyone off. Doctors? Forget about it, they're in bed with the pharmaceutical companies. Lawyers? No need to say another word on that. And you can't even watch the Oscars any more. Did you see who won Best Actress last year? You gotta wonder who she's doing. Or rather, whom she's doing. If you could close your eyes to the whole thing you wouldn't be so frustrated. But obviously you can't do that. You're an alert, concerned, interested person, so obviously you're going to read the paper and watch the news. Even in your own job, you can't help noticing what's going on, and because you are an interested, concerned person, it's going to bother you. And when you see you're every bit as qualified, and more talented and capable than most of these yokels who get noticed, anger kicks in. Then you're the fanatical, underground revolutionary who sees every man or woman in charge as a tyrannical, irrational, and immoral control fiend whose sole purpose is to keep you from achieving success.

You have every right to be honored for your achievements and efforts. But it's not that simple. You're disillusioned with the world, the cheapened values and lowered standards pervading society today. What passes for excellence and professionalism depends on TV ratings, box office receipts, and a faddist pandering to a fickle mob that is bloated with starch and devoid of all critical sensibilities.

A key question arises here that is the root of your whole problem and throws you into paroxisms of bitter resentment. Why do you seek approval from a society whose tastes you deplore? Why do you pursue acceptance by people you don't respect?

It's got to rattle and rile you when you're passed over for promotions, don't get reviewed, or somehow get dissed and ignored at the moments when you are craving, wanting, and needing the ego boost. Not even an ego boost, you say. Just a fair and honest appraisal. That's not what you want, though.

You hate those in power yet you're attracted to them. You're in conflict about being known, being on top, and making it. You are always in danger of creating yourself in an image you have come to loathe—the image of an irrational and controlling parent. This is a problem not only in business, but in setting up a family of your own. In fact, escape from your roots—or rather, the unrealistic wish to escape from your roots—could drive you to project some bogus identity to the public and present yourself as a hard-core driven career person, spending every waking moment thinking about career, politicking for position, wasting time getting noticed, begging and twisting yourself into the human pretzel version of someone you're not, just to avoid being what you perceive to be a beaten-down, feminized loser who couldn't make it and moved back to her hometown in Indiana to have kids and get married, not necessarily in that order. Your horror of scandal is just as strong as your wish to shock everybody in town. Even if you do do the Indiana thing and open up a greeting card shop (you'll have to do something to escape the cloying pressures of family), the whole political thing will happen again and it will be you against them, whoever they happen to be at that time.

Naturally none of this is news. You saw it in high school with the student council elections and you saw it at home. You were raised under a chaotic yet autocratic regime. Rules were changed without warning. Fairness and justice did not rule the household, madness did—not completely, of course, and that's where your madness lies. There was a semblance of order and normalcy, a respect for traditions, and a constant focus on respect for convention that you perceived to be stifling and fraudulent. Often when one parent is forced to perform the duties of two because of separation, death, drug addiction, or alcoholism, that parent attempts to be both the nurturer and the disciplinarian. The children are baffled and confused. If one parent is there but nonfunctional, or if gender roles are chaotically reversed, the children are baffled and confused. They lose respect for and faith in the people who are supposed to be guiding and protecting them. They grow silently resentful of parental authority. They can't wait to get out. Failing to be properly validated and recognized as children, they reject family values entirely and look for validation and recognition in the world. Baby goes out with bath water. Career becomes everything.

The loathing of authority, however, persists along with the vicious cycle of pandering and politicking followed by undermining and disappointment. The cycle needs to be broken.

A Key Relationship Issue

Who's on top? That is the big question. Relationships of any kind, business or personal, always require a delicate balance of power. In your case, sexual politics play a gigantic role in your future, and frankly, it's awfully hard to know which horse to bet on. Is it still a man's world? Or does any authority above you, male or female, set your teeth on edge, intimidate you, and make you buckle and go to your knees? Do you tend to think the opportunity of a lifetime is finally coming your way, only to be disappointed when it comes right down to it and the people who make the decisions completely ignore you? One of the major issues you have to come to terms with is this concept of having to make it in the world—or else. You are aware that time is passing you by and you've got to establish or reestablish your supremacy in the field, and sometimes you are willing to turn to desperate (even unethical) measures to secure a position for yourself. These are the tactics you abhor and yet are tempted to engage in. The very competitive cutthroat games men have always played to keep themselves in a superior position in business (and at home, by the way) appear to be the only means you think you have sometimes to achieve your ends. While this is not necessarily true at all, it is almost impossible for you not to fall into the trap of becoming the very things you have always despised in authority figures.

Issues to Resolve

Loving a bad reputation
Lack of credit
False sense of success
People who cheat people out of credit
Plagiarism
Society's repressive force
Mistrust of authority figures
Lack of faith in parents
Poor leadership in the home
Expecting punishment if you shine too brightly

Your Past Life (If There Is Such a Thing)

Maybe in your past life you were part of a system that was originally based on justice. As a leader, your intentions were pure. You were known the world over. Your name was on everyone's lips. You were loved, revered, and even worshipped. That was the problem. As time went on you became intoxicated with your position. You were so attached to your identity that you forgot how important it is to have a personal life with a home and family and people who love and nurture you. In fact, you became so enmeshed in the power that went along with position that you somehow lost the human element. Maybe you were a powerful magistrate or the judge who had become famous throughout the land, known for your stem yet just decisions. After a while you became synonymous with the law. In fact, you became the law. Your infallibility was never questioned. Your picture was up in every household and in every child's schoolbook.

Although you never lost your belief in your desire to be a good leader, you became an institution. Your edicts and pronouncements were taken as gospel. After a while they were never to be disobeyed. What began as justice became absolute power—like Caesar in ancient Rome, the Inquisition, the Salem witch trials, the French Revolution, the Empire in *Star Wars*. Any place in space or time where the rule of authority replaced human empathy. One day members of your own family were brought before another court in your country. Rather than show a chink in the wall of authority, you did not rush to their aid. As they were being taken away, you realized that the System you had so ferociously held and been a part of meant nothing without the people you loved. By then it was too late. You were addicted to your position. It was all you had come to know. You were successful but lost. There had to be a better way.

There was. And is.

Finding Your True North

Fame without a family will not bring you the happiness you desire. In fact, it will keep you from realizing your true potential, because without deep emotional bonds, you cannot take full advantage of your gifts or exploit them adequately. Although you will often try to escape domestic responsibilities and family ties, fearing they will keep you from your destiny, eventually you come to see they are an integral part of your destiny. Nobody likes to think they're dependent on the family name or the family money. Part of growing up is to dissociate from childhood and make a name for yourself in your own way in your own right. It's not a very exciting prospect to think that what ultimately awaits you is moving back to Tasmania and taking care of Daddy's dingos, or running the general store at Four Corners in Nowheresville, West Virginia. Naturally you aspire to greatness. Who's to say if you're just escaping your background by filling your head up with grandiose notions? You don't want to get all balled up in family business or stuck in the kitchen like the Beaver's mom back in the 1950s. A strong family life, however, is the path toward fulfillment, and the only road to becoming who you truly are destined to become.

Your destiny involves coming back to family and forgiving them their trespasses, changing your name if it makes you feel better, and finding some way to become recognized while preserving your anonymity. You need a secret method you can adapt so you can be both the public personality and the private citizen. It will always be a pull.

When the choice comes whether to stay in and cook or go out and eat in a restaurant, how often do you stay in? It's not the time it takes to cook and prepare meals the way you say it is. The aversion you have to being in the kitchen is directly related to your fear of being feminized, male or female. It's the a-woman's-place-is-in-the-home thing. Uh-uh, you think, "That ain't gonna happen to me."

Another irony. Mealtime. Finding yourself at the table with family is a strain, but it is the grown-up thing to do. You don't know how to do it naturally. It has to be learned and practiced. Becoming a parent is an even more daunting challenge, because you have to learn how to be in two places at once and struggle to be present for children when you'd rather be out playing world conqueror.

Domestic intimacy seems so easy for some people. They get married out of high school, have kids, go to church, deal with the in-laws and the mortgage and the rising price of gas and turkey, but they somehow seem to sail through life accepting their little niche, reveling in their cozy existence on the corner of Maple Edge and Foothills Road, and, barring a few hospital stays and funerals, live pretty much happily ever after.

For you a happy home life must be worked at. What seems anathema when you are younger begins to look mighty attractive as the days dwindle down to a precious few and your life rolls around to a metaphorical September. That quiet country place doesn't seem like a prison you'd choke to death in, it becomes a haven. In fact, you come to see that the safety of a nest is really all you need in life to make you truly happy. You want to be surrounded by loved ones who knew you when, who call you by your real name. That's another one of the great ironies of life: You spend half your life running away, creating this prosthetic persona and finally come home and want to sit around and watch a good movie on TV while eating a dish of blueberries and cream. As difficult as it is to accept, shopping for furniture can be fun. Even while you're rambling on about how you've been most recently done in by someone else's lack of competence or taste, any substance you are going to give your life requires you to turn your back on the vain search for glory and create a home for yourself. It doesn't have to be a palace. You need a place where you can sit by the fire with the dog asleep on the hearth and the world outside not even existing. You must learn how to appreciate rare moments of personal intimacy. Shopping for dishes and pillows at Pier 1, which once turned you off and seemed the last thing you'd ever have time to do, turns out to be the very activity you need to add depth to your life. Necessary, vital depth.

In strong contrast to the public adulation and political infighting that feeds some need you have to gain or maintain some position, the family turns out to be more of a source of support and joy than you ever imagined possible. You need to be able to go home and be real, no shoes, no makeup, just finally able to put politics behind you and sit on the deck with a cup of coffee and hear the birds twittering in the trees, and even an occasional deer poking its head out of the brush. It's not city. It's country. You need the balance. You need to be able to add nature to your life. Nature. It's the place to refresh yourself. You think it's a relief from city political, career pressures, when the opposite is true. Life in the country is the path.

How to Get Your Power Back

Whether you're the head of a nation or a regular person with a regular life, you want to be made to feel special. You want to stand out. You want to be noticed and recognized. That's natural. Male or female, you have a nurturing side that needs personal satisfaction as well. Your private and intimate abilities must eventually be developed. You need family, despite the fact that you run away from them. Not that you have to stay at home and breast-feed infants for the rest of your life, but staying out of the limelight and being more involved in setting up a home and developing a more fulfilling personal life would help immeasurably in curing your political addiction. Nowadays it is not cool to hang around with your family.

You could never be happy just roasting a big, fat goose for Christmas and sewing labels on your kids' clothes for summer camp. And yet, the older you get, the more empty the pursuit of cheap publicity actually turns out to be. Holding a position of power in a company is a thrill, especially if you've had to fight your way to the top. Even in a personal relationship, it's gratifying not to be in a weak and dependent state of childish need. The real power—strange as it may seem—is to be found in this maternal, nurturing, private, intimate side of you. Family will actually nourish you more than your public life, but that's something you have to find out for yourself.

Paths to Healing

Appreciating family (watching It's A Wonderful Life *without screaming)*
Resisting temptation to seize the floor
Avoiding dirty politics
Coping with dirty politics
Knowing what success is
Exposing fraudulence but not succumbing to it
Using a pseudonym to maintain anonymity

A Final Word to Send You on Your Way

It's fun to get out into the marketplace and compete—not only compete but to go head-to-head with the big shots, buck the System, and smash icons despite all the resistance, and still be able to hold your head up in public and say, "Yeah, that's me."

To develop fully, however, you have to turn away from the vain pursuit of personal glory, and abandon reason and the capacity to control every emotion in order to achieve the deep, intimate connection possible only through emotional and spiritual empathy. This connection cannot be bought or constructed artificially, and it has nothing to do with power, control, or worldly success. Intimacy adds dimension and depth to what would otherwise be a dry and empty existence. Intimacy is the achievement of oneness, shared histories, traditions, lifestyles, and common threads usually associated with blood ties and genetic, family bonds.

While it is not always found within the confines of a traditional family, you need to have this sense of oneness somehow. To do this you have to build a home, create the nest, and surround yourself with some form of family life. Empathic connections are not just therapeutic; they are vital to your health. Although they often make demands on your time and energy, they are actually providing you with a sense of belonging you can never find in a job or professional setting. Only when you have outgrown out of your fears of getting stuck in a kitchen can you start to appreciate the feeling of security and stability you find when surrounded by people who knew you when. They are the people who don't care whether you won or lost the election, or who screwed you at the office, or whom you killed in court or on the court. You need to bring people together, not divide them. These bonds will hold you in an embrace that will keep you safe from the assaults of a cold, cruel world and give you a haven of refuge with people you can trust and who can trust you to provide refuge for them.

Your Weird Image to Contemplate
*While watering his tomatoes, a movie producer
hears his picture did not win an Oscar*

Your Song to Sing in the Shower
"My Blue Heaven"

Your Magic Word for Happiness
Peace

FREEDOM

What Gives You Great Pleasure

Making a contribution to humanity

What You Tell Yourself, Your Shrink, Your Guardian Angel, but Nobody Else

Thank God for my friends—I don't know what I'd do without them or how I'd have gotten through some of the things I have been through. Even though, to tell the truth, there are times when I think, oh my God, where are they? And I feel like the Lone Ranger would have felt if Tonto just took off and sided with the Indians. Excuse me—Native Americans. It does bug me to feel like the oddball geek.

I will admit that sometimes the where-the-hell-am-I-going-and-what-am-I-doing-all-this-for thing hits me hard, as if somebody has whacked me across the back of my leg with a two-by-four. You know how it is: You bend over backward for people, you break your neck, you put yourself out, and they turn around and slap you in the face. It does hurt. When you think what an idiot you've been to care as much as you do and to get involved helping people, because somebody always comes along and has to ruin everything and you end up asking yourself if any of it was worth it. Believe me, there are people in this world (and I use the term "people" loosely), who get their jollies destroying things for others. But in a way I don't mind, I'm still what you would call a humanitarian. I've always been that way. I like to fight for the underdog, even though the underdog has bitten me more than once. I still hate to see people get screwed or left out. Believe me, I know all too well how it feels to be left out. Don't remind me.

Where You Go South

Your contributions to humanity could far outlive you, so while you may not always get the thanks you deserve, that doesn't mean you should ever stop trying. But just what are you trying to prove? That you're a good person? That you belong? That you shouldn't be left off the team or shipped off somewhere to Lower Slobovia? There's a heck of a lot more to your altruism than meets the eye. Tons more.

First off, you are ultrasensitive to people who get dissed and dumped. There's a darned good reason why you hate that with all your heart and soul: It's happened to you. More than once you've put your entire being into a cause you really believed in, only to see the whole thing fall apart and your contribution turn out to be a drop in a bucket with a big hole in it. Every time you wrap your head around something that at the time means so much to you and seems like you've found your true calling, just when you think you've found people who share your dreams and ideals and goals, it seems to disintegrate. That's a mystery. What is the mechanism that erodes your zeal to the extent that something that once meant the world to you becomes old news like yesterday's headline or an old TV rerun you couldn't possibly watch again.

Something happens to your hopes and dreams. In the distance they loom large and lofty. The closer they get, however, the shabbier and more mundane they start to seem. Why should that be? Why do you glom onto people the way you do, attach yourself to your little group, and drive yourself crazy trying to hold it all together single-handedly? There's got to be some way to understand how you could end up the scapegoat, playing the fool in the drama when all you ever wanted was to please the group, serve the people, create unity.

Your interests in group dynamics and human political interaction are noble, but they can easily lead you into situation after situation where you can be hurt and never learn your lesson. You seem to keep running back to, or at least falling into, a level where you are left out, even accused of being the force of disunity when you're actually trying to be just the opposite. The whole business of friendship is impossible to figure out. You're certainly a good friend. You try to be. You want that one best friend who can laugh with you and not at you, not judge you, and most of all not waltz off with the first new person to come along and leave you hanging. If there's one thing you absolutely detest, it is being that one person left standing there like an idiot when everyone else has been chosen for the team. There's nothing so horrible as that! You also know what it's like to put a team together and have something nice going and maybe not get blackballed yourself, and then to have to deal with somebody you totally can't stand, who doesn't belong there but refuses to get the hell out of there and make everybody happy.

There has to be a reason why you can't be totally, completely, 100 percent committed to a goal, an idea, or even a person without having some other option or outlet or place to run or thing to do or commitment elsewhere. And yet you desperately want that "thing"—that "cause," that "person" to catch you, hold you, embrace you, and take you on your path. But for some reason your need for freedom has often prohibited you from giving yourself totally, completely, and forever to any person, place, or thing. If you see someone on the side of a road with a flat tire in a snowstorm, you'll pull over and help in a flash, but if they ask you to get together and help them two weeks from Thursday, you'll say "Call me as the time gets closer. I don't know where I'll be."

Freedom can become an awful burden. An awfully empty feeling goes through you like a cold wind when friends dump you, die, fall in love and move away, or just get involved in their soap operas—or when your club disbands because of dissent and political infighting.

Suddenly you rush to fill the void with yet another new cause, new best friend, some "important" or radical purpose you simply have to convince the world of. It's not as if last Tuesday was the first time you experienced this very scary feeling of being all alone on stage, or just completely out of it and definitely not in the in-crowd.

One of the most awful moments in a kid's life can be when he sees a bunch of classmates frolicking in the snow right outside his window. Being the one left out, the immigrant, the alien, the one not tapped for the fraternity or sorority, or worse, the one who gets in trouble when everybody gets off—these are experiences you've got to remember from your childhood. In fact, right there in the family, you were the one who was "different," the Lone Ranger, the ostrich among flamingoes. In fact, there was something about you that actually was different, and you have made every effort since then to become part of the group, please the crowd, cover up the hump on your back. Was the hump there or were you just made to feel different? Was your uniqueness put down and frowned upon? What factors contributed to your overcompensating for being an outsider, the third side of a complicated relationship triangle that persists to this day? And why aren't you part of "the group"? Why do you feel left out when, if you are being truthful, you know you don't belong with them anyway?

A Key Relationship Issue

If "friends" have let you down and failed to be there for you when you really needed them, take heart. There may be a cosmic reason for it. Everybody needs good friends and you are no exception. Friends are those individuals who know all about you—the good, the bad, and the ugly. You can lean on them, confide in them, reveal different parts of yourself, confess sins and shenanigans you are reluctant to share even with your spouse. Friends accept you for who you are without jealousy or judgment. They provide you with a healthy outlet—an escape valve, if you will—from the pressures of your personal life. Besides, you have diverse needs that cannot be filled by one person and one person alone. And God knows, you demand the freedom to explore those various parts of yourself that cannot be satisfied by squeezing yourself into one tiny little life with just one person. You need the breadth and the scope and openness to seek adventures, look for your path, and make your contribution to humanity, whatever that may be. Your life loses balance, however, when you rely too heavily on friends who are not there or on friendships that don't work anymore. You may be clinging to associations that are already worn out, seeking companionship in empty connections, as a poor substitute for what you really and truly require emotionally, and thus risk losing yourself entirely in disappointing relationships and ultimately unfulfilling pursuits.

Issues to Resolve

Separations from dear friends
Being scapegoated
Being left out
Not wanting something once you get it
The disintegration of a tight group
Uncertain direction
The politics of democracy
Cliques and forces eroding group unity
Feeling you didn't belong (in the family as well)
Avoiding intimacy by finding safety in numbers

Your Past Life (If There Is Such a Thing)

Maybe in your past life you were a little too social. Maybe you were a public servant who gave your whole life to the common good. You lived, breathed, ate, and slept for the people. Maybe you were a big, idealistic Communist leader, perhaps shortly after the Russian Revolution. Like many revolutionaries, you were so wrapped up in the common good that you forgot the human need for personal achievement and love. Maybe you even crushed the individual, suppressed the individual's personal needs for the greater common good. Your desire to make a contribution to humanity was overwhelming. Filled with zeal, you devoted your whole life to realizing a dream everyone could share. You had no time for romance and children, pursuits you considered distractions that hindered your altruistic dreams. You cared only about the masses and ignored the people closest to you. Rigoletto, in the Verdi opera of the same name, sacrifices his own daughter in a blind effort to hide his deformity and please the nobles. Think about that and how in this life it's time to do something very different.

Finding Your True North

Are you trying to be different? Are you making a little too much of an effort to display your ideological, political, social, or even physical and emotional as a result of your childhood anger because of them? Making a big display of your social conscience may indeed lead to a unique contribution, but in fact it's your false path. The fact is you're scared of love. Or have been. It's territory you don't know how to tread well in this life. That's why you'll probably have to be older before you learn how to deal with children, or even have any.

The responsibilities that go along with intimate relationships, such as romantic attachments and children, may frighten you, but they'll turn out to be the true path you'll eventually want to follow. Whether you want kids or not, you'll eventually have to cope with them, the decisions they make, and the ways in which your attachment to them will curtail your freedom.

Afraid of love? Ridiculous. Who's afraid of love? Nobody's afraid of love. Everybody wants to be in love. What's to be scared of? In your case, for some reason you have sometimes disguised your love as friendship or have chosen to avoid love by hanging out with friends you don't really care about. Somehow or other, you may have confused romantic love with being burdened and trapped. Maybe that's why you have been able to hide your feelings of love in friendship where there are no commitments. Either you make sure you're busy with the bowling team or you're running out to bring orange juice over to a sick friend, or it's the other person who's not available. One or the other of you is usually committed elsewhere, often to some cause, political or otherwise. Your kids will end up calling their nanny "Mommy," if you even have kids, because of your avoidance of their needs. In fact, you're probably a much better parent when your children are older and more independent, just because they don't need you as much.

While it's easy to say that your path is to be able to handle intimate, romantic love, it is a strain for you to be saddled with children, or to be too cozy and close with a lover or mate without getting antsy like a cat that keeps jumping off a lap.

Does anybody know what true love is? Hollywood used to end the movies with a kiss. The guy got the girl and that was that. Happily ever after. Nobody was gay. If God forbid somebody strayed, they got a mysterious movie disease and died in the last reel. Your mission is love, real love, true love, which means cutting down on extracurricular activities and learning to be present in one-to-one situations without jumping up to make or take phone calls from a "friend." Cutting down on those little escapes may be possible but it won't stop your escaping completely. Love is kissing and hugging and holding and making love and being romantic, and flowers and candlelight and all the other frills that make you nervous—because you worry too much about where it's all going to lead.

Playing or having fun for its own sake seems a frivolous waste of time to you, and if you can't see the point in it, if it doesn't have a real, specific "goal," you get restless and jittery. Games of all kinds annoy you. Until you mature, playing games unnerves you totally. And that's the big challenge of this lifetime. Learning to play for its own sake. As soon as something starts to get too personal, you automatically and instantly detach, become objective, try to analyze, find some rational explanation to describe feelings and emotions you can't deal with. It's way easier to be "friends" with someone than to have to deal with the scramble of complex feelings that draws you into involvements that impede your freedom in any way. So you bounce between lovers and children—and friends who provide an escape from the pressures of intimacy.

During this lifetime, you are challenged to develop confidence in your talent, your ego, and your ability to love. You have to be able to handle intimacy without escaping into friendship, face your artistry and play the piano even if you don't get to Carnegie Hall, throw yourself into performing even if you think career is a ridiculous pursuit, and tolerate that you have ego needs that are no sin. They're healthy. You're not like other people and never will be. You've got to overcome your annoyance and arrogance, and understand that you may be special but your specialness gives you the responsibility to be a leader, whether your peers can tolerate that or not. You have to learn to tolerate those who can't seem to tolerate you.

It's the heart connection you need to tap into, without making fun of it because it's silly and romantic. Goo-goo eyes and hearts and flowers may make you gag, but guess what? The older you get, the more you'll have to deal with all of it, and that includes Valentine's Day.

How to Get Your Power Back

Whether you are a brand spanking new parent, saddled with terrifying teenagers, or your kids are turning forty, if you have children, they need you. As boring or bourgeois or profoundly annoying as it may seem, any stress caused by the needs of your kids has its roots in your own resistance to giving up your independence and being totally present for the nurturing and guidance children require. This is a paradox, the thought that you would gain power ultimately by giving up some freedom, but it's a fact that when you do finally surrender to love and intimacy, a rich reward will come back to you. It is quite difficult, however, to grasp the concept that power comes back to you if you lose a piece of your independence. You have to try it to see if and how it works.

On another note, if you're up for it an intimate love affair will do just as well, although it will scare the living hell out of you at the same time it fills you with ecstasy and a life-giving energy. Love recharges all your batteries as nothing else ever could. Creative artists often claim they get a similar charge by throwing themselves into their work and their performance. Nothing, however, cleans out your pipes, juices you up, and imbues you with a sense of confidence and power like a love that forces you to give up associations that have long since lost their meaning.

Paths to Healing

Accepting a parenting role
Overcoming fear of being close and needed

Enjoying romance without hiding behind groups and causes
Letting friends go when they must
Not testing people where you know they can't comply
Recognizing differences between people without judging them
Exploring creativity for its own sake
Giving up liberty for personal happiness

A Final Word to Send You on Your Way

Nobody can predict when the "big one" will come along, if ever. And if you wait around for it, you could be too old to enjoy it. Your number could come up at any time, whether in the three hundred million dollar lottery, or in the form of a truck that goes through a red light while you are crossing the street on the green. Who can say when a tornado will hit Kansas? Since there are a gazillion things you cannot foresee or control, you have only your heart to rely on. Most intelligent people agree that character is destiny, and that the more you develop yourself as a human being, the more a happy future is assured. When you have reduced the habits that erode character, and increased those that enhance it, you will have found a sense of yourself that can never be taken away from you. You have been born with gifts of strength, survival skills, and an innate knowledge of your worth, value, potential, and creativity. Despite whatever forces attempted to destroy your confidence in those qualities, your invincible Self remains intact. Fear of commitment is your enemy. It interferes with self-development on every level. Once you have dedicated yourself to the pursuit of your special talent, your commitments becomes stronger than your fear of missing out on an opportunity because you have made a wrong choice and given yourself to something or someone prematurely.

Once you have given yourself totally and completely, however, there is no need for fraudulent identities, no need to hide behind masks, engage in scurrilous activities or self-destructive behaviors. When you have found the courage to give yourself, your strength increases a thousand-fold. You don't have to bully or browbeat or lie to make yourself look good. Your performance speaks for you. Your warmth and honesty become marks of the true emotion that lies within you. Your productivity reflects the duality of all your efforts toward self-improvement. Most of all, your personal integrity becomes your badge, a brilliant beacon that shines, inspires, and guides others, and holds you up as an example of the highest form of self-expression and polished talent.

Your Weird Image to Contemplate
A loyal union worker is called out of the picket line to pick up her kids at school

Your Song to Sing in the Shower
"It Had to Be You"

Your Magic Word for Happiness
Honor

ESCAPE

What Gives You Great Pleasure

Getting away from it all

What You Tell Yourself, Your Shrink, Your Guardian Angel, but Nobody Else

I know if I could just sit here and work I'd be a thousand times better off. I know that in my head. But I can't stand it. I can't stand being a little pencil-pusher with no personal life. I feel like a goddamned leper. I so desperately need to be connected. I need to get away. I'm completely exhausted. Well, not totally. I don't feel sick or anything. I just feel emotionally exhausted. The pressure is killing me. And don't think I'm a slacker or anything, because I'm not. I show up. I always show up and do a damned good job, if I have to say so myself. And people know it about me. Oh, yeah, a couple of times I lied and said I was somewhere and I was really somewhere else because I just couldn't take working one more second. Besides, everybody goofs off once in a while. It's normal. It's human. It's natural to take a break. And I work a hell of a lot harder than most of the zombies hanging around the water cooler and pretending to be busy. And I do try to stay focused and centered, honest to God I do. But it's so hard to sit there and concentrate when the yearning is so great.

So great. The temptation. I know better. I know what a high is. I know how crummy I feel after the high. I know all that. I know that it's nothing. It's some stupid thing I'm chasing. But then again it's not. It's real. It's necessary. Every human being needs it. And it's not like me to be so distracted and restless. It's just that you can't just work all the time and not go crazy. I can't. Nobody can. You've got to have a little diversion, some fun. You've got to be able to get away once in a while and be—I don't know—be somebody else for a while. It's not just fun. It's necessary for some reason I don't even understand. It relieves pressure or something. And as I say, it's not because I'm a screw-up or I'm not responsible. Everybody knows how reliable I am. Or can be. But I have this need to do something secret once in a while. Is that wrong?

Where You Go South

No, it's not wrong and of course nobody can just be the perfect little elf performing unselfish service, or a robot clinking parts together on an assembly line in a silent factory full of other robots. Nobody in the world should be expected to dry up like that. We all need stimulation and repose, and sometimes we find that repose in removing the garments we wear in everyday life—taking off the uniform, and donning the clothing of some exotic "other" identity. It provides you with honest-to-goodness, necessary relief from a very stressful environment that requires you to be sober, disciplined, focused, and above all totally present. What we do know is that you will not be totally present, even when you are there doing your work. You'll be thinking about how, when you get off duty, you can do whatever it is that allows you to be shot out of a cannon into another universe for a while. You get into trouble when you become so hooked, and that's just what happens. You get hooked. What starts out as a necessary form of relaxation, begins to engulf your whole life and existence.

Work provides you with a vital structure that keeps you functioning healthily, but it demands a certain detachment on you part, most often at the expense of intimacy. It is this craving for intimacy which, albeit necessary for the balance of your system, becomes an overwhelming need. Because you feel deprived of it, you yearn for it more. The more escape you achieve, the more you need. Very soon your daily life is not punctuated by moments of relaxation and escape, but the opposite occurs. Your daily life becomes an annoying interference with the thing you are really loving—and that's escape.

You're like a kid who won't go to bed before going to the john three times, getting a glass of water, a cookie, and an apple. What is it with you that you just can't settle down?

You can, and when you do, you're actually able to accomplish a lot. When you are functioning properly you are doing what you should be doing. But you put yourself through the hell and high water before you get down to doing what you have to do, and even then you're looking around and thinking of thirty other things, not what you should be doing, but what you could be doing. What you "could" be doing are the thousand-and-one mental distractions that float through your kaleidoscopic mind with their sweet temptations.

You may tell yourself you're bored, but you're not really bored at all. You tell yourself you're bored to give yourself an excuse to punch out early, sneak out for a puff, and simply goof off. What you're probably resisting is the fact that you are not living a glamorous life. There's no flash, no glitz, and very little jazz. In fact, you're just plain angry because you have to work and not play. You are not free to do the intimate hideaway thing as much as you would like. You can't rely on magic or wait for a miracle when that's exactly what you would prefer to do. You tend to wing it through your orals, thinking your soul has absorbed the material, so if you get the gist and feel of English history you don't have to know about 1066 and all that. But oh, how wrong you are. This is a period in your evolution when you have to exercise your fingers, practice your scales, not just put a CD of Bach's *Art of the Fugue* under the pillow and think you're a master.

That's not to say that miracles don't happen. People snap out of comas, dance when they were told they'd never walk, and accomplish all sorts of wild feats you see on *Ripley's Believe It or Not*. Human beings defy reality and live to laugh about it all the time. You, however, can get way too rooted in fantasy. When you do, it's time for you to get into a cold shower, spiritually speaking, slip into something that doesn't show the dirt, and get out there and start picking that cotton.

You have to develop your powers of concentration and be present until you complete a task assigned to you without wandering off. You are so worried that you'll turn into a drone, or even worse, some dried-up old celibate workaholic. When you were a child, there may have been a lack of magic in the household. Maybe art and fiction were not considered to be valid forms of expression. There was an emphasis on practicality. Utilitarianism was valued, fantasy was not. Behind the scenes, however, someone was making secret forays, clandestinely practicing taboos, even abusing drugs or alcohol, so there was always a conflict between sobriety and intoxication. To this day sobriety scares you.

In your younger days you may have been afraid that sobriety would rob you of your edge, block your way out, trap you in a situation devoid of all spark, drain you of all inspiration and bliss. For this reason, until you come to value simpler joys, you will tend to live in exotic fantasies, and find all your pleasures in realms other than here on the planet Earth.

The good news: You have a fertile imagination and many sincere spiritual desires that support you and help you cope with the fact that life can get pretty dreary. It's dangerous, too, because although you think you're in control of when you can drift off or nod out, the fact is you are not. No one is. Before you know it, everyday life with its chores and errands becomes an annoying intrusion into what you think is a harmless form of release. Before you know it, you've spent the rent on coke.

The yearning to get away becomes the rush. Something is constantly pulling you away away away. It's not necessarily drugs or alcohol or any substance like that. For some people it's lying on a beach, or diving into a bowl of chocolate ice cream. It's really any rainbow you can't stop chasing. Whatever your way out happens to be becomes what you perceive to be the source of energy. Actually, it can start draining you of energy. You think it is nourishing you. You believe you need it to survive. After a while, it becomes your master. It stands ten feet tall, stands behind you, and just when you're about to get your life together, it bends down and kisses you behind the ear and whispers something nobody else can hear, and, baby doll, you're off and running. It takes the form of whatever you need to relax you and relieve the tensions and drag of everyday life. It's only dangerous when it becomes your primary relationship, when you start substituting it for the reality that demands your attention and energy.

It is the need for a transcendent experience, the urge to step out of your body and participate in a spiritual reality. This is a vital part of your life. It just must not take over. When it does—if it does—you can OD on anything and everything. In the worst cases the paranoia is overwhelming. Ghosts are coming out of the closet the minute you turn out the lights. Although you are gifted with insight into the underpinnings of life, and sensitive to undercurrents, you can lose yourself in other dimensions and start seeing Elvis at the gas station and link the sighting with UFO abductions and the crisis in the Middle East.

You can meditate, pray, put crystals on your forehead, play healing tapes while you sleep, drink water from the Ganges, and visit Lourdes, and you still keep smoking. You can get so intoxicated by existence in the "higher realms" that you cease to function effectively in this one. When your inner life, your private life, or your spiritual life starts screwing up your life in the here-and-now, you've got to realize it's time to snap out of it. You tend toward unhealthy escapes because of an inability to cope. So while nobody can predict which way you're going to go, one can only hope that as the years go on and you gain greater and greater maturity, you overcome your obsession with being glamorous and find greater fulfillment in wholesome, practical, nonfiction. Although you'll probably never be a saint there are paths to success that are actually easy to follow, once you decide to do the work.

A Key Relationship Issue

When you meet a new individual, a potential partner, or you connect on an exciting business level, especially if you have been feeling lonely or needy it's probably natural to fantasize, project all your wishes and hopes onto that someone and to imbue him or her with all the wonderful, magical qualities you need to make you happy and fulfilled. It's quite another, however, to land plop in the middle of a relationship with human beings whose appetites and instincts don't exactly jibe perfectly with yours. People are funny. They are often wounded, flawed, and full of conflicts that don't really involve you at all. So when they are unavailable, or critical, or try to control the situation, you have to remember that sexual politics are always in play. It's tempting to spend (read waste) too much of your time chasing dreams that not only won't come true but wouldn't fulfill you if they did. Those temptations and little forays into a nowhere you can't seem to give up are not bad or evil or wrong in themselves. They provide a necessary release from a life that is too normal, too pressured, too full of responsibilities, and in many ways, too lonely. As long as you keep your business to yourself and avoid sinking into an abyss of ultimately unsatisfying distractions, you are free to sneak around the back of the barn for a puff or two of escape. Besides, who's going to stop you when nobody knows what you are up to?

Issues to Resolve

Obsession with spooky sensations
Thoughts of something going on behind your back
The belief that pain can be avoided
Fantasies
Overinvolvement with fiction
Wrong medication
Sorrow nobody knows about
Religious versus spiritual training
The urge to deviate
Terror of hard work

Your Past Life (If There Is Such a Thing)

In a previous existence, you were not part of this world. You didn't have to be. All your needs were met and you were not obliged to soil your hands in any way. You were happily separated, cloistered, off in your own private universe. You may have been sheltered by a wealthy, conservative family who attended to your every whim and allowed you to pursue every capricious notion that entered your head. You may have been an actor who had hundreds of identities on stage, but none off. You may have slipped out of the hands of those who tried to protect you from yourself to no avail. Your wish to unite with oblivion was too great. Your wish to flee made it impossible to reach you. You were not interested in society at all. You believed that civilization was headed toward oblivion. You saw no point to participating in a world full of mad people who were incapable of making each other happy and loving each other. You found solace away from the world. Or, you could have been a monk or a nun who found God and lived apart from humanity in a convent or monastery way up in the mountains or woods somewhere, where you had fled the madness of the world to repent and find peace. One day, however, you knew it was time to come down from the mountain and do something. What it was you didn't know, but you knew you had work to do down there in the world of people.

Finding Your True North

Practicality. Simplicity. Service. Oh, that's hard. When there are so many delicious goodies in the bake shop window, only you know how difficult it is to hurry on by and prepare your tofu-spinach balls. There's no quick fix for this, because quick fixes have been your drug of choice.

For you there is the great challenge to remain sober, stay straight, and go clean, even when you don't even like to shower regularly. (You know you don't.) Physical hygiene, diet, and exercise are the places to start. Consistent work habits are next.

For some people it's easy. They wake up one morning, flush all the cigarettes down the toilet and never think of them again without disgust. For the rest of us, however, cheating on the diet is often a greater temptation than we can resist. We love chaos. It makes us feel we're not a bunch of obsessive-compulsive anal retentives. It's more fun being a bit of a slob. And it certainly is easier—until we have to start recycling our underpants. So while it's wonderful to be searching for meaning and piercing the veil of hypocrisy that shields the masses from what the government is "really doing," sometimes you just have to get in there and clean the damned kitchen. In fact, strange as it may seem, no matter how itchy, bored, anxious, hungry, or horny you are, very often it is the grunt work that will lift you out of your depression and send those goblins back wherever the hell it is they come from to knock you off your true course.

There's no recipe, though, except the will to be healthy and productive. It helps to think that what you are doing is performing a service, a useful service for other human beings. Somewhere down at your core, that idea switches on your motor. It gets you juiced when you come to realize that what you are doing is not lowly or menial but is the path you must take to develop mastery of a craft or restore purity to body and mind. Meditation helps, but so do fresh vegetables and regular eating habits.

You have to be in your body, more and more conscious of your body's needs and functions, and treat your body like a temple, not the town dump. Your body should be respected as a valued machine that needs care and proper maintenance. For that you have to develop a consistent eating regimen that not only gratifies but nourishes your body.

A work ethic is also vital to your happiness. Creating and maintaining a high sense of purpose will help you organize your surroundings, gain personal discipline, and fuel you to perform your duties consistently with excellence and clarity, so you're not just staggering out of bed and giving a shoddy substitute for actually being present. Do's: Every time you're excited by a dangerous situation, ask yourself why. What's your drug? Don'ts: You want to have a real shock? Make a list for one month of how much time you spend working, how much time chasing the escape.

Your trademark is the magic of a craftsperson; it is the way you do a job that can never be copied or matched or ripped off. It's your stamp of creativity. It demands you hold back and redirect many of your drives to escape and run away. Think of Michelangelo. Would the David ever have been finished, or the Sistine Chapel, if he had been running around all night doing God knows what so he couldn't concentrate in the morning? If you can carry on and have affairs and trash your bod and still produce a body of work so monumental, profound, and powerful that it can hold thousands of people in awe for hundreds of years, then fine. Go out tonight and have a ball. It's more likely to bring you fulfillment and happiness, however, if you can balance your addiction to living in romantic fiction with good old-fashioned work.

How to Get Your Power Back

There's a lot of truth in the old cliche that "All work and no play makes Jack a dull boy." It did drive Jack Nicholson's character crazy in *The Shin-*

ing. Nobody can submit to the daily grind incessantly without taking time away. There are people, however, like yourself, who have to curb the downtime and get back to old-fashioned productivity, even if you do punctuate it with a few naughty episodes. You must have already learned how important it is sometimes to pull yourself away from your own impulses to run away and force yourself to work. It may be boring and confining at times. It will certainly prohibit you from living out all your secrets and your escapist obsessions. Work is the saving grace. It holds you in place, keeps you sober, and makes sure you get to bed at a decent hour so you can get up in the morning and face the day. What you don't want to do now is let the day get away from you, so wake up with the Sun and your strength will be restored. You need your energy now to be able to fulfill all the excellent opportunities that are coming your way in your work. You cannot afford, therefore, to fritter away valuable time or to indulge in vices that sap your health, weaken your system, and corrupt your ability to perform your duties in the highest and most excellent way. Nobody can do the job as well as you can, but to do it, you have to be able to be present for five minutes without jumping up and running out.

Paths to Healing

Accepting daily life
Being able to receive as well as give criticism
Avoiding exit signs that lead to brick walls
Finding out there's no quick fix
Standing in the dark and leading blind souls
Trading romance for reality
Developing craftsmanship
Practical, detailed work
Finding fulfillment in the here and now
Returning to natural health
Diligence and discipline
Productivity
Utilitarianism

A Final Word to Send You on Your Way

Why bother to do anything at all? The politicians are dragging us all to ruin, and when they get through, an asteroid will eventually crash into the Earth. So what's the big whoop, and who cares whether you have one margarita or twenty? Such a philosophy ends up wrecking your body and sends you chasing after one stupid indulgence after another. The only thing that can resurrect you is the desire to do service. Fulfillment has nothing to do with the gratification of the ego at all. You'll find it in the joy you get knowing you have lightened the burden of another human being.

You are ignited by the flame of giving joy and restoring health and well-being to fellow men and women. Naturally, you don't want to be enslaved in a crappy job you hold onto just for the health insurance and a crummy two-week vacation in the summer that doesn't even give you a chance to unwind. In fact, when you are in service, it isn't even work. When you have found your true path, retirement isn't even an option, because it isn't even work.

The desire to serve is happiness itself. It is the only thing you need to hold you in place long enough to develop a skill, hone a craft, learn a performance that cannot be stolen or copied. When your engine is filled with this drive, creativity flows out of you. You have tireless energy that other people marvel at. You have no need for caffeine or stimulants of any kind. You remain healthy and useful all the days of your life. You'll stay youthful, too, since you too are being fed by the energy you put out for others. Your healing powers restore yourself as well as others.

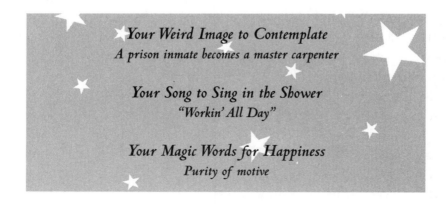

Your Weird Image to Contemplate
A prison inmate becomes a master carpenter

Your Song to Sing in the Shower
"Workin' All Day"

Your Magic Words for Happiness
Purity of motive

CONCLUSION

A Note from the Author

What is happiness? At the beginning of this book you were asked to jot down three ideas of what you considered happiness to be. After the long trip you have taken through the preceding pages, do you think that the information you found in this book has relevance to any of the three things you listed at the beginning of the book? I bet it has.

To tap into your core of health and vitality, and to realize all the potential that lies within the heart of your Sign, you have to go through a rite of passage that demands looking at the dark as well as the light side of your personality. As you have seen, there are things in life you are never going to get, no matter how much you want them, pray for them, scheme, or beg, no matter how many tantrums you have or deals you make with God. Fortunately, there are talents that you can explore and blessings you can embrace with love. It's easy to overlook the good stuff if you're too focused on what you can't have.

Happiness. For some people happiness turns out to be a simple recipe: just an evening with a special someone, cooking dinner and watching an old Hitchcock movie. Someone else may find fulfillment stepping out on a stage to ten thousand screaming fans.

For everyone, lasting happiness is the ability to make the most of your gifts, reduce your negative traits, and increase your positive ones. And it always comes back to your Sun Sign. Always. It's the heart and soul of everything you are trying to become and be. Once you have gotten a handle on how the Moon's path crosses your Sun's path, you have the weapons and resources you need to be who you have always been meant to be. People will feel it. You'll radiate something authentic and real that nobody can resist.

Of course, if we were perfect beings, we could manifest all our positive qualities and resolve all our conflicts immediately. But, hey, we're human. Very human. Nobody can stay on the True North path every minute, all the time. In fact, we follow that straight and narrow just as long as we have to, until we get a chance to head South. We all do it.

Why? True North can be very boring. It's not nearly as much fun as those other things we do, the stuff unauthorized biographies are made of.

When we're hooked on anything, we're attached, and when we're attached we can never be happy. As you've seen in this book, you are going to be happiest when you move away from ferocious attachments and needy longing, and let yourself be guided toward a more enlightened awareness of how damned stupid it is to wrap your whole life around things, relationships, even ideas and beliefs that bring little lasting satisfaction in the end.

We may not be ascended masters yet, but we are all destined to reach that shining, thrilling, blissful light that blazes from the heart of the Universe. Sooner or later, we are all going to get there, each at our own pace. Following the path of True North will lead you to that place of nonattachment and a feeling of oneness with the Universe. It will break through the crust of defense and longing, and tap into your vibrant core. This liberates your potential and helps you to realize your destiny.

On the way, though, we all do such idiotic, embarrassing things. You've got to be able to laugh at yourself. If SunShines has helped you laugh at some of those idiotic, embarrassing things, maybe you won't beat yourself up and take yourself so seriously if you screw up from time to time, take the bait, or are naughty when you know you should be good. Comfort yourself by this thought: The author of this book, the publisher, the person who sold it to you or gave it as a gift, your mom, your dad, your sweetheart, and your boss—all of us—are just as naughty as you are.

No matter what is going on around you or happening in the world, follow these simple rules and you will be happy for the rest of your life:

1) When the Universe keeps showering you with gifts you take for granted and don't even want because they interfere with your pursuit of something you're always chasing after but think you never get enough of, pay attention. You are being sent a message.

2) When it finally dawns on you that the Universe has stopped listening to your whining about the things other people seem to get so easily but you never have enough of, pay attention. You are being sent a message.

3) Limit the amount of time per day you spend thinking about or obsessing over the life you are not leading.

4) Embrace the opportunities the Universe is forever offering you, follow that path, and you will be happy for the rest of your life.

5) If need be, reread this book now.

May all beings receive joy.

Michael Lutin

APPENDIX

THE ASTROLOGY BEHIND IT ALL

The Solar Chart and House Systems

By now any astrologer who has studied this material must have figured out that when we talk about how the Sun Sign is affected by the path of the Moon around the Earth, we are talking about the Moon's Nodes. Astronomically and astrologically, the intersection of the Sun and the Moon's paths is called the Nodal Axis. Two points of special interest are the South and North Nodes. They define your deepest issues and determine what distracts you on your path to self-realization and what enhances your potential of getting where you should be going. There's always been a great deal of discussion around the meaning of these two points, but not much written about them. To make it easier for the reader to go right to the heart of his or her own personal story, I have elected to give each South Node a number and a key word.

You've already seen that *SunShines* is no mere Sun Sign book. The material in the preceding pages provides you with information about how the Moon's path affects both the Solar Chart and birth time chart.

Many astrologers refuse to consider the power of the Solar Chart at all, but as you have already seen, its accuracy can be profound and mind-blowing. The Solar Chart is a horoscope calculated by putting the Sun on the Ascendant, or Eastern, horizon, and placing the planets around the chart, according to their positions along the Zodiac. The charts in this book were calculated with the mean, not true node, and they were positioned by the whole sign house system. The whole sign house system is as valuable to the students of astrology as Placidus, Koch, or any other method you may use to divide up the chart into twelve houses.

If you want to gain further insight in the workings of the Nodes, beyond their effect on the Sun, go back to the beginning and reread the book, this time substituting your Rising Sign for your Sun Sign. The wisdom you can get from it will last for the rest of your life, in spite of the nineteen nervous breakdowns you'll have just because some of the material is so damned dark. You will be reading your birth time chart, calculated with whole sign houses.

You can even go through the book a third time, using the number in the chart corresponding to the house in which your Nodes are posited in whatever house system you use. For example, Taurus 12 corresponds to the South Node in the twelfth house. Aquarius 9 corresponds to the South Node in the ninth house. Try it. You'll find that the mystery of the Nodes is multilayered and textured, and that mystery takes a lifetime to solve.

Eclipse Births

If you were born with a Sun Sign Number 1 or 7, you will be strongly affected by the Nodes, because you were born near a solar eclipse. Not only do solar eclipse births describe bonds and separations, and spark especially intense feelings (positive or negative) toward your childhood and parents, but they will also manifest more powerful and complex characteristics you find described in the sections "Where You Go South" and "Finding Your True North."

Planets and Nodes

If you were born with planets on or near the South or North Node, you will have special life tasks and challenges to deal with, as well as special gifts and talents to develop. It is impossible to make sweeping generalizations and all-encompassing predictions about how—or if—an individual will develop talents and meet challenges. We are all presented with choices and dilemmas, and we will respond in our own individual ways.

You can only maximize your potential if you don't spend all your life heading South. If you do, you will waste all your time and energy trying to get in the present what you didn't get in the past.

Maybe the Nodes should be called the South Node and That Damned North Node, because to head north toward maturity and long-term fulfillment is a lot harder than repeating old patterns you should have outgrown years ago. Heading North means overcoming death anxiety, because it means you are heading forward, into the unknown.

Planets at or near the Nodes will be affected both by the nature of the planet and the Node it touches. Planets at the South Node can tend to keep you stuck in old habits and feelings of narcissistic, often childish needs for attention. They present a greater challenge to growth and change, especially because they are constantly presenting you with situations that force you to deal with an old sense of deprivation and thoughts of having been cheated way back in childhood.

Planets at the North Node, however, tend to make you grow up too early sometimes, as they force you into maturity and gave you added responsibility from the time you were very young. As annoyed as that makes you sometimes, such configurations bring you to a greater ability in adulthood to be a better parent, and to become a success in your chosen field, mainly because you have had so much practice at being responsible. Planets at your North Node seem to pick you up by the scruff of the neck and say to you, "For crissakes, what do you think you're doing? Grow up, already." And you do.

Synastry and the Nodes

The Nodes in your chart perfectly describe how you approach all relationships. They show you how you will tend to act in an infantile way, and how clinging, grasping, and impossible to satisfy you can be. They show you why you tend to stay in bad relationships too long and screw up the good ones. That's definitely where you "go South."

On the other hand, your North Node can show you (when you develop your natural talents in that area) how to find fulfillment and companionship as a responsible adult, not a petulant, needy child.

When comparing horoscopes, the position of another person's South Node in your chart will indicate the area that you should *not* focus on or obsess about, because it stimulates too much fantasy in you. A position in the North Node will show you how to get proper nourishment, and will give you the encouragement to follow the path you should be following. Sometimes that's easy to figure out, while at other times it makes your choices harder. But that's always the way with relationships. As much as you need them, they always complicate your life.

Cycles of the Nodes

The Moon's Nodes return to the positions they held relative to your Solar Chart (as well as to your birth time chart) roughly every nineteen years. These are periods during which you get the chance to revisit your old issues and get a fresh look at where you need be going if you are looking for lasting happiness and fulfillment.

Every nine and a half years, however, you are usually visited by temptation. You are tempted to lose sight of your real path. This is actually a course correction. It's a period when you will probably deviate from True North, have some fun heading South, and then, just in time, come to your senses. You realize you've put yourself under some kind of crazy spell and you'll thank God you realized it in time.

Special Note to Aries and Libra

Because of the way the Solar Charts are constructed, Aries, which is the first sign of the Zodiac, will get only one key word in this book. This doesn't mean Aries is less important, of course. It simply means that, according to astrology and the house systems we use, you need to develop special focus and stay on a more singular course toward success and happiness.

The Libra situation is a little more complicated. Because Libra is the natural seventh sign of the Zodiac, and because so many of your issues are worked out through relationships, you will find many more contradictions in the Libra section. It's often difficult to determine who is playing what role in your South and North Node issues.

Summing Up

As much information as we've provided in this book, there is a ton more to be gained by studying the effects of the Moon's path at the points where it crosses the path of the Sun through the Zodiac. *SunShines* has gone deeply into the talents and challenges you were born with, but, by referring to this book over the years, you can also predict how the Nodes will operate in the future. For example, in the year 2009, if you are an Aries, you will be an Aries 5, because the South Node will be transiting your Solar fifth house. In the year 2020, if you are a Virgo, you will be a Virgo 4, because at that time the South Node will be transiting *your* Solar fourth house.

You will have to modify some of the material, because the childhood issues described in the preceding pages may not apply to you in deailng with transits and you may well have already dealt with and overcome those issues. The rest, however, will definitely resonate and guide you on your journey. It has to be clear now that the Moon's Nodes deeply affect both the birth time chart and the Solar Chart. Enjoy this book forever.